How Ottawa Spends 1999-2000

How Ottawa Spends

1999-2000

Shape Shifting: Canadian Governance Toward the 21st Century

Edited by Leslie A. Pal

OXFORD
UNIVERSITY PRESS

OXFORD
UNIVERSITY PRESS

70 Wynford Drive, Don Mills, Ontario M3C 1J9
www.oupcan.com

Oxford New York
Athens Auckland Bangkok Bogotá Buenos Aires Calcutta
Cape Town Chennai Dar es Salaam Delhi Florence Hong Kong
Istanbul Karachi Kuala Lumpur Madrid Melbourne Mexico City
Mumbai Nairobi Paris São Paulo Singapore Taipei Tokyo
Toronto Warsaw

and associated companies in
Berlin Ibadan

Oxford is a trade mark of Oxford University Press

Canadian Cataloguing in Publication Data

The National Library of Canada has catalogued this publication as follows:

Main entry under title:

How Ottawa spends

1983-
Prepared at the School of Public Administration, Carleton University.
Issues for 1983- constitute 4th- eds.
Publisher varies: 1983, Lorimer; 1984-1987, Methuen; 1988-1997, Carleton University
Press; 1998- , Oxford University Press.
Includes bibliographical references.
ISSN 0822-6482
ISBN 0-19-541457-8 (1999-2000)

1. Canada – Appropriation and expenditures – Periodicals. I. Carleton University. School
of Public Administration.

HJ7663.S6   354.710072'2   C84-030303-3

Cover design: Brett J. Miller

This book is printed on permanent (acid-free) paper ∞

Copyright © Oxford University Press Canada 1999
1 2 3 4 - 02 01 00 99
Printed in Canada

CONTENTS

	Preface	vii
1	Shape Shifting: Canadian Governance Toward the 21st Century *Leslie A. Pal*	1
2	*Rethinking Government* As If People Mattered: From 'Reaganomics' to 'Humanomics' *Frank Graves*	37
3	Tectonic Changes in Canadian Governance *Gilles Paquet*	75
4	The Fourth Fiscal Era: Can There Be a 'Post-Neo-Conservative' Fiscal Policy? *Robert M. Campbell*	113
5	From Health and Welfare to Stealth and Farewell: Federal Social Policy, 1980-2000 *Michael J. Prince*	151
6	Taking Stock: Canadian Federalism and Its Constitutional Framework *Roger Gibbins*	197
7	'Coalitions of the Willing': The Search for Like-Minded Partners in Canadian Diplomacy *Andrew F. Cooper*	221

8	Negotiating Canada: Changes in Aboriginal Policy over the Last Thirty Years *Frances Abele, Katherine A. Graham, and Allan Maslove*	251
9	The Contested State: Canada in the Post-Cold War, Post-Keynesian, Post-Fordist, Post-national Era *Stephen Clarkson and Timothy Lewis*	293

Appendix A: Political Facts and Trends	341
Appendix B: Fiscal Facts and Trends	351
Abstracts/Résumés	369
Contributors	381

PREFACE

This edition marks an important moment in the life of one of Canada's most venerable public policy series. *How Ottawa Spends 1999-2000* is the 20th anniversary issue of a publication that began with the subtitle *Spending Tax Dollars* (the founding editor was G. Bruce Doern). At the time, there was a shortage of clear, critical analysis of federal government budgeting practices and spending priorities. The School of Public Administration at Carleton University saw an opportunity to contribute to public debate and public education. For almost an entire generation of Canadian students in the social sciences, *How Ottawa Spends* likely has been their first introduction to practical policy analysis, and their most detailed exposure to federal spending plans and priorities. It is a privilege to be the series editor both for the 20th anniversary issue, and the last volume of this century.

The coincidence of a significant anniversary with a 'millennial' shift suggested the idea of a special edition in the series. *How Ottawa Spends* is an annual, and authors are typically encouraged to concentrate on the current fiscal year. This year's edition has a wider focus: a smaller group of senior scholars was asked to examine broad areas of public policy and track patterns of change and continuity over the past twenty years or so. No specific format was imposed, but each chapter marks out the major shifts and changes that have so remarkably altered the practice of Canadian governance since the late 1970s. Indeed, as we exchanged chapters and ideas, it became clear how substantial the changes in federal policy and institutions have been. But while the changes have often been dramatic, they are sometimes belied by continuities and by certain comfortable constants. Canada's federal and parliamentary institutions, for example, look quite similar in form to what they were twenty years ago. In terms of substance and process, however, they are radically different. This combination of radical change and superficial similarity is captured in this year's overarching theme: *shape shifting*. Science fiction fans will recognize the idea of a single organism that can 'morph' into something dramatically different—and yet remain, somehow, the same. The essays in this volume demonstrate the metamorphosis that characterizes the last two decades of federal policy and politics, and peer ahead to discern where these changes may be taking us.

How Ottawa Spends by its nature imposes severe deadlines, but this year's demands were even greater because of the wider scope of the chapters. I would like to thank all the authors for their professionalism throughout the process. Readers will note that each author thanks a roster of readers, and I would like to express my gratitude as well to this small army of voluntary referees. Sandra Bach once again served as editorial assistant, reading chapters and compiling the hugely demanding Fiscal Facts and Trends and Canadian Political Facts and Trends (see Appendices).

The very existence of this book is unimaginable without the outstanding work of Jackie Carberry of the School of Public Administration at Carleton University. She organized the authors' colloquium in the fall of 1998, the conversion of word-processed text to camera-ready manuscript, and a ten-ring circus of authors, into a seamless outcome. Martha Clark, the School's Administrator, was once again an indispensable member of the editorial team, casting a practised and tireless eye over the manuscript as it developed into a book. Douglas Campbell again agreed to copy edit the manuscript, and once more performed with characteristic aplomb, patience, and professionalism. We are also grateful to Sinclair Robinson and Nandini Sarma for French translation. Oxford University Press, in the persons of Phyllis Wilson and Laura McLeod, was strongly supportive, despite the unusual features of our editorial and production process. I would also like to thank the previous editors of *How Ottawa Spends*—we owe to them not only the excellence of the series, but its very existence. They, and their respective authors, created an outstanding legacy that continues to nourish the series.

My final thanks go to my wife and children. They suffered all of the pressures of producing this volume, but remained true.

Leslie A. Pal
Ottawa,
April 1999

The opinions expressed by the contributors to this volume are the personal views of the authors of the individual chapters and do not necessarily reflect the views of the Editor or the School of Public Administration at Carleton University.

1

Shape Shifting: Canadian Governance Toward the 21st Century

LESLIE A. PAL

This edition of *How Ottawa Spends* marks the twentieth anniversary of the series—a series that has provided annual analyses of the federal government's spending and policy priorities. Moreover, it is being published on the cusp of the new millennium—in itself not terribly meaningful, but a useful point of focus for thinking about what has been and what may lie ahead for the country. Accordingly, it was decided to make this a special edition that would not only analyse federal policy and politics in the current year, but cast an eye back over the last twenty years, and try as well to peek forward to discern possible trends and challenges. A small group of senior scholars was asked to write essays analysing the broad sweep of changes and developments across key policy areas. Initially the approach was simply to assess patterns of change and possible developments, but as we exchanged ideas and insights, it became clear that the changes in the past two decades were not merely incremental, but in fact were tumultuous in their final implications for the nature and practice of the federal government and the Canadian state.

At one level, of course, the structure and nature of the federal state today are virtually identical to those of twenty years ago. Ottawa and the provinces remain the key constitutional players, and governments are still involved in the usual policy areas that define the welfare state (such as pensions, health, and employment-related programs). Closer examination reveals that these familiar features in fact mask some dramatic changes in form and function. Canadian federalism, for example, is now vastly changed, as a result of changes in spending, programs, and jurisdiction. The practical division of responsibilities and obligations between the two levels of government would be unrecognizable to someone familiar with the Canadian federalism of 1980. The same is true of policy toward and relations with Canada's Aboriginal peoples. The possible shift in paradigms toward treatment of Aboriginal peoples as equals, and moreover as nations, marks a change with potentially enormous implications. The content and practice of fiscal, social, and foreign policy all betray fundamental shifts as well. The Canadian federal state, in both structure and practice, is significantly different in 1999-2000. The odd combination of familiar features that have 'morphed' gradually but inexorably into patterns that are at times both odd and puzzling sets this year's theme: shape shifting.

Even Canadians who have lived through the changes described in this book might be surprised at their scope. However, the point about 'shape shifting' is that while the new patterns arise through gradual modifications in the old, those older patterns somehow remain and shimmer perceptibly in the new. It is this combination of old and new, of familiar and bizarre, that seems to best characterize the contemporary federal state. The shape has undeniably shifted in all fundamental areas, but without a consistent theme or outcome. In some areas government has become smaller; in others it grows. In some fields, government responsibilities and obligations have been simply abandoned, in others they have deliberately been expanded. A key strength of the essays in this 20th anniversary volume is the refusal to simplify the changes they describe into a single, grand pattern. The essays do isolate patterns, but they also take into account the complexities and the sometimes strange inconsistencies that underlie those patterns. This nuance provides a splendid basis for assessing the range of continued changes and shifts in shape and function that will doubtless occur in the next decades.

Traditionally, the introduction to *How Ottawa Spends* provides a brief synopsis of Ottawa policy and politics in the current year, a review of the federal budget, and a summary of the chapters. As a tribute to twenty years of indispensable analysis of federal fiscal affairs, and as a backdrop to the wider scope of this year's chapters, this introduction begins with a review of the last two decades, through the lens of the nineteen previous editions of *How Ottawa Spends*.

HOW OTTAWA SPENT, 1980-2000

The inaugural edition of *How Ottawa Spends* (entitled *Spending Tax Dollars*, edited by G. Bruce Doern) reviewed the short-lived minority government of Joe Clark and the newly elected majority government of Pierre Trudeau. Reflecting a key theme that would emerge over the decade, Doern noted that the federal debt increased that year as a percentage of budgetary expenditures, and that the cost of servicing the public debt was growing sharply. The Clark government had actually planned to increase expenditures by approximately 9 per cent— a figure almost inconceivable today—but the new Liberal government did them one better by releasing plans to increase annual spending by over 15 per cent.[1]

These spending plans were part of a remarkably ambitious agenda launched by the Liberals in 1980-4. Against the backdrop of a defeated sovereignty referendum in Quebec, the Trudeau Liberals decided to enhance the visibility and role of the federal government by connecting more directly to citizens through the patriation of the Constitution and the introduction of a Charter of Rights and Freedoms, through a wide array of economic development initiatives, and through a massive National Energy Program (NEP) that would micro-manage the Canadian oil and gas industry and insulate it from international market forces.[2] The Liberals believed that over the years transfers in social programs to the provinces had only succeeded in inflating the federal deficit and creating the impression that the federal government was mismanaged and irrelevant to the daily lives of citizens. The October 1980 federal budget set the government's course for the next four years: increased energy taxes linked to the NEP, muscular use of federal agencies to stimulate economic development, and reductions in social program transfers to the provinces under the recent Established Programs Financing Act. As Doern noted, the 1981-2 agenda reflected 'the most coherent assertion of political belief and principle by the Liberals since the early years of the Pearson Government'. It could not help but produce 'greater political conflict among Canadians'.[3] And indeed it did—the alienation of western Canada was massively intensified by the NEP, and the patriation of the Constitution strengthened the nationalist movement in Quebec. Both of these paved the way for Brian Mulroney to create a new Tory coalition of Quebec nationalists and western conservatives. This in turn set the backdrop for the failed Meech Lake and Charlottetown constitutional accords, and the eventual split of the Mulroney coalition into the western-based Reform party and the Quebec-based Bloc Québécois.

Liberal ambitions in 1980-4 eventually outstripped their capacities. This last hurrah of a strongly economically interventionist federal government soon foundered on the sheer size of the agenda and uncooperative international circumstances (energy prices went down and not up as the NEP had assumed, and US interest rates soared). Other difficulties had also arisen—the deficit was increasing, as was inflation, and in the 1982 budget Ottawa introduced its '6 and 5' program (public service wage increases were limited to 6 per cent that year and 5 per cent the year after, and these limits applied to federal transfers to the provinces as well). Recession hit the country hard as well in this period, and the Liberals found themselves developing special recovery programs and employment schemes. The hallmark of this period was confidence in the power of government at the outset, and confusion at the end as to how to tackle a wickedly complex range of economic and political problems.

As Allan Maslove pointed out in the 1984-5 edition, the combination of recession, increased expenditures, and high interest rates was driving the deficit and public debt charges rapidly up the political agenda.[4] The issue was seized in the first Tory Economic Statement in 1984 and later in the 1985 budget—key documents that laid out a consistent conservative vision of federal economic policy. As Michael Prince noted in the 1986-7 edition, the 'Tories not only want to reduce the size of government, they also want to redefine the role government plays in the Canadian economy. A strategic goal of the

Conservative agenda is to "depoliticize" the market economy in various sectors. This is to be done by reorienting (or what they call "reconfiguring") expenditure, tax and regulatory policies so that government programs do not distort or depress market signals. Federal programs must complement and reinforce the market-place.'[5]

The Mulroney period (back-to-back governments in 1984 and 1988) marks the beginning of the 'shape shifting' that is described in later chapters of this book. While in the end the Tories' record never matched their ambitions or their rhetoric, there can be no doubt that the intent was to re-orient the Canadian state and federal public policy. One of the first major Tory initiatives was a Program Review headed by Erik Nielsen to assess the efficiency and effectiveness of some 1,000 federal programs. While the Liberals had belatedly begun to concentrate on the deficit and public debt charges, the Tories made deficit reduction (at a gradual rather than a drastic pace) the centrepiece of their economic strategy. Whereas the Liberals in 1980-4 had tried to use government programs and agencies to create jobs and growth, the Tories flatly stated that deregulation and getting out of the market's way was the best method to stimulate growth. The Liberals had wanted to increase the visibility and role of the federal government vis-à-vis the provinces, but the Mulroney Tories were warm to decentralization and a greater provincial role, eventually pursuing constitutional initiatives that in the view of many would have emasculated Ottawa. While the Liberals had pursued nationalist economic policies, the Tories put out the welcome mat for international investors and launched free trade talks with the United States. And whereas the Liberals had frozen public sector wages but more or less preserved public sector jobs, the Tories looked to cut thousands of jobs in the bureaucracy. In sum, 'the Conservative view of national priorities shows a reliance on the private sector for job creation, a strong emphasis on deficit reduction and fiscal responsibility, a preference for downsizing and streamlining the federal public sector, and a belief in giving more room to the private sector in which to operate.'[6]

There were strong and visible indicators of each of these new orientations in the two Mulroney governments, but performance lagged for several reasons. Attempts to implement major changes in social programs foundered almost immediately in the face of strong opposition from affected groups (especially seniors, over cuts to pensions). The philosophical approach to expenditure reduction was gradualist to begin with, and so budgets continued to see high, if stable, deficits for some time before reductions were supposed to kick in. The governments were often mired in scandal, and internal mechanisms of fiscal control in the federal government were weak. Finally, in preparation for the 1988 election, the government began to ease up on its modest expenditure restraint and spend a bit more—all of which later compounded the deficit problem.[7]

Once safely elected in the tumultuous 'free trade election' of 1988,[8] the Conservatives returned to their preoccupation with the deficit in the 1989 and 1990 budgets. The February 1990 budget was particularly important in anchoring the government's objective, which was to 'restrict the role of the federal government and to create the image both nationally and internationally that what the federal government does, it does in a fiscally responsible manner'.[9] Deficit reduction through expenditure control (rather than increases in taxes, which had been a feature of the Conservatives' first mandate) was reflected in initiatives such as the freezing of federal transfers to the provinces for two years and cuts in funding to women's, Aboriginal, and multicultural groups. The strategy of cuts and freezes was continued in the 1991 budget, with further reductions in transfers to 'have' provinces, further reductions in general transfers to all provinces, reductions in programs such as social housing and in grants to individuals and businesses, tougher eligibility requirements for unemployment insurance, and caps on public sector wages.[10]

The second half of the Tory mandate continued to preach restraint, while emphasizing globalization and international competitiveness. Federal policies were ostensibly designed to facilitate the competitiveness of the Canadian economy through private-sector led growth. Frances Abele noted that by the early 1990s both governments and citizens were waking up to the altered context for governance:

> [T]he most arresting new elements are: 1) eroded national sovereignty, especially with respect to states' capacity to regulate; 2) permanently high levels of unemployment, through both booms and busts; 3) enormous, long-term pressures on the welfare state and the package of social safety net measures introduced in all but the poorest countries since the Second World War; 4) in many relatively wealthy countries, the growth of a permanently poor underclass, often of a different ethnic composition than the general population....These changes have

prompted a general revulsion against the neo-conservative enthusiasms of the 1980s: what remains is some consensus that the roles of public power and of markets must be rethought.[11]

The February 1992 budget continued the policy of cuts—reducing government spending by $1 billion in 1992-3 and promising a total of $7 billion per year over the next five years. The budget's projections for economic growth and for tax revenues turned out to be seriously flawed, and the Conservatives delivered an Economic Statement in December 1993, followed by a full-fledged budget in April 1993. The Economic Statement contained most of the bad news, while the budget was geared to a pre-election scenario. Despite some increases in expenditures (in infrastructural development, for example), the key motif of the Statement continued to be restraint. Departmental budgets were further reduced from the previous year, grants and subsides to interest groups were cut once again, unemployment insurance was further tightened, and a two-year wage freeze for public servants, employees of non-commercial Crown Corporations, cabinet members, parliamentarians, and the federally appointed judiciary were announced.[12] The April 1993 budget, in contrast, announced no major new cuts or taxes beyond ones that had been previously announced.

As is well known, the last two years of the second Tory mandate were disastrous for the party. The combination of constitutional failures, years of program cuts and expenditure reductions, recession, the GST, and scandals had made Brian Mulroney the most unpopular prime minister in history. He resigned in early 1993, and the party chose Kim Campbell as its leader and prime minister. She led the party to a historic defeat in the 1993 election—the Conservatives returned only two MPs and the Liberals won a strong majority. While there was general distaste for the Tories throughout the country, the election actually marked a strange sort of continuity for key policies pursued in the previous nine years. The victorious Liberals essentially agreed that the deficit was a critical problem and that it would have to be reduced. They accepted both the Free Trade Agreement and eventually the North American Free Trade Agreement (NAFTA), though with some qualifications that they successfully negotiated in the fall of 1993. The party seemed as well to accept the position that competitiveness in a global environment was the key to Canadian economic success. However, the party's campaign had also zeroed in on the most objectionable features of the previous regime—for example, the Pearson airport deal, cronyism, and helicopter contracts—and pledged fundamental change.

The great surprise of the last two Liberal mandates has been the extent to which the government has been committed to social and economic policies that could easily have come from their former adversaries. Ironically, this was initially masked in the government's first year, as it went about 'making change' in a host of policy areas (government integrity, a social policy review, more consultative foreign policy, management reform).[13] Indeed, in the 1994 budget the Liberals took a milder approach to deficit reduction than had the Tories, and proceeded to implement some campaign promises, such as new health programs, a $700 million infrastructure program, and research and development funding. These initiatives would be paid for through cuts in other programs, principally unemployment insurance, defence, and transfers to provinces.

By late 1994 Finance Minister Paul Martin was convinced by his officials that the deficit (over $40 billion annually, or 25 per cent of the budget when the Liberals assumed office) situation was extremely grave, and that it could not be addressed simply through incremental measures and the hope that economic growth would buoy government revenues: the solution also had to incorporate substantial expenditure reductions. Martin received the Prime Minister's support, and in cooperation with Marcel Massé, President of the Treasury Board, launched a Program Review exercise with the 1995 budget that eventually accomplished in three years what the Tories had not been able to achieve in almost ten—a balanced budget, and eventually a surplus, to pay down the accumulated federal debt. The 1995 budget was a clear signal of 'how the Liberals have shifted away from many of the fundamental values and principles of the Red Book to an all-consuming focus on deficit reduction'.[14] Beyond the focus on expenditures, however, the 1995 budget signalled a new vision of government:

> [T]hese cuts are much more than a frantic across-the-board slashing exercise. They have been portrayed as a change in philosophy toward reducing the role of the federal government by devolving responsibilities to other levels of government and to

the private and voluntary sectors; reducing transfer payments to provinces, individuals and businesses; and applying private sector management techniques to those federal government activities that remain.[15]

On the cusp of the 1997 election, which the Liberals won with a severely reduced majority, *How Ottawa Spends* editor Gene Swimmer summed up the Liberals' first mandate:

> Despite the Red Book's attempt to distinguish Liberal ideals from those of previous Conservative governments, Liberal policies, once in office, bear a much stronger resemblance to Tory Blue philosophy than to the Red Book [the 1993 platform]. The Liberals have performed well in economic management areas, like deficit control and trade promotion, with the important exception of employment policies. In the national unity field, they are barely passing, with another test yet to come. Their record is weak in social areas, such as child care, communications, and social housing, where the twin obsessions of deficit control and response to decentralist pressures are driving the policy agenda. Finally, in environmental protection and integrity agendas, Liberal performance has been mixed, but falls short of the expectations created by the Red Book.[16]

The 1998 budget was a triumph for Paul Martin and the Liberal government—for the first time in twenty years Ottawa had balanced its budget, and promised surpluses in ensuing years. As I noted in last year's edition, the post-deficit context has posed some challenges for the Liberals, since it has opened up the debate over spending priorities, and removed the relatively simple policy calculus of cuts and reduction. As I note later in this chapter, the Department of Finance has adroitly lowered public expectations over the 1999 budget, and underscored Canada's vulnerability to international currency speculation and economic turbulence, thus dampening debate about either substantial tax cuts or new investments in social programs.

This summary necessarily has omitted many details and sidebars in Canadian federal fiscal and policy developments over the past twenty years, but it provides a sketch of some of the key changes and developments that have gradually shifted the shape and nature of the federal state in this country. Several key themes emerge. The first is the gradual emergence of a political and societal consensus on the importance of tackling the deficit and the debt. The priority was already emerging at the close of the last Trudeau government, but it came to occupy rhetorical centre-stage with the Tories in 1984. By 1993 the Reform party had emerged as a vocal champion of expenditure cuts and deficit reduction, and within two years the Liberals had revised their middle-of-the-road approach to become hardened partisans of budget cuts and fiscal prudence. The ground was also prepared through vigorous lobbying by business-oriented interest groups and the rise of a number of fiscally conservative think tanks and journalists.

The second theme is the emerging sense that more, not less, decentralization and partnership among governments is what the country needs. There are strong opponents to reductions in federal powers and responsibilities, and they helped torpedo the Meech Lake and Charlottetown accords, but at the level of policy it is clear that the nature of federalism has changed fundamentally. The federal government transfers less money to the provinces than it once did, has less leverage over them, and is prepared, in effect, to devolve decision-making powers to them. In some areas and instances, of course, Ottawa has flexed it muscles—principally in manoeuvres to demonstrate resolve with respect to the Quebec sovereignty issue—but the broad pattern of decentralization is unmistakable. This emerging orthodoxy is not without its nuances, however. Poorer provinces are not especially enamoured of a decentralizing trend that leaves them with less support from Ottawa. Social policy advocates almost universally despise what they feel is the abandonment of national standards. Even federal authorities are prepared to intensify centralization in some policy areas (the economic union, for example).

A third theme is a change in the nature of government. The last two decades have witnessed a virtual revolution in the size, nature, scope, and activities of the federal government. After years of cuts, federal government expenditures account for no higher proportion of GDP than they did in the 1950s. Perhaps more important than mere size is the way in which the government and bureaucracy operate. Dozens of programs and agencies no longer exist. The ones that do, such as Employment Insurance or fiscal transfers to the provinces, have been radically redesigned. Others are offered in different ways—through partnerships with the private sector, by quasi-commercial entities, or by non-profit organizations. The philosophy underpinning this shift is one part fiscal conservatism—governments with fewer resources tend not to do some things, and do other things differently—but at least one part conviction that, given contemporary governance challenges, command and control mechanisms of governance are no longer adequate, if they ever were.

A fourth theme that emerges in this review of the last two decades is the gradual emergence of globalization as the primary context for Canadian policy-making. In many respects, globalization is the *El Niño* of public policy—just as almost every weather phenomenon seems explicable by *El Niño*, there is a temptation to argue that all fundamental policy changes somehow stem from the murky forces of globalization. But as one reads the last nineteen budgets and the analyses of former editors of *How Ottawa Spends*, it is clear that the international context has become an ever more important constraint and consideration in Canadian policy over the years.[17] Canada has always been a trading nation, and hence vulnerable to foreign (especially American) forces. But that exposure and vulnerability has increased dramatically in the last two decades. Just as importantly, however, many key policy objectives can no longer be pursued domestically. There is an ever greater international dimension to virtually every domestic policy issue—from social housing (the role of the United Nations in monitoring compliance with human rights conventions, for example) to resource management (for example, fisheries and forests). To some degree this constitutes a counter-trend to the decentralization of federal powers to the provinces. Globalization encourages a stronger international dimension in Canadian policy-making, and the federal state retains its jurisdiction as the main representative of Canada in international forums.

A fifth theme that runs through the last twenty years is the impact of these policy changes on community, cohesion, and democratic practice. Clearly, the constitutional file has been primarily about different visions of federal-provincial relations and their implications for nurturing national unity. The Trudeau strategy of a strong, visible national government assumed that the unity of citizens would be enhanced through direct contact with Ottawa. Despite the defeat of the two constitutional accords, their spirit of decentralization and of less rigidly symmetrical treatment of all the provinces seems to have gained ground. It is an open question, however, whether this formula leads to a stronger sense of national community or merely more robust regional/provincial identities. Outside of the constitutional file, there is the fundamental question of the impact of the changes described above on social cohesion and community. Pro-market policies and reductions in social spending have widened economic inequality. A more individualistically oriented social policy system that insists on a greater degree of self-reliance may weaken the bonds of mutual support and of the 'sharing community'. The harsh economic medicine of the 1990s may indeed have succeeded in fostering a more competitive economy, but at what price to community at the local, regional, and national levels?

This concern with cohesion is reflected in the sixth and final theme that seems to mark the last twenty years, the increasing concentration on the social and economic union.[18] Though few Canadians are aware of it, in 1994 Ottawa and the provinces signed an Agreement on Internal Trade to reduce economic barriers between provinces.[19] The agreement effectively prevents both the provinces and Ottawa from intervening in certain ways in the economy, thus ensuring greater market integration from coast to coast. The agreement's core chapters deal with government procurement, investment, labour mobility, consumer-related measures and standards, agricultural and food goods, alcoholic beverages, natural resources, energy, communications, transportation, and environmental protection. An agreement for a framework governing the social union (discussed in greater detail below) was reached in January 1999. It is not coincidental that the federal cabinet has only two policy committees—one for the social union and the other for the economic union. All policy proposals must be channelled through one or the other committee for decision. In this respect, federal policy-making at the end of the millennium is considerably more coherent and focussed than it was twenty years ago. Two decades of experience show that keeping the country prosperous, united, and strong has only two basic dimensions—economic and social.

This account may have given the misleading impression of a consistent shift rightward in policy and in governance. There has certainly been a shift to the right in terms of policy rhetoric, but results and outcomes depend on more complicated factors. We saw that in the last Trudeau government, a period of extraordinary commitment to active government, there was also an emerging concern about deficits. The Mulroney record was at best mixed in terms of the success of its fiscal program. More recently, as I argued in last year's edition, the Liberals had the advantage in 1993-8 of combining tight fiscal policy, decentralization through cuts in transfers, and national unity into a powerfully consistent policy paradigm driven by the Department of Finance. The post-deficit situation has posed new challenges for a government that still seems committed to fiscal prudence and a permanently reduced bureaucracy: what should the rationale be for new programs and new spending?

As the chapters in this edition demonstrate in greater detail, the changes in the past twenty years have been fundamental but not always coherent. The state has been downsized, but ordinary citizens and politicians recognize the need for core services such as health and education. Globalization has trimmed the state's capacities, but has also generated new demands for government policies to support and enhance competitiveness. A well-functioning economy requires market disciplines, but an economy founded on a fragmented and fractious community cannot be efficient. These realities create the paradoxical situation in which substantial change is combined with continuities, overlaps, and the retained if muted legacies of policies past.

A central question is what the future holds for this new, strange shape of governance at the end of the millennium. Given that even the federal New Democratic Party is searching for ways of redefining itself to accommodate a greater role for markets, it seems unlikely that we will see a return to Trudeau-style activist government. Small, lean, decentralized, partnered, and prudent seem here to stay. But in the absence of a consistent public philosophy to make sense of the appropriate balance of market and society, of compassion and competition, it is likely that policy will be driven less by ideology than by principled pragmatism. This is neither dramatic nor inspiring, but may be a typically bland Canadian compromise.

LIBERALS IN MID-TERM: UNCERTAIN AGENDA

In the past year the federal Liberals have had every incentive to work at defining a new public philosophy. The fiscal triumph of a balanced budget in February 1998 set the conditions for a substantive debate about national priorities. As I noted in last year's edition, this good news budget nonetheless created some tensions within the Liberals, since after years of proselytizing in favour of smaller, less activist and spendthrift government, it would hardly do to launch major programs. Accordingly, the budget offered a balance of some new spending (principally the Canadian Opportunities Strategy), modest tax relief, and payment against the debt. The economy, the government's integrity, and national unity came to dominate the later part of 1998, with the Liberal government appearing increasingly uncertain about its agenda and unclear about its priorities. This lack of decisiveness was reflected as well as amplified by a series of gaffes and weak public performances by the usually adroit Prime Minister. Jean Chrétien in many ways is a perfect symbol for the 'shape shifting' theme that marks this volume. A 1960s-style politician who abhors theory and broad policy ideas presides over a 1990s government, and looked increasingly bewildered through the year by the opportunities and challenges his own policies had wrought, such as the social union talks with the provinces.

Asia was to provide the Liberals with several headaches through the year. After the first balanced budget in two decades, one that predicted strong growth in the Canadian economy this year and next, the world economy developed serious difficulties. The Japanese banking system was seized by crisis in the late summer. By early fall most of East Asia was in deep recession, with GDP in free fall. The Russian ruble was also under pressure, and the government there effectively defaulted on its international loans. On Wall Street, share prices fell by almost $4 trillion, or the equivalent of Japan's GDP. Some of the gloomier economic forecasts anticipated global economic growth of less than 1.7 per cent, equalling the devastating recession of 1981-2. In September *The Economist* reported that its all-items commodity index had fallen 30 per cent to a 25-year low, and that the prices (in real terms) of industrial commodities were the lowest since the 1930s.[20]

Canadians watched in dismay as the loonie was buffeted and stock markets collapsed. By 27 August 1998, the loonie had plunged to a historic low of US$0.6331, against the backdrop of four consecutive months of contracting economic output. The fall in commodity prices and the crisis in the Asian and South American economies were slowing economic growth in North America and Europe. In mid-October the US Federal Reserve decided on a small interest rate reduction of a quarter of a percentage point in a cautious attempt to boost the world economy (through allowing rate reductions in other countries). Canada followed immediately with the same reduction, causing the loonie (which had climbed back up to US$0.6612) to fall to US$0.6473.

The currency crisis and the potential for a world economic recession was the backdrop to Finance Minister Paul Martin's *Economic and Fiscal Update* on 14 October 1998. Martin began by referring directly to the global economic context of shaken capital and financial markets in Asia, Russia, and South America, arguing that 'the Bretton Woods institutions, which have served the global economy for well over 50 years, are now in need of renovation'.[21] The impact of these global economic forces was evident in the Minister's growth projections. Whereas he was able to point proudly to remarkable progress on the deficit, inflation, interest rates, job growth, and employment over the past year—and reductions in federal program spending as a percentage of GDP that almost equalled levels last seen in 1949-50—growth projections for 1998 had to be scaled back, from 3.5 per cent to 2.9 per cent. The 1999 figures were down as well, from 2.9 per cent to 2.2 per cent.[22] Because of the Asian crisis, Canadian exports to that region were down by 30 per cent for the first seven months of 1998. So, despite a historic budget just seven months previously, and generally robust performance in 1997 and the first half of 1998, the Statement closed with a plea for caution and hard choices in the face of an uncertain global economic environment. In some respects, these new negative conditions made Martin's task somewhat easier, since he could maintain a hard fiscal line rather than be inundated with new demands to spend a ballooning surplus. The October projections for the coming year cut the anticipated surplus in half, from $10 billion to $5 billion.

As predicted in last year's volume, the 1998 balanced budget and its forecasts for future surpluses turned up the heat on federal-provincial negotiations on the social union. The provinces met though the spring and summer behind closed doors to hammer out a common position (Quebec did not participate, but did send observers). The Parti Québécois (PQ) position was that it would wait to see if the federal government accepted the provincial proposals—proposals that everyone knew would ask for limits on the federal power to spend in provincial jurisdictions such as health and education.[23] The PQ's strategy seemed at this point to be to stay away from anything that would make it appear that federalism could work. It came as a mild surprise in August at the Premiers' conference in Saskatoon that the Quebec government joined the others in a consensus document on the social union. The agreement proposed a closer partnership between the two levels of government in managing Canada's social programs, but also demanded significant limits to the federal spending power: (1) Ottawa could not change or create national social programs without majority provincial consent; (2) provinces that opt out of a federal program would get full financial compensation as long as they established a similar program; (3) national standards would be interpreted and enforced jointly; and (4) a dispute resolution mechanism would be established with provincial participation to resolve differences over standards and opting-out arrangements.[24] Quebec's key concession in the agreement was to accept that a province would only be compensated for opting out if it established a similar program; Quebec's traditional position had been unconditional compensation. The agreement posed a problem for Ottawa, particularly after the Quebec election was called for 30 November 1999. If it rejected the social union proposals, it would play into separatist hands by showing that Ottawa was unprepared for any limits on its powers. If it accepted them, then it would be undermining federal leadership capacity. As it turned out, while the PQ was expected to win handily against the Liberals in the provincial election, it was returned with 42.7 per cent of the vote, while the Liberals received 43.7 per cent and the Action Démocratique got 11.8 per cent.[25] Because of the electoral system, however, this neck-and-neck result in the popular vote gave the PQ 75 seats and the Liberals and Action Démocratique 48 and 1 respectively. The closeness of the popular vote—along with the fact that the PQ had dropped two seats from the previous election, when it had been led by Premier Parizeau—indicated that voters had repudiated the PQ's referendum strategy, and suggested that nationalism in Quebec was cooling if not tepid. The almost immediate result was a much tougher stance on Ottawa's part in the social union talks. By January 1999, it was tabling counter-proposals on such issues as stronger mobility rights. By February, as described below, it signed a deal with all the provinces and territories *except* Quebec.

The Quebec issue seemed to be the only bright spot on the government's agenda in the fall of 1998. The Supreme Court finally delivered its judgment on the reference on separation submitted by Ottawa in September 1996. The decision was that in the eyes of Canadian and international law, unilateral secession by Quebec or any other province was illegal, but that if a referendum on a clear question resulted in a clear majority in favour, the federal government would be obligated to negotiate. As ambiguous as this victory was, Ottawa lost no time in making firm public statements that the PQ's strategy of possible unilateral secession was forbidden by law.[26] The Quebec election at first seemed as if it might undermine Ottawa's position, but the final results suggested that the separatist project had suffered a setback and that Ottawa could safely assert itself without courting the danger of inflaming public opinion in the province.

Apart from Quebec, the fall was dominated by two other issues: the bank mergers and the APEC investigation. The bank mergers involved plans announced by the Royal Bank of Canada, the Bank of Montreal, the Canadian Imperial Bank of Commerce, and the Toronto-Dominion Bank. The news caused a furor, as well as a blizzard of reports and analyses. In September the MacKay Task Force on the mergers submitted a generally positive report. In November, the Liberal caucus issued a blistering report that argued that mergers would be a severe detriment to the Canadian public interest. The Competition Bureau, the Commons Finance Committee, and the Senate Banking Committee all delivered reports expressing varying degrees of support and criticism before December. Sensing the popular mood, and perhaps positioning himself as more of a populist after years of being the bearer of tough budgetary news, Finance Minister Paul Martin announced that he would not allow the mergers to go through at the present time. While leaving the door open for mergers in the future, he effectively and firmly shut the door for the short term.

The APEC inquiry was part farce and part comedy. On 25 November 1997, Jean Chrétien hosted the Asia Pacific Economic Cooperation summit in Vancouver, and among his guests were prominent dictators such as Indonesia's President Suharto. Protesters stormed barricades, and the RCMP responded with pepper-spray. The protesters in turn complained, and an RCMP Complaints Commission was struck to decide the issue. The Commission demanded the submission of documents that cast a sharp light on a variety of players—Terry Milewski, a CBC journalist who appeared to side with the protesters, and the government itself, which was shown to have had an unseemly interest in coddling international human rights violators. There were several small tempests in connection with the inquiry, such as the government's unwillingness to fund the protesters' legal costs, and the resignation of the Commission chair after charges of bias, but the worst event for the government was the loss of Solicitor-General Andy Scott. On a flight in early October 1998, Scott was overheard by NDP MP Dick Proctor making statements that suggested that Scott had prejudged the Commission's conclusions. Since Scott would eventually have to decide on the Commission's report, this had all the delicious elements of scandal. After several weeks of opposition badgering and government squirming, Scott resigned.

The resignation was a symbol of a fraying government agenda and perhaps even leadership incompetence. The Prime Minister appeared at several key fundraising dinners in the late fall looking weak, evasive, and tired. The end of the parliamentary session in December was almost merciful: the government had tabled little of legislative significance in the fall, had seemed to be riding the public policy agenda instead of setting it, and, except in relation to the banks and the Quebec issue, appeared bereft of ideas and inspiration. A counterexample of this vacuity was the Prime Minister's eleventh-hour intervention in the social union talks. By late January negotiations were at an impasse. Chrétien called a first ministers' meeting in Ottawa for 4 February, and worked the phones with his counterparts across the country. After a four-hour meeting, a deal was signed by all governments except Quebec. Ottawa kept its spending power in social policy areas, but agreed to consult provinces three months in advance of any initiatives. Ottawa also agreed not to introduce any cost-shared programs without at least six of the ten provinces agreeing; provinces that did not agree would not get any compensation. This satisfied a key Quebec (and provincial coalition) demand from the previous summer. Any differences would be worked out in a dispute resolution mechanism, and provinces would work to remove inter-provincial barriers in relation to employment, health care, and post-secondary education. There were several important elements to the agreement—for example, it was not a constitutional amendment, and it was valid only for three years—but the key was that Ottawa put about $2.5 billion in additional health care transfers on the table. Although it refused to sign, Quebec would still get its share of the booty.

Despite predictable claims about its 'historic character', the agreement was neither visionary nor especially courageous. Ottawa rightly calculated that Premier Bouchard was now weak as a result of the election, and could not credibly threaten repercussions. The other provinces jettisoned their principles as soon as money was on the table, though the agreement did meet some of their demands from the August premiers' agreement. The Prime Minister did not have to test his powers of cogitation or of persuasion—he simply flung a bag of money on the table. Nine of the premiers realized that the political terrain had shifted dramatically since 30 November—at best they could wring a few concessions from a newly invigorated federal government; at worst, Ottawa could fold its cards and still get away relatively unscathed. The opportunity was tailor-made for a Shawinigan-style deal: limited progress on principle, lubricated by wads of cash. The premiers took the money and ran. In an oddly poignant photo-op after the agreement was signed, Lucien Bouchard stood alone, the only leader to wear an overcoat, as though he were braving elements stronger than the winter, or merely readying himself to leave as quickly as possible.

Despite the Viagra-esque stimulus of the Quebec election, it was as though, after six years of changing the Canadian state and public policy in hugely significant ways, the Liberals had lost energy and vision. Their best hope was a new budget that might outline a fresh direction on the social union issue, and begin to reclaim some old Liberal ground by means of new spending programs. However, the shift that they had caused in the shape and nature of the Canadian state in the previous years would mean that they would also have to look to the other side of the political ledger—tax cuts and debt reduction.

THE 1999 FEDERAL BUDGET[27]

Paul Martin's February 1999 budget was a carefully crafted document that responded to a wide variety of pressures and demands, including fiscal prudence, a turbulent international context, and demands to spend some part of the 'fiscal dividend' (see the chapters by Robert Campbell and Michael Prince for details on the budget). As Martin put it in his speech, a successful society does not 'run on one cylinder'—clearly signalling that this budget would, like the previous one, move simultaneously on several fronts. He predicted a balanced budget 'or better' for the next three fiscal years. However, he emphasized the continued drain that the public debt placed on federal expenditures: the largest single federal expenditure category was the roughly $40 billion annual payment on the debt. Accordingly, Martin pledged to continue with the Debt Repayment Plan announced in the previous budget, a plan that hinged on conservative fiscal projections, a contingency reserve, and sustained payments against the debt.

On the spending side, the key initiative, tied to the social union talks held several weeks earlier, was an increase in health care transfers to the provinces. The Canadian Health and Social Transfer (CHST) was to be increased immediately by $2 billion, with a similar increase the year after. Subsequently, the top-up would increase to $2.5 billion for each of three successive years. As Martin noted, these increases would return the health component of the CHST to the levels prevailing before 1995, when the cuts began. The increases in the CHST would be supplemented by increased transfers under the Equalization program of approximately $2.2 billion, because of the fact that Ontario's economy is booming, and as its tax revenues increase, so does the base of the formula for equalization transfers. In addition to these transfers, Martin announced four new programs to improve systems for collecting and distributing health information: (1) annual progress reports to Canadians, (2) a National Health Surveillance Network, (3) a Canadian Health Network on the Internet to provide accessible and timely health information, and (4) initiatives to use information technology to deliver health care services. Other initiatives included a Canada Prenatal Nutrition Program, food safety, First Nations health services, additional funding for the Canadian Foundation for Innovation, and the Canadian Institutes for Health Research. Together, these non-CHST health initiatives would total $255 million in 1998-9, and increase to $589 million by 2001-2.

The rest of the budget's spending initiatives were loosely organized under the rubric of 'knowledge, skills and innovation', and together accounted for $5.3 billion in new expenditures. These are difficult to summarize, precisely because of their scattered nature. Martin argued that the budget's goal was to improve economic productivity, and that productivity depends on knowledge and innovation—the 'new raw materials' of the 21st century. Granting councils, for example, were promised an additional $120 million. A sum of $60 million over three years was to be devoted to 'Smart Communities' demonstration projects, and another $60 million would go to build GeoConnections (mapping technologies). Various initiatives were also announced to facilitate the commercialization of innovative research (such as increased funding for Technology Partnerships Canada and for the Business Development Bank of Canada).

The budget's third leg, after debt reduction and new spending, was tax relief. Calls for tax reductions had been coming all year, principally from the Reform party, the business press, and business-oriented lobby groups. Many believed that the Finance Minister would respond with large, visible cuts. But the scope of the cuts turned out to be quite modest. First, he raised the amount that Canadians can earn without paying taxes by $175 (the sum was modest, but Martin claimed that it would remove 200,000 Canadians from the tax rolls). Second, he eliminated the 3 per cent surtax on high-income earners effective July 1. Third, the Canada Child Tax Benefit was increased by $350 per child. In 1999-2000, these tax measures, along with reductions in Employment Insurance premiums, will cost $2.3 billion.

It is important to stand back and regard the budget from a broader perspective. As Robert Campbell argues in his chapter in this volume, the 1999 federal budget did not appear to be anchored in any one, single, clear fiscal philosophy. Apart from debt reduction and increased transfers for health care, the rest of the budget betrayed—by traditional Liberal standards—only a tepid commitment to government 'intervention' in the economy and society. Despite statements about new spending, federal expenditures will actually decline from $112.1 in 1998-9 to $111.2 billion in 1999-2000. They will increase by $2 billion in 2000-1, but revenues are projected to rise by almost $3 billion in the same period. The non-health spending initiatives amounted to $1.7 billion. However, when one compares debt reduction, new spending, and tax relief, it is clear that the February 1999 federal budget made choices. By some estimates, Martin was facing a potential surplus of about $11 billion in December 1998. The government's fundamental choice was how to 'spend' this surplus and reduce it to a balanced budget. Only $3 billion went to debt reduction, and only about $2.3 billion went to tax relief. The bulk of the dividend therefore was channelled into spending on new programs, the largest of which were for health care.

These choices might have been different with a different government in power—the Reform party would certainly have placed more emphasis on tax reduction. But it is likely that many aspects of this budget would have been supported by governments of a different stripe. The emphasis on the global context, the concern with debt, the focus on innovation and knowledge, the acknowledgment that taxes are too high—these seem to be the shibboleths of *fin de siècle* policy-making. The world has changed in twenty years.

THE BOOK

- **Frank Graves**'s chapter explores the shifting ground of Canadian public opinion concerning governments and governance. The key theme is the complex interplay in recent decades between declining levels of public trust and confidence in government and continued support for some sort of activist state. On the basis of original survey data from the Ekos Research Associates' *Rethinking Government* series, Graves is able to tap into a database consisting of 3,000 variables and 30,000 interviews over a five-year period. He shows that the conventional wisdom about declining trust in government is in large part true, but that this decline is tempered by a persistent support among the majority of Canadians for an active role by government in addressing collective problems such as health, education, and the impacts of globalization. Looking more closely, Graves is able to show that virtually all institutions in Canadian society have suffered declines in legitimacy. This has been accompanied in recent years by a growing tendency to give priority to humanistic values as opposed to purely instrumental concerns about prosperity and wealth. Minimal government is actually rated below these more normative concerns, such as a healthy population, freedom, and a clean environment. Canadians see government as a means for expressing core values. Ironically, Ekos' data show a 'normative rupture' between elite and public opinion in this regard—elites place much higher priority on values such as competitiveness, minimal government, and prosperity than does the public. They also rate public engagement lower than the public itself does, and, unsurprisingly, the public seems to have an appetite for recovering some power from media, big business, and the federal government and returning it to average citizens, small business, and community groups.

One of the most valuable features of Graves's chapter is his careful analysis of post-deficit public opinion about governance issues. According to Ekos' data, the public is not in fact as concerned about tax levels and tax cuts as conventional wisdom would assume. Citizens are more relaxed about public finances, and are prepared to support a more activist public agenda. At the same time, however, they do not want a return to big government. As Graves puts it, 'Canadians want to see a shift from paternalism to partnerships; they want clear accountability for targets and results; they want fiscal prudence and they want citizen inclusion in the selection of goals and means.' Canadians are sceptical about wealth redistribution and passive income support, and are likely to blame bad values for some social ills and to emphasize individual effort and self-reliance. This is a strange and in many ways unstable mix of public values, which both reveals how far Canadians have come in the last two decades in their views on government, and how challenging it will be in the future to arrive at a coherent public philosophy that reconciles the tensions.

- **Stephen Clarkson** and **Timothy Lewis** provide a magisterial backdrop to the other chapters in this volume. They trace the 'contested' Canadian state in its post-Cold War, post-Keynesian, post-Fordist, and post-national era in a narrative and an analysis that tracks the complex changes from the 'embedded' liberalism of the post-war consensus to the neoliberal state that emerged in the Mulroney/Chrétien eras. The analytical grid is supplied by the notion of a multi-tiered state that simultaneously operates at several levels: the global, the national, the continental, the sub-national (provincial), and the local. To understand how the nature and practice of the federal state has shifted in the last twenty years, it is important to see the shifts and recombinations among these five levels. The key point that Clarkson and Lewis make is that when the federal state is viewed through this lens, the reports of its evisceration appear to be much exaggerated. Ironically, the structural reforms required to establish and maintain a neo-liberal (less interventionist, more pro-market) regime often demand fairly extensive and vigorous government action.

Clarkson and Lewis present the shift in regimes across several policy areas: macroeconomic, social, industrial, trade, and environment. The emergent regime has changed the state's role in the economy, rearranged the distribution of power among the five levels, and seriously affected the redistributional role of government. The third section of the chapter, however, examines the contradictory political features of this new regime, from disgruntled citizens' groups, to a fractured party system, to a democracy deficit at the global level, and an increasingly robust and broadly gauged foreign policy. Their message is that a nuanced analysis shows that the federal state need not necessarily become a cipher in the neo-liberal paradigm, and moreover that in many respects this paradigm is not well equipped for many contemporary demands in respect to social policy and governance. Moreover, there remain substantial continuities with the past. The shape of the Canadian state has indeed shifted in remarkable ways in the last two decades, but the change has been complex and it is far from over. Indeed, a swing back in some respects to some elements of the previous paradigm is not out of the question. These themes are addressed in greater detail in subsequent chapters.

- **Gilles Paquet**'s chapter picks up several of the themes addressed by Clarkson and Lewis, but does so within the framework of 'governance'. Paquet argues that there has been a gradual but relentless shift in the Canadian mode of governance in the past decades, so that new practices are engraved on old institutions. Nonetheless, the changes are sufficiently dramatic that they amount to a 'tectonic shift' in the Canadian governance regime. The chapter explores evidence of this shift in three broad areas: (1) a changed philosophy of governance, (2) a rebalancing and reconfiguring of relations among the private, public, and civil society sectors, and (3) a retooling of public management and administrative practices. The shift itself is not unique to Canada—other countries and other systems are facing the same pressures, which arise from globalization, technological change, and a growing plurality of interests and values. In this new context, governments can no longer afford to be organized hierarchically, with rigid lines of command, control, and accountability. Flexibility, learning, and responsiveness are now the cardinal virtues, but they require different institutions and processes, ones organized around principles of decentralization and distributed networks of power and information. The first part of his chapter outlines the broad contours of these new, emergent forms of governance.

The second half of the chapter examines evidence for the rise of new philosophies, relationships, and practices in the Canadian governance regime. At the philosophical level, Paquet discerns growing support for the principle of subsidiarity—the idea that the level of government closest to a problem or issue should be responsible for dealing with it. At the level of roles and responsibilities, there is evidence of a growing acceptance of multi-stakeholder partnerships and collaboration. The old model, according to which the state goes-it-alone, is being replaced by a model in which multiple actors and players make contributions to the development of governance regimes in issue areas: government is only one player among many. At the level of management techniques, these changes in the philosophy and structure of governance have yielded major reform initiatives, from the PS2000 exercise in the late 1980s to the most recent renewal efforts led by Treasury Board.

The chapter closes with a valuable accounting of the resistance to these trends, a resistance that has hinged on concerns about excessive decentralization, and on internal political and bureaucratic reservations about a loss of power. Paquet remains hopeful, however, that a more distributed, flexible, and decentralized form of governance may yet triumph in Canada. Change is in air, according to Paquet, though both his essay and the one by Clarkson and Lewis admit the possibility that this change may be checked, and even possibly reversed, in the next decades.

- **Andrew F. Cooper** explores the changing nature of Canadian diplomacy and of the way in which this country pursues its interests on the international scene. As a nation that depends vitally on trade, but that remains nonetheless a 'middle power' in terms of economic, demographic, or military influence, diplomacy is crucial to Canada. The current impact of globalization makes the international context increasingly important for domestic public policy-making. Cooper's chapter argues that Canada has traditionally practised a dual mode of diplomacy—one side emphasizing the bilateral relation with the United States, and the other focussing on the search for partners among 'like-minded' states with whom to pursue a wider range of international objectives. In diplomatic terms, Canada has always been the quintessential 'joiner', working with a wide variety of countries to build international institutions. In recent years, through the Free Trade Agreement and the North American Free Trade Agreement, the bilateral relationship with the United States has, if anything, tightened. Cooper's chapter shows, however, that this has been matched by a corresponding 'loosening' in the practice of 'like-minded' diplomacy. In cobbling together 'coalitions of the willing', Canadian diplomatic practice has become more ad hoc, more fluid, populated with new players (among both states and non-state actors), and somewhat bolder in tweaking the United States (as in the land mines issue, where Canada led an international coalition that did not include the United States). The current Minister of Foreign Affairs, Lloyd Axworthy, is keenly interested in this more activist form of diplomacy, and has highlighted it as a counterbalance to the emphasis on trade in our foreign policy.

Cooper traces the evolution of the traditional paradigm of like-mindedness from the Pearson era in the 1960s to its expression in some recent cases, such as land mines and the

Zaire/Great Lakes initiative. In weighing the effectiveness of the new 'soft power' approach, Cooper argues that while pleasing to the Minister and certain segments of the public that applaud a morally driven foreign policy agenda, the long-term impact of these worthwhile Canadian initiatives is unclear. Despite this, however, Cooper concludes that this style of diplomacy will continue to attract support and interest. However much the new style may parallel the older Canadian tradition of like-mindedness, Cooper's chapter shows that form and function have subtly shifted.

- **Robert M. Campbell**'s chapter on the 1999 budget and fiscal policy starkly illustrates the notion of shape shifting in Canadian governance: Campbell sketches an emerging 'fourth era' fiscal policy paradigm that is a strange combination of elements drawn from pre-Keynesian, Keynesian, and neo-conservative periods. Pre-Keynesian fiscal policy emphasized small governments and fiscal prudence; Keynesianism as it was defined in the postwar period to the early 1980s was focussed on full employment and the extensive use of government instruments to manage the economy; the neo-conservative period of the last two decades was determinedly pro-market and anti-statist. Campbell shows how each of these eras succumbed to their own contradictions—and how the very success of the Liberals' first few budgets has created a policy vacuum that is being filled with an inconsistent mix of principles and maxims drawn from all three previous eras. The February 1999 federal budget did a little of everything— it protected its 'surplus', but cut taxes, spent more on core programs such as health, and reduced the debt. The key theme was flexibility and caution in the face of international pressures and an unpredictable global economy.

Campbell argues that the very absence of an overarching coherence in this fourth fiscal era may be its hallmark. Several factors account for this. First, there is much less faith in economic forecasting and much greater appreciation of uncertainty. Second, international forces seem both unpredictable and implacable—there seems very little that countries can do to insulate themselves. Third, there is increasing scepticism about the effectiveness of economic policy tools, from monetary policy to traditional fiscal policy tools. In a world where nothing seems to work quite right, a guiding maxim is emerging to limit governments' discretion: at least if they are tethered by formula, they might do less harm. Fourth, Campbell discerns a marked lack of consensus—even concerning the terms of debate—among the public and the policy-makers. Finally, Canadians themselves seem ambivalent about their expectations of government: they want lower taxes and high spending; less government but more security. Not surprisingly, policy-makers receive conflicting signals. Fiscal policy will likely evolve into a sort of domestic shock absorber against international forces, but will be marked by pragmatism. Nonetheless, fundamental issues of public purpose, such as productivity and the social security system, will have to be addressed, and Campbell sees debates over an appropriate public philosophy as inevitable in the long term.

- **Michael J. Prince**'s chapter on federal social policy and the Canadian welfare state highlights the complexities and inconsistencies in this policy field over the last twenty years. The overarching theme, of course, has been cutbacks and retrenchment, but Prince reveals a bewildering tableau of policy constants, embedded styles, shifting paradigms, and broad periods of coherent agendas of change. The shape and nature of the Canadian welfare state has been dramatically altered in many ways over these two decades, and while we still have recognizable social programs—and some that are clear legacies from the first stages of the Canadian welfare state—the edifice as a whole has been renovated and changed.

Prince argues that there have been four great phases of development in federal social policy since 1980: (1) the Trudeau government of 1980-4: reassurance and maintenance; (2) the first Mulroney government of 1984-8: restraint; (3) the second Mulroney government and the first Chrétien government of 1988-97: restructuring; and (4) the current Chrétien government and beyond: reparations. Prince's chapter is rich on the details of policy change in each period, but he makes the key point that while each period had its distinctive policy style, all governments relied in one fashion or another on the politics of stealth: 'changes to policy are made without a genuine process of public consultation or debate and are done through technical measures announced in budgets'. The reason for the reliance on stealth is obvious: federal social policy in the last twenty years has been primarily about cuts, and cuts hurt. The political fallout of restraint and restructuring can be blunted by stealth. The chapter shows how in each period, but particularly in the period of restructuring between 1988 and 1997, federal governments developed symbols, new discourses, and distinctive strategies to reorient public expectations and assumptions about the welfare state. As he points out in his conclusion, the result two decades on is an emergent paradigm that uses different imagery (the trampoline, for instance, instead of the safety net), and a very different structure (for example, compared to the early postwar period, the system is much more directly under provincial control and responsibility). Almost every bit of conventional wisdom about social policy-making has been overturned. Prince concurs with Campbell's analysis, however, in pointing out that the rhetoric of restraint sounds increasingly hollow in the face of budget surpluses. The Canadian welfare state has changed; and it is due for further fundamental change.

- **Roger Gibbins** reinforces the theme of shape shifting of the Canadian polity by emphasizing both the continuities and the changes in Canadian federalism over the past three decades. The continuities—demographic and institutional—are the bedrock of our collective sense that we occupy roughly the same political architecture today as we did yesterday. It is when he turns to patterns of change that Gibbins highlights the major renovations to that architecture that give most observers a sense of vertigo—the system looks similar, but clearly operates in fundamentally different ways. The patriation of the Constitution, for example, and the adoption of the Charter of Rights and Freedoms, dramatically altered the relationships of governments to each other, and of governments to citizens, and enhanced the role of the courts. Informal but important changes have occurred as well in the scope of provincial policy responsibilities. These patterns of change promise to challenge Canadians in the next few years. For example, Gibbins argues that Aboriginal governments (of which there may be as many as 70 in a few years) will have to be integrated into the Canadian intergovernmental system of negotiations. Local governments are also increasingly important, and it seems inconceivable that they will not demand a more visible role in Canadian intergovernmental policy-making. Gibbins argues that there is likely to be a complex interplay of heightened local sensibilities and more fluid, less territorially-defined identities. He closes with some reflections on the place of Quebec within Canadian confederation, a place that has been radically if informally redefined under the stewardship of the current Prime Minister, and which promises to remain contentious in the future.

- **Frances Abele**, **Katherine A. Graham**, and **Allan M. Maslove** explore the evolution of Canadian Aboriginal policy over the past thirty years, arguing that Canada's relationship to its Aboriginal peoples is fundamental to the nature of governance in this country. Policy has been guided by four paradigms: (1) the poverty paradigm, which treats Aboriginal peoples primarily as members of a disadvantaged and impoverished group; (2) the malcontents paradigm, which sees Aboriginal peoples as irresponsible and dependent; (3) the individual rights paradigm, which defines the 'Aboriginal problem' in terms of discrimination; and (4) the land paradigm, which sees use of and control over land by Aboriginal peoples as central to their survival and prosperity. The land paradigm is shared by almost all Aboriginal peoples, but the authors show how it has taken thirty years for that paradigm to become an important foundation for Canadian policy. They do this by tracing policy developments across three political periods, defined by the governments of Prime Ministers Trudeau, Mulroney, and Chrétien. The Trudeau period began with the attempt to literally extinguish Indian rights, and was driven by an emphasis on poverty reduction and individual rights. Some modest advances were made on the concept of self-government and on land negotiations. The authors argue that significant advances were made under the two Mulroney governments. Had the Charlottetown Accord been successful, it would have completely redefined the nature of Canadian-Aboriginal relations. But Tory governments made progress on land claims (most notably, Nunavut), and established the Royal Commission on Aboriginal Peoples. The Commission's report focussed on the centrality of land for Aboriginal peoples, and the Chrétien government has, in large measure, adopted its perspective as the foundation of its policies on Aboriginal self-government. After thirty years, this represents a major shift in policy—many more programs and dollars are managed directly by Aboriginal peoples themselves today than ever in the past. The change has been dramatic and positive; key framework agreements are either in place or being negotiated. Future progress will depend on hard work at the level of implementation.

CONCLUSION

Canadian governance in many important respects has changed radically in the last two decades. All the essays in this volume point out that there are substantial continuities as well—in public opinion (Graves), in Canada's role in the world (Cooper), in the possible rediscovery of more activist styles of government (Clarkson and Lewis, Campbell, and Prince), and in the main political institutions within which we live (Gibbins). However, all the essays in this volume stress the complex changes that are underway and that will pose the fundamental challenges at the beginning of the new millennium. Several essays allude to the greater diversity in Canadian society—in public opinion and values, in ethnic composition, and in demographics. As a society, Canada is more varied, more urban as well as more urbane, more rights-conscious, more tolerant in some respects (with regard to Aboriginal rights, for instance) and less tolerant in others (with regard perhaps to Quebec's nationalist aspirations). Globalization as a driving force shimmers behind every chapter in this volume—it has affected how we view policy issues, the capacities of our governments, the possibilities we envision, the collective projects to which we think it appropriate to aspire. Globalization is the *El Niño* of contemporary governance, and these essays demonstrate that it does have consequences that are both specific and far-reaching.

But perhaps the most remarkable and consistent, if sometimes implicit, conclusion of the essays in this volume is the peculiar nature of political and policy change in this country. To be sure, there have been grand and public episodes, such as the patriation of the Constitution in 1981 and the Charlottetown and Quebec referenda, episodes that entailed broad public debate and engagement. But the essays in this volume describe processes of change that typically are closed and opaque, and that were often arrived at through administrative fiat or subterfuge. As Frank Graves's chapter points out, there continues to be a gap between elite and public opinion on the value of citizen engagement, and a sense among citizens that they are shut out of political decision-making. Consider the following: the free trade and other international economic agreements described by Clarkson and Lewis; the decentralization and the managerial reform described by Paquet; the shift in diplomatic style and substance reviewed by Cooper; the new fiscal policy framework analysed by Campbell; the 'stealth' of social policy reform depicted by Prince; the quasi-constitutional response by Ottawa to Quebec described by Gibbins; the new era in Aboriginal governance outlined by Abele, Graham, and Maslove. The concept of shape shifting captures these changes precisely because they were changes of substance and content where form was often left untouched, changes with an informal character but vast formal consequences, changes that were agreed to by elites, implemented by functionaries, and largely obscure to the public. Shape shifting, in short, may express a peculiar syndrome of political and policy change in Canada—our cleavages are deep and varied, our institutions are sclerotic, our instincts centrist and syncretist. Change, if it is to occur, must occur by stealth or through bland administrative initiative. With rare exceptions, Canada is a country of paralytic progress, of incremental and quiet revolution, of reluctant reform.

As the essays show, this is not necessarily an impediment to change. Reforms to the social security system, whatever one might think of them, have been massive yet achieved by what Prince calls 'stealth'. Constitutional and managerial change have been equally far-reaching, though it is likely that few Canadians grasp their portent. First Nation governments in the next decades are likely to change Canadian federalism fundamentally, but outside of a few regions such as British Columbia, the scope of these potential changes is largely unrecognized.

If this diagnosis is correct, it suggests that our political institutions are not particularly adept at channelling and facilitating broadly-based, consensual change. Change occurs, but it is masked and managed, and ultimately masquerades as continuity. It is likely, however, that broadly-based, consensual change and adaptation are precisely what will be demanded in the first decades of the new millennium, both by external forces and by the citizenry. It is also likely, therefore, that the limits of shape shifting as a political strategy will be sorely tested in the years to come.

NOTES

I would like to thank Frances Abele, Bruce Doern, Michael Prince, and Gene Swimmer for their thoughtful comments on this chapter, and Sandra Bach for her research assistance.

1 G. Bruce Doern, 'Editor's Summary: Spending Tax Dollars', in G. Bruce Doern, ed., *Spending Tax Dollars: Federal Expenditures 1980-81: Analysis and Commentary on Canadian Federal Expenditures and the 1980-81 Estimates* (Ottawa: School of Public Administration, 1980), 18.
2 G. Bruce Doern, 'Spending Priorities: The Liberal View', in G. Bruce Doern, ed., *How Ottawa Spends Your Tax Dollars: Federal Priorities 1981* (Toronto: Lorimer and Company, 1981), 32.
3 Ibid., 1.
4 Allan M. Maslove, 'Ottawa's New Agenda: The Issues and Constraints', in Allan M. Maslove, ed., *How Ottawa Spends 1984: The New Agenda* (Toronto: Methuen, 1984), 26-27.
5 Michael J. Prince, 'The Mulroney Agenda: A Right Turn for Ottawa?' in Michael J. Prince, ed., *How Ottawa Spends 1986-87: Tracking the Tories* (Toronto: Methuen, 1987), 10.
6 Michael J. Prince, 'Restraining the State: How Ottawa Shrinks', in Michael J. Prince, ed., *How Ottawa Spends 1987-88: Restraining the State* (Toronto: Methuen, 1988), 12.

7 Katherine A. Graham, 'Heading into the Stretch: Pathology of a Government', in Katherine A. Graham, ed., *How Ottawa Spends 1988/89: The Conservatives Heading into the Stretch* (Ottawa: Carleton University Press, 1988), 10-12.
8 Richard Johnston, André Blais, Henry E. Brady, and Jean Crête, *Letting the People Decide: Dynamics of a Canadian Election* (Montreal and Kingston: McGill-Queen's University Press, 1992).
9 Katherine A. Graham, 'Tracking the Second Agenda: Once More with Feeling?' in Katherine A. Graham, ed., *How Ottawa Spends 1990-91: Tracking the Second Agenda: Once More with Feeling?* (Ottawa: Carleton University Press, 1990), 6.
10 Frances Abele, 'The Politics of Fragmentation', in Frances Abele, ed., *How Ottawa Spends 1991-92: The Politics of Fragmentation* (Ottawa: Carleton University Press, 1991), 18-19.
11 Frances Abele, 'The Politics of Competitiveness', in Frances Abele, ed., *How Ottawa Spends 1992-93: The Politics of Competitiveness* (Ottawa: Carleton University Press, 1992), 4.
12 Susan D. Phillips, 'A More Democratic Canada...?' in Susan D. Phillips, ed., *How Ottawa Spends 1993-94: A More Democratic Canada...?* (Ottawa: Carleton University Press 1994), 23-5.
13 Susan D. Phillips, 'Making Change: The Potential for Innovation Under the Liberals', in Susan D. Phillips, ed., *How Ottawa Spends 1994-95: Making Change* (Ottawa: Carleton University Press, 1994), 3.
14 Susan D. Phillips, 'The Liberals' Mid-Life Crises: Aspirations Versus Achievements', in Susan D. Phillips, ed., *How Ottawa Spends 1995-96: Mid-Life Crises* (Ottawa: Carleton University Press, 1995), 2.
15 Gene Swimmer, 'An Introduction to Life Under the Knife', in Gene Swimmer, ed., *How Ottawa Spends 1996-97: Life Under the Knife* (Ottawa: Carleton University Press, 1996), 2.
16 Gene Swimmer, 'Seeing Red: A Liberal Report Card', in Gene Swimmer, ed., *How Ottawa Spends 1997-98: Seeing Red: A Liberal Report Card* (Ottawa: Carleton University Press, 1997), 2. It should be noted that the Liberals' record on job creation and employment growth, even for younger workers, has been quite impressive in the last two years.
17 Globalization should be understood primarily as a technological and economic process driven by the revolution in telecommunications, economic production, and investment. Internationalization is linked to globalization, and refers to the varying degrees to which domestic policy-making is influenced by factors outside of territorial boundaries. See G. Bruce Doern, Leslie A. Pal, Brian Tomlin, eds, *Border Crossings: The Internationalization of Canadian Public Policy* (Toronto: Oxford University Press, 1996).
18 I owe this insight to Bruce Doern.

19 See Janine Brodie, 'Regulating the Economic Union', in Leslie A. Pal, ed., *How Ottawa Spends 1998-99: Balancing Act: The Post-Deficit Mandate* (Toronto: Oxford University Press, 1998), 81-98, and G. Bruce Doern and Mark MacDonald, *Free-Trade Federalism: Negotiating the Canadian Agreement on Internal Trade* (Toronto: University of Toronto Press, 1999).
20 'The World Economy', *The Economist* 5-11 Sept. 1998. Web site: http://www.economist.com/editorial/freeforall/current/index_sf1128.htm
21 Paul Martin, Minister of Finance, *The Economic and Fiscal Update: Strong Economy and Secure Society* (Ottawa: Supply and Services Canada, 14 Oct. 1998), 8.
22 Ibid., 41.
23 Elizabeth Thompson, 'Bouchard Urged to Co-operate with Conference', *The Ottawa Citizen,* 4 Aug. 1998.
24 Joan Bryden, 'Quebec Plays Along with Social Agenda', *The Ottawa Citizen*, 7 Aug. 1998.
25 'No Major Changes in Election Counts', *The Gazette* [Montreal], 3 Dec. 1998.
26 Reference re Secession of Quebec, Supreme Court of Canada. Web site: http://www.scc-csc.gc.ca/reference/hn.htm and 'Minister Dion Stresses the Need to Respect the Supreme Court's Decision in Its Entirety', *Press Release*, 26 Aug. 1996. Web site: http://www.pco-bcp.gc.ca/aia/ro/doc/eaug2698.htm
27 Unless otherwise indicated, this discussion draws on *The Budget Speech 1999* (Ottawa: Department of Finance, 16 Feb. 1999) and *The Budget in Brief 1999* (Ottawa: Department of Finance, 16 Feb. 1999).

2

Rethinking Government As If People Mattered: From 'Reaganomics' to 'Humanomics'

FRANK L. GRAVES

As the century closes, it is clear that we have witnessed a profound transformation in the nature of the relationships linking citizens, the state, and broader institutions in Canadian society. The depth of this 'shape shifting' can be established by even the most casual consideration of the nature of these relationships at the turn of the last century. In 1899, over 90 per cent of Canadians who were in the labour market were employed in agriculture, post-secondary education was a rarity, and women's suffrage was only a distant possibility. Apart from Aboriginals, the population was almost entirely composed of those of white European descent. Today, less than 1 per cent of the labour force works in agriculture, universal access to post-secondary education is a given, and a complex system of identity politics attempts to cope with a highly pluralistic and rapidly evolving society. Yet the basic political system of that earlier era—a system of elected representation in which decisions are made through elite accommodation on behalf of a deferential citizenry—is still in place. It is little wonder that Canada, like virtually all other advanced western societies, is experiencing intense public disenchantment with government.

In this chapter, we examine shifting Canadian attitudes to and values concerning the role of the state and broader societal institutions. The end of a century provides an opportunity for stock-taking and review. This is even more the case at the end of a millennium. Ekos Research Associates surveys[1] tell us that 60 per cent of Canadians believe that the millennium is a 'serious and momentous landmark', whereas only 40 per cent feel it is 'just a lot of hype'. It has been instructive to find that the 'landmark' view has grown in popularity as the actual date approaches.

The current blend of public attitudes and values concerning government and society is complex and turbulent. There are, however, some very important new points of consensus and contradiction that are well worth summarizing at this juncture. After all, the public and its collective interests are supposed to be the *raison d'être* for government—a notion that most members of the public view sceptically. Fewer than one in five Canadians believe that when governments make decisions they place the highest priority on the 'public interest'. Over 80 per cent believe that the interests of governments themselves, of big business, or of the friends of the powerful take real priority.

We begin with the 20-year period of 'shape shifting' selected as the theme for the volume. This period neatly coincides with that during which Ekos Research Associates has been studying public attitudes to and experiences with government. We will provide a brief summary of some of the key shifts in public attitudes evident over this period, drawing on both the literature and our own impressions from our internal research.

Our most detailed and rigorous conclusions will be drawn from the results of our ongoing *Rethinking Government* project. This research project was primarily supported by a consortium of governments. Now in its fifth year, *Rethinking Government* is based on an annual panel survey (this year, an initial random panel of 4,000 households). The database now includes nearly 3,000 variables and 30,000 interviews. In addition to this extensive quantitative telephone survey database, the study also includes a parallel survey of Canada's elites, in both the public sector and the private sector, as well as diagnostic qualitative research with sub-samples of original survey respondents to explore ambiguities and to deepen the understanding of the survey issues. This is one of the most exhaustive examinations of public attitudes, values, and behaviour related to government and other institutions ever conducted in Canada.

The study also constitutes a unique opportunity to provide a clear empirical profile of mature Canadian public opinion at the end of the period of fiscal 'crisis'. More than any other factor or event, the recent debate over the changing role of the state was focussed through the prism of the issues of debt and deficit. The *Rethinking Government* project straddles the most intense period of this debate and provides clear yet surprising conclusions about what Canadians really want from government in this post-deficit *fin de siècle*.

CYNICISM, INDIVIDUALISM, AND INSECURITY: THE LATE 20TH CENTURY

It is now a truism to note that Canadians have become more cynical and mistrustful of government over the past 20 years. The objects of this decline in trust are not restricted to governments, but also include broader societal institutions. Indeed, most Canadians think that there has been a broad erosion in the ethical standards not only of government and other institutions, but of individual Canadians themselves. Perceptions of a decline in interpersonal trust, particularly strong among those born after the Second World War, reinforce the mistrust of institutions.

The decline of trust in government may be the most striking feature of Canadian public attitudes to the state, but it is by no means restricted to Canada. International research vividly documents the consistency of this loss of faith in government in virtually all advanced western democracies.[2] A particularly revealing indicator of declining trust in government, drawn from the *American National Election Studies* of 1958 to 1996, shows a steady decline in the percentage of Americans who believe that they can trust the federal government 'always or most of the time' from over 70 per cent in 1960 to around 30 per cent in 1996.[3]

In Canada, public confidence in government is no lower than in other advanced western societies, but the fall from grace may well have been more precipitous. Analysts such as S.M. Lipset and others have commented that Canadians traditionally have had more deferential and respectful social values than Amercians.[4] This respect for authority and the search for order that accompanied it, was linked to the fact that a powerful elite regulated the political and economic order in a relatively quiet and occluded fashion.[5]

As Nevitte persuasively argues, the legitimacy of this elite has largely evaporated in the face of a rapid 'decline of deference'.[6] The depth of this decline and the diminution of the authority of the elite were vividly evident in Canadians' rejection of the Charlottetown Accord, notwithstanding the elite's clear consensual endorsement. Both Nevitte and Inglehart, using the 1981 and 1990 *World Values Surveys*, argue that there are many common features in public attitudes to government and institutions in advanced western societies.[7] Although there are also points of difference, most advanced western societies have witnessed this decline in confidence in government. There has also been a general rise in interest in politics, a rise in cosmopolitanism, a decline in religious observance, and a decline in materialism. Although it is less universally evident, there has actually been a significant *rise* in nationalism in North America, Canada in particular. Notwithstanding the claims of Thomas Courchene and others, nationalism is not yet being supplanted by regionalism, despite apparent shifts in trade axes from East-West to North-South.[8] Moreover, in spite of the diminution of federal policy, devolution, and increased sensitivities to 'fair share' arguments, Ontarians actually revealed declining attachments to province and much higher (and stable) attachments to country over the past two decades.[9]

This finding reflects the persistence of what Richard Gwyn has called 'state-nationalism' in Canada (that is, the unique role of the federal state in constructing a highly relevant source of national identity and belonging, particularly in English Canada).[10] This, along with a few other features, produces some additional layers of complexity that must be taken into account if attitudes to the state in Canada are to be understood.

In Canada, we have seen a number of interesting shifts in attitudes to the state and social and cultural policy. For instance, Ekos's data show a modest but significant decline in support since the 1980s for state intervention to support Canadian culture, despite the stable or rising attachment to country. In the early part of the 1980s, clear majorities of Canadians opposed quite modest reductions to Unemployment Insurance (from 60 to 57 per cent coverage). At the end of the decade, the majority supported much more dramatic reductions (to around 50 per cent coverage) and much tighter entrance restrictions as a step 'in the right direction'. The data also show rising support for trade liberalization and globalization. These longer-term shifts in the past couple of decades seem to be at odds with evidence of rising national attachment, and more recent evidence of a strong return of support for active 'investment' on the part of government.

Another important shift is rising individualism and, by corollary, declining collectivism. This is linked to increased emphasis on competitiveness, which is in turn linked to globalization. Most Canadians (two out of three) believe that we have become more individualistic and competitive. A similar large majority sees this as a trend for the worse, and they attribute it to growing 'Americanization'.

The issue of values becomes a central component of this debate. Authors like Nevitte and Inglehart place considerable emphasis on the role of 'post-materialist' values as major explanatory factors for understanding these changes. More basic demographic explanations, such as shifts in immigration, or population aging, do not really seem to have much explanatory force, and even the intuitively appealing 'contagion effects argument' that these changes in Canada are led by the United States is highly inconsistent with the data (many key shifts occurred in Canada or other countries earlier than in the US).[11] The 'rhythms of post-materialism' are rooted in declining respect for authority and the evolution of post-modern sensibilities. Rising rates of post-secondary education, shifts in workers' attitudes, and the ubiquitous influence of the media (particularly the increasingly critical tone of electronic mass media) have all exerted profound influences on citizen attitudes.

The often illiterate farm workers, miners, and fishermen of 1899 were largely content to elect their representatives and then trust them to deal with other elites in Ottawa to make decisions on their behalf. The much more educated, affluent, and cynical citizens of 1999 are bombarded with a daily deluge of information, much of it prurient in tone and often critical of politicians and other leaders. The public's perception of the media's unduly critical focus on the activities of politicians has had the ironic result of weakening trust in the media as an institution. Our research shows that the media have actually experienced the second steepest decline in legitimacy of all institutions in the past five years, including government (Fig. 2.1).[12]

Figure 2.1
Change in Performance of Institutions

'How has the performance of each of these institutions changed in the past five years?'

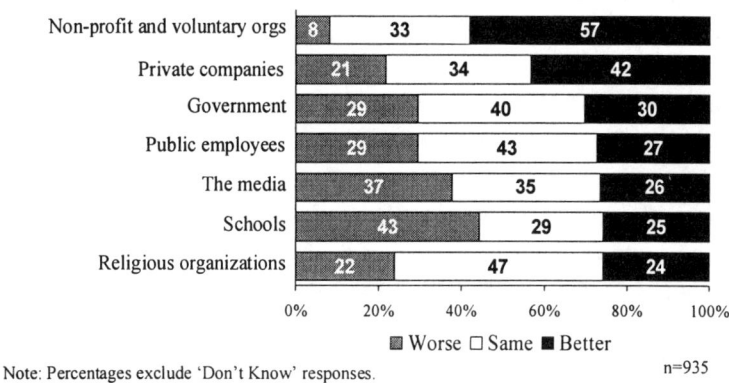

Institution	Worse	Same	Better
Non-profit and voluntary orgs	8	33	57
Private companies	21	34	42
Government	29	40	30
Public employees	29	43	27
The media	37	35	26
Schools	43	29	25
Religious organizations	22	47	24

■ Worse □ Same ■ Better

n=935

Note: Percentages exclude 'Don't Know' responses.
Source: Ekos Research Associates, *Rethinking Government*, April 1998

Part of this decline in trust is linked to concerns about the excessive and largely unaccountable power exercised by the media. Roughly three in four Canadians believe that the media exercise a lot of power, whereas only one in four think they should. Provocatively, roughly the same percentage of Canadians think their senior governments (that is, federal and provincial) exercise a lot of power but about the *same* percentage feel that they *should* have this much power. This underlines an important but often obscured point. Governments still enjoy legitimacy in terms of the power citizens think they should wield. When asked how to rebalance power to redress perceived public inequities, Canadians do not call for a reduction in government power. Rather they wish to see the power of the media and big business reduced and that of average citizens and small business elevated.

When asked to divide societal roles and responsibilities for collective action across different institutions (for example, media, business, third sector, schools, religions), governments are still identified as the prime agent for achieving societal goals. In fact, part of the anger toward government may be a sense of being held hostage to government in the absence of plausible alternatives. Governments are clearly seen as wasteful and self-serving, but few Canadians express confidence in the alternatives of the marketplace, the family, or the voluntary sector as a replacement for what are still seen as highly relevant goals for Canadian society (for example, security and protection, societal goalsetting, promoting economic and social security, ensuring a healthy population, promoting unity and identity).[13] In some important respects, undue focus on trust and legitimacy obscures the continued relevance of government as an institution for achieving collective goals and a sense of moral community. Once again, the issue of values is close to the heart of this discussion.

Insecurity is a defining feature of Canadian society, and over the past decade it has become 'unhinged'. It is highly volatile and a key predictor of a broad range of attitudes to government and society. 'Unhinged' is a characterization not only of the turbulence of our insecurity indicators but also of the perplexing disconnection between Canadians' perception of their economic situation and the official or statistical economy of gross domestic product (GDP) and unemployment rates. At various times over the last five years, far more Canadians have agreed that they have 'lost all control of their economic future' than disagreed, and no fewer than 30 per cent of Canadians have agreed with the statement during this time (Fig. 2.2). There has been a medium-term pattern of declining insecurity. We are also seeing similar findings with respect to the incidence of those who feel they could lose their jobs, despite macroeconomic indicators pointing to a relatively healthier situation.

Without discussing why Canada has so often been 'down' when GDP has been up, we offer the following observations:

- *Insecurity is broader and deeper than simple job insecurity.* Although connected to rational economic factors, particularly fears about rapid technological change and a 'workless' future, insecurity is also cultural in nature. Fears about

Figure 2.2
Tracking Economic Insecurity

'I feel I have lost all control over my economic future'

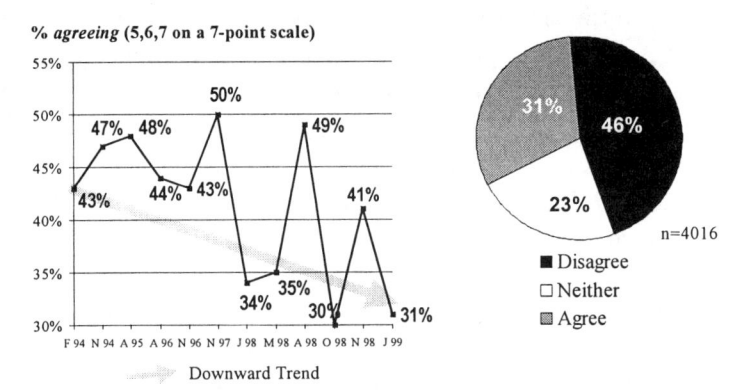

% *agreeing* (5,6,7 on a 7-point scale)

[Line chart showing percentages from F 94 to J 99: 43%, 47%, 48%, 44%, 43%, 50%, 49%, 34%, 35%, 30%, 41%, 31%, with downward trend indicated]

[Pie chart: Disagree 46%, Neither 23%, Agree 31%, n=4016]

Source: Government Communications Survey and *Rethinking Government*

identity, community, and values are directly connected to anxieties about the future.

- *Insecurity is unlikely to be 'solved' in the next few years and will continue to fluctuate.* The looming prism of the millennium is magnifying broader insecurities about meaning and identity in the next century.
- *Insecurity is increasingly polarized across social class and regional lines.* The East-West security divide is roughly demarcated by the Ottawa River. In part, insecurity is itself driven by fears of polarization. Our concluding section will show that two types of Canadians (the Anxious and Angry [21 per cent] and the Alienated and Disconnected [13 per cent])[14] find little comfort in strengthening macroeconomic performance.
- *Insecurity is seen as both a product of government action and a key reason for government.* Managing large-scale risks, and facilitating a smoother, more orderly transition to the future, are seen as key roles for government.

It is also interesting to note that *insecurity does not preclude optimism*. Many insecure Canadians are sustaining an uneasy mixture of hope and anxiety while looking to the national government for signals that it can help manage risk and create opportunity. In the past year, we have witnessed an impressive growth in optimism and a decline in longer-term economic insecurity. This new buoyancy, particularly pronounced among younger citizens, is linked to increased receptivity to a new 'practical vision' for Canadian government.

VALUES, POWER, PUBLIC JUDGMENT, AND CITIZEN ENGAGEMENT

How do the issues of values, power, public judgment, and citizen engagement relate to each other? Citizens are feeling more cynical and fractious and less compliant now than twenty years ago. In addition to cultural and demographic factors, part of this discontent is driven by discomfort with the distribution of power and privilege. Citizens' desire for greater inclusion in decision-making is rooted in a sense of relative powerlessness and a growing conviction that citizens can operate as equals to elites and leaders, particularly in the realm of values.

Canadians want to see more of their values reflected in government. Figures 2.3 and 2.4 show the most recent value hierarchy for government, with changes from five years earlier noted in brackets. Canadians espouse a mix of liberal and conservative values for the federal government. The continued low ranking of minimal government intrusions, in contrast to the high ranking accorded to values such as a healthy population and a clean environment, reflects a desire for active, humanistic government. At the same time, conservative values such as hard work, integrity and ethics, productivity, and family values, are now rated well ahead of egalitarian values, such as sharing wealth among rich and poor, redistribution of wealth, and social cohesion. This underlines the continued erosion of Canadians' faith in passive income support as a way of addressing social problems.

It is important to note that humanistic-idealistic values top the public's hierarchy. At the bottom of the list is minimal government. Equality values (based on redistribution) are also relatively lowly rated, as are values linked to wealth and competitiveness. One of our core conclusions is that the economy is really important, but that the economy

46 HOW OTTAWA SPENDS

Figure 2.3
Tracking Preferred Values for Federal Government (A)

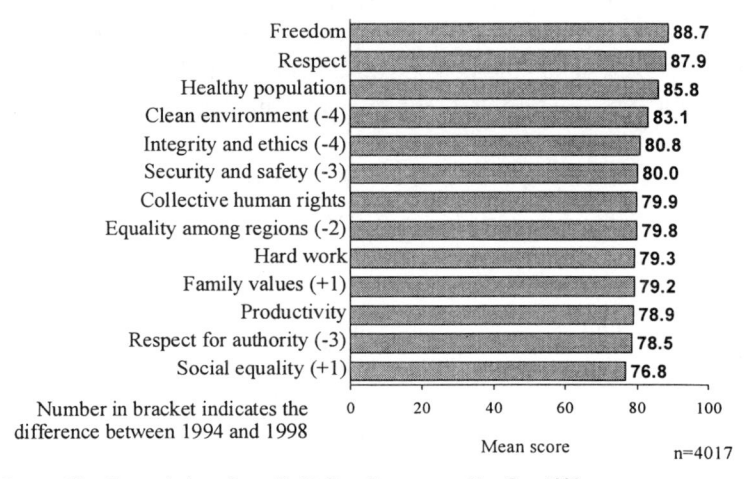

Value	Mean score
Freedom	88.7
Respect	87.9
Healthy population	85.8
Clean environment (-4)	83.1
Integrity and ethics (-4)	80.8
Security and safety (-3)	80.0
Collective human rights	79.9
Equality among regions (-2)	79.8
Hard work	79.3
Family values (+1)	79.2
Productivity	78.9
Respect for authority (-3)	78.5
Social equality (+1)	76.8

Number in bracket indicates the difference between 1994 and 1998

n=4017

Source: Ekos Research Associates, *Rethinking Government*, Nov-Dec 1998

Figure 2.4
Tracking Preferred Values for Federal Government (B)

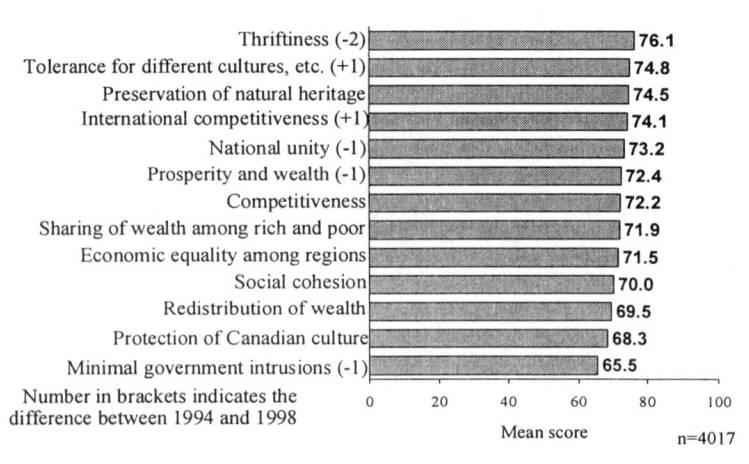

Value	Mean score
Thriftiness (-2)	76.1
Tolerance for different cultures, etc. (+1)	74.8
Preservation of natural heritage	74.5
International competitiveness (+1)	74.1
National unity (-1)	73.2
Prosperity and wealth (-1)	72.4
Competitiveness	72.2
Sharing of wealth among rich and poor	71.9
Economic equality among regions	71.5
Social cohesion	70.0
Redistribution of wealth	69.5
Protection of Canadian culture	68.3
Minimal government intrusions (-1)	65.5

Number in brackets indicates the difference between 1994 and 1998

n=4017

Source: Ekos Research Associates, *Rethinking Government*, Nov-Dec 1998

and economic values are seen as instrumental, not terminal values. Economic values such as thrift, productivity, and competitiveness are seen as tools for the achievement of higher order, humanistic goals (for example, healthy population, freedom, a clean environment). We think that the idea of 'humanomics' may help capture this rising sentiment.

Although yet another neologism to describe government is probably not an urgent need, we believe that the label 'humanomics' can help describe a growing public desire for an approach to an economy that recognizes the centrality of both real world human results (such as better health, higher skills, stronger quality of life), and human resource inputs (such as better human capital investments in health and education) as means for achieving these results. Humanomics can be a new blending of social investment and hard economic priorities such that government serves as a strategic broker linking citizens, the private sector, and other institutions. The notion of humanomics can help redefine the relationship between economic and social policy, not as competitors for scarce societal resources, but as complementary components of an overall plan to increase opportunity and reduce risks in the new economy. Citizens believe that humanism and economics can be synthesized to transcend some of the excesses and divisions that characterized the traditional focus on left and right. We also believe it can help solve the paradox of how it can be 'the economy stupid', when all of the top values and priorities for government are humanistic concerns. It may be the economy if economy means jobs, security, and people, but (for the public) not really the economy if that means only dollars and markets. Citizens want to see the economy harnessed for the well-being of average citizens—hence the promise of humanomics.

The study of Canadian society reveals a complex mosaic of cross-cutting values and sentiments that shape attitudes to government. Individualistic-libertarian values coexist with collectivist-conservative values—often within the same individuals. The new-found rejection of elite authority in Canada may be causing considerable internal conflict in the values of many Canadians. This is because of our historical tendency to respect authority—which the current research confirms as a still potent but declining core value in Canadian society. It would be a mistake to underestimate the potential for the happy coexistence of many seemingly internally contradictory values within the same individuals.

Our analysis of values, attitudes, and priorities leads to the conclusion that most Canadians see government as a means for expressing core values. In Canada, the country is a crucial source of identity and belonging (second only to family). As the *World Values Survey* and other sources confirm, attachment to country is actually higher in Canada than in any other advanced country, and it has risen over the past 30 years. Canadians seem to be seeking a higher-order moral community, and not merely a rational articulation of economic interests. There is a strong sense that the eighties' pursuit of materialistic-economic priorities has left Canadians disillusioned with the prosperity-minimalist government model, and searching for sources of meaning, values, and decency. The precise content and form of these post-materialist values remain vague, and there are a number of competing models of nationalism and moral community evident within the diverse Canadian publics. These range from traditional-conservative models stressing heritage and unity to the more social-activist, collectivist models such as the one underlying Quebec nationalism.

Elite Perspectives on Values and Government
The inaugural edition of *Rethinking Government* documented a 'normative rupture' separating the rated values of the public and the elites.[15] The comparison between the elites and the general public suggests that a profound gap exists between the public and decision-makers in the area of preferred government values (Fig. 2.5).

Decision-makers place a much lower value on most of the values discussed above. Competitiveness, minimal government, and prosperity appear near or at the top of the elite values for government—the opposite of their positioning for the general public. It is as though the elites look at government through the other end of the public's telescope. The elite are only weakly attached to their values, compared to the general public. Not only is the intensity of commitment to everything related to government reduced, it is also purged of its moral content. The elite perspective on government is more instrumental and more rational.

Figure 2.5
Values for the Federal Government

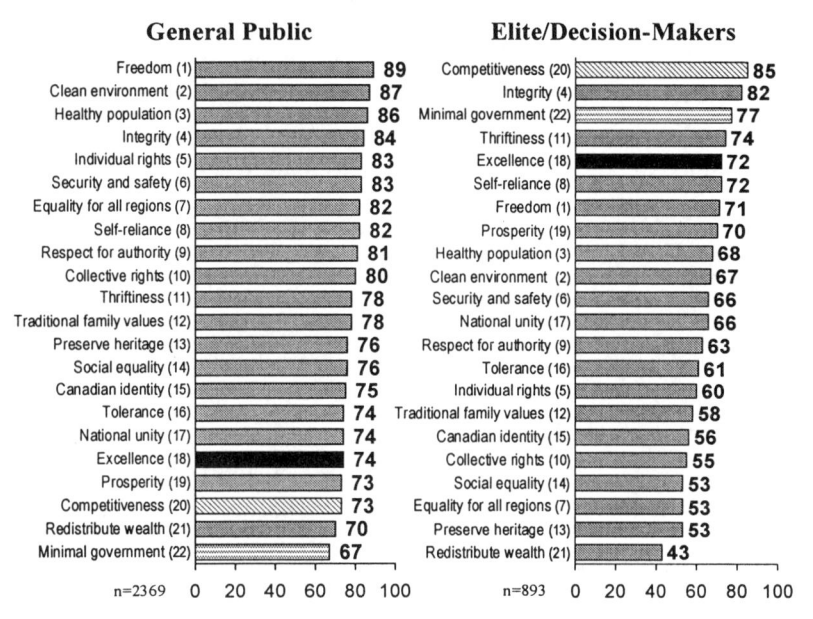

General Public

Value	Score
Freedom (1)	89
Clean environment (2)	87
Healthy population (3)	86
Integrity (4)	84
Individual rights (5)	83
Security and safety (6)	83
Equality for all regions (7)	82
Self-reliance (8)	82
Respect for authority (9)	81
Collective rights (10)	80
Thriftiness (11)	78
Traditional family values (12)	78
Preserve heritage (13)	76
Social equality (14)	76
Canadian identity (15)	75
Tolerance (16)	74
National unity (17)	74
Excellence (18)	74
Prosperity (19)	73
Competitiveness (20)	73
Redistribute wealth (21)	70
Minimal government (22)	67

n=2369

Elite/Decision-Makers

Value	Score
Competitiveness (20)	85
Integrity (4)	82
Minimal government (22)	77
Thriftiness (11)	74
Excellence (18)	72
Self-reliance (8)	72
Freedom (1)	71
Prosperity (19)	70
Healthy population (3)	68
Clean environment (2)	67
Security and safety (6)	66
National unity (17)	66
Respect for authority (9)	63
Tolerance (16)	61
Individual rights (5)	60
Traditional family values (12)	58
Canadian identity (15)	56
Collective rights (10)	55
Social equality (14)	53
Equality for all regions (7)	53
Preserve heritage (13)	53
Redistribute wealth (21)	43

n=893

Source: Ekos Research Associates, *Rethinking Government*, 1994

Elites are fairly homogeneous in their values and in their attitudes about government. This finding is likely due both to their shared social class and to the internal cohesion produced by the current fiscal situation. The elite consensus and the wide discrepancies between the public and the decision-makers suggest that a chasm exists between those charged with governing our country and those being governed. Whether elites are correct in their beliefs or not, they are clearly disconnected from the views of the mass public, and this disconnection serves to underline the growing rift between the comfortable and the insecure segments of Canadian society.

Our tracking of the normative rupture separating elite and mass public values suggests that the extent of the gap has narrowed over the past five years. This narrowing may reflect a convergence that is based on elite recognition that public values may well be different from elite values, and that public decision-makers must understand and reflect citizen values more fully. Perhaps as a result of the elites' having recognized their declining legitimacy, elite 'pollmanship' may have produced survey responses that appear to narrow the gap. One large gap that persists concerns views on one of the prime remedies proposed for redressing public exclusion—citizen engagement.

Citizen Engagement
If a key engine of discontent with government is a perception that it has lost its focus on public interest, that citizens are excluded from real power and decision-making, and that public values are inadequately reflected in government, the 'citizen engagement' model becomes a theoretically attractive remedy for these problems. Our recent work on citizen engagement[16] shows that only about one in four Canadians think that average citizens have a lot of power, but three in four think that they should. This is roughly the opposite of their views on the power balance for big business and the media. Some of the more promising remedies proposed for citizen powerlessness are various expressions of the notion of citizen engagement as discussed by such authors as Daniel Yankelovich and James Fishkin.[17]

Overall, the general public is more likely than decision-makers to perceive a need to engage ordinary citizens in public issues (Fig. 2.6).

Figure 2.6
Perceived Need for Engagement

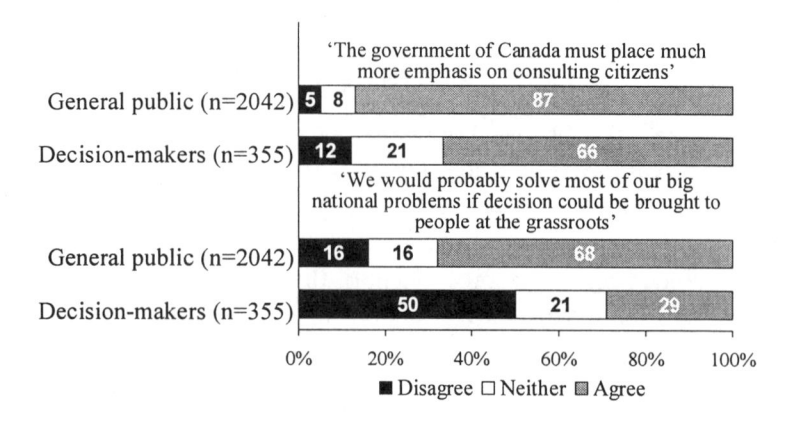

'The government of Canada must place much more emphasis on consulting citizens'

	Disagree	Neither	Agree
General public (n=2042)	5	8	87
Decision-makers (n=355)	12	21	66

'We would probably solve most of our big national problems if decision could be brought to people at the grassroots'

	Disagree	Neither	Agree
General public (n=2042)	16	16	68
Decision-makers (n=355)	50	21	29

Sources: Ekos Research Associates, *Rethinking Government*, June 1998, and *Rethinking Citizen Engagement*, March 1998

PUBLIC OPINION   51

Elites and public share roughly the same qualitative views on consultation or engagement, but elites are clearly more tepid in their support. According to the other survey indicator (originally drawn from the Lortie Commission), most members of the public (68 per cent) agree that we would solve most of our big national problems if decisions were brought to people at the grassroots. Elites are clearly unconvinced, with less than one in three agreeing. This underlines continued elite-public attitudinal cleavages, and probably reflects resistance on the part of elites to abandoning their traditional hold on power in Canada.

How Would Canadians Realign Power?
If Canadians were provided with the opportunity to redesign the distribution of power in Canadian society, how would they proceed? Survey respondents were presented with a list of 12 actors and asked to rate how much influence each actor actually has and how much each *should* have on how decisions concerning major public issues are made (Fig. 2.7).

Figure 2.8 combines these data to produce an 'influence gap' index. This shows who Canadians would like to elevate, humble, or leave

Figure 2.7
Influence of Various Actors
'How much influence do/should each of the following have?'

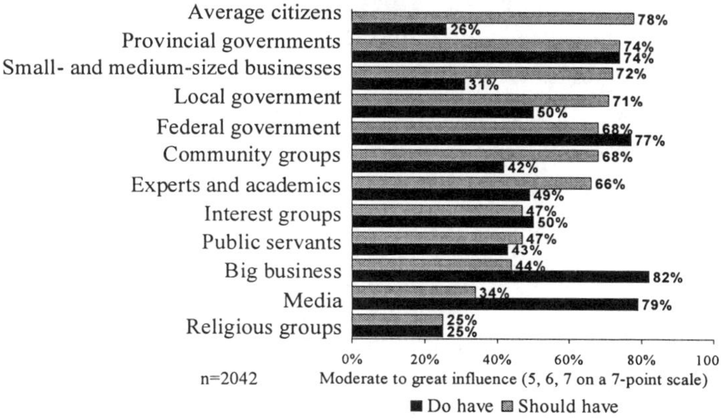

Actor	Do have	Should have
Average citizens	26%	78%
Provincial governments	74%	74%
Small- and medium-sized businesses	31%	72%
Local government	50%	71%
Federal government	68%	77%
Community groups	42%	68%
Experts and academics	49%	66%
Interest groups	47%	50%
Public servants	47%	43%
Big business	44%	82%
Media	34%	79%
Religious groups	25%	25%

n=2042   Moderate to great influence (5, 6, 7 on a 7-point scale)

Source: Ekos Research Associates, *Rethinking Citizen Engagement*, March 1998

alone in the current hierarchy of power and influence. Overall, there is a surprising degree of balance in the perceptions of who should and who does exercise power, with only four groups perceived as being egregiously under- or overpowered.

Figure 2.8
The Influence Gap

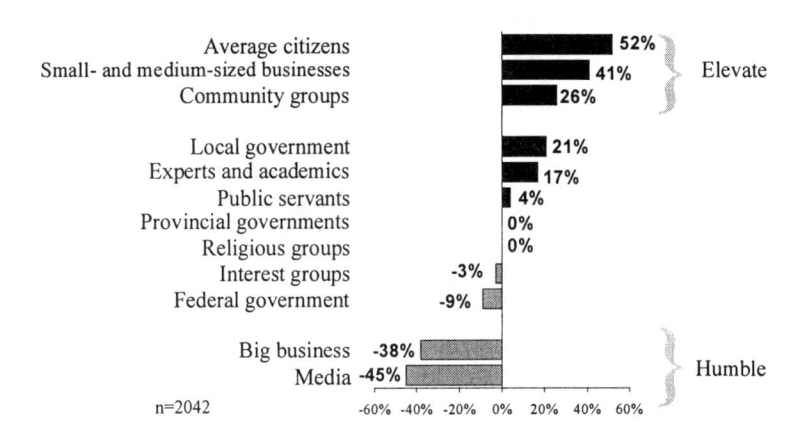

Group	Value	
Average citizens	52%	Elevate
Small- and medium-sized businesses	41%	
Community groups	26%	
Local government	21%	
Experts and academics	17%	
Public servants	4%	
Provincial governments	0%	
Religious groups	0%	
Interest groups	-3%	
Federal government	-9%	
Big business	-38%	Humble
Media	-45%	

n=2042

Source: Ekos Research Associates, *Rethinking Citizen Engagement*, March 1998

Not surprisingly, the largest gap is for average citizens (52 percentage points). This influence gap is at the root of the demand for greater inclusion and engagement. There is also a strong preference to elevate small business (which may be a reflection of relative popularity and empathetic resonance with the public).

There is a strong desire to reduce the power of the media and big business. The relatively broad range of agreement with respect to perceptions and preferences concerning government power is fairly impressive, although there appears to be a mild desire for rebalancing power downward to the local levels.

Noteworthy also is the position of voluntary and third-party representation. Notwithstanding rising criticisms of identity politics and interest group representation, the survey evidence suggests that most Canadians see a healthy balance existing here—the somewhat provocatively described 'interest' groups are seen as at a balance point, and 'community groups' are seen as candidates for increased power.

What results from these tests is three broad classes of political actors: potentates, the moderately influential, and the disenfranchised. These can be further classified according to whether their power is seen to be legitimate or illegitimate. Figure 2.9 illustrates this classification.

Figure 2.9
Canadians' Attitudes Toward Legitimacy and Power: Three Broad Classes

I. The Potentates
- Big business } Illegitimate
- The media

- The federal government } Legitimate
- Provincial governments

II. The Moderately Influential
- Community groups
- Local governments } Legitimate and to be advanced
- Experts and academics

- Interest groups } Legitimate and balanced
- Public servants

III. The Disenfranchised
- Small business } Legitimate and to be advanced
- Average citizens

- Religious groups } Legitimate and balanced

The fact that many actors are roughly at a point of equilibrium, and that there is a reasonable balance between those who should be advanced and those who should be humbled is mildly surprising. It suggests that legitimacy problems for governments may not be at the crisis level we might assume when simply examining trust and confidence indicators. In the next section we will show that, notwithstanding persistent trust and confidence issues, there is a clear resurgence of interest in government activism—albeit a very different form of government activism from the parental statism that characterized government 20 years ago.

POST-DEFICIT PUBLIC JUDGMENTS ON GOVERNMENT

What does the public really want from government in 'post-deficit' Canada? Those seeking a simple answer to this question will be disappointed. They may also be bewildered by the apparent inconsistencies in the conclusions of many polls claiming to answer this question. A series of high-profile media polls in recent years has argued that Canadians are demanding immediate broad-based tax relief, and that this demand is rising and outstrips other public policy priorities.[18] These polls and the accompanying editorial comment are typically linked to calls for minimal government. Our extensive *Rethinking Government* project is uniquely poised to provide a more neutral and complete answer. We have compiled a very detailed database and an ongoing time series asking the same questions at different points in time.[19]

Canadian attitudes to government are complex and turbulent and often there is no societal consensus on this issue. Moreover, the artificial framing of this issue in terms of tax relief, debt reduction, or more spending, risks reducing the question to terms that miss or distort the public understanding of why government exists. Nonetheless, the arguments for tax cuts and minimal government versus, for example, those for renewed active investments in health and education serve as proxies for some of the more fundamental underlying issues.[20]

In our view, the survey evidence, properly analysed, supports some fairly clear conclusions about public judgment at the end of a period when the fiscal crisis has dominated the debate about government and society. Here we attempt a catalogue of some core conclusions.

Conditional Receptivity to New Activism
In some important respects, the focus on trust and values obscures some more important areas of public judgment about government and society. Despite deep scepticism about the effectiveness, efficiency, and fairness of government, Canadians are clearly now looking for a return to an active agenda. Relaxed fears about public finances, growing concerns about the social costs of retrenchment and globalization, and a desire to preserve a unique Canadian identity are all fuelling guarded acceptance of a bigger role for governments in general and the federal government in particular. More recently, rising levels of economic optimism have further reinforced this 'active shift'.

In the past few years, we have seen Canadian public opinion stabilizing at a consensus that Canadians want both levels of government to increase or maintain their level of involvement across all policy areas (Fig. 2.10).[21] Desire for increased involvement for both levels of government far outstrips demands for reduced or eliminated involvement. This sentiment has grown since 1995, when 25 per cent were calling for reduced or eliminated involvement. This year, this number has declined to 10 per cent, with nearly half of all Canadians calling for increases and another roughly 40 per cent calling for the *status quo*. Even when we randomly alternated the word 'spending' instead of 'involvement', we got the same result.

Figure 2.10
Future Government Involvement Across All Priorities
'Overall what would you like to see the federal/provincial government do in the future?'

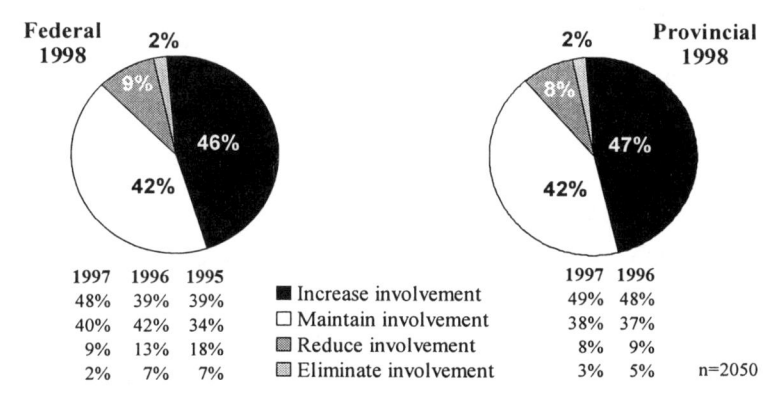

Federal	1997	1996	1995		Provincial	1997	1996
1998: 46% Increase	48%	39%	39%	■ Increase involvement	1998: 47%	49%	48%
1998: 42% Maintain	40%	42%	34%	□ Maintain involvement	1998: 42%	38%	37%
1998: 9% Reduce	9%	13%	18%	▨ Reduce involvement	1998: 8%	8%	9%
1998: 2% Eliminate	2%	7%	7%	▥ Eliminate involvement	1998: 2%	3%	5%

n=2050

Source: Ekos Research Associates, *Rethinking Government*, Nov-Dec 1998

When Canadians say they want increased activism, it does not mean that they have abandoned fiscal prudence, nor does it mean that they want a *holus bolus* return to the 'big government' models of a couple of decades ago. This new activism is highly conditional. Governments will be expected to meet important public conditions for renewed government activism. In very simple terms, Canadians want to see a shift from parentalism to partnerships, they want clear accountability for targets and results, they want fiscal prudence, and they want citizen inclusion in the selection of goals and means that reflect public values.

There are some significant divisions underlying these views. There is a very sizable gender gap, with women favouring a human agenda much more than do males, who emphasize a fiscal-economic agenda. There are also significant regional and social class effects, which see the more vulnerable and insecure portions of society favouring more activism. We will conclude with a typology that summarizes some of the patterns of difference in the public's attitudes to government (see Appendix).

A Rejection of Neo-Conservatism, but ...
One of the more striking features of the 1980s and early 1990s was the rise of neo-conservatism (or what is labelled neo-liberalism in Europe). The elections of Ronald Reagan and Margaret Thatcher, and to a much lesser extent that of Brian Mulroney in Canada, were linked to the weakening of the traditional left, social democratic styles of government. Traditional left and centre-left social democratic governments had featured big parental government, an ever-widening 'cradle to grave' set of social services, heavy utilization of passive income supports, a 'value-free' theory of social pathology, and highly impersonal, bureaucratic delivery systems linked to core values of equality of outcomes and social justice. Conditioned by a range of factors, but perhaps most tellingly by the sheer public costs of maintaining this state edifice, the 1980s and 1990s saw growing concerns about the efficacy, efficiency, and fairness of these post-war models of government. More and more concerned over tax burdens and the cost of big government, citizens—particularly more economically secure citizens—began to seriously attack the traditional liberal-capitalist paradigm of government. California's Proposition 13 tax revolt in the early 1980s may well have marked a watershed, where the legacy of the Democrats' Great Society began to give way to Reaganomics and new Republicanism. Thatcherism also successfully displaced Labour in Britain, and in Northern Europe many other social democratic governments fell.

At the same time the traditional right was further reinvigorated by a moral critique of progressive liberalism for its blindness to the role of values as either a cause or effect of social pathology. For example, in progressive eyes, poverty was seen as a product of environmental factors that could be corrected through wealth redistribution. The new right argued that social problems reflected problems of poor values (a poor work ethic, for example), and that passive income support had the ironic effect of exacerbating the very problems it was designed to alleviate (for example, by encouraging dependency and reducing self-reliance).

Essential Ingredients of Neo-Conservatism
Although it is subject to a variety of different interpretations, the vernacular meaning of neo-conservatism tends to embody the following elements:

- *Across-the-board tax cuts* and, in particular, tax relief for the middle class.
- *Increased emphasis on values and morality* in dealing with social problems such as poverty and crime (expressed in programs such as workfare, and bootcamps for young offenders).
- *Minimal government*, purged of waste, duplication, and abuse.
- *Private sector models for public sector reform* (for example, entrepreneurial systems of incentive and delivery of public programs, as well as increased commercialization of public services).
- *Trickledown economics*, according to which rising economic tides will lift all ships.
- *Largely unregulated private markets.*
- *Increased emphasis on the family, the community, and the voluntary sector* as sources of solutions for social problems.

This list is an incomplete and stylized depiction of neo-conservatism, but it nonetheless provides a useful checklist for our discussion. The items on this list have never persuaded the majority of Canadians. Now that the deficit crisis is over, and despite an intense diet of editorials (often supported by the apparently neutral narrative of 'scientific' polls funded by right-leaning media moguls), the neo-conservative movement has faltered and is in decline. In Canada, it is noteworthy that the plurality of Canadians (around 40 per cent) identify themselves as small-l liberals and about one in four identify themselves as small-c conservatives (many small-c conservatives reject some neo-conservative attitudes). By contrast, in the US less than 8 per cent of the public will accept a 'liberal' label.

On virtually every indicator and test that we examine, the neo-conservative wave—always overstated in terms of public support—is in collapse. For example, 'level of taxation' as a priority for federal action was rated highly by only 64 per cent of the Canadian public in January 1999, down from 75 per cent five years earlier. Health care as an issue was rated as a high priority by 85 per cent in early 1994. In January 1999, it received a high priority rating from 91 per cent of the public. This sizable advantage for active human investments over tax cuts also extends to areas such as child poverty, education, and unemployment. Furthermore, in hard trade-off choices, tax cuts, also lose to human investment options, and the sizable advantage for social investment priorities over fiscal priorities (taxes and debt) has actually widened over the past five years.

A tiny minority of Canadians agree with the proposition that now that the economy is strengthening, child poverty problems will also improve (a rough proxy for the trickledown thesis). On the other hand, 80 per cent of Canadians agree that now that the economy is strengthening, we should invest more to deal with problems of child poverty. We also find Canadians similarly sceptical about assuming that private sector practices are best for reforming the public service.

Indelible Impacts of Neo-Conservatism
Despite the rejection of neo-conservatism as a new dominant political ideology, the neo-conservative debate has had indelible impacts on Canadian attitudes to government and social policy. It clearly has reshaped public views on the role of the state. For example, Canadian political culture now takes fiscal prudence as a given. The old progressive model of wealth redistribution, passive income support, and a heavy state apparatus is also in disrepute with the public. Many Canadians believe that both the marketplace and governments have exerted a corrosive influence on the quality of Canadian society. Some core neo-conservative values such as thrift, hard work, and self-reliance have risen, while some traditional liberal values, such as com-

passion, equality, and statism have declined. Moreover, there has been a growing desire to link values, morality, and social policy.

For example, many believe that 'poor values' underlie problems of poverty and that simple income support may not only fail to solve social problems, but may well worsen them (Fig. 2.11). This dependency critique of social assistance has found favour, and many now view the social safety net as something of a hammock.

Figure 2.11
Factors Producing Poverty in Canada

'Which of the following problems is the most important factor producing poverty in Canada?'

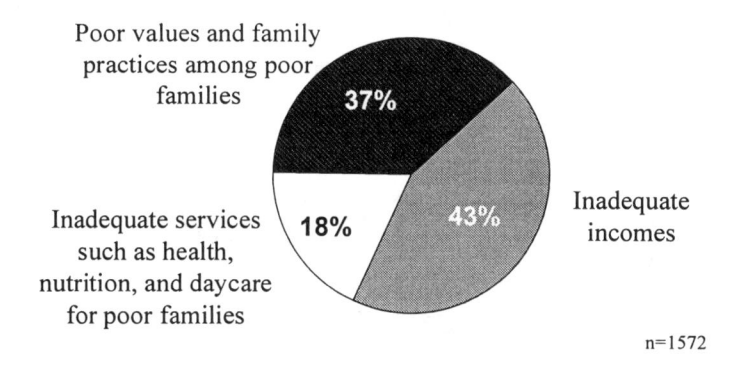

- Poor values and family practices among poor families: 37%
- Inadequate incomes: 43%
- Inadequate services such as health, nutrition, and daycare for poor families: 18%

n=1572

Source: *HRDC Child Poverty Survey*, October 1997

THE COLLISION OF INTEREST AND VALUES:
HEALTH CARE AS A SYMBOL OF BROADER PUBLIC
JUDGMENT ON THE ROLE OF THE STATE

The recent debate about health care and the 1999 federal health care budget provide a vivid illustration of the direction in which the public (and governments) are moving in post-deficit Canada. Health care has been a top public priority for some time. In early 1994, it was essentially tied, with jobs and the deficit, as one of the top public priorities. Since the current government originally took office in 1993, the issue of health care has become the key public priority. How and why did this occur and what does it mean?

Perhaps the most important visible expression of the emerging public judgment about government occurs in the health care field. Despite recent predictions to the contrary, Canadians are clearly opting for a 'one-tier' national health care system. Notwithstanding grave fears about declining quality, the incidence of those supporting a two-tier system has declined sharply (Fig. 2.12), and the vast majority of Canadians are urging governments to preserve a national, accessible, public health care system.

Figure 2.12
Tracking Beliefs Surrounding Two-Tier Health Care

'Individuals should be allowed to pay extra to get quicker access to health care services'

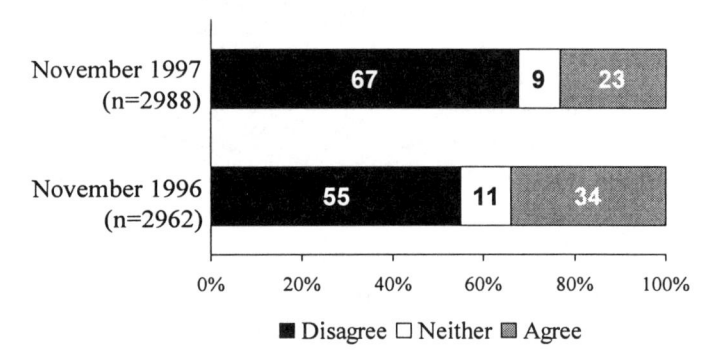

	Disagree	Neither	Agree
November 1997 (n=2988)	67	9	23
November 1996 (n=2962)	55	11	34

Source: Ekos Research Associates, *Rethinking Government*

In January 1999, health care had clearly consolidated its position as the dominant public priority. In the fall of 1998, there had been growing claims that the declining Canadian dollar, global market meltdowns in Asia and South America, and an apparently shrinking federal surplus would dampen the public's clear preference for health care reinvestment over fiscal priorities such as debt reduction and tax relief. The public recognized these external economic problems but they did not alter their clear preference for a health care budget. The issue of health care actually rose in importance progressively from the early part of the decade. From the fall of 1998 to January 1999, the public advantage for health investment over fiscal priorities widened further.

In some respects, this advantage occurred not so much as a result of the dramatic rise of health care (it only rose moderately), but rather as a result of a progressive decline in fiscal priorities and a more recent decline in concern with jobs and unemployment. Health care is strongly linked to other human investment priorities such as children and education (statistically, in a factor analysis of priorities, it loads on the same human investment dimension). Why, however, did health care emerge with such clarity as the top public priority in post-deficit Canada?

The answer does not lie in a direct, objective decline in the quality of the system. It is worth recalling that only two years ago, the health care system was seen as the outstanding public sector success story. It was a source of great pride and achievement, an icon of national unity and identity. There is little evidence that the actual system has declined as precipitously as has public confidence. Although there has been a recent plateau and perhaps a slight rebound in public confidence, most Canadians felt the system was in a virtual freefall. Both surveys and focus groups vividly documented a decline in public confidence that was linked to dire images of growing waiting lists, crowded emergency rooms, and the closing of hospitals. These fears were reinforced by extensive negative media reports. The premiers and, to a lesser extent, doctors had been successful in linking perceived decline to federal funding cuts through the Canadian Health and Social Transfer (CHST).

There were certainly real reasons for public concern; cuts were dramatic, and some of the reported problems were indeed real and worsening. The decline, however, was not as breathtakingly rapid as the public believed. Our surveys showed that the actual experiences of users of the system were still largely satisfactory, contrary to the imagery in the public consciousness.

Concern for health care also fit prominently into the unique demographic configuration of Canada. With the largest baby boom in the Western world, and a creeping recognition that the population of the aged was going to double over the next 20 years, the swollen boomer cohort became increasingly concerned with issues of health and mortality (both theirs and that of their parents, many of whom were now encountering the system). All of this occurred against the backdrop of deep cuts in federal CHST spending (the primary federal vehicle for funding health care) and earlier cuts to provincial spending. The public approved of some of these measures (particularly in theory) in the middle part of the decade, when concerns with debt and deficit were dominant. Now, the painful but necessary retrenchment of the mid-nineties seemed to be producing the demise of arguably the most cherished public institution in Canada. All of this debate occurred in the realm of both the highest practical stakes (health, life and death) and the highest core values of Canadians (health, equal access, caring, national identity). In a real sense, the debate became both a metaphor and a hard real world test for the future of Canadian society. In the 1997 federal election, every major party (perhaps reading the same polls) made health care, and the preservation of medicare, centrepieces of their platforms. This remarkable political consensus further reinforced public focus on the issue.

Another factor shaping the debate was that the provinces had managed to unload some of their perceived public responsibility as the chief causes of this problem. The federal government had been effectively damaged by the apparent consensus among the premiers. In the debate concerning health care, and the associated discussion on social union, the provinces were beginning to have some success in presenting themselves as 'national' champions. The federal government, which had previously owned the national standards and equal access issues, was seen as increasingly absent. Ottawa was anxious to re-establish some connection with Canadians and to renew its eroding moral authority in this crucial area.

The 1999 federal budget response, based on a blend of sizable renewed multi-year funding, a number of innovations, and a longer-term plan linked to accountability and integration, was conditioned by these factors. The public's initial response to these steps was approving and receptive. The longer-term impacts are uncertain.

Lest the significance of the health care debate be lost, let us restate it in stark terms. During the deficit crisis, Canadians accepted numerous cuts to social programs, in view of fiscal exigencies. As public finances returned to a state of equilibrium and a surplus ensued, Canadians faced a very real choice—tax cuts and increased private health care, or reinvestment in the publicly-funded system. In the court of public judgment, they clearly opted for reinvestment in publicly-funded health care over the obvious neo-conservative alternatives.

IS THERE A BOTTOM LINE?

Although polls are not physics, they are not astrology either. There should be some big-t truths about what the public is really thinking concerning the future role of government. Our research leads us to disagree with the view that support for tax cuts and minimal government is growing. Contrary to claims based on other recent national media polls, our evidence points to *declining* concerns about the level of taxation and *rising* support for active government.

When asked what priority the federal government should assign to 'level of taxation' in relation to other priorities, such as unemployment and debt, we find that it registers much lower as a public concern (Fig. 2.13). These patterns have continued into 1999 and are reinforced by numerous other tests and evidence.

Figure 2.13
Longer-Term Tracking of Priorities

'Thinking not just of today but over the next five years, what priority should the federal government place on each of the following areas?'

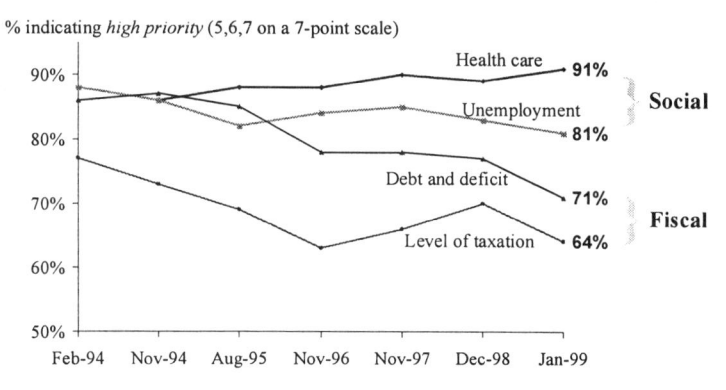

% indicating *high priority* (5,6,7 on a 7-point scale)

- Health care — 91% (Social)
- Unemployment — 81% (Social)
- Debt and deficit — 71% (Fiscal)
- Level of taxation — 64% (Fiscal)

Feb-94, Nov-94, Aug-95, Nov-96, Nov-97, Dec-98, Jan-99

Note: 'debt and deficit' replaced by 'debt and public finances' in January, 1998
Source: Government Communications Survey and *Rethinking Government*

Furthermore, there has been a consistent and progressive pattern of declining concern with level of taxation since the last federal election. At the same time, we are finding evidence of rising concern for others (Fig. 2.14) and increased receptivity to the role of government as an agent to address problems in our collective life. We also see a clear rejection of trickledown economics.

Figure 2.14
Concern for Others

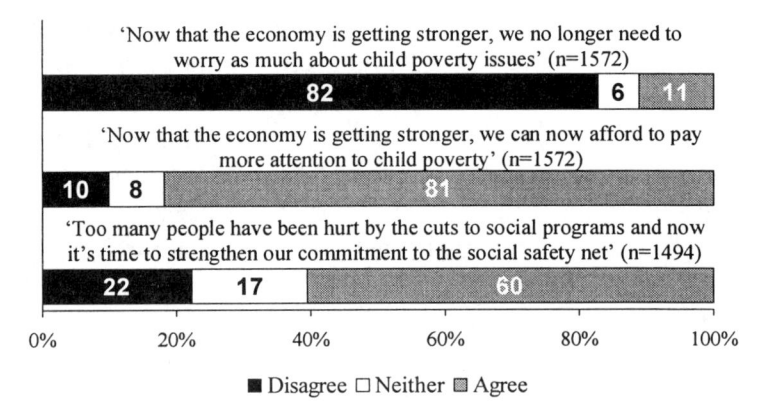

'Now that the economy is getting stronger, we no longer need to worry as much about child poverty issues' (n=1572)
Disagree 82 | Neither 6 | Agree 11

'Now that the economy is getting stronger, we can now afford to pay more attention to child poverty' (n=1572)
Disagree 10 | Neither 8 | Agree 81

'Too many people have been hurt by the cuts to social programs and now it's time to strengthen our commitment to the social safety net' (n=1494)
Disagree 22 | Neither 17 | Agree 60

■ Disagree □ Neither ▨ Agree

Source: *Rethinking Government*, November 1997, and HRDC Child Poverty Survey, October 1997

The public's desire for a return to active government is, however, highly conditional. The public resists a return to old-style government, and seeks a new style of governance that acknowledges the importance of targets, results measurement, fiscal discipline, and partnerships. The public does not want to reduce governments' role solely to that of an accountant. They also want government to help plan, coordinate, and protect. Despite reservations, Canadians still want government to help deal with the really big problems that are too onerous for them to manage on their own. Children, the next generation, and the growing gap between rich and poor are key examples of topics Canadians are deeply concerned about, and do not believe will be fixed by tax cuts or minimal government.

So why the confusion about taxes and government in post-deficit Canada? First, the culture of discourse of elites, which dominates the debate, is different from that of the general public in terms of both values and interests. Second, there are problems of methodology. The complex issues of the blurring boundaries across the state, citizens, and other sectors of society cannot be reduced to a couple of indicators.

We see the coexistence of two apparently contradictory core conclusions. First, most Canadians feel that taxes are too high, government does not work well, and we suffer enormous debt. The second, less visible conclusion, is a recovery of concern for others and strong support for an active government role in dealing with collective life. The public sees the possibility of reconciling these two sentiments through the use of a new style of government, which substitutes performance warranties for rhetoric, and strategic partnerships for parentalism. Time is, however, limited, and if new styles of government fail to deliver observable results, then, undoubtedly, Canadians will revisit the issue of tax cuts and minimal government with more vigour.

The next challenge for Canadian governments will be to offer a new model of government that incorporates the new public conditions for active government. In Britain, Tony Blair and the 'new Labour' have been successful in developing a 'third way'.[22] The Clinton administration has sketched out an analogous vision for the US. Canadians are increasingly receptive to a new but practical vision of a 21st century government that manages the unique blend of values and priorities expressed in Canadian society. Perhaps the notion of 'humanomics' (rather than Reaganomics) can capture the blending of new human investment priorities with a focus on creating overall winners in the new economy, rather than perpetuating the chronic division of society into those who pay and those who benefit from government. The challenge for the federal government will be to develop a plausible plan for managing risk and creating opportunity in the 21st century.

Despite the allure of a new consensual model of a humanomic state, there are deep divisions underlying this potential consensus. The rapid social, economic, and cultural change of the late 20th century has seen the emergence of an incipient underclass in Canada and deep disagreements among the economically comfortable classes. In the Appendix, we present a new segmentation of the public that underlines the extent of these differences and the depth of the challenge of seeking a new consensus.

APPENDIX

Beneath Consensus: The Shifting Structure of Political Class Culture in Canada

Five years ago, in the inaugural edition of *Rethinking Government*, Ekos constructed a typology of Canadian society that produced five ideal types of citizens. The typology was focussed on attitudes and values regarding the changing role of the state in Canadian society. It came in the midst of intense public debate focussed upon jobs and public finances. The original typology produced five types of Canadians:

- *relatively affluent insiders* (in favour of fiscal conservatism and less active government);
- the *secure middle* (contented, middle-class);
- the *insecure middle* (anxious members of the middle class, linked to the 'old economy'); and
- two classes of *economically distressed* Canadians:
  – *disengaged dependants* (still looking to government); and
  – the *angry and alienated* (who felt betrayed and abandoned).[23]

Five years later, the debate about government has matured and there are some fairly stable areas of public judgment concerning the role of the state. In the wake of declining fears about the state of public finances and rising optimism about the longer-term future, we see a strong consensus that active government—albeit a more fiscally responsible variant—has survived the clamour for major tax relief and 'minimal' government. Yet, there are still deep cleavages underlying this highly simplified summary of public judgment on the eve of the millennium. Once again, we have generated five idealized types of citizens. These types are presented along a continuum of both socio-economic status and the relative desire for more or less government (Fig. 2.15).[24]

The typology shows important areas of similarity and continuity, but also some revealing shifts, and what might be seen as a reflection of the evolving class structure of Canadian society. While not an exact reproduction of the original exercise, we believe that this exercise provides a useful synthesis of the varieties of Canadian political experience and culture at the close of the century.

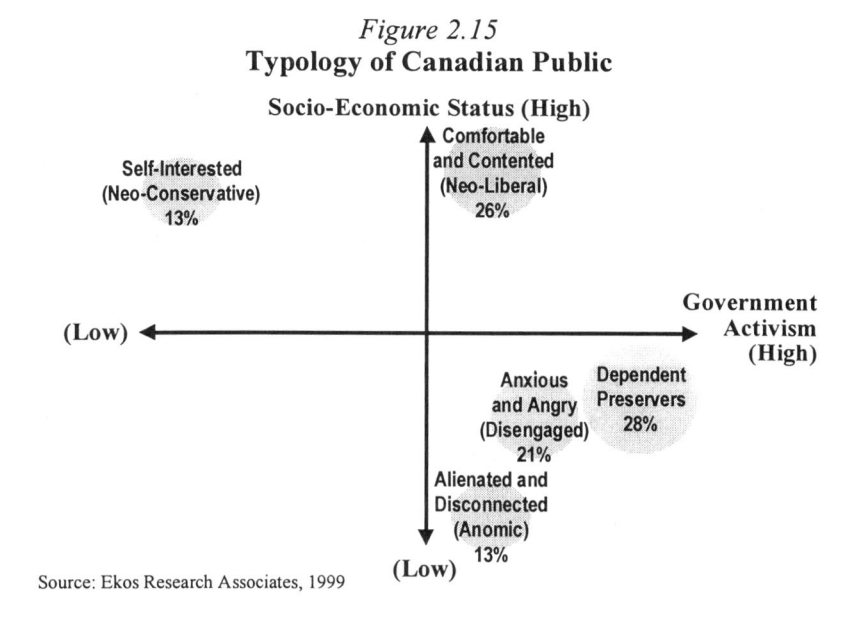

Figure 2.15
Typology of Canadian Public

```
                    Socio-Economic Status (High)
                              ▲
                         Comfortable
    Self-Interested     and Contented
    (Neo-Conservative)  (Neo-Liberal)
         13%                26%
                                                        Government
(Low) ◄──────────────────┼──────────────────► Activism
                                                          (High)
                              Anxious    Dependent
                             and Angry   Preservers
                            (Disengaged)    28%
                                21%
                            Alienated and
                            Disconnected
                              (Anomic)
                                13%
                              ▼
                            (Low)
```

Source: Ekos Research Associates, 1999

The Self-Interested (Neo-Conservatives) (13%)
The neo-conservative movement has exerted a profound influence on Canadian and broader Western political culture. In our view, the movement has crystallized within a highly cohesive segment of Canadian society. Unfortunately for the movement, it is equally clear that it has failed to expand its support or convince the mainstream of Canada. Some of its central tenets and beliefs have registered indelible impacts on the broader political culture, but the size of the cadre of core supporters who embrace the movement *in toto* has remained flat at best over the past five years.

One of the chief distinguishing features of the self-interested segments is their unremittingly rational and economic perspective. The realm of national symbols and the normative domain are of little significance to neo-conservatives. In addition to being self-interested, they emphasize self-reliance both for themselves and for the society writ large. They do not reveal any adherence to many of the traditional positions of liberalism in Canada. They oppose bilingualism as not critically connected to the country, and are the least compassionate of all groups toward poverty and social justice issues. They are also much less likely to come in contact with the federal government than other segments. This group is highly antipathetic to government in general, and federal government in particular. They are individualistic and mistrustful of institutions. They see government as co-opted, self-interested, and wasteful.

The demographics of this group are not terribly surprising but they are revealing. The group constitutes roughly 13 per cent of the Canadian population (roughly the size of the hard right in Canada). It is dominated by secure white males. They are evident throughout the country, but occur more frequently in Western Canada. They tend to be relatively well educated, but are not the best-educated Canadians. Their household income is quite high, and they are very likely to be baby boomers. Those evident in Quebec tend to be sovereigntists. In terms of political orientation, Canadians of this type are, not surprisingly, small-c conservative, and eschew small-l liberalism. This is the centre of Reform party support, and individuals from this segment reveal much stronger than average trust in leaders such as Preston Manning, Gary Filmon, and Mike Harris.

Comfortable and Contented (Neo-Liberals) (26%)
At 26 per cent, the comfortable and contented (neo-liberal) segment is one of the largest and is clearly the most powerful of all segments. This is the new dominant professional class (what some sociologists have called the 'new class'). Together with the neo-conservatives, the neo-liberals define the centre of authority and affluence in Canadian society. This group is differentiated from the self-interested (neo-conservative) segment on a number of key fronts, most notably a system of political values that reflects continuity with traditional liberalism and aversion to neo-conservatism. In key respects this segment sees a coincidence between its interests and values and the overall interests and values of the broader society. Its members represent the leadership and centre of Canadian political culture, and their views are moderate and supportive of current directions.

Unlike the self-interested, this segment is highly nationalistic and highly supportive of the current government. Together with the dependent preserver segment, they form the centre of new Canadian political attitudes, and bedrock for the current Liberal government.

Neo-liberals are the most affluent, educated, and professional of all segments. Alvin Gouldner[25] predicted a split of the new class into a technical intelligentsia and a humanistic intellectual wing. Some of these characteristics are evident respectively in the neo-conservative and the neo-liberal segments. In addition to enjoying the most privileged position in the current class order, the comfortable and contented are the most secure and confident in their economic futures. Their strong support for the current order reflects their core values and interests as the dominant class.

This segment is strongly connected to country, and still reflects the legacy of Trudeau (whom it holds in high regard). Members of this group have significant contact with the federal government, are generally satisfied with their contact with all governments, and welcome the state as a legitimate institution. They also approve of bilingualism and multiculturalism. Canadians of this group are proportionately spread in all regions and are overrepresented in the lower age cohort.

Dependent Preservers (28%)

At 28 per cent, dependent preservers are the largest single segment. Considerably less affluent and educated than the self-reliant or comfortable and contented segments, they are the strongest supporters of more active government and hold nostalgic views of the welfare state. They see themselves as highly reliant on the state, and their core values and interests are aligned with big government. Similarly to the comfortable and contented, they are strong (actually the strongest) supporters of the current government. Their views on fiscal versus human investment priorities lean decidedly more to the human investment side than do upper socio-economic status segments.

This segment is highly normative in orientation. They rate all values highly and they are particularly attracted to social activism. They espouse a mixture of traditional and liberal values and identify themselves as small-l liberals. This group seems to be the most attracted to the idea of government as a source of moral community. They are also highly connected to country and other sources of belonging. They could be described as fiercely nationalistic.

The demographics of this group are revealing and show a connection between their interests and their values. The group includes a high incidence of more economically vulnerable Canadians. Women, the less well-educated, and ethnic minorities (slightly) are overrepresented in this segment. This is not the lowest socio-economic status group, but its members have modest educations, below-average incomes, and lower skills. This group contains a higher concentration of blue- and pink-collar workers than the others.

Anxious and Angry (Disengaged) (21%)
Nearly one in five Canadians fall into this economically insecure type. Unlike the dependent preservers, the anxious and angry are highly insecure, and disenchanted with the current order. They are almost unanimously (nine out of 10) convinced that government has completely lost sight of the needs of average Canadians. They feel angry, abandoned, and betrayed by government. Unlike the neo-conservative segment, they do not have the skills, financial resources, or confidence to adapt without the aid of government. As such, they feel they have lost control of their futures (the most economically insecure) and hold governments (and cutbacks) responsible in that respect (the lowest level of satisfaction toward government). Nonetheless, this segment tends to be similar to the Dependent Preservers (but weaker) in its expectations for government activism (especially in human investment) and values. Anxious and Angry are the least tolerant of immigration.

This segment reveals high levels of stress, and poor health. Part of their hostility is driven by a sense of low political efficacy. Their demographic profile underlines some of their views. They tend to be women, live in single-parent/non-traditional households (slightly), are very poorly educated, and have very low incomes, well below the national average. Their skill levels and resources are such that they are unlikely to succeed in the 'new' economy. In fact, many are out of the labour force or retired. They are more likely than other segments to support the NDP, to the degree that they are politically engaged.

Alienated and Disconnected (Anomic) (13%)
This smaller segment (13 per cent) may represent the emergence of a hardening underclass in Canadian society. What is striking about this group is the virtual absence of value orientations or sense of belong-

ing to anything (world, country, province, or ancestry). They provide a classic illustration of what Durkheim called *anomie*. They feel no sense of solidarity or integration with the local or national community, and feel no sense of shared interest or values. In that respect, this group of Canadians is alienated and disconnected from governments (for example, this segment is the least likely to have contacted the federal government in the last three months).

This disturbing group generally is very poorly educated (most have less than high school). They have very low incomes, poor skills, high unemployment, and the highest level of under-employment. They often live in non-traditional, single-parent families and are much younger than the anxious and angry. They tend to be white and to express high levels of xenophobia. This group is overrepresented in Quebec (and underrepresented in Ontario), and to the degree that they are politically involved they lean toward the Bloc in Quebec and are the most likely to support Quebec independence options.

NOTES

Whereas any errors in this paper are the responsibility of the author, its potential contribution is highly indebted to a number of colleagues. I would like to thank Leslie Pal for kindly inviting this submission and for his highly constructive comments. My colleagues at Ekos have been extremely helpful. In particular, Alfred MacLeod has been developing these ideas with me over the past year or so. Patrick Beauchamp, Christian Boucher, and Andrew Sullivan have all provided helpful advice, analysis, and ideas, all of which are reflected in this paper. Sheila Redmond has provided excellent editorial input. I would also like to thank the many sponsors in federal and provincial governments who have been generous in providing both intellectual and financial resources for the *Rethinking Government* project. My close colleague, David Zussman, has been instrumental in developing this entire project and I would also like to thank Paul Reed, who helped develop some of these ideas. Finally, I would like to thank the thousands of Canadians who patiently endured surveys and focus groups on these topics.

1 The major part of the following discussion is based on a number of nation-wide Ekos surveys: *Rethinking Government, Rethinking Citizen*

Engagement, and *The Information Highway and the Canadian Communication Household*. Some parts of the analysis have been previously published in reports and other articles or will be appearing shortly. The analysis builds on the previous work, looking at the data from a new angle, and creating a deeper insight into the relationship of Canadians to their governments.

2 Ronald Inglehart, *Culture Shift in Advanced Industrial Society* (Princeton: Princeton University Press, 1990); Neil Nevitte, *The Decline of Deference* (Toronto: Broadview Press, 1996); Joseph S. Nye, Philip Zelikow, and David C. King, eds, *Why People Don't Trust Government* (Cambridge Mass.: Harvard University Press, 1997).

3 As quoted in Gary Orren, 'Fall from Grace: The Public's Loss of Faith in Government', in Nye et al., *Why People Don't Trust Government*, 81.

4 Seymour Martin Lipset, *Continental Divide: The Values and Institutions of the United States and Canada* (New York: Routledge, 1990).

5 See, for example, John Porter, *The Vertical Mosaic: An Analysis of Social Class and Power in Canada* (Toronto: University of Toronto Press, 1965).

6 Nevitte, *Decline*.

7 Nevitte, *Decline*; Inglehart, *Culture*.

8 Thomas Courchene, with C. Telmer, *From Heartland to North American Region State* (Toronto: University of Toronto Press, 1997).

9 Frank L. Graves, with Tim Dugas and Patrick Beauchamp, 'Identity and National Attachments in Contemporary Canada', in Harvey Lazar and Tom McIntosh, eds, *Canada: The State of the Federation 1998-99, Vol. 13: How Canadians Connect* (Kingston Ont.: Institute of Intergovernmental Relations, 1999), forthcoming.

10 Richard Gwyn, *Nationalism Without Walls: The Unbearable Lightness of Being Canadian* (Toronto: McClelland and Stewart, 1995).

11 Nevitte, *Decline*.

12 *Rethinking Government IV*, September 1998.

13 Frank Graves and Paul Reed, 'Canadians and Their Public Institutions', *Optimum: The Journal of Public Sector Management* 28, 4 (1999), 1-8.

14 See Appendix, 'Beneath Consensus: The Shifting Structure of Political Class Culture in Canada', 66-71.

15 For the purposes of *Rethinking Government* surveys, the power elites are defined as the key agents of decision-making in society. Ekos' operational definition of elites is virtually identical to that used by John Porter in *The Vertical Mosaic*, with the exception that he included former Privy Council members, whereas Ekos uses current members of federal and provincial legislatures.

16 *Rethinking Citizen Engagement*.

17 Daniel Yankelovich, *Coming to Public Judgement: Making Democracy Work in a Complex World* (Syracuse: Syracuse University Press, 1991);

James S. Fishkin, *The Voice of the People: Public Opinion and Democracy* (New Haven: Yale University Press, 1995).

18 A recent illustration of this sort of conclusion was a February 1999 *National Post*/Compass poll under the headline 'Federal Tax Cuts Top Pre-budget Wish List: Poll; Tax Rage Rife...'.

19 The methodology for each year of the *Rethinking Government* study typically involves the following components: an initial telephone interview of over 200 questions with a random sample of 3,000 Canadians 16 years and over; a second detailed telephone interview (over 150 questions) with approximately 1,500 of the original 3,000 public survey respondents; a third survey of the general public (over 150 questions) with approximately 1,300 of the original 3,000 panel respondents, and 200 general public respondents; six follow-up focus group sessions with respondents from *Rethinking Government*; and a survey of the top governing and economic decision-makers in Canada.

20 The recent public consensus about health care and the 1999 federal budget response provide an interesting illustration of this debate (see the discussion beginning on page 59).

21 Survey respondents were asked to indicate whether the federal government (and provincial government separately) should 'increase', 'maintain', 'reduce', or 'eliminate' its involvement in a series of 20 different policy areas. The findings discussed here are based on the aggregate responses of respondents across all individual policy areas explored in the question.

22 See Anthony Giddens, *The Third Way: The Renewal of Social Democracy* (London: Polity Press, 1998).

23 See *Rethinking Government 94* for a fuller description.

24 This typology is based on a large set of questions and was constructed in four steps. First, various factor analyses were performed to identify underlying structures and latent dimensions. Second, scaled dimensions were created that are based on the various factors identified in the first step. Third, a cluster analysis was developed that used the following 11 scaled dimensions: social class, economic security, government activism, performance, human, fiscal, identity and diversity investment priority, tolerance to immigration, liberal, neo-conservative, and traditional values. Fourth, five segments were identified by means of the cluster analysis and graphed in the above Fig. 2.15 along government activism and social class axes (both axes are z-scored; the origin points [0,0] represent the mean of both axes). See *Rethinking Government V* for the survey questions used to construct these scales and a profile of each of the segments across demographic, attitudinal, and political characteristics.

25 Alvin Gouldner, *The Future of Intellectuals and the Rise of the New Class* (New York: Seabury Press, 1979).

3

Tectonic Changes in Canadian Governance

GILLES PAQUET

> In Canada, practice now sprints ahead of theory.
> Don Lenihan

Governance is about guiding. It is the process by which an organization or society steers itself. It is my basic argument that the pattern of governance has shifted dramatically in Canada over the last few decades. The shift has been gradual if relentless, and the new is engraved in traditional institutions, so that old forms often mask the new emergent forces. This transformation is due to three sets of forces:

- major transnational and technological forces, which have strained the old order;

- the epiphany of a culture of diversity, which has completely undermined the traditional foundations of social cohesion; and
- the interaction between the first set and the second set of forces, which has acquired a dynamics of its own.

In section 1 of this chapter, I distinguish between governing and governance, and suggest the contours of a social learning dynamic. This dynamic underlines the various dimensions of Canadian governance that have been modified in the recent past. Section 2 examines the broad features of the discontinuity undergone by the Canadian pattern of governance in the last few decades, and argues that there has been a transformation in the underlying assumptions at work, and in the social rules and mechanisms. This corresponds to a tectonic change in the Canadian governance regime.

To support this hypothesis, I examine:

- evidence of a *reframing* of the philosophy of governance (from egalitarianism to subsidiarity);
- evidence of a *restructuring* of the governance process (a new division of labour among the three sectors, private, public, and civic, a new emphasis on sub-national forums, and a significant increase in the range of relevant stakeholders); and
- evidence of a *retooling* of public management and of the ways in which the public sector is administered.

Section 3 documents some of the resistance and the learning blockages that have been experienced in the transition period on the three fronts: cognitive dissonance of leaders and citizens alike, but also ideological, political, and bureaucratic resistance to the new governance. This has translated into a weakening of the governing institutions, and has generated more divisive debate than is either necessary or desirable.

GOVERNANCE AND SOCIAL LEARNING[1]

Traditionally, governing signifies the use of certain instruments to steer a system that has some autonomous existence. It presupposes an agent or a purposeful organization in charge. But as diversity, complexity, interdependencies, and turbulence increase in modern societies, there are important governing failures. They stem from unrealistic assumptions about the system to be regulated or governed, and bad choices of governing instruments, but also from all sorts of unintended consequences of governing action that result from unpredictable or counter-intuitive reactions to governing activities in complex societies characterized by deep network interdependencies. This has led to greater and greater pessimism about the governability of complex social systems by the state or by any other single agent. Nobody appears to be in charge any longer.

Modes of Governance
As Kickert puts it, '[G]overnance is the achievement of a balance between governing actors.'[2] This 'balance' can be achieved by a variety of means: by some hierarchical control or traditional structures of authority, methods, and instruments, but also by alternative arrangements in which public authorities play an ever-diminishing role, and the citizen an ever-increasing role, with the control forms and the normative bases (that is, the key mechanisms that regulate the system) ranging from rules based on 'the will of the people' to self-regulation and self-development. While the traditional hierarchical model represents one pole, the dynamic process of continuous self-reorganization through social learning represents the other.[3] These alternative arrangements can be described in terms of a few dimensions summarized in Table 3.1, adapted from Beck Jorgensen.

To survive in the new dynamic, complex, and diverse environment generated by globalization, accelerated technical change, and greater cultural diversity, private, public, and civic organizations have been forced to develop a philosophy of continuous improvement and innovation, to become learning organizations. In this world, organizations must become capable of learning both new goals and new means as they proceed, and this can only be done by tapping the knowledge and information that others possess, that is, through consultative co-ordination and co-operation with other stakeholders. This has meant a shift in the governance process.

Governance as a mode of social coordination refers to a pattern of relationships that is likely to emerge rather than be crafted, and that

Table 3.1

Models of Governance

Models of governance	Roles of the governor	Roles of citizens	Control forms	Normative bases
hierarchical	implementation	subject	rules	will of the people
autonomous	safeguarding of rights and values	protected	peer group control	standards
negotiated	mediator	member of interest group	negotiation	consensus
responsive	listening	client	dialogue	service
self-governing	setting framework	co-producer	self-regulation	self-development

provides the stakeholders in varying degrees with an opportunity to share information and to partake collectively in the process of steering and learning. As one moves away from hierarchical governance, the illusion that a leader is in charge or has a monopoly on the governing of the organization disappears: for the organization to learn quickly, everyone must take part in the conversation and bring forward each bit of knowledge and wisdom that has a bearing on the issue. The governance process becomes more and more a game without a master.

Discontinuity

In globalized, dynamic, and pluralistic environments, the pattern of governance has to be flexible and adaptive. This does not mesh well with hierarchical structures and bureaucratic procedures. So the pattern of governance must become non-centralized. Managers must strategically exploit all the favourable environmental circumstances in the same way as the surfer uses the wave—to learn faster, to adapt more quickly—and make use of each team player in each task force-type project at the local level.

This paradoxical outcome—globalization *cum* localization—has been analysed by Naisbitt and christened *glocalization* by Courchene.[4]

As globalization proceeds, the increased economic integration across borders generates increased economic disintegration within borders, as 'the component parts of the system become more numerous and smaller and more important'.[5] This reinforces growing cultural diversity. And the central challenge is how to organize for faster learning. It would appear, according to Naisbitt, that the game of learning generates more innovation if governing organizations confronted with different local realities are empowered to take decisions on the spot. In this way, globalization encourages localization of decision-making, empowerment, the dispersion of power, and a more distributed governance process.

Distributed governance does not mean only a process of dispersion of power toward localized decision-making within each sector. It also entails a dispersion of power over a wide variety of actors from the private, public, and civic sectors. This is because the best learning experience in a context of rapid change comes through decentralized and flexible teams, woven together by moral contracts and reciprocal, negotiated partnerships.[6] In distributed governance, the social system does not require an external authority: in the limiting case, the system self-organizes and self-steers as a result of interaction among stakeholders from the various sectors, but also among stakeholders at different levels of organizations. The relationships are not hierarchical, but they are not necessarily horizontal either. They may be transversal and embrace different layers of private concerns, government structures, civic associations, and the like.

Effective governance
To be effective, distributed governance through social learning requires not only new structures (more modular and network-like), but also more trust on which to build integrated, informal moral contracts. For learning entails 'the mutually consistent interpretation of information that is not fully codified, and hence not fully capable of being transmitted, understood, and utilized independently of the actual agents who are developing and using it'.[7] This calls for conventions and relational transactions to define mutually coherent expectations and common guideposts, though these conventions differ from sector to sector. They provide the requisite coherence for a common context of interpretation.

Such coherence is a major source of the nimbleness of the network society. Yet a good learning network must not be too coherent: the nodes should not be too similar, nor the ties too strong or too routinized. This is the sense in which one may speak of 'the strength of weak ties':[8] a certain degree of heterogeneity might foster a higher potentiality of innovation, because the different parties bring to the 'conversation' a more complementary body of knowledge. More fruitful synergies ensue.

Recently, the dual set of pressures emerging from the turbulence of the international environment and from the increased heterogeneity of national populations has led public, private, and civic organizations to adopt strategies calling for lighter, more horizontal and modular structures, for the creation of networks and informal clan-like relations, for a move away from a fixation on goals and controls, and for more fundamental reliance on intelligence and innovation. In the private sector, the 'virtual corporation' and the 'modular corporation' are now the new models of governance.[9] And they are most effective. The same can be said about the public and civic sectors: the hierarchical model is being challenged, but the governance regime has not evolved completely toward self-governance.

A CHANGE OF KIND IN CANADIAN GOVERNANCE[10]

To overstate somewhat, the difference between the prior and latter governance regimes in Canada is that between an anti-democratic, centralizing, homogenizing, and hierarchical regime ruled by elites, and a more communitarian, non-centralizing, and distributed governance regime.[11] There is no clean break between these two regimes: in many ways, the two institutional arrangements overlap and are intermingled. The prior regime is still present in our values, ideologies, institutions, and policies, and indeed it has been reinforced by the Charter of Rights of April 1982,[12] but the latter regime is making inroads and the illiberal nature of the prior regime is being challenged on a variety of fronts, although the challenge is often delivered *sotto voce*.

If one had to put a label on the prior governance regime, one might use Stephen Carter's label, 'the liberal constitutional project', and define it as built on (1) the priority 'to get the answers right, not to worry too much about the process through which the answers are obtained', and (2) a model that holds that 'the central government (where decisions on matters of right or wrong are made) is more likely than anybody else to find the answers that are right'.[13] As for the latter emerging governance regime, one might label it 'the distributed governance scenario'; it is built on a reduced and transformed role of the state, a greater reliance on governance mechanisms from the private and civic sectors, and a scattered and multi-layered distribution of power. The word 'scenario' is used to emphasize the fact that it is still in the process of unfolding, and that it is in no way certain that it will unfold exactly as we suggest.[14]

The Prior Governance Regime Under Stress
The prior governance regime is approximated rather well by the hierarchical mode of governance, with its top-down enforcement of rules by a governor who claims to represent the will of the people and who treats the citizen in an imperial way. The main weaknesses of this brand of centralized governance have been well documented. They may be subsumed under a few headings:[15]

Overgovernment and government overload: Seven million Canadians were born between 1951 and 1966, and they have created a phenomenal demand for public goods. This Big Generation also put some pressure on markets and led to an immense regulatory effort in response to market failures. Finally, the demographic boom tested the civic sector in areas such as education and health, and led to the transfer of many responsibilities to the state. As a consequence, the state sector grew exponentially and became 'a kind of arthritic octopus, an inept leviathan', unable, despite massive growth, to do much to meet the demands of the citizenry. This state of affairs has resulted in disgruntlement, weakened citizen compliance, growing civic indifference, and much disillusionment. In most of the OECD countries, these feelings led to growing pressures for a reduction of the public sector and a redeployment of state activities toward the private and civic sectors.

A legitimation deficit: Public confidence in political leaders, governments, and public institutions since the mid-1970s has been low, and levels of trust have declined. Globalization has made traditional macroeconomic policies increasingly less effective, and government's inability to respond effectively to persistent problems such as unemployment, and public scandals such as the Somalia affair or the tainted blood system, have increased the perception that 'governments cannot do anything right'.[16] It seems that the public has by now ceased to believe that the state has any moral authority or technical ability to deal with the major issues at hand.

A fiscal crisis: This crisis emerged in the 1970s, but was largely ignored until the mid-1980s. It has apparently been resolved by massive cutbacks in program spending, but this resolution has revealed the incapacity of the state to reconcile its dual obligations to attenuate social difficulties on the one hand, and on the other to foster the process of capital accumulation without generating fiscal deficits that are in the long run unbearable. As it stands now, there is both a decline in living standards (especially of the most destitute) and a stagnation of productivity growth that can only mean that the fiscal crisis has been resolved only at a superficial level.[17]

Social limits to growth: It has become evident over the last decade that the three crucial dimensions of our social organization (liberal capitalism, mass democracy, and a very unequal distribution of both material and symbolic resources) cannot coexist easily—democratic egalitarianism (in society) generates compulsive centralism (in the polity), in order to redistribute more and more resources; it has little success in reducing inequality, but it imposes ever more burdensome shackles on the productive capacity of the economic system.[18] States face

> a crisis, because they appear incapable of carrying out established and expected tasks, tasks which they have over the years accepted, because of the absence of necessary resources, *both financial and civic*, or because they cannot meet claims and expectations fostered by the economic and social systems themselves.[19]

How did such a situation develop? In Canada and elsewhere, the central reason would appear to be found in the world of values. The public institutional framework built in the postwar era was designed for instrumental purposes: to combat a depression, to raise standards of living, to provide public goods not otherwise produced, or to assist the needy. As a result, citizens came to define the state in terms of the claims they could make on it: '[C]laimant politics began to overshadow civic politics.' By comparison, 'the activities of the private sphere were seen as ends pursued for their own sake.' It is hardly surprising that the instrumental goods of the public sphere were regarded as subordinate to the intrinsic goods of private life.[20]

Even though governments were major funders, underwriters, and regulators of postwar prosperity in Canada, and therefore were the fundamental bedrock on which the economy and society prospered from the 1940s to the 1970s, Canadians have continued to ignore the importance of the state: '[T]he dominant strains in our culture ... [remained] a vigorous individualism, a suspicion of interest groups as self-serving and subversive of democracy, and a skepticism about pervasive social and economic planning by the state'.[21] This ideology of individualism has continued to prevail, despite the fact that government activities had grown so much by 1980 that very little remained absolutely private in a meaningful sense.

In a more globalized context, the Canadian private sector made ever greater demands on public institutions for protection and regulation, at a time when the capacity to supply public services could no longer expand. This limitation on the capability of the public sphere was due to the fact that participation, trust, and creative interaction (on which politics and the public sphere are built) had all but disappeared, as had the sense of community that underpinned civil society and the collective/private ways of meeting the needs of strangers.[22]

In this world of rugged individualism, where most citizens were strangely unaware that the government has been the prime mover in the postwar period of prosperity, private enterprise at public expense became the rule. The lack of commitment of emotional, intellectual, and financial resources to refurbish the public infrastructure could only lead to demand overload, and the frustration generated by the policy failures of the 1970s set the stage for citizens to suggest that the best way to strengthen both democracy and the economy was to weaken government.

Yet, with ever-growing complexity and interdependence on a world scale, the need for collective decision-making is growing. The solution therefore is not less government, but a different sort of government. There is a need for a new framework, for a transformation in our governance, but this new framework, capable of guiding us in the years ahead, has not yet been articulated fully in Canada. One may point to efforts by Bill Clinton in the United States and by Tony Blair in the United Kingdom to rebuild the state on lines appropriate to the late 20th century. But even in those cases, the sort of inclusiveness that has been defended and the types of coalition that have been struck have not yet crystallized into a new governance regime. We know what these new regimes are not, but we do not yet know what they are.[23]

The Emerging Scenario

At the core of the strains on the prior governance regime is a moral vacuum. The notion of public purpose is alien to us. So at the core of the new regime what is needed first and foremost is a philosophy of public intervention, a rationale for the new sort of governance, a philosophy of the public realm.[24] However, this new philosophy cannot materialize mechanically. It is emerging as a two-stage process: first, a growing recognition that there is a moral vacuum to be filled with an 'ethic' that will underpin the new governance regime; and second, the development of the sort of design principles that are likely to underpin the social architecture of this new strategic and learning governance regime.

Though it is not fashionable to say so, the state is a moral agent and not a morally-neutral administrative instrument. This strikes quite a blow at the core belief of the gospel of functional politics. Both on the left and on the right, there is a longing for civil society and its component communities to organically provide the well-defined codes of moral obligation that underpin the realization of the good society.[25] However, the 'built-in restraint derived from morals, religion, custom, and education' that were considered by Adam Smith as a prerequisite before one could safely trust men to 'their own self-interest without undue harm to the community' are no longer there.

It is futile to hope for some replacement for these values to come about by 'immaculate conception' in civil society. Thus many have called on the state and on political leaders to accept the responsibility to act as second-best moral agents.[26] This means that political leaders are called upon not to impose values on a community, but to provide a framework, a sense of direction, a commitment to ideals, together with the public philosophy to realize these goals. This public philosophy would not necessarily be the least constraining one available, but one that would be chosen by citizens if they had 'the fullest attainable understanding of the experience resulting from that choice and its most relevant alternatives'.[27] The challenge is to bring about that sort of 'fullest understanding' in the population. Government can no longer operate in a top-down mode, but has a duty to institute a continuing dialogue with the citizenry. This requires a language of common citizenship, deeply rooted in civil society: citizens have goals, commitment, and values that the state must take into account, and they want an active role in the making of policies supposedly designed for them.[28] Only through a rich array of institutions that enhance citizens' competence in communication is an enlightened understanding likely to prevail—both as a result of, and as the basis for, a reasonable armistice between the state and the citizenry.

The state, in the past, has played housekeeping roles and served offsetting functions. These roles and functions required minimal input from the citizenry. The state in complex advanced capitalist socioeconomies must now play new central roles that go much beyond these mechanical interventions. It must become involved as a broker, as an *animateur*, and as a partner in participatory planning, if the requisite amount of organizational learning, co-evolution, and cooperation with economy and society is to materialize. This involvement will pave the way to a participation-society (where freedom and efficacy come from the fact that the individual has a recognized voice on matters of substance and procedure in the public realm, and more importantly an obligation to participate in the definition of such matters). The citizen will refuse to be confined to a rights-society, where the dignity of individuals resides exclusively in the fact that they have claims.[29] The citizen will become a co-producer of governance.

But one cannot develop such a philosophy of the public realm unless social cohesion is refurbished, unless one can build on shared values and communities of interpretation. And both in social commentaries and in public documents, it has been argued that social cohesion has been declining and that much depends on the capacity of public institutions to build a consensus around a new definition of common purpose, to build the requisite social capital.[30]

The design principles for a social architecture in keeping with the guiding values mentioned above are clear. First is the principle of subsidiarity, according to which 'power should devolve on the lowest, most local level at which decisions can reasonably be made, with the function of the larger unit being to support and assist the local body in carrying out its tasks.'[31] The rationale for this principle is that the institutions closest to the citizen are those likely to be the closest approximation to organic institutions, that is, to institutions that are likely to emerge 'undesigned', to emerge from the sheer pressure of well-articulated needs, and likely to require minimal yearly redesigning. Subsidiarity reduces vertical hierarchical power and increases in a meaningful way the potential for participation.

This is not the death of central government, but the demise of big government. When the ground is in motion, the bulkier and the more centralized the government, the more it will flounder. The lean new central strategic state must deal with norms, standards, general directions, and values. The process of ministering to the public and of delivering a service well adapted to its needs must be devolved to the local level. Such a government would provide services within a framework agreed to nationally, and would support self-development.

The second design principle is that of an effective citizen-based evaluation feedback to ensure that the services produced, financed, or regulated by the public realm meet the required standards of efficiency, economy, and effectiveness, and are consonant with agreed standards or norms. This is a central cybernetic loop in refurbished governance. It is essential if organizational learning is to proceed as quickly as possible, and it entails a transformation of the audit and evaluation functions in the decision-making process. Instead of being limited to untimely *ex post* efforts at identifying abuses, these functions become part of *ex ante* strategic decision-making in a citizen-centred governance regime. Perfunctory consultation will not do: what is required is the creation of 'chaordic organizations'.[32]

This sort of evaluation ensures that the process of participation is significantly strengthened. It partially provides some content to the implicit contract between the state and the citizenry. This sort of feedback cannot be presumed to materialize organically, but once it is in place its objective is to ensure that state activities, standards, and rules have legitimacy in the beneficiaries' eyes, and that they are compatible with everyday morality, rather than incentives for the citizens to lie or misrepresent their situations. It would allow the ordinary citizen, in a way, to be heard better, for 'politics is not only the art of representing the needs of strangers; it is also the perilous business of speaking on behalf of needs which strangers have had no chance to articulate on their own'.[33]

Shift at Three Levels
Donald Schon has suggested that any system (and the Canadian governance system is one) is composed of a structure, a technology, and a theory.[34] The structure consists of the set of roles and the relations among members of the organization. The technology refers to the tools used by members of the organization. The theory is the view held by members about the system—its purposes, its environment, its future. These dimensions hang together, and any change in one affects the others.

The drift in the Canadian governance regime has materialized along these three dimensions. And while we may not yet have a clear picture of what will be the new institutional order embodying the new structure, the new technology, and the new theory, there is sufficient evidence to determine roughly in what direction they are evolving, and the likelihood that they will mesh in the new regime.

I will argue that Canadian governance is espousing more and more a philosophy of subsidiarity, that its structure is being transformed more and more into a web of partnerships among the private, public, and civic sectors, that its technology echoes more and more the doctrine of managerialism and the realities of the new world of work, and that these three sets of trends mesh rather well to define the contours of the new Canadian governance regime.

At the level of theory, one may identify a dramatic drift in Canadian governance.[35] One might characterize the drift in the underlying philosophy of Canadian governance as a movement from egalitarianism to subsidiarity. Over the last 125 years, circumstances have often threatened Canadian prosperity. Canada has had to learn ways and means to cope with these challenges. The economic culture that evolved from the 1870s to the 1970s was based, as Herschel Hardin has put it, on the extensive use of two fundamental elements: public enterprise, and inter-regional redistribution of the economic surplus.[36] These two root stratagems have been used repeatedly from the very early days of the federation.

Over the recent past, both these tenets of the Canadian economic culture have come under attack. First, not only have governments sold off their enterprises (Canadair, de Havilland, Air Canada, Teleglobe, etc.), but there has also been a 180-degree change in the perception of public enterprise. This has culminated in the 'alternative service delivery' initiative, which is built on the presumption that most of what the public sector does can be done more efficiently by the private sector.[37] Second, the massive inter-regional redistribution of resources has been under attack. After an orgy of regional development programs and generous equalization programs that proved much less effective than had been anticipated, there has been a shift away from *place prosperity* toward *people prosperity* in the design of public policy. Mobility has become more important. Indeed, with the deficit and debt threats, transfers from the federal to the provincial governments were frozen during the Mulroney years and dramatically reduced with the creation of the Canada Health and Social Transfer in 1996. At the conceptual level, this was seen as a shift away from the welfare state toward the strategic state.[38]

The north star of the philosophy of the welfare state is egalitarianism. This philosophy argues that equalization of outcomes is a desirable objective and strives to provide each citizen with all the resources required to ensure equality. Even though in practice this could never be achieved, and perhaps was never intended, this rights-based philosophy of governance acquired an extraordinary symbolic importance as the rationale for the federal-provincial equalization payments scheme, which was designed to equalize the fiscal potential of the different provinces.[39] This rationale had been advanced at various times, by the Rowell-Sirois Commission, for example. This is hardly surprising. As Tocqueville suggests, '[D]emocratic peoples ... have an ardent, insatiable, eternal, invincible passion for equality.'[40] This strong taste for equality of outcome is still echoed, for example, in opposition as a matter of principle to two tiers in the health care system.

The coexistence of egalitarian rights and considerable and even increasing real inequalities could only lead to resentment.[41] The welfare state found itself in a vicious circle: redistributive attempts to achieve equality of wealth became increasingly expensive, and that rising expense in the service of an impossible goal simply generated more resentment among citizens seduced by egalitarianism. As a result, the social security compact came under attack. At first, the attacks on the legitimacy of the social security compact were countered by technical adjustments of the existing mechanisms. Only in the 1990s was Canada forced by its fiscal crisis to question the old philosophy of governance.

Elements of a new philosophy of governance, of a new compass, are visible in the fabric of Program Review, which was announced in the February 1994 budget[42]—a process of critical examination of the activities of federal departments and agencies by means of a series of six tests (does the activity serve a public interest? is a government role necessary? is the current role of the federal government appropriate or is there a case for realignment with the provinces? can it be transferred in whole or in part to the private or voluntary sector? could its efficiency be improved? can we afford it?). However, there has not yet been a public debate of consequence concerning this new orientation.[43]

Much of the national debate in relation to the Meech and Charlottetown accords had to do with ways in which there could be orderly devolution in Canada. But these debates occurred at a time when the population remained somewhat schizophrenic: while trust in government was declining, the high degree of dependency that forty years of the welfare state had fostered meant that Canadians had not been weaned from the Samaritan state. Therefore, any massive devolution could only be regarded with suspicion, since it would of necessity entail a weakening of the inter-regional redistributive role of the state.

Consequently, a philosophy of subsidiarity, built on the centrality of active citizens who must take primary responsibility for their own welfare and that of their families, was not generating enthusiastic support. In this new world of subsidiarity, the authority of governments to intervene is not based on any rights or entitlements ordained from above, but stems from the citizens' need for help. Thus governments act in a subsidiary way, in the same way that a reserve army intervenes in case of need. This new governance system calls also for decisions to be made at the lowest, most local level, where they can be made with reasonable efficiency and effectiveness. The task of the higher order of government (regional, federal, etc.) is to assist the individual and the local authorities in carrying out their tasks.

The full extent to which this new philosophy of governance has impregnated *de facto* the work of the federal bureaucracy can be gauged by the fact that by 1996, in the definition of the basic scenarios shared by the Deputy Minister Task Forces, the preferred 'Renaissance' scenario (as opposed to the business-as-usual and market scenarios) was characterized by a 'wide distribution of responsibility for governance amongst civil society, private and public sectors; distribution is essentially along the lines of the subsidiarity principle— Federal government focuses on those matters that cannot be handled by civil society, the private sector, local and Provincial governments.'[44] But it remained a principle that would not be shared widely with the citizenry, because it is abhorred by a significant portion of the federal Cabinet, including the Prime Minister.

At the structural level, a transformation of Canadian governance is underway.[45] This new philosophy calls for a redefinition of roles and responsibilities by stakeholders. One cannot examine here all the structural changes generated by the reframing of the basic philosophy of governance, but since this process of restructuring has worked by fits and starts, it is possible to underline the broad phases in the redeployment of activities into networks linking the different sectors.

The strains that the Canadian governance system experienced from the 1970s on did not lead to a full-fledged effort at restructuring until the Mulroney years. An early effort at restructuring occurred with the creation of the Nielsen Task Force on Program Review by the Mulroney government in 1984, to explore how government might dispatch its work more economically, efficiently, and effectively. Several multi-stakeholder task forces (including an equal number of private and public sector representatives) reviewed the full range of government programs and made recommendations for change. Reporting delays meant that the Nielsen Task Force failed to inform the early actions of the new government, and consequently its impact proved negligible. Many of the critiques and recommendations put forward by the 'amateurish outsiders' asked to examine the federal programs were often easy prey for 'well-informed professionals on the inside'.[46]

During the late 1980s, the Mulroney government wrestled with many urgent issues: the Meech Lake Accord and the challenge of bringing Quebec fully back into Confederation, negotiating the Canada-US Free Trade Agreement, and designing a tax reform package (reducing income tax rates and introducing the Goods and Services Tax). The restructuring of the governance system was relegated to the second mandate.

A new bout of restructuring efforts was launched early in the second mandate with two initiatives: the Public Service 2000 (PS 2000) process and the creation of Special Operating Agencies (SOAs). PS 2000 was announced by Prime Minister Mulroney in December 1989, and was intended (1) to clarify the accountability relationships in human resources management; (2) to improve service to the public; and (3) to design and implement human resource policies to enable institutions and employees to better meet the challenges of a changing world. Ten working groups, composed mainly of senior public servants, were established to examine issues as diverse as classification, remuneration, the executive group, service to the public, staff relations, staffing, and human resource development.

At the same time, Robert de Cotret, then President of the Treasury Board, announced the creation of five SOAs. The SOAs were new administrative units developed for entities delivering well-defined services within departments, in order to provide additional flexibility in the management of financial and human resources within the federal public service. The SOA experiment may not have been nearly as important in Canada as it was in the United Kingdom, but it echoed a significant change in attitudes.

In December 1990, a White Paper—informed by the work of the task forces—was released by the Prime Minister's Office. Perhaps its most striking feature was the extent to which managerialism infused the analysis and the recommendations of the government and senior public servants alike. At the most general level, managerialism rests on the assumption that management is a separate activity, that there is no fundamental difference between the private and public sectors, that both need better management, and that it is progressive to redefine the citizens who interact with public sector organizations as customers.[47] This new philosophy of management affected the consciousness of the Mulroney government, but rather slowly. The rhetoric was strident at times, but the actions on this front were relatively temperate. Change was guided by a cosmology of reform: senior public servants would design and implement reform in an evolutionary way and emphasize the adoption of new values, while relying on selective statutory and institutional changes. This approach stood in stark contrast to the radical reforms launched, for example, by the governments of New Zealand and the United Kingdom during the 1980s.

It was only with the change in government in 1993 that the process of structural change in keeping with the new philosophy of governance moved into high gear. Program Review (which by all accounts was just an improved version of the Nielsen exercise) triggered some profound rethinking of the governance process. The fact that it did not accomplish all that was intended (and in the end was much more focussed on expenditure reduction than on an overhauling of the governance process) does not mean that it did not significantly transform the governance structure.

Program Review was action-oriented. Each department and agency had to set specific plans that were reviewed, criticized, and revisited. These plans led to serious structural transformations in many departments and locked them into further plans of action in subsequent years. More importantly perhaps, the Program Review exercise was followed by a wide-ranging series of activities included under different rubrics and masterminded by the Treasury Board Secretariat (for example, the Quality Initiative, the 'alternative service delivery initiative') that was explicitly presented by the federal Treasury Board Secretariat as a framework meant to 'support the implementation of Program Review decisions'.[48]

Indeed, a generous interpretation of the rhetoric that accompanied these initiatives in the mid-1990s might even lead one to conclude that they were meant to be mechanisms to implement the philosophy of subsidiarity that underpins the process of federal program review. But these diverse and diffuse structural initiatives were never presented under a single rubric. The rationale and rhetoric of efficiency and managerialism were given much prominence in public discourse and deflected attention from the governance implications of all these initiatives. It is only *ex post* that these structural reforms have appeared as means to implement the new philosophy of governance. These organizational changes slowly but surely have transformed the traditional cosmology of the Canadian public service.

At the technological level, the public service has been transformed. The changes in the philosophy and structure of the governance regime directly challenged the management practices and the traditional cosmology of a career public service. Both the new philosophy of subsidiarity and the new structures building on new networks of collaboration with the private and the civic sectors did much to legitimize the new managerialism and to challenge traditional practice.

Ken Kernaghan, when exploring how the ideas central to the PS 2000 exercise would affect existing precepts, suggested that a career public service is based on the following practices:

- appointments to the public service are made with a view to preserving its political impartiality;
- appointments to, and within, the public service are based on merit, in the sense that the person appointed is the one who is best qualified;
- as far as possible, appointments are made from within the public service; and
- public servants are assured of assistance in selecting their career goals and the path to those goals.[49]

While political impartiality and merit might be not be regarded as impediments to efficiency and effectiveness, the priority given to internal candidates and the emphasis on self-designed career paths in a context of total job security would appear incompatible with the new organizational requirement for nimbleness and flexibility.

In the December 1990 White Paper released by the Prime Minister's Office,[50] several proposals, such as single operating budgets, carry-overs, new classification systems at the managerial and staff levels, and more options in common services, were clearly designed to increase flexibility for managers. Other proposals, such as service standards, a focus on results, acknowledging the need for risk management, shifting resources from management to front-line workers, and more consultation with clients and citizens, reflected greater concern about the effectiveness of programs.

It would appear logical to think that, along with espousing managerialist values and recognizing the changes in the world of work in the private sector, there would have been a sharp questioning of the traditional cosmology of a career public service. Yet, the White Paper and the First Annual Report of the Clerk to the Prime Minister on the Public Service of Canada contained strong commitments to a 'career public service'[51] and to efforts to attract the best talent for those careers. Despite evincing earlier reservations and caveats about the meaning of a career public service, the PS 2000 Task Force on Staffing re-affirmed that employment in the public service was 'largely predicated on the concept of a career public service', which was 'essential to Canada's national well-being'.

The sharp questioning would emerge after a certain lag. The Second and Third Annual Reports to the Prime Minister on the Public Service of Canada[52] reveal a clear discontinuity in the operational cosmology of a career public service. In the Second Annual Report, dated March 1994, while the term career public service is not used, there is a continued 'commitment' by the Prime Minister to a 'real partnership with the Public Service', and mention of 'a loyal and professional body of public servants'(4). The Third Annual Report of 1995 is revisionist. Its general tone suggests that a fundamental change has occurred between the fall of 1993 and the fall of 1994: a 180-degree turnaround vis-à-vis the traditional perspectives on the public service has been effected.

Ian Clark, then Secretary to the Treasury Board, had expressed concern in the summer of 1994 that the basic public sector bargain, whereby public servants accepted less than private sector pay in return for greater security of tenure, was at risk.[53] He suggested that if the federal government could no longer provide full employment security, it had to be seen to be striving to maximize employment security—which implied redeployment of officials to new jobs in the public service, along with an increased commitment to training—and treating redundant employees fairly. But in the fall of 1994, the message had become sharper. The Personnel Renewal Council (consisting of departmental representatives appointed by the heads of personnel) released a discussion paper entitled *The Way Ahead for the Public Service,* which concluded that a career public service is no longer 'necessary or affordable', and that, in any case, 'it is an unhealthy expectation' (5). Indeed, the paper recommended moving away from the concept of a career public service altogether (17). The ultimate message was delivered in the 1994-5 Annual Report of the Public Service Commission, which stated as a *fact* 'that the implicit employment contract which guaranteed relative job security to employees has been abrogated' (13).

The combination of the new philosophy of subsidiarity *en émergence*, the significant transformation of the division of labour between the private, public, and civic sectors, and the new technology of governance effected by the slow penetration of managerialist thinking, would appear to mesh perfectly to bring forth the new regime of governance. The new philosophy, the new structures, and the new technology reinforce one another. One might therefore have expected that the transition from the prior regime to the new governance system would be effected rather quickly. But this would fail to recognize that any governance regime embodies a set of rules and arrangements that benefit some actors and groups to the detriment of others. Consequently, any modification of the governance regime is bound to be resisted by the coalition of shared interests benefiting most from the prior governance regime. This rearguard action may be more or less effective, depending on the relative power of these forces of dynamic conservatism.

RESISTANCE ON MANY FRONTS

Schon has exposed in vivid detail the power of dynamic conservatism. He has shown that social systems (whether a naval ship, an industrial firm, a community, or a policy compact) have a tendency to fight to remain the same, and that this tendency is not ascribable to the stupidity or venality of individuals, but is a function of the system itself. It may take the form, for example, of selective inattention, containment, co-option, or minimal compliance.[54] Donald Michael has also explored the psychodynamics underpinning these sources of obstruction—for example, alternative rationalities, reference to dominant values and non-rational reasons, and denial.[55]

Ideological resistance[56]
The erosion of the old economic culture in no way diminished the propensity to centralize among a major segment of federal political and bureaucratic elites. This is not just a Canadian trait. It is a widely shared bias that Mitchell Resnick has analysed in detail. He explains how, in an era of decentralization in every domain, centralized thinking remains prevalent in our analysis of problems, and in our search for policy responses: 'Politicians, managers and scientists are working with blinders on, focusing on centralized solutions even when decentralized approaches might be more appropriate, robust, or reliable.'[57] This centralized mindset would appear to be stronger in Canada than elsewhere, and the strategies to immunize the traditional centralized mindset from challenges and erosion have been very sophisticated. These have gone through many phases.

First, there was the denial posture. Using public spending patterns as benchmarks, many have argued that Canada is one of the most decentralized countries in the world. They base their argument on the relative importance of provincial/local government revenues and expenditures as a percentage of the total government revenues and expenditures in Canada. This is hardly a measure of the true relative importance of the different levels of government. The many liens and controls that the federal government imposes on provincial/local spending (national standards or other conditions) truly entail that the federal government has much more effective control than these percentages would appear to indicate.

A second line of defence suggests that there cannot be more devolution, because it might well disastrously balkanize the country, a line of argument defended by John McCallum.[58] J.L. Migué has shown rather persuasively that this argument does not hold water. Balkanization is a very precise word: it refers to the artificial differential generated between regional costs and regional prices that blocks or slows down the normal inter-regional adjustment flows of human and financial resources. The action of the federal government to impose standardized levels of services in the different regions (whether they can afford them or not) and the equalization of fiscal resources among regions to allow them to finance this normalized standard of services, acts to prevent normal inter-regional adjustments. It is centralization and not decentralization that is the source of balkanization in Canada. Migué has suggested that 60 per cent of federal spending had this 'balkanizing effect' in 1960 and that it had increased to 75 per cent in 1990.[59]

A third argument is that decentralization is necessary but that it must be postponed until we have uncovered the 'Canadian core values' that might be used in determining the nature, extent, and character of 'acceptable' decentralization. Judith Maxwell does not argue against decentralization, but expresses a fundamental if somewhat elusive unease about jumping into a devolution process before knowing what might ensue.[60] This is easily understood when one realizes the extent to which the welfare state has conditioned Canadians to believe that there are important benefits to the centralized and redistributive management of the federation. Canada's social cohesion is seen as potentially threatened by devolution.

A fourth defence mechanism is along related lines. It suggests that the glue that binds this country together is the egalitarian economic culture of redistribution: federal standards (presented as national standards) are the 'fabric' of this country, so central control cannot be reduced without threatening the very existence of the Canadian social glue. The central government must also retain the role of enforcer, so the argument goes, because of Canada's commitment to international agreements.[61] This fourth argument is subtly built in three stages. First, it is suggested that income and wealth redistribution is necessary and sufficient for a community to be constituted. Second, social programs are then presented as the basic tool to feed and reinforce this sense of community. Third, it is suggested that national norms imposed by the federal government on provinces are the only safeguard against Canada's degenerating into a 'community of communities', where inequalities would increase because there is no federal equalizer. This argument is false for many reasons. First, there is more to a community than egalitarianism. Second, there is no reason to believe that 'an inter-regional laundering of money' (Banting's apt phase) is necessary to maintain the community. Third, the use of federal coercion is neither necessary nor sufficient for a strong social and cultural Canada to survive.[62]

A soft egalitarian philosophy remains omnipresent in the Canadian psyche and it has been used as a most effective lever by many federal ministers, senior federal bureaucrats, and members of the elites who have been strongly opposed to devolution. It has been used in particular to rationalize and defend unilateral moves to assert the prerogatives of the federal centre (as in the case of the Millennium Fund). This sophistry builds on a very profound public sentiment (that is only very slowly being eroded) that one cannot be 'equal and different'. It has been a powerful force in recent interprovincial deliberations and constitutional forums around the country: it represents a fundamental mental block to discussing the possibility of any viable asymmetric governance regime in Canada, it provides a ready-made rationale for any unilateral move by the federal government to enforce so-called 'national' standards, and it fuels a certain paranoia that makes any rational debate on devolution difficult.

Bureaucratic and political resistance
Even though the administrative state (politicians and bureaucrats in their daily activities) is overshadowed if not occluded by the bells and whistles of constitutional conferencing, it constitutes an effective, if more pedestrian way of addressing difficult issues. A most divisive and explosive issue like universality could never have been handled in constitutional forums or in an electoral campaign, but it could be adroitly managed by the administrative state: new arrangements that all but eliminated universality have come to take its place without a major national confrontation. Many of the real, as opposed to the symbolic, concerns being agonized over by the different parties could be handled in this manner. Indeed, it has been said that about 70 per cent of what Charlottetown and Meech were trying to achieve could be accomplished through administrative re-arrangements.

The Efficiency of the Federation initiative introduced late in 1993, and Program Review in 1994, were promising instrumentalities for this sort of work. The minimal success of these initiatives up to now should not be interpreted as an indication that these instruments lack potency, but as evidence that they can also be used, when the government in power and a contingent of senior federal bureaucrats have a centralized mindset, to delay, contain, and obstruct change.[63]

Those in the political and bureaucratic elites most opposed to a transformation of the Canadian governance system have embraced alternative service delivery (ASD) and the drive to a quality-service and citizen-centred federalism as a most attractive manoeuvre designed to give an appearance of transformation of the federal governance apparatus without any substantial reduction of federal hegemony. In the original model, the ASD initiative was meant to look at (1) the rationale for the program under scrutiny, (2) the appropriateness of the roles and relationships among the different stakeholders in the program, and (3) the machinery of service delivery. The evaluative framework for the programs in search of alternative delivery schemes had to trade off mandate, accountability, and efficiency. In fact, the ASD initiative has focussed much less, if at all, on the first two dimensions and has emphasized the machinery of delivery *stricto sensu*.

Such a focus (rather surprising for what was meant to be the implementation arm of Program Review) results from the implicit assumption that the structures and theory of governance are given, or may even be regarded as in some sense optimal, and that therefore they do not call for direct redress. Moreover, the ASD initiative, by 'inventing' (so to speak) a notion of public interest built on the requirement that the federal government continue 'fulfilling federal obligations and interests', can only bolster the existing centralized institutional order.[64] In this dark scenario, which, it must be said, is valid only for a portion of the federal scene, obfuscation is increased: Ottawa's central agencies might even be able to increase their power base.

The assumptions of those who view the ASD initiative in this way have tended to immunize many fundamental issues concerning the policy process from critical scrutiny. There has been no serious examination of (1) the reasonableness of separating policy formation, program design, and delivery mechanism; (2) the sacred nature of the Westminster model of government and the consequent dogma that public servants are accountable through the minister to Parliament, and must remain untouched as the process is amended; and (3) the presumption that explicit detailed contracts are sufficient to ensure that the policy intended by the senior executives (political and bureaucratic) will be carried out. If one adds the over-ride clause that permits any initiative to be disallowed if, in the opinion of the federal government, it prevents Ottawa from fulfilling its obligations, or if it does not serve the interests of the federal government, it becomes clear that there is ample room for political and bureaucratic obstruction.[65]

Resistance to the new covenant in the public service[66]
There is also much scope for resistance through delay and containment in the development of new rules of operation for the Canadian public service that would fit the requirements of the new philosophy of governance. On this front, the failure to develop new, clear, and legitimate rules can only mean that the old rules remain in force. And this entails of necessity that even the new initiatives may be corrupted or derailed in the implementation phase by the lack of a new overall framework to redefine what we mean by 'public service'.

The Public Service Commission—the agency charged with the overall role of preserving on behalf of Parliament the merit principle in government personnel recruitment, hiring, and promotions—has tried to strike a new balance: abandoning the old 'career public service' concept while re-affirming traditional public service principles (that is, political impartiality, merit-based appointments and promotions, hiring from within the public service, and support for career development). However, there is much cynicism about the application of these principles.[67] And this cynicism will only grow, in that the powers of the Public Service Commission would appear to be eroding to such an extent (in particular in connection with *La Relève*—the initiative to refurbish the public service by a variety of measures such as fast-tracking and training—for it was an initiative that was orchestrated explicitly to fall outside the authority of the Public Service Commission) that there have been rumours that it might even be abolished altogether.

The slowness in designing a refurbished concept of accountability in keeping with the new circumstances has generated a real crisis. While there has been some talk about the importance of the new moral contracts of public servants with the citizen, with partners, and the like (as networking, new alliances, and joint ventures develop to provide the requisite flexibility and nimbleness), there is no sign that the notion of accountability has escaped from its Westminster linear, top-down straitjacket. Consequently, there is some lip service paid to the notion of the multiple loyalties of the public servant (for example, to

Parliament through the minister, to partners, to his/her community of practice, to citizens, and so on), but the very existence of multiple accountabilities is neither recognized nor even acknowledged in these new partnerships and alliances. The rigid, linear top-down Westminster model of governance is still regarded by a large majority of public servants as the only model that has any legitimacy in Ottawa. This means not only that there is no effort to define the new moral contracts required, but the very protocol used to select the new cohort of pre-approved assistant deputy ministers in the *La Relève* process of leadership renewal has made it very unlikely that the emerging bureaucratic elite might see the world differently from the old. The determining importance of the views of the old-guard deputy ministers in the selection process of the new-guard (a final interview of the candidates with three deputy ministers was the most important element in the process) and the relative absence of any meaningful inputs by the other stakeholders can only suggest that the top-down accountability framework is the only one in good currency.

Yet 360-degree accountability (with all its paradoxes and its elusiveness) must be a central feature of the new government bureaucracies in a citizen-centred governance built on partnerships with the private and civic sector.[68] Moreover, their very elusiveness explains why such accountabilities cannot be defined in strict and rigid terms. They must of necessity be based on 'moral contracts', leaving much to be determined according to circumstances and therefore depending much on trust.[69] But even if these relationships are considered central features of the new model of distributed governance, there are still no guidelines for the process of arriving at new trust mechanisms or workable conventions for the new governance regime, nor even any interest in giving any priority to the clarification of the concept of 360-degree accountability.

The traditional shackles are still imposed on new organizational arrangements, and the all-important compensation strategy in vogue is in no way designed to reward those employees whose policy skills and political savvy are not geared entirely to serving the whims of their superiors, irrespective of their service to stakeholders and partners.

To require any employee to work differently without a transformation of the hiring practices, of the system of promotion, or of the compensation package, can only be regarded as dysfunctional and counter-productive. It is bound to choke any true change and to generate immense morale problems for the most dynamic elements in the public service. Yet, the very slowness of these adjustments and the systematic weakening of the central agencies from which a transformation might emanate (the Public Service Commission, but also in some way the Treasury Board Secretariat, as *de facto* departments and agencies that have become freer to manage in their own way) can only lead one to the conclusion that such developments may well constitute a reasonable strategy of containment for those intent on delaying and weakening the devolution process.

CONCLUSION

How far have we travelled down the road from the centralizing, homogenizing, and hierarchical prior governance regime? Are we moving toward a more non-centralizing, distributed, and associative governance regime? It is difficult to be very precise in answering this question because of a certain confusion on the national scene.

If one were to assess the state of affairs strictly by reference to the statements of the Prime Minister, one would have reason to believe that the process of change has been derailed, and that we are slipping back to the old caesarism of the Trudeau years. In the debates preceding the recent Social Union agreement and the new transfers to the province for health care purposes, the Prime Minister sounded like Louis XIV when, musing in public, he said, in effect, 'Sometimes on Monday I feel like giving the provinces more money, and then on Tuesday not.' It is not excessive to say that in the recent past dissent, even though it has often pertained to minor events, has been quashed, and when convenient, liberties have been limited. The uncanny continuity from Trudeau to Chrétien is most striking when one considers the extent to which circumstances have evolved. We would still appear to be in the throes of a rule by self-righteous elites claiming to know better.

Yet if one observes the daily administration of the Canadian federal system, and interviews federal public servants, one sees an evolving administrative apparatus that slowly drifts toward a more distributed governance. Citizen engagement, consultation, inter-sectoral partnering, and federal-provincial negotiated arrangements are blossoming everywhere. *De facto*, the Canadian governance regime is being devolved. Consequently, it is putting more and more power in the hands of people, and even the population is beginning to understand that devolution is the only radical way to 'truly place power in the hands of people'.[70]

Change occurs by fits and starts, and there are signs that, after decades of denial and procrastination, some reframing of the Canadian governance regime may emerge from a seemingly marginal set of events. Our evolving arrangements with the First Nations are likely, in my opinion, to act as an important catalyst in the transformation of our *weltanschauung* and of our philosophy of governance. The process of accommodation with the First Nations may indeed be the only route that is likely to lead toward a rediscovery and a formal recognition of cultural diversity and toward a more balanced polyarchy, where differences and dissent will be less systematically suppressed. James Tully has shown how these debates are likely to create an intercultural common ground, a new lexicon capable of dealing with diversity. This may hold the key to a broader capacity to deal with interculturalism.[71]

Members of the federal Liberal caucus freely admit that even if a significant portion of the Chrétien cabinet stands firmly with him in his defence of the prior governance regime (Sheila Copps and Stéphane Dion, for example), there is also a solid plurality of restive cabinet members (Paul Martin, Pierre Pettigrew, and others) who would gladly move forward to a new distributed governance regime. The balance of power is still with the defenders of the prior regime. Yet, forces are at work that are slowly tilting the balance the other way. *De facto*, the silent activism of the administrative state is bringing forth much change in the governance regime. And the spasmodic efforts of Canadian citizens to defend the right to dissent, the right of communities to follow their own ways, though still quite muted and tamed, can now be heard. These forces are the *premiers balbutiements* of a new philosophy of governance based on freedom and communities.[72]

Perestroika is in the air. So, as Donald Michael would say, 'There are reasons to hope—not to be optimistic, but to hope.'

NOTES

I am grateful to Leslie Pal for his most extensive and valuable comments on an earlier draft of the chapter, to my colleagues at the

Centre on Governance, in particular Jeffrey Roy, for their help, and to Anne Burgess for her editorial assistance.

1. A short segment of this section has been excerpted from the introductory chapter in G. Paquet, *Governance Through Social Learning* (Ottawa: University of Ottawa Press, 1999).
2. W. Kickert, 'Complexity, Governance and Dynamics: Conceptual Explorations of Public Network Management', in J. Kooiman, ed., *Modern Governance* (London: Sage Publications, 1993), 195.
3. T. Beck Jorgensen, 'Modes of Governance and Administrative Change', in J. Kooiman, ed., *Modern Governance*, 219-32.
4. J. Naisbitt, *Global Paradox* (New York: Morrow, 1994); T.J. Courchene, 'Glocalization: The Regional/International Interface', *Canadian Journal of Regional Science* 18, 1 (1995), 1-20.
5. Naisbitt, *Global Paradox*, 16.
6. N. Nohria and R.G. Eccles, eds, *Networks and Organizations* (Boston: Harvard Business School Press, 1992); J. de la Mothe and G. Paquet, 'The Dispersive Revolution', *Optimum* 25, 1 (1994), 42-8.
7. M. Storper, 'Institutions of the Knowledge-Based Economy', in *Employment and Growth in the Knowledge-Based Economy* (Paris: OECD, 1996), 259; P.G.W. Keen, 'Transforming Intellectual Property into Intellectual Capital: Competing in the Trust Economy', in N. Imparato, ed., *Capital for Our Time* (Stanford: Hoover Institution Press, 1999), 3-35.
8. M. Granovetter, 'The Strength of Weak Ties', *American Journal of Sociology* 78, 6 (1973), 1360-80.
9. 'The Virtual Corporation', *Business Week*, 8 Feb. 1993, 98-103; S. Tully, 'The Modular Corporation', *Fortune*, 8 Feb. 1993, 106-14.
10. A segment of this section has been excerpted from G. Paquet, 'The Strategic State', *Ciencia Ergo Sum* 3, 3 (1996), 257-61 (Part 1); 4, 1 (1997), 28-34 (Part 2); 4, 2 (1997), 148-54 (Part 3).
11. The use of the word 'anti-democratic' may generate some unease, so some clarification is in order. Our governance regimes are complex and unstable mixtures of four broths: the democratic tradition anchored in ancient Athens, the republican tradition rooted in imperial Rome and certain medieval Italian cities, the liberal tradition traceable to medieval Europe but more clearly to Locke and Montesquieu, and the tradition of the rule of law, together with 'the existence of state agencies that are legally empowered—and factually willing and able—to take actions ranging from routine oversight to criminal sanctions or impeachment in relation to possibly unlawful actions or omissions by other agents or agencies of the state'. Any undue weight given to one or another of these components may corrupt the mixture. And without the possibility of redress when there is encroachment by one state agency upon the lawful authority of another, caesarism is near (see G. O'Donnell, 'Hori-

zontal Accountabilities in New Democracies', *Journal of Democracy* 9, 3 (1998),112-26, especially 115-17). When we use the expression 'anti-democratic', we suggest that there has been a tendency in the prior regime, during the Trudeau years for instance, but also in the recent past, for top-down unilateralism to be regarded as legitimate. And the lack of authoritative agencies willing and able to stop the encroachment of one state agency upon the lawful authority of another has also been deplored. This situation—fuelled by the centralized mindset of many governments over the last decades, but also by the immensely greater bureaucratic power at the disposal of modern Caesars—has been denounced in the United States and Canada. See S.L. Carter, *The Dissent of the Governed* (Cambridge: Harvard University Press, 1998), and G. Paquet, 'Governance and Social Cohesion: Survivability in the 21st Century', in *Transactions of the Royal Society of Canada*, Sixth Series, 9 (1998), forthcoming.

12 For a very enlightening demonstration of the illiberal character of the Charter, see F.L. Morton, 'The Charter of Rights: Myth and Reality', in W.D. Gairdner, ed., *After Liberalism* (Toronto: Stoddart, 1998), 33-61.

13 S.L. Carter, *The Dissent of the Governed*, 20.

14 G. Paquet, 'States, Communities and Markets: The Distributed Governance Scenario', in T.J. Courchene, ed., *The Evolving Nation-State in a Global Information Era: Policy Challenges*, The Bell Canada Papers in Economic and Public Policy 5 (Kingston: John Deustch Institute for the Study of Economic Policy, 1997), 25-46.

15 G. Duncan, 'A Crisis of Social Democracy?' *Parliamentary Affairs* 38, 3 (Summer 1985), 267-81.

16 D. Zussman, 'Do Citizens Trust Their Governments?' *Canadian Public Administration* 40, 2 (1997), 234-54.

17 G. Paquet, 'Canada as a Disconcerted Learning Economy: A Governance Challenge', *Transactions of the Royal Society of Canada*, Sixth Series, 8 (1997), 69-98.

18 F. Hirsch, *Social Limits to Growth* (Cambridge: Harvard University Press, 1976).

19 Duncan, 'A Crisis of Social Democracy', 274.

20 R.N. Bellah et al., *The Good Society* (New York: Alfred A. Knopf, 1991), 60-61.

21 K. Banting, ed., *The State and Economic Interests* (Toronto: University of Toronto Press, 1986), 23.

22 On the economic costs of the erosion of social capital at a time when trust is becoming an ever more important asset, Quebec is a particularly interesting case in point. See G. Paquet, *Et si la Révolution Tranquille n'avait pas eu lieu ...* (Montréal: Liber, 1999).

23 For a look at the different frameworks that are discussed in the recent literature, see Leslie A. Pal, 'Policy Analysis as Soulcraft', *Canadian Public Administration* 39, 1 (1996), 85-95.

24 D. Marquand, *The Unprincipled Society* (London: Fontana Press, 1988).
25 M. Walzer, 'The Idea of Civil Society', *Kettering Review* (Winter 1997), 8-22; E.J. Dionne, ed., *Community Works:The Revival of Civil Society in America* (Washington DC: Brookings Institution Press, 1998); for a look at the difficulty of selling this idea in Canada, see G. Paquet, 'André Laurendeau et la démocratie des communautés', *Cahiers d'histoire du Québec au XXe siècle* 10 (1999) (forthcoming), and G. Paquet, 'Governance and Social Cohesion' (forthcoming).
26 L. Mead, *Beyond Entitlement: The Social Obligations of Citizenship* (New York: The Free Press, 1986); A. Wolfe, *Whose Keeper?* (Berkeley: University of California Press, 1989).
27 R.A. Dahl, *Democracy and Its Critics* (New Haven: Yale University Press, 1989), 180.
28 A. Sen, *On Ethics and Economics* (Oxford: Blackwell, 1987).
29 At least a significant and growing segment of the population makes this choice, while a non-insignificant if declining segment insists on living explicitly by the ethics of claimant politics. C. Taylor, 'Alternative Futures', in A. Cairns and C. Williams, eds, *Constitutionalism, Citizenship, and Society in Canada* (Toronto: University of Toronto Press, 1985), 183-229.
30 J. Maxwell, *Social Dimensions of Economic Growth*, The Eric John Hanson Memorial Lecture Series 8 (Edmonton: The University of Alberta, 1996); Policy Research Secretariat, *Growth, Human Development and Social Cohesion* (Ottawa: Privy Council Office, 1996).
31 Bellah, *The Good Society*, 135-6.
32 D.W. Hock, 'The Chaordic Organization', *World Business Academy Perspectives* 9, 1 (1995), 5-18. Hock uses the word 'chaord' (from chaos and order) to refer to a 'self-organizing, adaptive, non-linear, complex system, whether physical, biological or social, the behavior of which exhibits characteristics of both order and chaos or, loosely translated to business terminology, cooperation and competition' (6). As founder of VISA, he has created a company that is 'an inside-out holding company', in which the 23,000 financial institutions that create its products are 'at one and the same time, its owners, its members, its customers, its subjects and its superiors' (14). This sort of organization not only embodies subsidiarity as a founding principle ('[N]o function should be performed by any part of the whole that could reasonably be done by any more peripheral part, and no power vested in any part that might reasonably be exercised by a lesser part' [13]), but also the principle that the chaordic organization is owned by its members, and that it must embrace diversity and change, but that no individual or institution, and no combination of either or both, should be able to dominate the deliberations. In order to ensure that this is the case, VISA has had to ensure continuous learning through continued feedback loops.
33 M. Ignatieff, *The Needs of Strangers* (New York: Viking, 1985), 12.

34 D.A. Schon, *Beyond the Stable State* (New York: Norton, 1971).
35 G. Paquet, 'Slouching Toward a New Governance', *Optimum* 27, 3 (1997), 44-50.
36 H. Hardin, *A Nation Unaware* (Vancouver: J.J. Douglas, 1974). Canadian public enterprise began with the building of the Lachine Canal in 1821 and continued through the canal- and railway-building eras to the establishment of public utilities, the CBC, Air Canada, and the other Crown corporations as we know them today. Interregional redistribution began in the BNA Act, with the federal per capita subsidies to bolster the provinces' municipal tax base, continued with the National Policy, which brought subsidized railroad development eastward and westward but brought manufacturing development to Central Canada at the expense of captive markets in Western Canada and the Maritimes, and culminated with the tax equalization payments instituted in 1957.
37 R. Ford and D.R. Zussman, eds, *Alternative Service Delivery: Sharing Governance in Canada* (Toronto: IPAC/KPMG, 1997).
38 G. Paquet, 'The Strategic State', in J. Chrétien, ed., *Finding Common Ground* (Hull: Voyageur Publishing, 1992), 85-101; for a much more elaborate statement of the same general argument see G. Paquet, 'The Strategic State', *Ciencia Ergo Sum* 3, 3 (1996), 257-61 (Part 1); 4, 1 (1997), 28-34 (Part 2); 4, 2 (1997), 148-54 (Part 3).
39 J.H. Perry, *A Fiscal History of Canada: The Postwar Years* (Toronto: Canadian Tax Foundation, 1989), 434-40.
40 A. de Tocqueville, *De la démocratie en Amérique* (1840; Paris: Gallimard, 1961), 2: 104.
41 P. Laurent and G. Paquet, 'Intercultural Relations: A Myrdal-Tocqueville-Girard Interpretative Scheme', *International Political Science Review* 12, 3 (1991), 171-83.
42 G. Paquet and J. Roy, 'Prosperity Through Networks: The Bottom-Up Strategy That Might Have Been', in S. Phillips, ed., *How Ottawa Spends 1995-96:Mid-Life Crises* (Ottawa: Carleton University Press, 1995), 137-58; G. Paquet, 'Le fruit dont l'ignorance est la saveur', in A. Armit and J. Bourgault, eds, *Hard Choices, No Choices: Assessing Program Review* (Toronto: Institute of Public Administration of Canada/Canadian Plains Research Center, 1996), 47-58; G. Paquet and R. Shepherd, 'The Program Review Process: A Deconstruction', in G. Swimmer, ed., *How Ottawa Spends 1996-97: Life Under the Knife* (Ottawa: Carleton University Press, 1996), 39-72.
43 One finds numerous references to subsidiarity in Canadian debates in the 1980s, but mostly referring to the European experience. The philosophy of governance implicit in the concept was in line with the ideological stand of the Mulroney government (a government intent on re-inventing government and on redeploying activities away from government to the private and civic sectors), but very much as in the case of the deficit and debt, Canadian citizens suffered from major learning

disabilities. It took many years of didactic efforts by the Mulroney government before the realities of the deficit and debt challenges took hold. Even in the 1993 election, the Liberal party trod very carefully with regard to this issue, because a major segment of the citizenry still felt that the country could spend its way out of the recession of the early 1990s. In the case of the dependency on the state for universal programs, the learning was even longer and more difficult for Canadians. So, the reality of subsidiarity casts a big shadow on the debates of the late 1980s and early 1990s, but in a manner that is extremely diffuse. Even with Program Review, we have a subsidiarity agenda that does not dare to say its name. It is only in 1996, in the work of the Policy Research Committee (*Growth, Human Development, Social Cohesion*) and in the Deputy Ministers Task Force Reports on diverse subjects (policy capacity, ethics, horizontality, etc.) that the word subsidiarity is used formally for the first time, and in those instances its use was orchestrated by the Privy Council Office. It will be found in speeches of Stéphane Dion later. But one would be ill-advised to assume that this change in usage means that the new philosophy is now in good currency. At a meeting in Ghent early in 1999, Stéphane Dion's deputy minister could declare that neither subsidiarity nor devolution could be regarded as useful ways to amend Canada's governance. Indeed, it is not clear that Canada's federal cabinet is less schizophrenic than the Canadian citizenry on this front: while subsidiarity and devolution would appear to be the way of the future for some, others fear it like the plague and would like to preserve the present top-down arrangements in the name of the so-called social efficiency of this form of centralization. See K. Banting, 'Notes for Comments to the Deputy Ministers' Luncheon', 5 Jan. 1996, 1-14; for a critical assessment of this point of view, see G. Paquet, 'Gouvernance distribuée et habitus centralisateur', *Transactions of the Royal Society of Canada*, Série 6, 6 (1995), 93-107.

44 Deputy Minister Task Force on the Future of the Public Service: The Governance Scenarios (draft 26 Feb. 1996).

45 J. Jabes and G. Paquet, 'Réforme administrative dans la fonction publique fédérale au Canada: préliminaires à une évaluation', in M. Charih and M. Paquin, eds, *Les administrations publiques à la recherche de l'efficacité* (Québec: Ecole nationale d'administration publique, 1994), 27-47; G. Paquet, 'Alternative Program Delivery: Transforming the Practices of Governance', in R. Ford and D.R. Zussman, eds, *Alternative Service Delivery: Sharing Governance in Canada* (Toronto: IPAC/KPMG, 1997), 31-58.

46 V.S. Wilson, 'What Legacy? The Nielsen Task Force Program Review', in Katherine A. Graham, ed., *How Ottawa Spends 1988-89: Conservatives Heading into the Stretch* (Ottawa: Carleton University Press, 1988), 23-47.

47 C. Pollitt, 'Managerialism Revisited', in B.G. Peters and D.J. Savoie, eds, *Taking Stock: Assessing Public Sector Reforms* (Montreal: McGill-Queen's University Press, 1998), 45-77.
48 Treasury Board Secretariat, *Framework for Alternative Program Delivery* (Ottawa, 1995), 2.
49 K. Kernaghan, 'Career Public Service 2000: Road to Renewal or Impractical Vision?' *Canadian Public Administration* 34, 4 (1991), 553.
50 *Public Service 2000: The Renewal of the Public Service in Canada* (Ottawa: Supply and Services Canada, 1990).
51 *Public Service 2000*, 63; P. Tellier, *First Annual Report to the Prime Minister on the Public Service of Canada* (Ottawa: Supply and Services, 1992), 51.
52 G. Shortliffe, *Second Annual Report to the Prime Minister on the Public Service of Canada* (Ottawa: Supply and Services Canada, 1994); J. Bourgon, *Third Annual Report to the Prime Minister on the Public Service of Canada* (Ottawa: Supply and Services Canada, 1995).
53 I.D. Clark, 'Restraint, Renewal, and the Treasury Board Secretariat', *Canadian Public Administration* 37, 2 (Summer 1994), 209-48.
54 D.A. Schon, *Beyond the Stable State*, 32, 48-50.
55 The first root of obstruction is easy enough to recognize. Any reframing is bound to dispossess a number of stakeholders. Alternative rationalities give a higher priority to the protection of organizational turf than to rational decision-making. As a consequence, allowing the debate to proceed on issues that might unmask this alternative priority becomes taboo. The second root of obstruction is the nexus of nonrational reasons that may be invoked, such as different values, cultural norms, and beliefs about what is 'acceptable'. These values, norms, and beliefs claim to supersede any considerations of efficiency or rationality. The third root of the obstruction has to do with the psychodynamic processes that operate unconsciously and express themselves as anger, denial, face-saving, etc., when leaders in particular are forced to attend to the necessary agenda. In such cases, leaders use all their powers to ensure that some topics are not dealt with, because of the danger that, if such topics were ever addressed head on, the leaders' ignorance would be exposed, they would lose face, and they might be disowned. D.N. Michael, 'Reason's Shadow: Notes on the Psychodynamics of Obstruction', *Technological Forecasting and Social Change* 26 (1984), 149-53.
56 G. Paquet, 'Distributed Governance and Transversal Leadership', in John E. Trent, Robert Young, and Guy Lachapelle, eds, *Québec-Canada: What Is the Path Ahead?/ Nouveaux sentiers vers l'avenir* (Ottawa: University of Ottawa Press, 1996), 317-32.
57 M. Resnick, 'Changing the Centralized Mind', *Technology Review* 97, 5 (1994), 36.

58 B. McKenna, 'Ottawa's Grip on Economy at Issue in Debate over Powers', *The Globe and Mail* [Toronto], 13 Nov. 1995, B1-2.
59 J.L. Migué, 'The Balkanization of the Canadian Economy: A Legacy of Federal Policy', in F. Palda, ed., *Provincial Trade Wars: Why the Blockade Must End* (Vancouver: The Fraser Institute, 1994), 107-30.
60 J. Maxwell, 'Build on Core Values', *The Ottawa Citizen*, 15 Nov. 1995, A17. This is not an unreasonable position, but when nothing is proposed as a suggestion concerning what these core values might be, it can only provide moral support for delay tactics. It is also a common line of defence used as a last resort by those who consider that top-down enforcement of federal norms is the very 'fabric' of the community.
61 K. Banting, 'Notes for Comments'. See above, note 43.
62 G. Paquet, 'Gouvernance distribuée et habitus centralisateur', *Mémoires de la Société Royale du Canada* Série 6, 6 (1995), 93-107.
63 G. Paquet, 'The Downtrodden Administrative Route', *Inroads* 5 (1996), 21.
64 Treasury Board Secretariat, *Framework for Alternative Service Delivery* (Ottawa, 1995).
65 G. Paquet, 'Alternative Program Delivery'. This ominous 'federal obligations and interests' clause is even more explicit in the French version, where it reads, 'remplir les obligations du gouvernement fédéral et en protéger les intérêts'.
66 G. Paquet and L. Pigeon, 'In Search of a New Covenant', in Evert Lindquist, ed., *Government Restructuring and the Future of Career Public Service in Canada* (Toronto: Institute of Public Administration of Canada, forthcoming, 1999); E. Lindquist and G. Paquet, 'Career Public Service Under Stress: The New Governance and the Federal Public Service', in Evert Lindquist, ed., *Government Restructuring and the Future of Career Public Service in Canada* (Toronto: Institute of Public Administration of Canada, forthcoming, 1999).
67 L.W. Slivinsky and P. Faulkner, *Merit in the Public Service* (mimeo, 1995).
68 M.A. Harmon, *Responsibility as Paradox: A Critique of Rational Discourse on Government* (Thousand Oaks Calif.: Sage, 1995).
69 G. Paquet, 'Betting on Moral Contracts', *Optimum* 22, 3 (1991-2), 45-53. These 'moral contracts' between the different stakeholders correspond to different loyalties: for instance, in the case of a public servant, the loyalty to his superior and through him/her to the minister, the loyalty to his/her community of practice (professional engineer, etc.) and its own codes of ethics, the loyalty to partners, the loyalty to the citizen, etc. The Social Union agreement might be regarded as a sort of moral contract between the federal and provincial governments.

70 S.L. Carter, *The Dissent of the Governed*, 144.
71 J. Tully, *Strange Multiplicity* (Cambridge: Cambridge University Press, 1995).
72 W.D. Gairdner, ed., *After Liberalism* (Toronto: Stoddart, 1998).

4

The Fourth Fiscal Era: Can There Be a 'Post-Neo-conservative' Fiscal Policy?

ROBERT M. CAMPBELL

When Paul Martin stood up in the House of Commons on 16 February 1999, he was delivering the last federal budget of this century and of this millennium. Given the occasion, the budget appeared to be innocuous. It was finely crafted, balanced, and pragmatic. It addressed without surprises the various fiscal and economic concerns and options that had been rehearsed since the 1998 budget. It comprised an incremental mix of spending and taxes initiatives that, while debatable, was hardly earth-shattering.

Yet this was an unsettling budget in many ways. It was the first 'post-deficit' budget and its logic was elusive, almost serpentine. Framed by the desire to continue to avoid deficits and to reduce the debt, it evoked the values of pre-Keynesian Classical economics—of balanced books, sensible fiscal finance, and economic equilibrium in the self-regulating market. But this was six decades after the close of the Classical era. The budget hardly noted its own likely impact on inflation, unemployment, and economic circumstances. Yet it was presented with a hearty mix of self-congratulation and confidence, addressing Canadians' continuing need to be reassured that their government was taking charge in an uncertain and perilous world. This latter point injected a note of anxiety in its otherwise positive theme, a reminder that unanticipated global forces could swiftly bring disruption to the Canadian economy—unless the government and Canadians were on guard. The budget expressed assurance and purpose, but articulated a sense of limits, both self-imposed and imposed on it by international markets. In this, it lacked a sense of finality; its conclusion read, 'to be continued'. Keynesian, post-Keynesian, and neo-conservative elements and sensibilities abounded, but not in any essential or consistent way. The budget looked to the long term, but shrewdly reflected short-term and other political calculations. It was a budget that echoed the trials and tribulations of budget-making over the last half-century, and presented itself as a work-in-progress for fiscal policy in the new millennium.

The 1999 budget thus presented an intriguing mixture of the mundane and the curious, the predictable and the uncertain, the assured and the cautious, the past(s) and the present. It reflected the 'shape shifting' character of policy at the end of the millennium, combining ingredients of past policy eras, while adopting eclectic and contradictory policy elements. Its morph-like mixing produced a mélange evocative of policy past, but simultaneously like no other policy past. The 1999 budget is inherently transitory, setting out an uncertain trajectory to a new fiscal policy era.

There were three fiscal policy periods in the postwar period, and the millennium marks the beginning of the fourth. Each had a central *raison d'être*, a strategy and tactics, and an Achilles heel that led to its demise. The Keynesian period (1945-75) focussed on unemployment, was organized around countercyclical policy and the welfare state, and ended with inflation and stagflation. The post-Keynesian era (1975-84) focussed on stagflation, and was organized around economic planning and development, but ended in deficits and debt. The neo-conservative era (1985-98) focussed on the elimination of deficits, comprised rolling back the state and embracing globalization, and is ending with modest economic optimism, and policy anomie and anxiety about the future.

The 'post-neo-conservative' period does not yet express a full or coherent rationale or strategy at a theoretical level, and remains relatively shapeless. This new fiscal policy era continues to be framed by the discourse related to deficits and the debt, but this no longer provides an animating force. Neo-conservatism's sensitivity to the limited capacity of state economic management persists, but there is an emerging desire to articulate a public policy purpose and to move policy into strategic domains. The new policy era embraces globalization and the demands it makes on fiscal policy to get the domestic economy 'in order'. But it also understands the dark side of globalization and wants to initiate policies that adjust and respond to global forces. The debt and deficit discourse and globalization insist on restraining the welfare state, but the new fiscal policy era simultaneously champions essential elements of that state. The new era responds to economic circumstances but tentatively looks to shape them; it is passive generally, but active strategically. All of this evokes a curious sense of Keynesian and post-Keynesian *déjà vu*. Fiscal policy at the end of the millennium is still in the process of becoming, marked by the absence of an all-embracing theory or rationale but appearing poised to combine elements of past fiscal policy strategies and changed tactics in a new, shape shifting policy mix.

This chapter will present the 1999 budget as a prism through which fiscal policy's past can be seen to inform its present rationale as well to shape its possible future. The chapter will proceed in three parts. First, it will situate the 1999 budget in the context of the closing of the third era of postwar fiscal policy, review the process leading to its formulation, and present its main features. Second, the chapter will unpack the 1999 budget, addressing how the budget speaks to and reflects the major issues that have informed fiscal policy over the last decades. Third, the chapter concludes by anticipating how the next era of fiscal policy may take shape at the beginning of the next century.

THE 1999 BUDGET: THE END OF THE NEO-CONSERVATIVE ERA?

The broad contours of the 1999 budget were set by the 1995 and 1998 budgets. When returned to power in 1993, the Liberals accepted pragmatically the neo-conservative agenda that had been established internationally by the Thatcher and Reagan governments in the United Kingdom and the United States and by the previous Conservative government of Brian Mulroney. Neo-conservatives argued that unwarranted government interventions in the economy had caused the sluggish growth, weak productivity, stagflation, and rising deficits of the 1970s. The neo-conservative agenda proposed slashing government spending and eliminating deficits, deregulating the economy and selling state enterprises, reforming the tax system and cutting back on welfare and social security, pursuing a neutral fiscal policy and a disciplined monetary policy, and liberating domestic and international market activity. The Conservative governments of Brian Mulroney (1984-8, 1988-93) pursued this policy mix with some commitment but limited success. When the Liberals re-entered office, they confronted a neo-conservative *fait accompli* that they did not undo. They also faced a federal public debt that had doubled under the Conservatives to $500 billion and a $45 billion annual deficit.

Its 1993 electoral Red Book[1] committed the Liberals to reducing the deficit to the European standard of 3 per cent of GDP from the inherited 6 per cent level. Minister of Finance Paul Martin's first budget included some spending cuts, but deficit reduction was to be pursued mainly through economic growth. This benign strategy was upset by events, particularly the Mexican *peso* crisis of 1994. This further weakened an already weak Canadian dollar. Subsequent interest rate increases threatened to sabotage economic growth. Martin's 1995 budget was one of Canada's most significant, in that it committed the government to a dramatic course of action that changed the contours and fabric of Canadian society and politics. Program spending would be cut by more than $25 billion over the next three years, tax revenues were increased by $3.7 billion, and 45,000 public service jobs were eliminated. Subsequent budgets reduced the deficit targets to 2 per cent and 1 per cent of GDP. An equally significant budget in 1998 saw Martin deliver the first balanced budget since 1969-70 and commit the government to balanced budgets in the next two years. Budgetary surpluses could be anticipated, given conservative assumptions and the creation of a $3 billion contingency reserve. When the books closed on the 1997-8 fiscal year, the government recorded a budgetary surplus for the first time in 28 years—$3.5 billion—to be applied against the debt.[2] The 1998 budget operationalized the Liberals' 1997 electoral commitment[3] to allocate surpluses on a

50:50 basis—half to tax cuts and debt reduction and half to spending—in a mix of moderate spending increases ($11 billion over 4 years), tax relief ($7 billion), and debt repayment ($9 billion).

Martin's 1999 budget was formulated in circumstances different from those of his previous ones. The 1998 budget had already committed the government to producing a balanced budget in 1999. Moreover, the results of the 1997-8 fiscal year suggested that the challenge for Martin was less balancing the books than what to do with the 'fiscal dividend'.[4] But the relative calm of the previous years had been replaced by stormy economic weather. 'The world has become an inhospitable place', Martin observed before the House of Commons Finance Committee, and characterized economic conditions as 'a period of turmoil not seen for a very long time.' George Soros, the billionaire capitalist turned philanthropist, said that the global capitalist system was 'coming apart at the seams', and President Clinton declared this 'the biggest financial challenge facing the world in half a century.'[5]

The changed budgetary context was first set in the summer of 1997, when the Thai *baht* was floated and sunk quickly. This incident led to a chain of investment outflows, currency problems, and interest rate increases across Thailand, the Philippines, Indonesia, and South Korea. The Hong Kong stock market fell, economic riots forced Indonesia's President Suharto from office, and Japan's economy went into reverse as its banks failed.[6] The 'Asian flu' spread through the world, half of which entered a recession. A North American stock market panic in the summer of 1998 saw almost $3 trillion in value disappear on Wall Street in five weeks, the equivalent of the economy of Germany. By early October, the Toronto Stock Exchange fell to its lowest level in two years and bond prices hit a record low.[7] The Asian flu rocked the Canadian dollar, which had already been on a 20-year downward trajectory, tracking the decline in world commodity prices. Currency traders bet against the loonie, calculating that Canadian commodity exports would suffer, since Asia purchased one quarter of the world's commodities. The loonie fell by over 10 per cent against the US dollar over the year, hitting new record lows with each passing week.[8] After a year of dollar deterioration and policy passivity, the Bank of Canada finally intervened. It traded a record US$5.8 billion in August to support the loonie, and raised its lending rate by 1 per cent to 6 per cent. After a further dip to US$.6331, the dollar subsequently stabilized at around $US.65 and then jumped back up to $US.67 in February 1999.[9] To the puzzlement but relief of observers, the world economy did not plunge into recession, even though the stabilization of international conditions was later rocked by a currency crisis in Brazil.[10] The US Federal Reserve Board cut interest rates three times in October and November, which helped global liquidity and international capital flows. The Bank of Canada followed suit quickly, undoing the interest rate increase it had introduced in August. The leading industrial nations—including Canada—acted to assist the International Monetary Fund (IMF) in repairing the damaged Asian and Latin American economies to stem the international tide.[11] These rapid and jarring international developments had a surprisingly modest impact on the advanced economies, but their prospects for economic growth declined substantially.[12]

The Asian flu, the stock market decline, the plight of the loonie, and recession anxiety sobered the government's views while it was preparing the budget. When a $5.8 billion first quarter surplus was announced, Martin exhorted Canadians not to count these chickens before they were hatched. 'We've been prudent because we live in an interdependent and highly charged world', asserted Martin, 'as we've seen events over the course of the last month.' Martin had to tread a fine line between dampening expectations about the size of the surplus and causing anxiety about a recession. He reported to the Finance Committee that falling growth forecasts halved the original estimates of the fiscal dividend to $5 billion.[13] While critics, interested parties, and the opposition lined up like kids in a candy store, offering advice on how to spend the surplus, Martin remained cautious: 'In the current environment, it is difficult to predict with sufficient confidence the size of future dividends.... What is clear now is that any dividend will be very small. That is why we need to continue to be cautious and have a debate over priorities.' Reform party leader Preston Manning accused Martin of being over-cautious and gouging Canadians.[14]

Discussions revolved around the Liberals' proposed 50:50 split, between spending on the one hand and tax cuts and debt reduction on the other. The government made fewer and fewer references to this electoral promise over the course of the year, for reasons to be discussed below. Whatever framework for priority-setting it might have offered was neutralized by Finance officials, who characterized it as 'a rule of thumb for planning purposes over the mandate—the annual allocation will vary from year to year'.[15] This issue spoke to the question of priority-setting in the post-deficit age. What rated higher: Diminishing the tax burden? Reducing the accumulated debt? Targeting priorities for spending? And what principles or plan would guide these choices?

The three broad possibilities all enjoyed popular support, and it was a question of the proportion of available dollars that would be assigned to each. The polls were ambiguous in their identification of the public's preferences. Some showed that debt reduction was valued over increased federal spending. But when the question was framed in terms of a priority list, health care came out on top. Canada's debt-to-GDP ratio remained above the OECD average; it was, in fact, second only to Italy's. But enormous provincial pressures complemented public pressure to restore health care transfers. Martin was sensitive about not having paid sufficient attention to health care, and his former deputy minister, David Dodge, was now deputy minister at Health. The Prime Minister effectively crossed the policy Rubicon when he declared that 'our next major investment in this mandate will be in Medicare.' There were frequent federal-provincial meetings during the fall and early winter about a proposed 'health accord' and a new 'social union'. This culminated in a First Ministers' meeting at the Prime Minister's residence in January 1999, where the federal government sweetened the health care pot by an undisclosed amount of money in return for certain provincial 'guarantees' that the money would be spent on health care.[16] The 1999 budget would be a 'health care budget'.

This had not been the choice of Finance officials in the first instance, for whom 'health is just politics and tax cuts are good policy'. But the construction of the budget is as political a process as it is a technical or economic one. The Business Council on National Issues (BCNI) suggested a spending freeze and exhorted the federal government not to give in to provincial demands on the health front. The Canadian Chamber of Commerce looked for a freeze on total spending, with increased health spending financed by spending cuts elsewhere.[17] Cabinet ministers were offered a 'wish-list' opportunity to vote for their top five spending priorities, knowing that only a few would be chosen. Eighty projects were proposed, ranging from increased expenditure on highways, defence, and foreign aid to selected spending on native health and research and development—with aid to beleaguered farmers topping the list.[18] The Reform party called for spending restraint, particularly in business subsidies, but Martin insisted on maintaining investment in 'the infrastructure of the new economy' lest the economy remain in the 'horse-and-buggy age'.[19]

There was considerable pressure to cut taxes, whose proportion of GDP had risen from 29 per cent in 1979 to 39 per cent, which was around the OECD average but high relative to the US's 32 per cent. Increases in tax revenues had played a far greater role in taming the deficit than had spending cuts, particularly because of the de-indexing of taxation in the 1980s. Among others, the C.D. Howe Institute urged large tax cuts, arguing that Ottawa could afford a $4.6 billion cut in each of the next five years; *The Globe and Mail* took up this theme in its pre-budget editorials.[20] Where to offer tax relief was also a puzzle: indexation, the basic personal exemption, child tax benefit, the surtax, lower, middle or upper band rates, a general cut? Each tax option represented an enormous amount of revenue foregone: a $100 cut for all taxpayers ($1.45 billion); a $100 increase in the personal exemption ($350 million); a 1 per cent across the board cut in personal taxes ($3.6 billion); removal of the surtax from higher income earners ($1.1 billion); indexing the personal exemption ($1 billion); full indexation ($2 billion); each 1 per cent cut in the lower band rates ($2.1 billion); a 1 per cent cut in the mid-income band ($1.2 billion); a 1 per cent cut in the GST ($3 billion).[21] Martin cautioned against initiating too many and too large tax cuts, which could lead to a return to a deficit situation if the economic situation deteriorated.

A side issue was what to do with the groaning, $20 billion surplus in the Employment Insurance (EI) Fund. These surpluses had been blended into the Consolidated Revenue Fund since 1986, and had been used to pay down the debt. The provinces, particularly Ontario, insisted on a cut in EI premiums of up to one-third. But this would cost $7 billion, and Martin argued that there were better things to do with this money: 'Everybody has got their wish list.... And EI isn't at the top of anybody's wish list.' While the C.D. Howe Institute urged a cut to offset an impending increase in Canada Pension Plan (CPP) premiums, business groups like the BCNI and the Chamber of Commerce recommended tax cuts instead.[22]

The Liberals promoted an approach that balanced spending, tax cuts, and debt reduction. The Prime Minister stated, 'I'm a Liberal... It's always a balance. You know, 50-50—it's very much Liberal.' Chrétien insisted that both spending and tax cuts were possible: 'We can walk and chew at the same time.' The Liberals seemed to back away from their 50:50 formula, sensing that the market would not be keen on permanent increases in expenditures.[23] The House of Commons Finance Committee recommended a balanced approach: $3.58 billion in tax cuts, $1.85 billion in spending, and $6 billion in cushions and contingencies for debt reduction.[24]

As pre-budget discussions unfolded, a 'technical' problem emerged concerning how to spend the surplus, which indicated two possible decision biases. This problem related to how the government set up its fiscal management framework, which comprised four elements: (i) a two-year horizon for budget planning; (ii) prudent economic assumptions; (iii) a $3 billion Contingency Reserve buffer; and (iv) payment on the debt when the Reserve is not needed.[25] The actual fiscal surplus would not emerge in concrete form until after the books were closed for the year. By this time, though, it would be too late to 'spend' the money, for the year would be over. This is what happened in 1997-8, with the $3.5 billion surplus going to pay down the debt. It would be a calculated risk for the government to 'spend' the money before year-end. If its forecast turned out to be wrong, it could face the embarrassment of presenting a deficit. Thus, the fiscal dividend process was biased to one of two choices: debt reduction (the passive choice) or one-time spending at the eleventh hour. The latter comprises spending that does not enter the budget base as an ongoing expenditure. The Millennium Scholarship Fund ($2.5 billion in 1997-8) and the Innovation Fund ($800 million in 1996-7) were policy decisions made at a relatively late time, which involved large amounts of money and did not require ongoing commitments. Any increase in program spending ($3.9 billion), as well as substantial budget savings ($1.5 billion), were directed to $5.5 billion in one-time spending in 1997-8. The Auditor-General queried and challenged this creative accounting, according to which spending that was accounted for in one year took place in another. There were pre-budget rumours that Martin would use part of the 1998-9 surplus to sweeten the health care pot for the provinces.[26]

In sum, two issues played hard on Martin's budget calculation. First, how would international economic circumstances impact on the Canadian economy, the government's finances, and the fiscal surplus? Second, what approach should the government take in using the fiscal dividend? The first was an issue over which it had little or no control—save to the extent that it was optimistic or pessimistic in its forecasts. The second issue was basically political, and required a strategic rationale as guidance, which was not yet evident to observers or perhaps to the government itself.

The 16 February 1999 Budget

By the time Martin delivered his budget, its broad contours had already been widely rehearsed, articulated, and defended, reflecting the more 'open' budget process of recent years. There were some modest surprises, and these may foreshadow the emerging shape of fiscal policy in the fourth era.

A half-dozen budgetary themes surprised no one. First, Martin continued to sound a cautious note about persistent international economic uncertainty and lowered growth prospects. This caution framed the presentation of his conservative fiscal estimates and easy targets, which guaranteed another 'unexpectedly' large surplus in February 2000.[27] Second, he presented a balanced budget for 1999-2000 and extended the government's balanced budget commitment to 2000-1. This represented four consecutive balanced budgets for only the third time in Canadian history. Third, the budget comprised balanced initiatives on the spending, tax, and debt fronts: '[A] successful society does not run on one cylinder....We must never become a single issue government.'[28] There was no mention of the 50:50 ratio of spending to tax cuts and debt reduction, although the figures came fairly close to hitting this ratio.[29] Fourth, Martin continued to reject the idea of an aggressively activist government: 'Behind us forever is the era of governments promising more than they could deliver and delivering more than they could afford.'[30] The budget did not explore or mention its impact on unemployment, inflation, and economic circumstances. Fifth, Martin declared that within a modest government role, it still had to set priorities. This budget 'acts strongly on the highest priority Canadians have—strengthening their system of health care.'[31] The 1999 budget was very much a health care budget. Sixth, Martin used his creative, end-of-term accounting and spending to clear out an 'unexpectedly' large surplus by means of large amounts of one-time spending (see below).

Two budgetary ingredients could be characterized as surprises—the size of tax cuts and the amount of spending increases. The tax cuts were smaller and fewer than had been anticipated. Martin did not pursue the options on the expensive end of the continuum, such as indexation or across-the-board cuts. He extended the 1998 budget's increase in the tax threshold to all taxpayers, and increased it by another $175; this gave all taxpayers a tax cut, albeit a modest one. Martin also eliminated the 3 per cent tax surplus on incomes above $50,000, but the 5 per cent surtax on incomes above $65,000 remained. These two initiatives provided $1.5 billion of tax relief in 1999-2000, rising to $2.8 billion and $3.4 billion in the next two years. The government also expanded benefits under the National Child Benefit System, increasing support by $350 per child over a two-year period and pumping in $300 million in support for modest- and middle-income families. Editorial, business, and public reaction was critical; given the size of the government's surplus, the feeling was that the government could have gone much further in offering tax relief. On the other hand, it was recognized that each of the proposed alternatives was hugely expensive and that public pressure to spend on health care had narrowed the government's fiscal space. Moreover, political observers shrewdly calculated that the government was likely 'saving' fiscal room for major tax cuts closer to the next federal election.[32]

A second surprise was the amount and direction of government spending, which Martin increased by $18 billion. Relative to debt reduction and tax reduction, this was a considerable sum of money. Martin maintained a $3 billion contingency reserve, proposing to use the reserve to pay down the debt if it were not needed. The debt to GDP ratio had fallen and would continue to fall with economic growth. But Canada's ratio remained above the OECD average, second only to Italy's. The debt-servicing charges were poised to actually increase by a few billion dollars in future years even as the ratio declined (because of higher interest rates).[33] Thus, taxes and the debt were being cut only modestly, and a large proportion of the fiscal surplus was spent on government activities. Martin committed a huge amount of money to increased health care transfers, over $11 billion in all.

There were some surprises as well in the specifics of how Martin decided to carve up the fiscal dividend. With respect to the 1998-9 accounts, Martin confronted an $11.7 billion surplus in December. The budget reduced this to $8.5 billion for year-end by factoring in economic developments over the remainder of the year (equalization transfers, corporate tax collection, and so on). $3 billion of the remainder represented the Contingency Reserve (to be applied to debt reduction). Martin had to do 'something' with the remaining $5.5 billion, lest the year end with this amount going to debt reduction as well. As in past years, Martin chose to spend the money, primarily in one-time spending initiatives. Some of this had been announced before the budget, such as the cut in the EI premium that was finally settled in December,[34] costing $300 million in 1998-9. Also, $1 billion was allotted to the agricultural and fisheries sectors under the Agricultural Income Disaster and Canadian Fisheries Adjustment and Restructuring Programs (these were not ongoing budget commitments, although there would be some spending commitment in the next fiscal year). This left $4.2 billion to spend in the 1999 budget speech. $700 million of this was consumed in a hodge-podge of spending: $255 million in health initiatives, $35 million for Parks Canada, $13 million for crime prevention, $12 million for environmental challenges, $100 million for the Canada Foundation for Innovation, $41 million for the closing of Devco, and so on. Much of this money would not actually be spent in 1998-9. But the biggest ingredient was a 1998-9 $3.5 billion CHST supplement to be paid into a 'third-party trust in 1999-2000, on passage of authorizing legislation', which would be available to the provinces and territories over the next three years.[35] This unusual device saw the government clear out $3.5 billion of budgetary surplus in 1998-9 without spending one dollar in 1998-9, and without this spending entering the base budget. The Finance Department received preliminary blessing from the Auditor General on this initiative after a series of pre-budget meetings, but the practice was widely criticized in the press.[36]

With respect to 1999-2000 and beyond, Martin assigned incremental increases to targeted areas like foreign aid, Aboriginal spending, and the armed forces. But the most significant and substantial increases in government spending focussed on two areas: health and innovation. With respect to health, Martin committed the government to increase transfers to the provinces by $11.5 billion over the next five years. $3.5 billion of this was a one-time but immediate injection. Over and above this, Martin also presented a number of strategic federal initiatives in the area of health information, research, and prevention, totalling $1.4 billion through the next three years. These included construction of a system of 'progress reports' in selected areas, a National Health Surveillance Network, a Canada Health Network, development of information technology on health delivery, rural and community health support, prevention programs, food safety, diabetes, Aboriginal health, the Canadian Institute for Health Research, and the Canadian Health Services Research Foundation.

Martin also provided for significant strategic spending in the area of productivity, innovation, and support to the 'knowledge based economy', totalling $1.8 billion over the next three years. 'Breakthroughs don't just happen', Martin observed, 'they require sustained investment.'[37] To this end, Martin provided extra cash over the next three years to the Canada Foundation for Innovation ($200 million), the research councils ($120 million), Networks of Centres of Excellence ($30 million a year), Technology Partnerships Canada ($50 million a year), and bio-technology research in government departments ($55 million). He also expanded the Youth Employment Strategy by 50 per cent and allocated $430 million to the Canadian Space Agency.

In his concluding budget comments, Martin used Wilfrid Laurier's famous declaration that the 20th century would belong to Canada to suggest that the 21st century would also belong to Canada.[38] The 1999 budget was a 'back to the future budget', in that it evoked elements and values of budgets past as it pieced together fragments of a strategy for the future. Four consecutive budget balances have established this Classical policy element as a foundational element for the future, and the budget declares again the death of Big Government. At the same time, the government presents the budget balance and debt reduction as means of increasing Canada's capacity to absorb international shocks and to take advantage of economic opportunities. The budget resisted tax cuts in favour of the use of fiscal resources for strategic, albeit limited, spending and interventionist initiatives in the movement to the knowledge-based economy. The 1999 budget comprised Keynesian, post-Keynesian, and neo-conservative touches that, together, struggle to take shape as a fiscal strategy or vision for the post-neo-conservative era.

THE 1999 BUDGET AS METAPHOR

The 1999 budget can be viewed as a prism by means of which to analyse and reflect on postwar fiscal policy and to anticipate the character of future fiscal policy. It represents a transitional moment to the postwar period's fourth policy era. This is an era that is in the process of taking on shape and rationale. Indeed, this millenium moment may be marked precisely by the absence of hard-edged characteristics. As noted in the introduction, each era had a rationale, a strategy, and a weakness. The Keynesian era (1945-75) was framed by the Depression and the Second World War, focussed on maintaining economic and social security by means of demand analysis and countercyclical policy, and was undone by its asymmetry: it was easier for governments to cut taxes and raise spending when the economy weakened than it was to increase taxes and cut spending when inflation developed. The second era (1975-84) focussed on supply issues (efficiency, productivity, and growth), and tended to a planning framework, with interventionist tools and institutions (Crown corporations, agencies, and controls). Its Achilles heel was the deficit, which exposed the schizophrenia inherent in an expensive pseudo-planning process that basically respected market autonomy. Instead of productivity gains and growth it produced increased expenditures, decreased tax revenues, and burgeoning deficits. The neo-conservative era (1985-98) was born of these eras. It focussed on rolling back the state's role in the economy and eliminating the deficit, which was symbolic of that earlier role. Its policy framework was the Classical one associated with free market economics: balancing budgets and liberalizing markets. Its Achilles heel was its ultimate aimlessness and lack of purpose, particularly in the globalized world it helped to create.

The fourth fiscal policy era will be informed by the three previous eras. It will combine elements of each, which will make the era simultaneously familiar and unfamiliar. The era will be sceptical of tools that did not seem to work, such as Keynesian countercyclical budgeting and economic development policies, and will be anxious about inflation, deficits, and unregulated globalization. On the other hand, the era will address the disobliging features of globalization and deregulation inherited from the third policy era, but in a pragmatic, ad hoc, and at times contradictory fashion. This era remains somewhat lacking in overall coherence as it shifts its shape in response to circumstances—and this may be its eventual character. One can highlight and analyse those conditions that have framed its experiences—as in the process leading up to the 1999 budget. In this way, one can begin to anticipate how the present shape shifting of fiscal policy might emerge as a new policy paradigm in the next millennium.

Analysing and Understanding Economic Circumstances
Finance Minister Martin's prudent economic forecasting has become legendary and an easy target for critics. Between budgets, Martin has avoided making hard forecasts or commitments. He mocked the easy confidence of private economic forecasters, whose early year predictions of 4.7 per cent growth had to be revised to 3 per cent by the fall.[39] 'The dramatic downward revision in private sector forecasts illustrates ... why we simply cannot afford the risks associated with changing planning assumptions so drastically, month by month.' The Prime Minister himself cautioned that 'even if we're doing relatively well in Canada, we don't know where we will be in February.'[40] Martin refused to commit to tax cuts, because it was impossible to predict the size of the surplus. The 1999 budget in turn was founded on extremely conservative forecasts.

The analysis of economic conditions is at the core of fiscal policy. Policy analysts use statistical and analytical techniques to forecast economic conditions and formulate appropriate policy responses. The development of economic techniques and statistical tables such as the national accounts were part and parcel of Soviet- and French-style planning and the emergence of the Keynesian idea of managing the economy. The growth in sophistication of analytical techniques and the accumulation of statistics have been countered by the persistent decline in optimism about the efficacy of economic forecasting and the capacity to understand economic conditions—indeed by the crisis in economic theory and economics itself.

The absence of 'economic certainty' has led to getting policy wrong. A famous Keynesian-period example was the 1957 budget. The Liberal government received contradictory advice from two of its departments. It followed the advice of the one that cautioned against inflation, with the result that it initiated a tight fiscal policy at the start of an economic downturn. The start-stop experiences of the 1960s and 1970s were plagued by lags in policy information, such that policy often lagged behind economic conditions. As a generalization, when governments were confronted with economic uncertainty, they tended to be biased toward dealing with inflation rather than unemployment.[41] Martin has in the 1990s tended to choose conservative estimations, with a bias toward debt reduction, one-time spending, and the re-emergence of the problem of year-end spending scrambles.

This uncertainty applies as well to an understanding of current economic conditions. The development of stagflation in the 1970s (a combination of high unemployment and high inflation) defied economic comprehension, and policy became, in effect, a matter of educated guesswork. The data were available, but there was no consensus on what they meant. Three recent examples exemplify this phenomenon. First, policy observers were struck by the irrationality and unpredictability of international developments in the summer, fall, and winter of 1998-9, which seemed outside of comprehension and control. There was no consensus as to why conditions later stabilized. The cycle of 'good' and 'bad' times seemed to have collapsed from years into a matter of months. Second, it was difficult to explain the performance of the Canadian dollar. An Organization for Economic Co-operation and Development (OECD) study suggested that the 'true' value of the Canadian dollar (in terms of what it should buy) was over US$.80, rather than around US$.65 to $.67. The sense was that the market had the wrong image of Canada as being a resource-based commodity exporting country, when only 35 per cent of its exports are of this character. Martin insisted that the loonie's performance 'simply does not reflect the true economic picture of Canada'. He insisted that 'financial markets do not always get it right. They travel in herds, they run on rumour, they often ignore fundamentals, and all too often they overshoot.'[42] Third, Canada's poor productivity performance was a concern (as was the issue of its relation to the declining value of the dollar). An OECD report concluded that Canada's relative income advantage within the OECD (10 per cent at present) was likely to fall to a 15 per cent to 25 per cent disadvantage over the next 20 years, as a result of its declining productivity. The report expressed puzzlement about this, given the extensive economic reforms that had been initiated in Canada over the last decade, which should have had the opposite result.[43]

Fiscal policy has been made daunting, if not impossible, by the declining confidence in economic forecasting and analytical comprehension of economic conditions. It is difficult to debate or make fiscal policy in an intelligent or effective way when the technical and empirical basis of discussion and policy is uncertain. We will suggest in the concluding section that this analytical uncertainty will likely result in fiscal policy that is fairly unambitious, focussed on the 'basics' and the short term, and more open to public discussion.

The International Context

The run-up to the 1999 budget was fraught with uncertainty and anxiety generated by the Asian flu and turmoil in the international economy. As stock markets plunged, observers described the scene as 'utter bedlam', with the world capitalist system 'coming apart at the seams' and the international economy on the 'brink of a financial precipice'. Martin declared that 'negative developments in far-off corners of the world are having immediate repercussions everywhere. Very clearly, the global economy has entered uncharted waters.' Jeffrey Simpson reported a 'widespread sense of helplessness that now pervades Ottawa', and the Canadian government looked anemic, if not hopeless, in dealing with the plummeting dollar.[44]

Canada's susceptibility to international developments has been central to its experience as a trading nation. It has lived by—and died with—the twists and turns of the global economy. With few exceptions, this has been accepted as a fate that Canada must endure. The Keynesian approach embraced liberalization of trade, capital flows, and exchange rates as a means of increasing national income. The postwar White Paper on Employment and Income acknowledged that 'the conditions under which post-war trade can reach higher levels than before are not, in any large degree, under the direct control of the Canadian government.'[45] When the Canadian economy weakened in 1949-50, 1953-4, and the late 1950s, governments tolerated the rise in unemployment. They maintained that they had no control over European reconstruction, the end of the postwar sellers' market, and increasing international competition, which impacted negatively in Canada. During the second fiscal policy era, governments confronted huge supply-side shocks in energy and agriculture. There were some attempts to insulate the Canadian economy by means of economic development policy, but the international constraint on fiscal policy was accepted as a given. The third fiscal policy era saw Canadian governments embracing globalization as a good-in-itself, and they negotiated international free trade agreements to this end. Governments accepted a reduction in their capacity to influence economic conditions in return for the economic benefits that were anticipated from globalization.

The fourth fiscal policy era has inherited the consequences of the trend to economic internationalization. The globalized economy makes open, trading countries like Canada more sensitive to distant conditions (such as the health of the Thai *baht*). Speculation against domestic currencies seems to have increased as a result of economic interdependence and increasing computerization and speed of transactions. Martin characterized the Asian flu and its fallout as 'the first real test of the stability and sustainability of globalization'.[46] At the same time, the third fiscal policy era reduced what little domestic fiscal policy resources that Canada possessed to deal with globalization (such as fiscal policy in a flexible exchange rate world). Stabilization policy in the era of globalization requires an international as well as a domestic framework for evaluation and action. But international institutional developments have lagged behind global economic developments. As economist John McCallum put it, 'We are moving to a system of global finance but we don't have a global government.' There was a degree of coordinated global response to the international turmoil. Governments granted extra resources to the IMF, bailouts were extended to many economies in Southeast Asia, Latin America, and Russia, and the US cut interest rates to ease the global liquidity squeeze. There was discussion but no immediate action to check the flood of cross-border money in emergency situations to keep otherwise healthy economies from collapsing.[47] While discussions at the World Economic Forum in Davos, Switzerland suggest that there is agreement that the international financial system is outdated, no clear plans emerged. This crisis may see the emergence of new institutional mechanisms to mitigate such problems in the future. Canada made a number of its own proposals in this regard, and efforts to solve this problem will be a central feature of Canadian action in the fourth fiscal policy era.[48]

Increasing Policy Scepticism
In his pre-budget appearance before the House of Commons Finance Committee, Martin distanced himself from an interventionist approach to economic management: '[W]e must never again allow short-term preoccupations to blind us to the long-term needs of the nation. The fact is, that's what governments have done all too often.... Governments focussed on fine tuning economic performance to smooth out bumps in the road. What they didn't do was look far enough ahead to see that the road was in fact a dead end.' Instead, he articulated a 'common sense' approach to the economy, with government responsible for putting 'fundamentals' in place to allow the market to work efficiently. These fundamentals included reducing interest rates, the debt to GDP ratio, government spending, and taxes. Martin distanced himself from economic theory and models: 'We have not been doing any of this because it satisfies some textbook definition of good economic fundamentals. We are doing this because it speaks to the fundamentals that really count for Canadians.'[49] Given the increasing sophistication of economic analysis and technique, this position was ironic if not startling. Martin's position reflects scepticism that economic tools can be used to improve circumstances—indeed a loss of faith in economic theory as a guiding framework or discipline.

This development has its origins in the early postwar period. When the economy weakened in the late 1940s and early and late 1950s, governments concluded that using expansionary fiscal measures would not mitigate economic weaknesses caused by changing international economic circumstances, technological change, or regional or seasonal factors. Later, Walter Gordon did not follow President Kennedy's 1960 tax cut, asserting that its benefits would accrue to foreign economies when Canadians increased their consumption of imported products. Policy-makers lost faith in the restrictive capacity of fiscal policy in the inflationary 1960s. Raising taxes to contain inflation would worsen inflation, as those with 'market power'—large corporations, unions, and professional associations—would pass on the increase by means of higher prices or wages. By 1975, there was a consensus that Keynesian tools lacked the capacity to deal with international conditions, supply-side factors, market power, and inflation. In the second era, governments embraced a combination of policy instruments, including monetarism, expenditure formulae, and economic controls. Some of these instruments extended the government's role in the economy, albeit in a half-hearted way that interfered with but did not alter market development. Canadians and their governments have always been schizophrenic about the extent to which politics should dominate the market. While development and control policies proliferated in this period, and government spending and deficits rose, Canadians were unimpressed by the mixed economic results. They eventually embraced the neo-conservative agenda in 1984.

From the second through the third fiscal policy eras, there was a shift in policy authority from fiscal to monetary policy, which coincided with a diminished role for the former in a flexible exchange rate system. This reflected a sense that fiscal policy had limited capacity, and also that government could abuse it in an undisciplined way. From the perspective of containing inflation, monetary policy was seen to be a more effective and disciplined tool, insulated from political interference. Confidence in the efficacy of monetary policy has been undermined considerably, as a result of Canada's absorption into the world economy, which limits its potential independence and effectiveness. Interest rates have always had to be synchronized with American rates, lest there be short-term outflows of speculative capital. Ironically, even as monetary policy plays by the rules, the dollar seems now to be valued almost randomly, and independently of what takes place within the Canadian economy. A telling moment in the tumultuous summer of 1998 was the Bank of Canada's attempt to stem the loonie's decline. In late August it raised interest rates by a full percentage point. The result? The loonie fell half a cent to a record low $US.631. The Bank of Canada subsequently followed the US Federal Reserve Board's three cuts in interest rates, and the earlier interest rate increase was more or less undone.[50]

Globalization has constrained Canada's capacity to pursue an independent monetary policy. To the extent that governments choose to respond to the disobliging features of globalization, fiscal policy may have to re-emerge as an instrument that could be used to some effect. This scenario is unlikely to unfold, for the reasons expressed by Martin above. The policy experiences of the past cast an inhibiting shadow over future fiscal and economic policy. The first fiscal policy era ended with Keynesianism in disrepute, while the second policy era ended with a revolt against government intervention in the economy. The growth of the deficit and the debt are seen as symbolic representations of past government failures. For the immediate future, it is inconceivable that a government would dare present a deficit budget, save in a dire emergency.

A major theme in the transition from the second to the third policy era was a decline in policy discretion. Policy formulae and targets were introduced to limit government's ability to act in a discretionary and potentially undisciplined way. This tendency represents a frustration with lack of policy success, a desire to impose simple solutions on complex situations, and a demand for increased public accountability. The first stage in this evolution occurred in 1975, when the Liberal government imposed wage and price controls, embraced monetarism, and instituted a kind of expenditure control plan. Limiting the growth in government expenditures to the growth of the economy was the first example of setting spending targets related to a formula. Monetarism embraced the same sort of formulaic approach to monetary growth. Wage and price controls were an extreme example of the imposition of a formula.

The formula approach continued in the third policy era. The Mulroney government extended the policy of monetarism. In 1991 it joined forces with the Bank of Canada to set a series of formal inflation targets, to reduce inflation to 2 per cent by the mid-1990s. The Liberals continued the approach and extended until 2001 the formal commitment to keep inflation within the 1–3 per cent range. The Mulroney government introduced spending limits in its Expenditure Control Plan in 1990. This was initially a modest plan that limited spending to a 3 per cent per annum level of growth, which would hardly put a dent in the deficit. Later, it legislated a Spending Control Act, which mandated that spending not exceed a level set in 1991. The Liberals later introduced a more forceful plan. Martin now reports routinely the extent to which government operating spending has declined as a percentage of GDP. A decline in this ratio has become an informal target, and it is hard to imagine that a government could easily raise it. The Liberals embraced an expenditure management system, which requires that any new spending initiative be financed out of savings from existing initiatives. The formulae here are less rigid and formal, but are increasingly public and are presented as accountability targets or criteria. The most fundamental or primary formula is the balanced budget target, which is now central to fiscal policy. It boxes governments into a tight policy corner and limits their policy options and discretion. The balanced budget has become an accountability target for the public—independent of economic circumstances. The federal government has not yet gone so far as to put this balanced budget requirement into some sort of legislative form. Newfoundland, Prince Edward Island, and Ontario are the only provinces that do not have some sort of formal fiscal rules on balanced budgets, debt reduction, and tax increases, from four-year cumulative balanced budget requirements to annual balanced budget obligations. Ontario has recently introduced legislation to deal with this matter and the public seems to be increasingly amenable to the idea.[51]

Two other formulae feed into the non-discretionary policy mix. The first is the debt-to-GDP ratio. Governments will feel obliged to reduce this ratio yearly for the foreseeable future, although economic growth might do this for them automatically. The second is the Liberals' 1997 electoral commitment to use any fiscal dividend or surplus in a formulaic way—50 per cent to tax cuts and debt reduction and 50 per cent to spending. It is unlikely that the Liberals will feel bound by this formula, and may actually impose a tighter one on themselves. It would be extremely difficult for the government to sell spending increases to the public (and to the market) that had to match the amount of tax relief and debt reduction. This would require billions of dollars of spending. This 50:50 formula was ill-conceived, and is being increasingly ignored by the government. It was not mentioned in the 1999 budget and will likely be jettisoned in due course, to be replaced by an alternative formula.

Increasing scepticism about the effectiveness of policy tools, coupled with anxiety about governments' lack of discipline, has resulted in demands for accountability and restraints on government. The imposition of formulae and controls on governments—thereby limiting their policy discretion—is likely to continue and strengthen in the fourth fiscal policy era. What is uncertain is how long this policy objective will be sufficiently satisfying as an end purpose around which all government policy will revolve.

Absence of Consensus
A broad public and expert consensus has evolved that the government should continue to balance budgets and reduce the accumulated debt and taxes. But beyond that there is little policy agreement about overall policy strategy or particular tactics on most economic topics. In the decline of Keynesianism, planning, and neo-conservatism, the movement through the first three policy eras has left the fourth one with a theoretical or framework lacuna and an absence of vision. There is no grand theory or policy saviour on the horizon. Ironically, now that the deficit has been tamed and a fiscal dividend attained, the harder questions remain about the ultimate purpose or goals of policy.

In the Keynesian policy period, the public insisted on the government's responsibility for economic and social security; there was agreement on the likely benefits of countercyclical budgeting and the welfare state, and an acceptance that reducing unemployment was a central or defining policy goal. There was not a total paradigmatic dominance, but there was a shared discourse and vision. In the second fiscal policy period, there was a movement to a nationalist-inspired strengthening of the economy against international and technological changes. There was never anything approximating universalism, but there were elements of a shared discourse and framework. In the third fiscal policy period, a gradual understanding and acceptance evolved concerning the need to reduce deficits and the debt and to reconsider the extent to which government involvement in the economy was necessary. Not everyone adopted neo-conservativism, but its language and discourse became predominant.

Elements of all three frameworks exist in Canadians' current vocabulary and thinking. But none of them predominates and no shared language or discourse has evolved. The predominance of the most recent framework—neo-conservatism—has weakened for a number of reasons. First, there is increasing anxiety about its costs, particularly in social services such as health care. Second, its broader economic results have not been overwhelming, particularly with respect to productivity and the standard of living—which appears to have declined through the 1990s. Third, with the deficit tamed, the *raison d'être* of neo-conservatism seems to have passed, but nothing has been presented to replace it. The closest thing is Martin's common sense pragmatism, as illustrated earlier. But this lacks the precision or depth to guide Canadians through complex circumstances or to provide answers to important economic questions.

This state of affairs has been illustrated recently in a series of incidents. The public was ambivalent about how the government should respond to the dollar crisis in 1998. It alternated between the view that there was little that could be done and the view that the government had fumbled the ball. Expert advice was as ambivalent. It ranged from the option of doing nothing, to raising interest rates and cutting taxes or both, to pegging the exchange rate or even adopting the US dollar. When the government chose the first option, it was criticized for being irresponsible. When the Bank of Canada finally raised interest rates, commentators and economists were deeply divided. Some endorsed the move, some were scathing in their criticism of the government for harming the economy, while others sympathized with the government's impossible situation. This range of divided opinions reflected the absence of agreement on the cause of the loonie's decline. Some (such as the Bank of Canada) said that falling commodity prices drove it down. Others (such as Martin) insisted that the markets had got it wrong. Others related the decline to Canada's weak productivity or high taxes. Once markets stabilized, experts were still bewildered as to why this had happened and disagreed about where the economy was heading.[52]

Given the absence of a shared vision or framework, there was a wide variety of opinions about the best way to spend the fiscal dividend. Health care spending topped the polls and was obviously favoured by the provinces. But what was the appropriate amount? Business called for substantial tax cuts and the BCNI encouraged the government to freeze spending, including health care transfers. Finance officials themselves favoured tax cuts. The Reform party demanded lots of everything while Prime Minister Chrétien opted for a little of everything. There was an equally wide division of opinion on which taxes were the most appropriate to cut. Some experts recommended focussing on low-income earners. Others argued that relief should be offered to middle- and upper-income earners, whose personal taxes were high relative to those in the US. There was considerable support for indexing the tax system. Some premiers and opposition parties demanded that EI premiums be cut, particularly to neutralize the impending rise in CPP payments. Others argued that there were better ways to spend the EI surplus, noting that Canadians enjoyed one of the lowest payroll taxes in the world. In sum, discussion about tax and spending options was random and ad hoc, and not tied to telling arguments or cases provided by a shared discourse or framework. This feature of the present policy conjuncture was described candidly by Scott Clark, deputy minister of finance: 'As we turn the corner now to having balanced budgets or surpluses, there is no consensus in the public as to what is good policy or what we should do.'[53]

There was little available by way of institutional alternatives or their tools for the government or the public to draw on. Economic policy is dominated by the executive branch of the majority party in government, traditionally through the Department of Finance and the Bank of Canada. There are alternative sources of information and advice, in think tanks and institutions, but fiscal policy authority is highly centralized. Its framework at the end of the century is not substantially different than it was in the pre-war period, nor does it offer more resources or possibilities. The Keynesian commitments made little or no institutional demands. Some degree of fiscal centralization seemed warranted and was pursued during and after the war. But Canada's centrifugal forces slowly and surely decentralized fiscal resources. Ottawa had 70 per cent of government revenues and spent twice as much as the provinces in the mid-1950s. By 1975, though, the provinces were spending more than Ottawa. Indeed, the federal government's present level of program spending comprises but 12.7 per cent of GDP—about the level that existed in the late 1940s. Even if there were a will to use federal spending and taxation powers there would not be a significant economic impact, given its insubstantial economic presence. The provinces have collectively accumulated increased fiscal powers, but there has been little in the way of co-ordinated inter-provincial fiscal development or initiatives.

There was a plethora of institutional developments in the second fiscal policy period associated with government planning and supply-side interventions. There was also some effort made at business-labour-government collaboration, if not corporatist initiatives. These concertation efforts were limited by the absence of any Canadian tradition or experience and by the reality that neither business nor labour was concentrated sufficiently to make such a system work. Many economic agencies, regulatory bodies, and Crown corporations were dissolved in the third fiscal policy period, as a result of the neo-conservative agenda of privatization, deregulation, and downsizing. There was little public outcry at the dissolution of these boards and agencies, and the Chrétien government did not feel pressure to reinstate them.

Public discussions in the lead-up to the 1999 budget confirmed the extent to which no dominant discourse or overarching framework has emerged to guide debates, set a policy agenda, or give authority to any policy approach. Nor are there competing or alternative institutions to draw authority away from the dominant economic policy-making agencies. In the previous three policy eras, unemployment, inflation, and the deficit respectively dominated or framed the agenda. There is currently no central goal or idea around which the policy process or agenda can be organized or revolve. Martin's calculus of pragmatism is anti-textbook and anti-ideological, and does not offer a policy vision, comprise a public philosophy, or set a public agenda. At most, what this pragmatism suggests is that globalization and increased competition constitute an inevitable reality, and that if Canada is to survive and prosper it must act to adjust and respond to this reality. As Martin suggests, this comprises getting the 'fundamentals' correct, such as having the fiscal house in order, so as to be ready and able to take advantage of opportunities when they arise. This strategy will be discussed further below.

Public Ambivalence

Canadians seem schizophrenic about what to expect from governments in the economic realm and what their own role in the policy-making process should be. There has been a modest policy 'democratization' process in Canada through the three fiscal policy eras, particularly in the period since the failed Meech Lake Accord. Notwithstanding its ongoing central role, the Department of Finance has lost a considerable amount of its Talmudic authority over the postwar period. This is partially the result of the perception that the Department is fallible, that it can and does make mistakes. There is a public understanding that there are limits to the knowledge and comprehension of economic circumstances, such that Finance can no longer hide behind a curtain of scientific mystery. Moreover, Finance is not the only player in the game of economic analysis and policy development. Various think tanks have arisen—from the C.D. Howe Institute and the Institute for Research on Public Policy to the Caledon Institute and the Canadian Centre for Policy Alternatives—that house expert staff, produce regular reports, and offer informed policy advice. The banks, investment houses, and major interest associations contain economic intelligence units, whose spokespersons are regularly called on to comment in the media. Their analysis is often more accurate than government's, and they provide competing points of view.

Fiscal policy discussions have been widened by an extensive pre-budget consultation exercise, which departs from traditional budget secrecy. The House of Commons Finance Committee seeks input and ideas from groups and individuals, and the finance minister meets provincial representatives, individuals, and groups in an elaborate exercise through the fall and early winter. As 'economics' and economic analysis are found wanting, it makes sense for a finance minister to seek wider advice. By the time the budget appears—as in February 1999—there are relatively few surprises, and the process has generated some degree of understanding and legitimacy.[54] But the process also constrains Finance to a degree. Despite these more open processes and a wider range of players, fiscal policy still remains the exclusive responsibility of the finance minister and the prime minister and is under their authority. There are suggestions that the process should be made more collaborative. This is ironic, in that it takes place at a time when Canadians' expectations of fiscal policy have declined, and when they maintain that governments should play a limited role in the economy. This evolution can be more accurately described as an 'accountability' trend rather than a democratic or participatory one. There is a growing demand for, and emphasis on, performance targets and measurable outputs.

Canadians remain deeply ambivalent about the respective roles and authority of governments and markets. The Canadian version of Keynesianism in the first fiscal policy period was a 'free enterprise' sort of Keynesianism, so aptly described by historian Jack Granatstein.[55] Comprising a modest extension of the role of the state in economic life, it socialized uncertainty more than it socialized the means of production or the major decisions of the market. When this approach was found to have limited effectiveness, Canada faced a choice between extending the state's economic role and rolling it back to allow the market to sort things out. The former strategy was pursued for a decade in the second fiscal policy era, and was then rejected for the pursuit of the latter in the third fiscal policy era. At the turn of the millennium, Canadians continue to want it both ways. They desire strong and effective federal economic leadership in an efficient and free market economy. Canadians need periodic assurance that economic life is going to be all right and that the authorities are alert, aware, and ready to act to protect their interests. Ekos research shows that Canadians expect fiscal prudence, feel that taxes are too high, and are suspicious of heavy state interference and old-style government. On the other hand, research shows also that neo-conservatism has lost a considerable amount of its resonance, and that Canadians want their government to deal with big collective concerns such as security and health care—which rank ahead of tax cuts in surveys.[56]

Paul Martin reflects these Canadian sensibilities. He has rejected the 'big government' approach to social and economic affairs, but he also rejects the view that 'our society and economy should be left to twist in the winds of globalization'. In the 1998 budget, he insisted that 'there is more to taking care of the nation than simply taking care of the books. Canada is not just a market place. It is a community.'[57] In this, Martin may be feeling his way toward the 'third' or 'middle way' popularized conceptually by American President Clinton and British Prime Minister Blair. What remains unclear, though, is how to concretize and operationalize this path.

THE FUTURE

The 1999 budget was informed by a series of pressures and conditions that have buffeted fiscal policy over the last half-century. These pressures have generated three distinct periods of fiscal policy-making, each with its own character, rationale, strategy, and tactics. Each was undone by a set of specific constraints and failures that set the parameters for the next era. The 1999 budget stands poised at the dawn of the new millennium, and at the beginning of a new fiscal policy era. What shape will this fourth era take? What will emerge is unlikely to be a solid paradigm, with hard-edged parameters and boundaries. Fiscal policy will very much be of a shape shifting character for a considerable period, and this may very well define this fourth era. It will be influenced by the experiences of earlier eras, and comprise some elements of each, as well as some new ingredients. For this reason, it will not appear to be totally distinct. Four particular themes have emerged from the previous policy eras that will frame the complex character, rationale, and tactics of the next fiscal policy era. These are economic uncertainty, public scepticism, internationalization, and public ambivalence.

Globalization, rapid technological change, and intense international and domestic competition are likely to continue in consequential ways for the foreseeable future. Takeovers and mergers, international partnerships, and the intensive application of new technological processes may lead to short periods of economic normalization, if not calm. Until that time, policy-makers will continue to confront economic circumstances that are rapidly changing and difficult to comprehend. Uncertainty will make fiscal policy a highly perilous business. Policy-makers will proceed with caution, and an element of pessimism will prevail about the capacity of policy to influence economic circumstances. Indeed, uncertainty will also encourage policy-makers to accept the main features and results of market activity. Policy will involve pragmatic responses to economic circumstances, and will eschew ideological or theoretical consideration of how to transform these circumstances. The concrete policies that are chosen will depend greatly on specific conditions and circumstances. The overall policy orientation will be toward preparing to take advantage of what circumstances offer. This will result in eclectic, ad hoc, and seemingly unambitious policies. Uncertainty will limit policy to short-run responses and programs, with a bias toward one-time spending programs. Policy will emphasize simplicity, economy, flexibility, and getting the 'fundamentals' right—that is, ensuring the correct conditions for maximum market reaction and performance. Governments will have to 'sell' this modest role to the public, even as circumstances display signs of crisis. On the other hand, the public itself may play as important a role in dampening governments' sense of what policy can do.

There is little evidence that the public will jettison its scepticism about policy capacity. At most the public will continue to be ambivalent about the respective roles of governments and markets. This will produce a limited terrain for fiscal policy, but a terrain nonetheless. A Classical orientation and a balanced budget framework will persist for a considerable time. This will limit political choices and constrain government opportunities. Any initiatives will have to be focussed, well defined, costed, and introduced only after considerable legitimating and prioritizing consultation exercises. Continuing public scepticism will insist on more and finely tuned targets and formulae that will limit action but also provide legitimacy—and possibly effectiveness—to the policies pursued. Major government initiatives may result from time to time. This will reflect the ongoing public expectation that the government should deal with big, pressing, and priority items—like health care in 1999. It is unlikely that the amount of government spending will rise, because its proportion of GDP will be an accountability proxy for evaluating government performance. But continuing public consultation and accountability exercises might generate a slightly more ambitious vision of the role and scope of government.

The international impact on domestic economic circumstances and possibilities will grow, and the public will appreciate that there are limits to domestic responses to globalized activity. On the one hand, this will lead governments and the public to push for international responses and solutions to international events and problems. Canada will strive for greater international collaboration, to the end that international agencies and organizations will regulate the international economy and mitigate its harsher edges. On the other hand, increasing recognition and appreciation of international realities will result in a broader acceptance of the general policy approach appropriate to this condition—one oriented toward making the Canadian economy flexible and adaptable to international competition and opportunities. This approach—combining adjustments to international changes and responses to opportunities—will generate an eclectic and sometimes contradictory mix of policies. Some will roll back the state to encourage liberalization and modernization, while others will increase the role of the state to strengthen parts of the economy in order to exploit economic opportunities. The result will be a constant re-setting of policy in a series of ever-changing shapes and sizes.

Finally, there will likely be an extended struggle to define a new public philosophy for the 21st century. This process will reflect a number of variables. First, the public's ambivalence about the roles of governments and markets will express itself politically—as priorities for action, as a rejection of some features of globalization, or simply as some national or international aspiration. In the immediate 'post-neo-conservative' era, there is an existential policy emptiness that needs to be addressed. Once the budget is balanced and the debt is under control, what will be the public purpose for governments? Second, some economic conditions are evolving that may be unacceptable to Canadians. For example, if Canada's productivity crisis is not attended to, there will be a further decline in Canadians' standard of living. Recent employment growth notwithstanding, there has been a decline in labour market participation and a growth in part-time employment, which may see a jobs or income crisis arise in the near future. The collapsing relative value of the Canadian dollar is a chicken that will eventually come home to roost. The health, pension, and social security systems seem shaky, and one does not have to be Cassandra to anticipate that they may come undone. Debt and deficit reduction has been achieved, but this success has not been matched by an improvement in Canadians' standard of living. Any of these developments may force a public debate and the formulation of a more ambitious public economic strategy. Third, politicians themselves may take the lead in formulating a new public philosophy. Pragmatically, political parties need to differentiate themselves, as they cannot all fight over the political centre forever. On the federal level, they need to create a differentiated ongoing role for the federal government—lest they find themselves without a purpose. Internationally, the electoral pendulum has swung away from conservative parties to social democratic ones, albeit in an environment where the centre has shifted far to the right. In the European Union over two-thirds of member governments are social democratic. The 'third way'—between the 'old' left and the 'new' right—is an abstract idea in the process of becoming.[58] It may emerge as a framework for debate in Canada, the result of which could help further define and concretize the shape shifting character of the fourth fiscal policy era.

NOTES

This research is supported by the Social Sciences and Humanities Research Council. I would like to thank Bill Coleman, Timothy Lewis, Leslie Pal, and David Wolfe for their helpful comments.

1. Liberal Party of Canada, *Creating Opportunity: The Liberal Plan for Canada* (Ottawa, 1993).
2. Government of Canada, *Briefing Book: The Economic and Fiscal Update* (Ottawa, 14 Oct. 1998).
3. Liberal Party of Canada, *Securing Our Future Together: Preparing Canada for the 21st Century* (Ottawa, 1997).
4. On the concept of the fiscal dividend see Michael J. Prince, 'New Mandate, New Money, New Politics: Federal Budgeting in the Post-Deficit Era', in Leslie A. Pal, ed., *How Ottawa Spends 1998-99: Balancing Act: The Post-Deficit Mandate* (Toronto: Oxford University Press, 1998), 31-55, and *Policy Options Politiques* 19, 1 (Jan.-Feb. 1998).
5. Government of Canada, *Briefing Book*, 53, 62; Brian Milner, 'Fear and Loathing of a Global Recession', *The Globe and Mail* [Toronto], 19 Sept. 1998, B1, 5.
6. Susan Smith, 'Thai Tale of Unravelling Began Canada's Reversal of Fortune', *The Globe and Mail* [Toronto], 29 Aug. 1998, A11.
7. Marion Stinson, 'Rates Rise, Stocks Plunge', *The Globe and Mail* [Toronto], 28 Aug. 1998, A1, 10; Marion Stinson, 'Dollar, Markets Plummet as Global Woes Deepen', *The Globe and Mail* [Toronto], 2 Oct. 1998, B1, 7.
8. *The Economist*, 15 Aug. 1998, 61.
9. Sean McCarthy, 'Ottawa Faces Tough Choice on Dollar', *The Globe and Mail* [Toronto], 8 Aug. 1998, A1, 6; Guy Dixon, 'Selloff Swamps Global Markets', *The Globe and Mail* [Toronto], B1, 4; Marian Stinson, 'Dollar Soars to Best Close in Months', *The Globe and Mail* [Toronto], 5 Feb. 1999, B1, 4.
10. Guy Dixon, 'Brazil Rocks Dollar', *The Globe and Mail* [Toronto], 14 Jan. 1999, B1, 4; Heather Scoffield, 'New Crisis Feared as Brazil Devalues Currency', *The Globe and Mail* [Toronto], 14 Jan. 1998, A1, 13; Heather Scoffield, 'Brazilian Real Finally Floating Freely', *The Globe and Mail* [Toronto], B1, 10.
11. Heather Scoffield, 'G7 Unveils Plan to Tackle Global Financial Crisis', *The Globe and Mail* [Toronto], 31 Oct. 1998, B3; Heather Scoffield, 'IMF Fails to Boost Brazil', *The Globe and Mail* [Toronto], 1 Feb. 1999, B1, 12.
12. Michael M. Phillips, 'IMF Lowers Its Forecast for Worldwide Growth', *The Globe and Mail* [Toronto], 22 Dec. 1998, B9; Bruce Little, 'Recession or Recovery in 1999', *The Globe and Mail* [Toronto], 30 Dec. 1998, B1, 10.
13. Edward Greenspon, 'World Events, Budget Linked, PM Says', *The Globe and Mail* [Toronto], 19 Aug. 1998, A3; Edward Greenspon, 'Turmoil Threatens Ottawa's Nest Egg', *The Globe and Mail* [Toronto], 28 Aug. 1998, A1, 10; Government of Canada, *Briefing Book*, 63.

FISCAL POLICY 145

14 *Briefing Book*, 28; Edward Greenspon, 'Use Surplus to Cut Taxes', *The Globe and Mail* [Toronto], 21 Nov. 1998, A4.
15 *Briefing Book*, 32.
16 Edward Greenspon, 'Health Care Issue Bonds Rival Ministers', *The Globe and Mail* [Toronto], 6 July 1998, A1, 4; Edward Greenspon, 'Health Care Tops List of Concerns', *The Globe and Mail* [Toronto], 11 July 1998, A4; Edward Greenspon, 'World Events, Budget Linked, PM Says', *The Globe and Mail* [Toronto], 19 Aug. 1998, A3; William Walker, 'Chrétien Promises to Treat Medicare', *The Toronto Star*, 19 Sept. 1998, A9; Shawn McCarthy, 'Alberta Says Martin Supports Province', *The Globe and Mail* [Toronto], 23 Oct. 1998, A3; Shawn McCarthy, 'Rise in Health Funds Possible, Rock Hints', *The Globe and Mail* [Toronto], 4 Nov. 1998, A11; Edward Greenspon, 'Premiers Put Heat on Ottawa for Health-Care Money', *The Globe and Mail* [Toronto], 9 Dec. 1998, A1, 8; Edward Greenspon, 'Federal Offer Plays Well at Social-Union Talks', *The Globe and Mail* [Toronto], 13 Jan. 1999, A1, 5; Daniel Leblanc, 'PM Sounds Warmer to Health Transfers', *The Globe and Mail* [Toronto], 21 Jan. 1999, A4; 'Canadians Rank Health Care as Top Priority for Leaders' Attention', *The Globe and Mail* [Toronto], 2 Feb. 1999, A4; Edward Greenspon and Graham Fraser, 'PM Finds Cash to Woo Provinces', *The Globe and Mail* [Toronto], 3 Feb. 1999, A1, 7; Anne McIlroy and Brian Laghi, 'PM Gets Social Union Deal but Quebec Won't Sign', *The Globe and Mail* [Toronto], 5 Feb. 1999, A1, 8; Shawn McCarthy, 'Canadians' Message to Martin: Keep Cutting the Debt', *The Globe and Mail* [Toronto], 8 Feb. 1999, A1, 3.
17 Edward Greenspon and Shawn McCarthy, 'A Dilemma for Martin', *The Globe and Mail* [Toronto], 9 Sept. 1998, B1, 4; Heather Scoffield, 'Council Advocates Spending Freeze', *The Globe and Mail* [Toronto], 10 Sept. 1998, B9; Shawn McCarthy, 'Business Group Fears Martin Pushed to Spend', *The Globe and Mail* [Toronto], 8 Feb. 1999, A3.
18 Erin Anderssen, 'Heat on Indian Affairs to Deliver Extra Funding', *The Globe and Mail* [Toronto], 18 Jan. 1999, A1, 4; Shawn McCarthy, 'Manley Falls Short in Bid to Get Millions for Aerospace', *The Globe and Mail* [Toronto], 1 Feb. 1999, A5; Kevin Carmichael, 'Federal Budget Will Provide Funds for Native Health Problems', *The Globe and Mail* [Toronto], 1 Feb. 1999, A15; Jeffrey Simpson, 'Stumbling Towards Tomorrow', *The Globe and Mail* [Toronto], 5 Feb. 1999, A12; Edward Greenspon, 'Farm Crisis Tops Cabinet's Private List of Priorities', *The Globe and Mail* [Toronto], 5 Dec. 1998, A1, 13.
19 Shawn McCarthy, 'Martin Rejects Calls to Cut Spending', *The Globe and Mail* [Toronto], 2 Feb. 1999, A4.
20 Bruce Little, 'Tax Cut Battle Looms', *The Globe and Mail* [Toronto], 1 June 1998, B1, 6; Bruce Little, 'Ottawa Seen Affording Middle-Class

Tax Break', *The Globe and Mail* [Toronto], 9 Dec. 1998, B5; 'Ottawa Could Cut Taxes, Report Says', *The Globe and Mail* [Toronto], 18 Dec. 1998, B5; Jeffrey Simpson, 'The Stealth Tax', *The Globe and Mail* [Toronto], 17 Dec. 1998, A26. See the pre-budget editorials in *The Globe and Mail* [Toronto], 12, 18, 20, 22, and 26 Jan. 1998.
21 *Policy Options Politiques*, Dec. 1998, 4.
22 Shawn McCarthy, 'Martin Pitches Plan to Keep EI Windfall', *The Globe and Mail* [Toronto], 24 Sept. 1998, A1, 13; 'EI Kitty May be Used to Cut Income Tax', *The Globe and Mail* [Toronto], 27 Sept. 1998, A11; Bruce Little, 'Cut UI Premiums to Offset CPP Increases, Ottawa Urged', *The Globe and Mail* [Toronto], 14 Oct. 1998, B5; Shawn McCarthy and Edward Greenspon, 'UI Premiums Can Fall 33%', *The Globe and Mail* [Toronto], 30 Sept. 1998, A1, 2; Shawn McCarthy and Edward Greenspon, 'Martin Hopeful for UI Rate Agreement', *The Globe and Mail* [Toronto], 13 Nov. 1998, B3.
23 Edward Greenspon, 'Cutting Debt Top Priority: Chrétien', *The Globe and Mail* [Toronto], 14 Sept. 1998, A1, 8; Edward Greenspon, 'Arithmetic Hints Liberals 50:50 Plan Is History', *The Globe and Mail* [Toronto], 17 Sept. 1998, A4; Edward Greenspon, 'PM Admits Being Off Course on Surplus Split', *The Globe and Mail* [Toronto], 11 Nov. 1998, A8; Daniel Leblanc, 'PM Sounds Warmer to Health Transfers', *The Globe and Mail* [Toronto], 21 Jan. 1999, A4; Government of Canada, *Briefing Book*, 2-4.
24 Shawn McCarthy, 'Commons Committee Urges Tax Cuts on Above-Average Incomes', *The Globe and Mail* [Toronto], 1 Dec. 1998, A1, 12.
25 Government of Canada, *Briefing Book*, 31.
26 Edward Greenspon, 'Liberals Soften on Cutting National Debt', *The Globe and Mail* [Toronto], 10 Nov. 1998, A1, 10; Jeff Sallot, 'Auditor Raps Martin Over Accounting Practice', *The Globe and Mail* [Toronto], 19 Nov. 1998, A12; Bruce Little, 'A Few Weeks to Spend a Few Billion', *The Globe and Mail* [Toronto], 24 Jan. 1999, A2; Shawn McCarthy, 'Clash Looms over Liberals' Bookkeeping', *The Globe and Mail* [Toronto], 4 Feb. 1999, A9.
27 Paul Martin, Minister of Finance, *Budget Speech* (Ottawa: Public Works and Government Services Canada, 1999), 4, 8.
28 Ibid., 5.
29 RBC Dominion Securities broke down the surplus allocation to 43 per cent spending, 29 per cent tax reduction, and 28 per cent debt reduction. See Neville Nankivell, 'A Bad Time for Feds to Resume Spending', *The Financial Post*, 18 Feb. 1999, C7.
30 Martin, *Budget Speech*, 28.
31 Ibid., 3.

32 Eric Reguly, 'Martin Merely Tinkers with Taxes', *The Globe and Mail* [Toronto], 17 Feb. 1998, B2; Jeffrey Simpson, 'The Year of the Health-Care Budget', *The Globe and Mail* [Toronto], 17 Feb. 1999, A16; Lawrence Martin, 'The Lost Issue of Living Standards', *The National Post*, 18 Feb. 1999, A14; Jeffrey Simpson, 'Real Liberals Don't Cut Taxes', *The Globe and Mail* [Toronto], 18 Feb. 1999, A16.
33 Paul Martin, Minister of Finance, *The Budget Plan 1999* (Ottawa: Public Works and Government Services Canada, 1999), Table 1.1, 18.
34 Shawn McCarthy and Edward Greenspon, 'UI Rate Could Be Cut Far More, Actuary Says', *The Globe and Mail* [Toronto], 2 Dec. 1998, A1, 9; 'Thief Label Spurred Martin's UI Reversal', *The Globe and Mail* [Toronto], 5 Dec. 1998, A15.
35 Department of Finance, *The Budget Plan 1999* (Ottawa, 1999), 84, 141.
36 Hugh Winsor, 'Wizard Made Use of Hidden Helpers', *The Globe and Mail* [Toronto], 17 Feb. 1999, A14; Alan Toulin, 'Blessing Given to Health Spending', *The National Post*, 17 Feb. 1999, A12. For editorial criticism of the practice, see 'Curing the Santa Clause Syndrome', *The Globe and Mail* [Toronto], 17 Feb. 1999, A16, and 'Show Us the Money', *The National Post*, 17 Feb. 1999, A16. The Auditor General's acceptance of this device was related to a number of considerations, such as that the spending was related to an existing program, that it was targeted, that there was a federal-provincial agreement about it, and that it would be given parliamentary approval.
37 Martin, *The Budget Speech*, 18-19.
38 Ibid., 28-9.
39 *Briefing Book*, 63-4.
40 Edward Greenspon, 'World Events, Budget Linked, PM Says', *The Globe and Mail* [Toronto], 19 Aug. 1998, A3.
41 These examples of postwar fiscal policies, and others cited below, are taken from Robert M. Campbell, *Grand Illusions: The Politics of the Keynesian Experience in Canada 1945-1975* (Peterborough Ont.: Broadview Press, 1987), and *The Full Employment Objective in Canada 1945-85: Historical, Conceptual and Comparative Perspectives* (Ottawa: Economic Council of Canada, 1991).
42 Mark MacKinnon, 'Dollar Undervalued, OECD Study Finds', *The Globe and Mail* [Toronto], 22 Sept. 1998, B2; Corey Goldman, 'How Far Does a Dollar Go?' *The Globe and Mail* [Toronto], 19 Oct. 1998, B1, 8; *Briefing Book*, 59.
43 Bruce Little, 'Faltering Productivity Cited for Lower Living Standard', *The Globe and Mail* [Toronto], 16 Oct. 1998, B4; Bruce Little, 'Economy Is Lagging, Canada Is Warned', *The Globe and Mail* [Toronto], 3 Dec. 1998, A1, 11.

44 Marion Stinson, 'Rates Rise, Stocks Plunge', *The Globe and Mail* [Toronto], 28 Aug. 1998, A1, 10; Jeffrey Simpson, 'What the Hell Is Going On', *The Globe and Mail* [Toronto], 28 Aug. 1998, A16; Brian Milner, 'Fear and Loathing of a Global Recession', *The Globe and Mail* [Toronto], 19 Sept. 1998, B1, 5; *Briefing Book*, 53-5.

45 Department of Reconstruction, *Employment and Income with Special Reference to the Initial Period of Reconstruction* (Ottawa, 1945), 7.

46 *Briefing Book*, 54.

47 Barrie McKenna, 'Economic Powers Try to Avoid Calamity', *The Globe and Mail* [Toronto], 3 Oct. 1998, A1, 6; Barrie McKenna, 'World Economic Storm Spurs Another Rate Cut', *The Globe and Mail* [Toronto], 16 Oct. 1998, A1, 16; Heather Scoffield, 'G7 Unveils Plan to Tackle Global Financial Crisis', *The Globe and Mail* [Toronto], 31 Oct. 1998, B3.

48 Terrence Roth, 'Global Finance Review Creates Discord', *The Globe and Mail* [Toronto], 1 Feb. 1999, B9; Alan Freeman, 'Schroeder Calls for Controls on Capital Flows', *The Globe and Mail* [Toronto], 2 Feb. 1999, A14. For Canada's six-point program in this regard, see *The Budget Plan 1999*, 26.

49 *Briefing Book*, 67, 56.

50 Bruce Little, 'Economists Divided over Rate Hike', *The Globe and Mail* [Toronto], 28 Aug. 1998, B1, 4.

51 Richard Mackie, 'Ontario Introduces Bill to Force Balanced Budgets', *The Globe and Mail* [Toronto], 15 Dec. 1998, A4. In an Angus Reid poll, 62 per cent of Canadians supported the idea of passing a law to make it illegal for governments to have a deficit. See Shawn McCarthy, 'Canadians' Message to Ottawa: Keep Cutting the Debt', *The Globe and Mail* [Toronto], 8 Feb. 1998, A1, 3. For a survey of provincial and territorial legislation, see Organization for Economic Cooperation and Development, *OECD Economic Surveys: Canada 1998* (OECD: Paris, 1998), 143-4.

52 Shawn McCarthy, 'Ottawa Faces Tough Choice on Dollar', *The Globe and Mail* [Toronto], 8 Aug. 1998, A1, 6; Edward Greenspon, 'Turmoil Threatens Ottawa's Nest Egg', *The Globe and Mail* [Toronto], 28 Aug. 1998, A1, 10; Edward Greenspon, 'Poll Finds Ottawa Blew Dollar Crisis', *The Globe and Mail* [Toronto], 3 Oct. 1998, A6; Shawn McCarthy, 'Thiessen Links Loonie's Plight to Commodities', *The Globe and Mail* [Toronto], 21 Nov. 1998, B4; Jeffrey Simpson, 'The Productivity Puzzle', *The Globe and Mail* [Toronto], 20 Nov. 1998, A24. *Briefing Book*, 58-59.

53 *Policy Options Politiques* 20, 1, (Jan.–Feb. 1999), 15.

54 Gord McIntosh, 'Nothing About Martin's Budget Left to Chance', *The Globe and Mail* [Toronto], 8 Feb. 1999, A2.

55 Jack Granatstein, *The Ottawa Men* (Toronto: Oxford University Press, 1982), 167.
56 See Chapter 2 in this volume. Edward Greenspon, 'Health Care Tops List of Concerns', *The Globe and Mail* [Toronto], 11 July 1998, A4.
57 Paul Martin, Minister of Finance, *Budget Speech* (Ottawa: Public Works and Government Services Canada, 1998), 6.
58 See Anthony Giddens, *The Third Way: The Renewal of Social Democracy* (Cambridge: Polity Press, 1998).

5

From Health and Welfare to Stealth and Farewell: Federal Social Policy, 1980-2000

MICHAEL J. PRINCE

> We have not yet solved the great social problems facing our country. The distribution of income in Canada is largely unchanged despite all the social policy changes of the 1960s and 1970s. Crime and poverty have not disappeared. Today, Canada has more poor children than ten years ago and the problems of many pensioners are still with us. The majority of Canadians still have no pension coverage other than that financed through the public sector.
>
> Jean Chrétien, Minister of Justice and Social Development
> House of Commons Debates, 16 June 1980

The statement that appears above is a useful entrée to the topic of this essay, which looks at Canadian social policy changes of the 1980s and 1990s. It is an intriguing passage not only because of who said it, but also because of its implicit criticism of the earlier Liberal administrations of Lester Pearson and Pierre Trudeau, and for the language used in talking about social troubles and social justice. It is a revealing statement of our times. A speech like this by a senior minister of the government has not been the current fashion. Further, it is a disturbing statement given where we are as a country a generation later with respect to inequality, poverty, and insecurity. This paper seeks to shed light on federal social expenditures, policy processes, and trends over the last two decades of the twentieth century. It examines what has happened to the Canadian welfare state, where we stand today, and where we may be heading. The more social programs have been cut back, dismantled, and restructured, the more these social problems have persisted, if not worsened. In addition to exploring changes in the practice of social policy, the paper considers how the theory behind Canadian social policy has also been challenged. What we understood to be the functions and political stature of social programs has altered significantly.

The story of federal social policy over the period 1980 to 2000 is 'a mingled yarn of good and ill together: our virtues would be proud if our faults whipped them not'.[1] Both Conservative and Liberal governments actively engaged in restraining, reforming, and retrenching social programs. Some changes to benefits and services were incremental, either maintaining or eroding provisions, while other changes were radical, eliminating fundamental elements of a social security system built up over the previous four decades. Overall, there has been a further 'residualization' of social policy in Canada, of the federal government's role specifically, and of public provisions more generally.[2]

Changes in social policy have changed Canadian federalism. The reverse relation has also been much in evidence over this period. Much of contemporary federal-provincial/territorial conflict and co-operation has been about human and social development issues. These include reforms to the Canada Pension Plan (CPP); cuts to intergovernmental transfer payments for health care, welfare, and post-secondary education; the offloading of federal program costs and deficits; and the devolution of labour market and social housing programs. It is too simplistic to characterize the last 20 years of federalism as a pendulum-swing toward decentralization. This is certainly an appropriate image for fiscal decentralization, the absence of a national child care strategy, and the transfer of certain program authorities and resources to provinces and First Nation governments. At the same time, however, we have witnessed the entrenchment of the Charter of Rights and Freedoms in the Constitution, the introduction and enforcement of the Canada Health Act, and the exercise of the federal spending power with respect to social assistance and other program fields. Neither centralized federalism nor peripheralized federalism are adequate terms to capture the reality of intergovernmental relations. Indeed, for a number of years over the 1980s and 1990s, fiscal constraints limited the influence of both the federal and provincial governments. Contested federalism, marked by activist governments at both levels, is a more accurate depiction of the social union.

Since the mid-1980s, successive federal governments have surreptitiously woven a tangled web of social policy 'reforms'. Sweeping and far-reaching changes and cuts to social programs have been made through a process of 'stealth'.[3] Though this term was coined to describe and to condemn the prevailing style of social policy-making by the Mulroney Conservative governments, the Chrétien Liberal governments have continued to use tactics of stealth in restructuring and restraining social transfers and benefits. I will outline the key elements of this style of policy formation, including its consequences for the political system and the public.

If the 1960s and 1970s are portrayed as a period of social reform in Canada, how are we to describe and interpret the 1980s and 1990s as a period for social policy? The last 20 years cover the final Trudeau government, the two Mulroney governments, and the two Chrétien governments.[4] Relative to the 1960s and 1970s, the status of the social policy field has changed dramatically. Chapters in early editions of *How Ottawa Spends* referred to 'the attack on social policy', and asked, 'whatever happened to compassion?' By the 1990s, not only have social programs changed, but the social union itself has been severely altered. Chapters in more recent editions of *How Ottawa Spends* speak of 'lowering the safety net', 'weakening of the bonds of nationhood', and 'lowering the boom on the boomers', and ask whether these changes reflect 'renovation or abandonment'. Canadian social policy has been on the defensive for this entire period. The 1980s were deeply conservative for federal social policy, first, in respect to the effort to maintain social programs in the face of a major economic recession and rising deficits, and second, in respect to restraints on the growth of social expenditures. For much of the 1990s, change to federal social policy has been abrupt and transformational. The landmarks include the end of universality in family and elderly benefits, the end of direct federal government financing of the unemployment insurance system, the unilateral capping of the Canada Assistance Plan (CAP), the eventual termination of both it and the Established Programs Financing (EPF) agreement, and the replacement of both by the Canada Health and Social Transfer (CHST). By the late 1990s, many of the pillars of federal social policy had disappeared or were much diminished. Core Canadian beliefs about the nature of the social union have changed substantially. After 20 years we still have something that is recognizably a welfare state and a social union, but the content and architecture of the system is fundamentally different.

Informing and shaping these actions and beliefs has been the policy paradigm of fiscal stress and restraint. In the current post-deficit period, however, we are witnessing the very early steps of a paradigm shift. Recent budget surpluses and fiscal dividends are the logical and intended result of the restraint paradigm. These budgetary achievements were expected, although perhaps not so soon. If sizable surpluses continue at the federal level, the reigning paradigm of restraint and restructuring becomes increasingly incongruent with healthy public accounts. Indeed, Finance Minister Paul Martin has been trying to extend the restraint paradigm to fit the new fiscal circumstances. Meanwhile, various policy actors and institutions, including federal cabinet ministers, the opposition political parties, provincial premiers, business and labour organizations, and poverty and women's groups are challenging the necessity of the restraint paradigm. This questioning and challenge will continue for several years, and will perhaps result in a new paradigm of public finance and governance in the early decades of the new millennium. Even if we move into a new paradigm, however, changes made to social policy and budgets in the last decade alter the starting point of any 'paradigm shift', and from a policy legacy viewpoint we cannot expect a return to the more expansive 1960s.

SOCIAL POLICY BOUNDARIES, PHASES, AND STYLES

The academic literature is filled with discussions on the meaning and content of social policy. In an authoritative political sense, however, the field of social policy is whatever a government defines it to be in budgets, cabinet committee systems, and departmental portfolios. A look at Canadian government records reveals that there is no long-standing definition of social expenditures and programs. Over the last 20 years, the social policy field in the federal budgeting system has been redefined four times, with the result that it is difficult to track trends and measure public spending in social programs as a share of total expenditures or of the economy. The recent history of the social policy field within federal budgeting systems is as follows: in 1979-80, with the creation of the Policy and Expenditure Management System, a Social Affairs envelope was established; in 1985-6, a Social Development envelope was created, comprising the former Social Affairs and the Justice and Legal Affairs envelopes; in 1989-90, with the death of the envelope system, Social Development was broken down into Social Programs, Communications and Cultural Programs, and Justice and Legal Programs. Then, in 1994, with another transition in governments, the budgetary concept of social policy shifted somewhat again under the Expenditure Management System and the related Program Review exercise.

In the early 1980s, the federal government embraced an organizationally integrated approach, according to which social policy was to be coordinated and planned across departments, with the support of a central agency. Over time, federal governments moved away from this approach, toward a more departmentalized one, focussing on individual programs or small sets of related programs usually located within particular portfolios. This less than holistic approach to thinking about social policy was apparent in the 1994-5 Social Security Review undertaken by the Chrétien Liberals. If the idea of a social policy envelope has survived, it is not so much in the dreams of policy planners as in the dictates of Finance and Treasury Board ministers and officials. Paradoxically, the departmentalized concept of social policy has been subject to considerable direction from Finance Minister Martin and Prime Minister Chrétien.

Federal social policy manifests itself in several ways. These include direct expenditures, transfer payments, provision of services, tax expenditures and other tax measures, laws, and regulations. In addition, shifting ranges of structures, clients, and interest groups, and of ideas, goals, and priorities, are involved. The languages or discourses in which social issues and policy stances are talked about are important too. In addition to government decisions and actions, social policy also involves non-decisions and defeated proposals. Major social policy 'non-events' of the 1980s and 1990s include:

- a significant expansion of the CPP, following several years of the Great Canadian Pension Debate;
- the retreat from the attempt to partially de-index Old Age Security (OAS) benefits in 1985;
- the death of the planned national child-care strategy in 1987;
- the lack of social adjustment programs in response to the economic upheavals that were caused by the free trade agreements;
- an unwillingness on the part of successive federal governments to restore full indexation of income tax brackets;
- the cancellation, in 1998, of the proposed Seniors Benefit, which was to replace several cash and tax benefits for the elderly in 2001; and
- the failure to achieve the objective embodied in the unanimous motion passed by the House of Commons in 1989, to eradicate child poverty in Canada by the year 2000.

Federal social policy over the last 20 years may be divided into four phases of development. These phases correspond roughly to government mandates, and each refers to a dominant strategy of social policy change and direction apparent at the national level. The four phases are:

1. *Maintaining the social safety net: 1980-4.* The final Trudeau government espoused a strategy of defending the status quo of social programs against calls for cutbacks. In general it was a politics of reassurance. Most benefits and services were on a holding pattern, while there were some cuts and a few small improvements.
2. *Restraining social program costs: 1984-8.* The first Mulroney government focussed on limiting the growth of social spending. Within this politics of restraint, the Conservatives pursued a strategy of containment rather than neo-conservative dismantlement.

3. *Restructuring the social role of government: 1988-97.* The second Mulroney government and the first Chrétien government both undertook fundamental retrenchments and reconstruction of social programs. The federal role in the Canadian welfare state was itself transformed, as was social politics, to a politics of retrenchment and dismantling.
4. *Repairing the Social Union: 1997 and beyond.* With the emergence of budget balances and surpluses, the second Chrétien government is injecting additional resources into certain social programs. With this new fiscal era comes a new politics of reparation.

Each phase contains elements of the primary strategy of the other periods, but is defined by the dominance of a particular approach. In the first phase, for example, the introduction of the Canada Health Act, which prohibits extra-billing and user charges, exemplifies the strategy of maintaining a core sector of social policy. This phase also saw a few modest reforms, such as the enrichment of the Guaranteed Income Supplement for low-income seniors in 1980 and again in 1984, as well as restraint measures directed at other social benefits. The entrenchment of a Charter of Rights and Freedoms in the Constitution in 1982 illustrates a restructuring of not only the social union but also the political and governmental systems.

Over these four periods, certain federal budgets were epiphanies that marked a sudden and important shift in policy style, policy direction, or both. Without doubt, for federal social policy the 1985, 1989, 1995, and 1998 budgets were epiphanic financial and political plans. These budgets, far more than others, were turning points that ruptured routines and set out new conceptions of the federal role. These budgets were vehicles for advancing new arguments and fashioning new governmental identities. In the 1980s and 1990s, therefore, the politics of social policy went from reassurance, through restraint, then restructuring, and now, at the turn of the century, to reparation. In comparison to social initiatives of the 1960s and early 1970s, social policy-making in the 1980s and 1990s was more conflict-ridden, because of stable or shrinking expenditure budgets, rising tax burdens, and the lack of progress in income growth and in the reduction of income inequalities. Metaphorically, social policy has gone through four seasons: the 1980-4 phase was the late summer of the welfare state, the 1984-8 phase of restraint its autumn, and the 1988-97 phase of restructuring its long and harsh winter; the nascent post-deficit era promises a new spring.

Every policy sector 'tends to develop a particular style of public policy-making, with a distinct set of pre-established preferences for particular types of instruments and sets of policy claims or problems'.[5] For the federal social policy sector, that style has been aptly called 'policy change by stealth'. Ken Battle introduced the concept of social policy by stealth in a critique of Conservative government expenditure and tax measures.[6] Battle argued that the 1985 federal budget ushered in a new style of changing policies and programs. Core elements of this style are that changes to policy are made without a genuine process of public consultation or debate and are done through technical measures announced in budgets. The *political* reason for stealth, from a governmental perspective, relates to the challenge of cutting social benefits in the face of growing economic insecurity and substantial public opposition.

Features of the stealth style are outlined in Table 5.1. Battle did not suggest that the Conservatives were the first—or would be the last—government to make policy changes in this fashion, rather that they had 'made much more use of these methods than previous governments and ... done so in a deliberate, calculated manner that defines their style'.[7] In fact, as will be argued later in this chapter, the Mulroney Conservatives were not the last federal government to practice social policy change by stealth. Despite condemnations and disavowals of the stealth tactics by senior Liberal ministers, the style has continued under the Chrétien governments.

Of course, not all changes to federal social policy over the last 20 years have been done by stealth. Other styles of changing social programs and taxes have been used. Some changes have been made in a relatively more open, consensual, and negotiated fashion. Examples include reforms to the CPP, which were agreed to among federal and provincial governments in 1987 and again in 1997; the National Child Benefit reforms over the 1996-8 period; amendments to the Constitution regarding education in Quebec and in Newfoundland in 1997; and the harmonization of the Goods and Services Tax and provincial sales taxes in certain provinces. Moreover, not all social policy changes

Table 5.1
Key Elements of the Stealth Style of Social Policy Change

Policy paradigm:
Acute fiscal stress, if not financial crisis, in the public sector, demanding retrenchment of government. Influenced by neo-conservative thinking.

Main goals:
Eliminating government deficits and reducing the national debt.

Policy instruments:
Cutting social expenditures on benefits to persons and transfers to other governments, and raising income tax revenues through surcharges and limited indexation of tax brackets. Examples are the partially indexed Goods and Services Tax Credit and the personal income tax system. Also the highly selective presentation of statistics on the effects of reforms.

Relations between state and society:
Relatively high autonomy of government in framing the problem and imposing the solution on the public and other governments. No notice or open consultation regarding the changes.

Lead government structure and process:
Social policy changes by stealth are inspired by and introduced by the Department of Finance through the hidden and closed process of budgets. Changes are usually expressed in arcane and technical language involving amendments to obscure legislation or regulations. Social policy departments and Parliament play little if any meaningful role.

Outcomes:
1. Silent and automatic declines in the value of benefits (and, conversely, increases in tax burdens) over time through the device of partial indexation against inflation.
2. Regressive impacts on low- to moderate-income Canadians, since benefits are a larger share of their disposable resources.
3. Further complication of the tax system, social programs, and fiscal federalism.
4. Cuts of billions of dollars in social spending and substantial revenue increases with virtually no political cost to the government.
5. The stifling of public and media awareness of and debate over social policy reform, so that it is harder to engender opposition to such changes.
6. Public susceptibility to government propaganda and the opportunity for governments to announce occasional 'increases' to eroded benefits and/or 'relief' from elevated taxes.
7. A unilateral *de facto* reform of the federation, as a result of the erosion of federal cash transfers to the provinces.

made through budgets are regressive and stealthy. For instance, numerous changes to the tax system unveiled in budgets since the mid-1980s have had a generally positive impact for people with disabilities. These changes have typically flowed from consultations among the Finance and Human Resource departments and groups of and for people with disabilities.[8]

There are instances, some of which are discussed here, that are policy-making 'by accident'. The concept of stealth, then, may ascribe more foresight to, and control by, policy-makers than is warranted by practice.[9] The Charter of Rights and Freedoms, for example, has had massive implications for social policy areas such as health (abortion), pension benefits (gays and lesbians), and gender relations (equity policies and pornography). Yet Canadian politicians had little idea how it would affect policy outcomes, social rights, and the role of the courts. The Social Union talks in the later 1990s is another instance of the contingent and partly unplanned nature of policy results.

What makes the stealth style noteworthy is that it stands in sharp contrast to liberal democratic views of the state, public policy-making, and collaborative federalism. In the stealth approach, the policy process is largely a closed and monopolistic process, a far cry from an open and clear style of governance. In the strongest formulation of the stealth concept, there is no clear mandate from the voters, no consultation with the public or other governments, and no bargaining with clients or interest groups. The state dominates the agenda-setting and problem-definition stages of policy formation. Policies changed by stealth are imposed, rather than negotiated and decided upon by consensus. Even where there have been consultations, most groups in the social policy sector have felt that their ideas and concerns were ignored.[10] Decisions are responses to fiscal imperatives as defined by federal policy-makers, whether those definitions encompass social program excess, population aging, or global market pressures. The Department of Finance is like the secret ministry of frost, hanging social programs and tax measures up like icicles, to melt silently in the winds of inflation. This is a slower and subtler whittling away of social programs, as compared to the direct dismantlement of programs, and it is thus more difficult to oppose the attack.[11]

Employing the tactics of stealth, Ottawa has been a significant power in its own right within the social union, acting unilaterally and generating considerable tension and forceful reactions by provincial governments.

MAINTAINING THE SOCIAL SAFETY NET: 1980-4

The final Trudeau government of 1980 to 1984, together with the penultimate one from 1974 to 1979, was a period for Canadian social policy that can be characterized primarily as one in which the social safety net was maintained. The approach involved carrying on with existing social programs rather than tearing them down or building new ones. A serious breach of this strategy of maintenance was the declining commitment by the Liberals, through the 1970s, to a high and stable level of employment, a central idea of the postwar welfare state in Canada and other industrial countries (see the chapter by Campbell).[12] For the Trudeau Liberals, the maintenance of Canada's welfare state meant an affirmation that the federal government would cope with the economic problems of inflation and recession without relinquishing its support for social benefits and services.

In the 1980-4 period especially, the Trudeau Liberals both professed and, for the most part, practised a project of defending and keeping social programs. In 1981, in perhaps his last major speech on social development, Prime Minister Pierre Trudeau pledged that Liberals would never abandon their long-time commitment to a compassionate social policy, especially in favour of neo-conservatism.[13] A principal secretary to Trudeau, Jim Coutts, has written, 'In some respects, the Trudeau years were a time of consolidation, rather than creation. But the Trudeau administration held the line against growing conservative elements that wanted to tear down the systems that had been built by previous governments.' Coutts adds that

> [P]articularly during the latter part of the Trudeau administration, the attack on established social policy was heightened to levels not seen since the early part of the century. The battle became jurisdictional as well as ideological. The business and professional community heated up their attack on the cost and so-called waste of social programs. Some provinces fought long

and hard against the introduction of new national programs, while others did their best to undermine the programs that were already in place.[14]

These attacks and battles certainly existed, but the final Trudeau administration inherited a fiscal situation largely of its own making, including significant lost revenues resulting from tax breaks given in Liberal budgets in the 1970s. Most of the major social policy initiatives by Trudeau governments were taken in the early to mid-1970s. A number of these initiatives were either then scaled back, as were Family Allowance and Unemployment Insurance (UI), or eliminated under fiscal restraint measures, as were the Opportunities for Youth and the Local Initiatives Program, during the 1974-9 administration. Bruce Doern has described the provision to tax the universal income benefits of the Family Allowance and the eventual adoption of the Child Tax Credit in 1979 as done by stealth rather than by open debate. Unlike later examples of stealth, however, this change can be regarded as a progressive change in social policy, which directed greater resources to lower-income families within the context of a universal program.[15]

Aside from pension reform and the protection of medicare, the latter really being an afterthought near the end of this period, social policy did not figure in the strategic agenda of the last Trudeau regime. That agenda concentrated on constitutional reform and a charter of rights, a national energy program, economic development, Quebec and the aftermath of the 1980 referendum, and western Canada in light of the paucity of Liberals in that region following the 1980 federal general election. The agenda was activist, interventionist, and nationalist in orientation and intent. The strategy was aimed at 'making the federal government more pervasive and visible in the lives of individual citizens and thus to reinforce the allegiance of citizens to the national political community.'[16] By comparison, the Liberal stance toward social programs was at best defensive and protective.

The high confidence, strong sense of purpose, and comprehensive set of policy measures in these other fields were absent in the social development sector. In part, this may have happened because the early 1970s essentially completed the postwar vision of a comprehensive social security system. In addition, subsequent years had witnessed oil-pricing crises, relatively high rates of inflation and then stagflation, the election of a separatist government in Quebec, and declining political effort and agreement among the federal and provincial governments to advance new social reforms. This was also true for the main opposition parties of the day. In 1983 I wrote,

> Social policy is the Cinderella of Canadian parliamentary politics in the 1980s. The social policy field has become the neglected stepsister of economic development and energy policy, especially by the Tories who give relatively slight attention to social affairs and considerably less than full support to social welfare values. The NDP is playing the role of the fairy godmother by trying to rescue social policy from cutbacks and by advocating extensions in several program areas. Whether the social welfare system in Canada will revert back to rags after midnight, as a result of Liberal government actions and inactions, is an open question according to both opposition parties.[17]

A significant social policy action by the Liberals was the increase in basic benefits for the Guaranteed Income Supplement once in 1980 and twice again in 1984, advantaging over 700,000 low-income seniors and helping to reduce poverty among them. A significant inaction was the lack of legislative reform of the occupational pension system at the federal level.

At the outset of the 1980-4 period, the Trudeau Liberals placed 'a much lower priority on real expenditure restraint and reduction of the deficit than did the Conservatives during their brief stay in office', yet the Liberals still saw themselves as financially constrained, with few new resources for launching new programs.[18] With respect to social policy, the Liberals' expenditure plan was to hold the growth rate of the social affairs envelope below the rate of growth in total outlays and at a rate less than that of the economy as a whole. The wished-for outcome, therefore, was that social spending would decline as a percentage of both the federal budget and the Gross Domestic Product (GDP). The social affairs envelope was not given any policy reserve of funding for new initiatives. The Liberals intended to maintain and, as resources permitted through reallocations, to improve the social security system. In 1981, James Rice and I observed that '[t]he attack against social policy is definitely planned. The federal government intends to shift resources away from social affairs to economic and energy development. However, it must be noted that while the Liberals officially project a decline in relative social spending these are projections which could partially come undone.'[19] In fact, the projections did come undone.

By the 1984-5 fiscal year, the rate of growth for social programs was above the rate of growth in total program outlays, primarily because of the impact of the 1981-2 recession and the effect of automatic and discretionary counter-cyclical measures in social assistance, unemployment insurance, housing, and job creation. By economic criteria, the recession of 1981-2 lasted 15 months, with a rise in the official unemployment rate of 5.9 percentage points over 16 months, peaking at 12.8 per cent, and an actual drop in the GDP of 6.7 per cent over 18 months.[20] The majority of the 560,000 job losses were permanent layoffs. Canada's first food bank began in Edmonton in 1981. The final expenditure plan of the Trudeau era noted that 'social safety nets have been maintained over the past fiscal year, and in some cases enhanced, despite the fiscal pressures of a severe recession that have led many other western governments to limit or even reduce their commitment to social security.'[21] From 1979-80 to 1985-6, the average annual rate of growth of social development spending was 11.2 per cent, compared to 10.8 per cent for all program outlays. Thus, the social development envelope's share of the expenditure plan stayed fairly steady at around 47 per cent of the federal budget.

The pattern of maintaining social programs was apparent in this period in other ways too:

1. The Ministry of State for Social Development was created in 1980, a professional staff agency to advise the Cabinet Committee on Social Development. The policy process rested on the principles that new priority programs be financed largely out of the proceeds from the elimination of other expenditures; that ministers must make conscious trade-offs among possibilities; and that the choices of such programs should benefit from the advice of all ministers within the sector.
2. The attempt in the 1981 budget to reduce the value of several tax expenditures for better-off Canadians produced what Doern has justly called a 'failed social policy', since the planned benefits did not go in large measure to low-income

Canadians. 'The Budget purported to tax the rich by closing off the lucrative tax expenditures and distributing benefits to as many as twelve million Canadians in the form of reduced taxes. This proposal provided for an infinitesimal gain to the members of a dispersed constituency of largely middle class and upper income Canadians. It provided losses to powerful and cohesive economic interests. It rightfully earned the Liberals little support and much criticism.'[22] Consequently, in subsequent budgets most of these tax measures were quickly dropped, quietly withdrawn, or revised.

3. Under the '6 and 5' anti-inflation program announced in the 1982 budget, the indexation of personal income tax exemptions, public service pensions, Family Allowance, and OAS benefits were limited to increases of 6 per cent in 1983-4 and 5 per cent in 1984-5. To shelter those most in need from the anti-inflation program, the Guaranteed Income Supplement was augmented to offset the limitations on the OAS payments, and the Child Tax Credit remained fully indexed, as did veterans' pensions and allowances.

4. Section 36(1) of the Constitution Act, 1982, commits federal and provincial governments to 'promoting equal opportunities for the well-being of Canadians; furthering economic development to reduce disparity in opportunities; and providing essential public services of reasonable quality to all Canadians.' Further, section 36(2) expresses the commitment of the federal government to 'the principle of making equalization payments to ensure that provincial governments have sufficient revenues to provide reasonably comparable levels of public services at reasonably comparable levels of taxation.' This section gives constitutional expression to a set of pan-Canadian goals and fiscal practices that date from the 1940s and 1950s, as well as legitimating the federal spending power into the future. This represents the maintenance of social policy-making at a fundamental level of governance.

5. The Canada Health Act, 1984, perhaps best illustrates the Liberal strategy of maintaining the social safety net, in this case the publicly insured medical care system across the country. The principles of accessibility, comprehensiveness,

portability, public administration, and universality, expressed in earlier pieces of federal hospital insurance and medical care legislation, were consolidated, clarified, and backed by financial penalties if a province allowed the application of user charges or extra-billing. All jurisdictions that had been allowing such practices quickly complied with this aim of the Canada Health Act.

In summary, the Liberals' stance in the early 1980s was to hold the line on social policies and programs in the face of growing talk internationally as well as domestically of overloaded government and a fiscal crisis. At a macro level, the stable pattern in federal social spending also reflected the impact of the most severe economic recession since the Great Depression of the 1930s, and of political factors such as ministerial interests, client groups, and provincial governments. Combined, these conditions yielded little room for the government to manoeuvre. Reviewing the evidence on budgetary expenditures, Allan Maslove, in the 1984 edition of *How Ottawa Spends*, concluded, 'total federal spending is composed of existing programs that are characterized by strong inertial forces. Once in place it is very difficult and slow to cut back, reallocate, or eliminate a spending program, at least through the established budgetary processes.'[23] The next phase of social policy, from 1984 to 1988, revealed, however, that through a different budgetary process—the stealth style—inertial forces could be bypassed, and cutting back programs and raising revenues became less difficult politically. Through the 1990s, it became increasingly obvious that federal social spending programs were far more malleable and vulnerable than conventional social policy theory held or hoped.

RESTRAINING SOCIAL PROGRAM COSTS: 1984-8

On social policy, the first Mulroney Conservative administration concentrated on reshaping certain programs and limiting the growth rate of spending. The years 1984-8 should be considered a separate phase because they represent not the introduction of restraint—that had already occurred under the Trudeau Liberals—but an intensification of it. The Conservatives were ideologically more disposed to regard the growing federal deficit as a grave threat, and to take further restraint actions. What happened under Mulroney's first government can also be distinguished from the marked shift toward more severe forms of restraint implemented in the 1988 to 1997 period.

The first Mulroney government used four types of restraint most readily in the social policy sector. These were dissuasion, restriction, freezes, and revenue generation. Dissuasion consists of government efforts, through language and symbols, to alter public and private attitudes and behaviour in order to discourage reliance on government and the public purse. Dissuasion includes advocating self-reliance, extolling the virtues of charity and voluntarism, and arguing for the acceptance of program cutbacks. It can result in a narrowing of the sense of government responsibility for human and social development. Restriction is the mildest form of expenditure or revenue restraint. This approach involves maintaining the base budget but slowing down the rate of growth in expenditures, personnel, service, or taxes. This is still budgeting by addition, but to a more limited extent than otherwise. A third approach to restraint is the freeze. This is restraint as retention—keeping a status quo, but one that melts in quality or value over time. Tax increases may not seem to be a restraint type at all, but revenue generation can be an important way of reducing the government's cash requirements and the public deficit. In the stealth style of policy-making, tax reforms can mean tax increases for those with modest incomes and tax decreases for those with higher incomes.

Retrenchment, termination, and privatization are more severe forms of restraint, and all relate to the downsizing of the state and the public service in absolute terms. Retrenchment is the withdrawal of resources from the base budget of an agency, policy, program, or activity. Under the termination approach, policies, programs, and staff are not simply cut back, they are cut out. Government cancels or eliminates public services. Privatization involves the residualization of public provisions, by turning them over, or returning them, to the family, the community at large, or private sector and market forces. These three forms of restraint are examples of what is often meant by the terms 'dismantling the welfare state' and 'the neo-conservative attack on social policy'.

The Mulroney Conservatives came to power strongly supportive of the pro-market liberalism of the Thatcher government in Britain and the Reagan administration in the United States. But, in the context of the mid-1980s, this support was mellowed by the early experience of the other two countries, by inherent features of the Canadian political economy, and by mixed beliefs within the Progressive Conservative party. The Mulroney government was philosophically committed to support of the private sector, opposition to the Ottawa-based bureaucracy and to Trudeau-style centralism, and an eagerness to practise a new form of federal-provincial reconciliation. The Mulroney government's manner of expressing its main policy preferences was much milder than that of its fellow practitioners of the neo-conservative version of politics, policy-making, and budgeting.[24] It spoke of fostering economic renewal by removing government obstacles to growth. It sought to reduce the federal deficit gradually, better manage government programs, and downsize the federal public sector.

The key strategic document that influenced the first Mulroney mandate declared, 'The current and projected size of the deficit is simply too large. It implies steadily rising debt/GNP ratio, which will have serious consequences for interest rates, private investment, and the government's room to manoeuvre. In short, the federal deficit is a major obstacle to growth, and the government must take immediate action to deal with it.'[25] The Conservatives' focus was on reducing the growth of federal spending in three areas of transfers: to persons, to other levels of government, and to other groups, such as Aboriginal, cultural, and women's organizations. Their goal was to reduce the growth of transfers in an enduring fashion, downsizing the federal budget by $10 to $15 billion by the end of the 1980s. This is the restriction type of restraint identified above. At times, the Conservatives also spoke of not just restricting the growth of social transfers, but reshaping them as well, so as to enhance their effectiveness in meeting changing societal needs and their efficiency, in a period when government's financial capacity is heavily constrained. Such reshaping reflects retrenchment, a potentially far more substantial and controversial type of restraint.

The Conservatives sought to redesign social programs so that resources were directed first to those in greatest need, in other words, to increase the selectivity of benefits. As Finance Minister Michael Wilson stated in the 1986 *Budget Speech*, 'This government is not prepared to dismantle social programs. The best ways to reduce the cost of social measures are to make sure that spending and tax assistance are targeted effectively and to reduce the need for such support—by keeping the economy growing and creating jobs so that greater opportunities are provided to those Canadians now in need.'[26] After sharp increases during the 1981-2 recession, the rates of unemployment, poverty, and inflation all declined during the Mulroney Conservatives' first term. Within this context of improving economic conditions, the Conservatives were able to raise tax revenues, target the design of some programs, and pursue a relatively more cooperative approach to intergovernmental relations.

During this period of restraining the welfare state, as with the earlier Liberal phase, the Canadian approach was less extreme than those in Thatcher's Britain and Reagan's United States. Frank McGilly noted in 1990 that, in responding to the fiscal pressures and the critiques of state intervention, 'Canada has followed the trend, though perhaps with characteristic moderation'.[27] Social expenditures continued to increase over this period, though relatively more slowly than in the early 1980s and the 1970s. McGilly describes the approach taken as containment, with perhaps some reduction in public commitments for social welfare. Universal programs may have been chipped and dented, but they were not demolished. Ramesh Mishra similarly observed in 1990 that changes in Canada's social programs and safety net during 1984-8 were conservative in nature rather than inspired by the more radical neo-conservative or New Right ideology in evidence in Britain and the United States. First, as Mishra pointed out, there had been no *deliberate* policy attempt to retrench services and benefits for the poor, such as social housing and the Canada Assistance Plan. Second, the Mulroney Conservatives adopted and practised a consultative and conciliatory style of government, in contrast to the Thatcher and Reagan approaches. A third difference is that Canada's was the only national government of the three in the 1980s contemplating the introduction of a major new social program, namely child daycare.

Mishra's analysis of this record of moderate conservative restraint is that the Mulroney Conservatives initially flirted with a neo-conservative approach to social policy retrenchment, but then hastily retreated in the face of strong public protest. Examples of the flirtation with radical change and then retreat to 'the centrist consensus in Canada over social protection' are:

- Raising the idea of income-testing the universal Family Allowance and OAS programs in 1984-5, and then reaffirming the principle of universality.
- Proposing in the 1985 budget to partially de-index the OAS benefits in relation to annual cost of living increases and then retracting the proposal weeks later in the face of widespread criticism.
- After expressing concerns about costs and labour disincentives, creating a Commission of Inquiry to review the UI scheme, but then deciding in 1986 not to implement the majority report's recommendations.
- Instituting a review of the CAP by a panel of business and government officials, who confirmed the vital role served by this safety net program for low-income Canadians.
- Reforming the tax system in a way that added to the regressivity of the system but also included some equitable changes.[28]

McGilly, Mishra, and other commentators determined that, compared to retrenchment policies in Britain and the United States, the 1984-8 Mulroney record on social policy cuts was moderate. A further inference drawn in the social policy academic literature was that universal social programs were less vulnerable to retrenchment efforts by conservative governments, because these programs served a broad and articulate constituency of the population. Experience also appeared to show that 'grey power' had arrived in Canada, and that no political party proposing the retrenchment of universal social programs could win a national election. However, that the Mulroney cuts to social programs were moderate, that 'grey power' now was a potent force in Canadian politics and federal policy processes, and that universal programs are durable if not irreversible, are all somewhat misleading conclusions. Their limitation derives from focussing on a series of well-publicized policy retreats, on the resiliency of a few universal income security programs, and on short-term program cuts. The concept of social policy change by stealth alerts us to policy and program restraints that were successfully implemented, though not widely recognized and protested, changes that had major longer-term consequences for social programs, the government treasury, and the disposable income of individuals and families, elderly and non-elderly alike.

For the style of changing social policy, the 1985 federal budget was an epiphany at two different levels, at the same time a highly public, politically dramatic event and a relatively hidden occurrence. The public event dealt with the modified indexation of OAS payments proposed in that budget. As part of the Mulroney government's plan for reducing the federal debt, the budget announced that from 1986 the indexation of OAS benefits would be altered, with benefits increasing yearly by the annual change in the consumer price index in excess of three percentage points. Therefore, old age pensions would no longer be fully adjusted for increases in the cost of living. The proposal incited a strong outcry by seniors' groups, social policy organizations, some provincial governments, and even business lobbies. Barely four weeks after the budget had been delivered, the Finance Minister withdrew the OAS de-indexation measure. This spectacular and rapid reversal of a budgetary measure, a rare event in Canadian parliamentary politics, was interpreted by many commentators as a result of the emergence of grey power, the strong influence of seniors' groups on policy-making, and the inexperience and incompetence of the governing party. The neo-conservatives blinked and retreated to a more moderate approach to restraint. If the 1985 budget is remembered, it is because of this visible policy reversal that dealt with a single program and a 'deserving' client group, in a process where the media, interest groups, and legislators featured. This incident, however, was just the tip of an iceberg; far more danger to social programs lay below the surface.

The 1985 budget had another dimension with much greater fiscal and policy significance. It laid the basis for considerably greater cuts to social spending and increases in taxes than was appreciated. This entailed a largely invisible policy process, which achieved substantial retrenchments across several programs and various client groups, and which the federal finance bureaucracy effectively dominated. This second side to the budget was not widely appreciated until several years later, when it was given the name 'stealth' by Battle, and critically examined in subsequent articles by Battle and others. Characterizing the Conservatives' style of restraint as social policy by stealth, Battle outlined the main features in the following terms:

> It relies heavily on technical amendments to taxes and transfers that are as difficult to explain as they are to understand and thus largely escape media scrutiny and public attention. It camouflages regressive changes in the rhetoric of equity in an attempt to convince Canadians that tax increases are tax cuts and that benefit cuts are benefit increases. By further complicating an already complex labyrinth of taxes and social programs, the stealth style of policy-making confuses the electorate and so insulates itself from criticism.... [F]or every positive action, there is an equal and opposite negative change. As a result, the goal of a fairer, simpler and more rational system of taxes and transfers remains as distant as ever.[29]

The 1985 budget decreed 'a fundamental shift in social and tax policy because it abandoned full indexation of child benefits and the personal income tax system for partial indexation. Family allowances, the Children's Tax Exemption, the refundable tax credit (including the income threshold for maximum benefits) and the income tax system's exemptions, deductions, credits and tax brackets would be adjusted each year only by the amount that inflation exceeded 3 percent, rather than by the full amount of inflation.'[30] The indexation formula for transfers to the provinces and territories for health services and post-secondary education was also reduced. Reducing the index formulas for these taxes and transfers meant that over time Ottawa was spending billions less in outlays and collecting billions more in revenues than people realized and than otherwise would have been the case. In part, the stealthy nature of this style lay in the secrecy and complexity of the budget process and changes. In large measure, it lay in the fact that the central tool of de-indexation operated automatically year after year, routinely generating benefit restrictions and tax hikes, without further need of presentation in budgets, parliamentary approval, or public debate.

RESTRUCTURING THE SOCIAL ROLE
OF THE STATE: 1988-97

The third phase of policy change represented a deepening and widening of the restraint of social programs and corresponded to the second Mulroney government as well as the first Chrétien government. Social policies and programs were more directly challenged and some were actually dismantled. Under both Conservative and Liberal administrations the stealth style continued to operate. No doubt as a result of the accumulation of past restraint measures, but also because of the escalation of cutbacks and systemic retrenchment in this period, the social role of the federal government itself was diminished.

Restructuring implies more than the incremental erosion of programs and service from years of neglect and under-funding. It implies more than increasing welfare recipients' incentives to take training or seek work. It goes beyond restricting the resources for programs and transfers, to actually reducing and redefining the role of government. For social policy, restructuring involves major alterations of the basic features of public social provision, with immediate ramifications for communities, families, First Nations, voluntary agencies, and other institutions. Universal programs are replaced with selective programs; federal standards are removed from transfers to other governments; age-old distinctions between deserving and less deserving clients are revived. Relationships change between the federal government and provincial and territorial governments (and, in turn, provincial and municipal governments), as do the rules of the game in fiscal federalism and the social union. Longstanding expectations and practices are abruptly ended, generating intense acrimony in intergovernmental and constitutional politics. Likewise, the federal social policy role in relation to the economy and to the citizenry is transformed. Under restructuring, the stabilization function of Keynesian-style economics virtually disappeared, as did the social solidarity function of universal family benefits. This phase was also defined by the economic recession of 1990-2, which lasted longer and had greater long-term unemployment and more permanent job losses than the 1981-2 recession.

Three general features of the social policy record of the second Mulroney government stand out. First, while the Conservatives seemed fearful of social reforms in their first mandate, they were much more decisive and active in their second mandate in altering the social safety net. Second, the Mulroney government consciously made some fundamental shifts in the very foundations of Canadian social policy that were laid down in the 1940s, 1950s, and 1960s: the open-ended and equal cost-sharing agreement on social assistance was unilaterally capped in 1990; the universal Family Allowance program was terminated at the end of 1992; the universality of the OAS program was effectively abolished by 1991; and the federal government's direct contribution to financing the UI program was ended in 1991. Third, several of these changes were done in the stealth style of policy-making, in particular in the 1989 budget.[31]

As part of its restraint and restructuring strategy, the Mulroney government introduced an Expenditure Control Plan in the 1990 budget. Originally a two-year restraint program, this plan was extended to five years in the 1991 budget and then was deepened by further measures in the 1992 budget. Rice and I estimated the total fiscal impact from expenditure control measures on federal social program spending at some $51 billion from 1990-1 through 1995-6, an average of $8.5 billion a year in cutbacks. The most notable perhaps was the declining share of transfers to other levels of government as a portion of federal social expenditures. The position of the Mulroney Conservatives, like that of the previous Trudeau government, was that transfers to the provinces were too large to be exempt from expenditure restraint. Reductions and freezes in the growth of EPF cash transfers and limitations of federal CAP contributions to the three 'have provinces' of Alberta, British Columbia, and Ontario were imposed by the second Mulroney government.

Cuts in intergovernmental transfers were so substantial that concerns were raised as to the ability of the federal government to enforce the provisions of the Canada Health Act through the deduction provision of that legislation. The federal share for health funding had declined from about 50 per cent in the early 1980s to closer to 30 per cent in the early 1990s. Were federal transfers now too small to serve as a penalty if they were withdrawn in the event of the re-appearance of extra-billing or user charges in the health care system? The Conservatives established, through the Budget Implementation Act of

1991, the authority to withhold other cash transfers to the provinces and the territories, beside those under the EPF, to encourage compliance with the principles of the Canada Health Act. The 'cap on CAP' was initially presented as a two-year expenditure control measure. In fact, it was extended through the rest of the Mulroney mandate and into the first three years of the Chrétien government before the program was replaced. The length of the cap, and the fact that it occurred during the 1990-2 recession, meant that what was originally a short-term restraint move resulted in a longer-term and structural change in this major social program.

The most important social policy non-event of the final Mulroney government was the broken promise on child care reform. In their first mandate, the Conservatives had proposed $4 billion in operating and capital grants over seven years for a federal-provincial child care agreement. The legislation for this died on the order paper when the 1988 federal election was called. In their first budget after re-election, the Conservatives announced that a new Bill was being postponed, even though the child care strategy figured prominently in the Conservatives' free trade election campaign. The Prime Minister argued that because of the fiscal situation, the federal government was not in a position to proceed with the $4 billion for the 200,000 additional daycare spaces, but insisted that the government remained committed to meeting daycare policy reform objectives within its second mandate. That commitment was never honoured.

The reframing of social issues is a symbolic side of the restructuring of the welfare state, but it is a no less potent dimension, as child care demonstrates. Reframing involves redefining what, if anything, the public policy response to an issue should be, by changing the portrayal of the nature of the issue itself. This, in turn, alters the relative priority of the issue on the governmental agenda. Over the 1988-90 period, Conservative cabinet ministers changed the image of the national child care strategy from 'we will do it' through 'we will do it when budgetary resources permit' to 'we don't want to pay for the yuppie couple.'[32] In the last few years of their mandate, Conservative policy-makers increasingly spoke of 'children at risk' and 'parental choice', and eschewed any talk of a publicly provided and regulated system.[33] A residual and regressive image emerged that replaced the image of a government dedicated to helping those in need of social assistance in order to end welfare dependency and encouraging greater private sector involvement in the provision of daycare spaces. Federal support of child care through direct expenditures remained within the CAP, the last-resort program of welfare, while through tax expenditures, benefits were offered to higher-income families. That federal contributions to child care services continued under the CAP meant that many modest- and middle-income families received no assistance in meeting pressing daycare needs. For the three larger provinces, it meant a declining share of federal resources through the early to mid-1990s for welfare poor and working poor families.

The first Chrétien administration (1993-7) turned out to be a government of the times: Liberal ministers with neo-conservative measures. From their first budget in 1994, the Liberals emphasized expenditure restraint and deficit reduction, including further cutbacks of $725 million to the beleaguered UI program. The free trade agreements were accepted, the dreaded Goods and Services Tax was not replaced, and the private sector was acknowledged as the prime creator of economic opportunities and jobs, good or bad. A Program Review of federal services and agencies reaffirmed what was referred to as the 'core mandates' of social policy departments: 'The current levels of staffing and funding for some programs are decreasing as the departments make changes to get closer to these core mandates. The departments will place more emphasis on rationalizing costs, recovering more of the costs of certain government services from users and directing benefits and services to those in greatest need.'[34] While Finance Minister Martin promised in his first budget to end the tactics of stealth as practised by the Conservatives, his very next budget was the ultimate in stealth.

The 1995 budget was an epiphany in fiscal federalism and national social policy with the surprise announcement of the termination of the EPF and the CAP and their replacement with the more 'flexible' and much smaller CHST. This announcement astonished the provinces and shocked many in the social policy community. It was also a 'bolt from the blue' for the House of Commons standing committee that had just completed an extensive nationwide consultation on the social security review discussion paper, in which this new development had been neither identified as an option nor implicitly supported in public consultations. Federal spending on the overall social program sector was forecast and planned to decline in absolute terms over the next few years. The 1995 *Budget Speech* proudly declared that the reductions in federal spending were 'unprecedented in modern Canadian history', indicating that the country has 'put the era of band-aid budgets behind it'.[35] Not just the size but the very purpose and role of government itself was being redefined, and the Finance Minister pointed to this as the main achievement of the 1995 budget.

Many commentators regarded that budget as a full-scale attack on Canada's social security system, some viewing it as worse than anything the Mulroney governments had done. Jane Pulkingham and Gordon Ternowetsky observed that 'the Liberals are not simply continuing the Tory tradition of social program through "social policy by stealth".... [R]ather they are escalating this process, moving beyond "tinkering" to undertake a more fundamental transformation of the role of the federal and provincial governments.'[36] According to the Caledon Institute of Social Policy, the 1995 budget indicated that 'the Liberals are basically following the Conservative road toward the new social policy—with a diminished role for the federal government, more power to the provinces, cuts to UI and greater variability in provincial welfare systems.' The Institute concluded that

> [t]he 1995 federal Budget represents a fundamental turning point in Canadian social policy. It was the Liberals who created the foundation of our social security system in the 1950s, 1960s and 1970s. It was the Conservatives who fundamentally weakened that foundation in the 1980s by putting federal transfer payments to the provinces on a down escalator. It is now the Liberals of the 1990s who are shaking that foundation to the core—making it smaller and extracting the cement that holds the essential building blocks in place.[37]

The Canadian Council on Social Development called the CHST the most serious revamping of social policy since the 1960s, pointing out that it fundamentally changed the social safety net and the federal government's role in the field of social policy.[38] In similarly dramatic language, the National Council of Welfare commented that '[f]ederal social policy hit rock bottom in the 1995 budget speech', and that the CHST symbolized Ottawa's 'backing away from a leadership role'.[39]

The CHST replaced the previous arrangements of federal transfer payments for social assistance and social services, created in 1966 under the CAP, and, for health and post-secondary education, under the EPF agreement, which was first signed in 1977. The CHST is a single block fund of a smaller amount, in the name of federal restraint, and with fewer federal conditions attached, in the cause of 'flexible federalism'. Total federal cash transfers for these strategic social policy fields were initially targeted to decline by 30 to 35 per cent. To provide a degree of budgetary certainty, a cash floor was included to ensure that the CHST transfer would total at least $11 billion a year over the five-year agreement. This bottom line of cash transfers makes the CHST, for the next several years, an established part of Ottawa's program expenditures and our system of fiscal federalism. It does not prevent, however, any unilateral actions by the federal government to increase or reduce this commitment. During the 1997 federal election, in response no doubt to the strength of concerns voiced especially with respect to health care, Chrétien announced that a new Liberal government would raise the cash floor of the CHST from $11 billion to $12.5 billion. This was done in the 1998 budget, increasing cash payments to the provinces and territories by $700 million in 1998-9, $1.4 billion in 1999-2000 and 2000-1, $1.3 billion in 2001-2, and $1.2 billion in 2002-3.

Under the CHST, the federal government intends to uphold the core principles of our national health insurance system as before, though with respect to social assistance and social services only one of the five principles under CAP—access to welfare payments without minimum residency requirements in a province—is retained. This change raises serious concerns about the future of social assistance and social services previously funded under the CAP. Among the misgivings are:

1. The substantial and continual decline in federal social transfers by itself exerts additional financial pressure on provincial and territorial governments to cut social assistance rates for basic needs and special assistance.
2. The move to a block fund from a cost-sharing arrangement with matching federal funds means the loss of a direct incentive to the provinces, territories, and municipalities to support and develop income assistance and social services. Indeed, the

block funds need not be allocated to these social program areas at all.
3. The loss of the CAP means the loss of a specific statutory base and of standards at the national level for social services and welfare. As a result of this relinquishment of a federal role many Canadians are concerned about the future of rights to assistance for all persons in need, and rights to appeal decisions made by provincial and territorial or municipal authorities in relation to income support.
4. Placing federal transfers for social services and income assistance into a single block fund with health and post-secondary education will increase competition among these program areas, and on a very uneven political field. 'And, in making tough budgetary choices, provincial governments would be less likely to direct adequate resources to any area of policy with low visibility or lacking public support.'[40]
5. As an open-ended matching grant program, the CAP involved Ottawa in sharing the costs of offsetting the impact of economic downturns on provincial, territorial, and municipal welfare rolls. As a closed-ended block fund, the CHST lacks this stabilization feature. Come the next recession, the federal government no longer will automatically meet half the cost of rising provincial welfare expenditures.
6. The CAP was the primary national policy for addressing housing needs and was also an important vehicle for supporting home-based support services. Over half of direct public expenditures on housing in Canada had been through the shelter component of social assistance programs, 56 per cent in 1995-6, for example. Cutbacks to already inadequate shelter allowances in welfare systems, as happened in some provinces prior to the CHST, and occurring in some in the CHST era, certainly mean further hardships.

The CHST also has implications for the child care policy agenda in Canada. For the 1993 federal election, the Liberals had formulated a fairly modest pledge on child care, yet four years later the promise was unfulfilled. Sandra Bach and Susan Phillips have convincingly argued that 'neither the provinces nor the state of the economy were responsible for the demise of the child care commitment, although both could be seen as accomplices.' Instead, they suggest that the idea of a national child care policy was 'the first fatality of the construction by the federal and provincial governments of a New Social Union', of which the CHST 'represents a foundational pillar'.[41] Bach and Phillips clearly see the CHST as part of a wider restructuring of the welfare state in Canada, a process that 'has shifted the balance from primarily public to greater private provision of social services, from direct state funding of services to reliance upon the tax system for redistributing income to individuals and families, and from a moderate degree of federal involvement in social services and welfare to emphasis upon the primacy of the provinces'.[42] One result of the CHST is that a shared-cost national child care program is virtually impossible to achieve in the foreseeable future. The ramifications are troubling on several counts—'impeded healthy child development, increased demands for the social welfare system, and adversely affected future labour markets. The policy consequences for women and their equality in the labour force will be particularly onerous.'[43]

If the lack of real child care reform is in part a labour market policy non-event, the main labour market policy occurrence of the 1990s was the application of cuts to the UI program and then the replacement of that program by the Employment Insurance (EI) system in 1996. Under the Mulroney Conservatives in the 1988 to 1993 period, UI was subject to two bouts of reductions, and employers and employees were subject to a series of premium increases necessitated by Ottawa's withdrawal from financing key elements of UI. Eligibility requirements were raised, the maximum duration of benefits was shortened, and the relative value of benefits was reduced, with the earnings replacement rate lowered in 1993 from 60 to 57 per cent of insurable earnings. Under the Liberal government of 1993-7, UI was restrained further and restructured into the new EI system. Important features of EI include the following:

- Every hour of work is insurable, so that income benefits are now based on hours rather than weeks worked, which is a more flexible and inclusive measurement of work effort.

Workers have a full year to build up the minimum number of hours to qualify for benefits, from 420 hours to 700 hours, or the equivalent of 12 to 20 weeks, based on a 35-hour week. The actual number of hours needed depends on the unemployment rate of the region in which the individual claimant lives.
- Benefits are lowered from 57 to 55 per cent of a person's insurable earnings, though for lower-income claimants with dependents the earnings replacement rate was raised to 60 per cent. Consequently, the maximum weekly benefit decreased from $448 to $413 and is frozen at that level until 2000.
- The maximum duration of benefits is reduced from 50 weeks to 45 weeks.
- Claimants with an annual income of $48,750 or more have to reimburse up to 30 per cent of their benefits to the federal treasury, thus weakening the connection between premiums paid and benefits retained, a connection integral to social insurance programming.

Because of the repeated cuts to UI/EI through the 1990s, as well as changes in the nature of work and the labour market, the proportion of unemployed Canadians who actually receive regular insurance benefits dropped dramatically, from 83 per cent of unemployed Canadians in 1989 to only 42 per cent in 1997. In many cities, the social insurance net shrunk to the point that it offered income protection to 30 per cent or less of unemployed people.[44] This is a shocking development given the fact that the official national rate of unemployment in Canada has not been below 8 per cent since 1989 and has averaged over 9 per cent for the 1990s so far. The incredible shrinking protection offered by the EI system intensifies the anxieties of many Canadians in insecure jobs or industries.

The new EI system is the most important set of changes to this policy area in 25 years. By constraining the basic income protection function and at the same time allocating some of the savings from the cuts to employment measures, the Canadian government is transforming the system from what conventional rhetoric calls a 'passive safety net' that catches those temporarily unemployed into a 'springboard' or 'trampoline' that helps claimants into the workforce sooner. To take advantage of this 'pro-employment system', however, many claimants must work longer to become eligible; they are collecting lower benefit amounts, for shorter periods of time. In the context of our own modern social policy history, the new EI system is less beneficent and inclusive than the old system. The federal government has been, and will continue to be, under political pressure from high unemployment regions of the country, in particular Quebec and the Atlantic provinces, to liberalize rules on eligibility and benefits for seasonal workers.

In the 1990s, labour market policy was directly influenced by political efforts to amend the Canadian Constitution and transfer further powers and resources from the federal government to the provinces. Labour market policy reform was also affected by the move away from Keynesian management of the aggregate demand for labour at the national level, and the belief that Canada's economy today is a series of loosely connected regional and urban economies. A notable example of this was the change in federal minimum wage legislation in 1996, the first increase in the federal rate in 10 years. From being a standard $4 per hour across the country, the federal rate is now adjusted in each province and territory to that jurisdiction's general adult minimum wage rate. This has resulted in increases in federal minimum wages in each jurisdiction, ranging from a 19 per cent rise in Prince Edward Island and Newfoundland to a 70 to 75 per cent increase in Ontario and British Columbia. These increases affect the lowest paid workers in private sector industries that are inter-provincial or international in scope, such as banks and telecommunications, and some federal Crown corporations.[45]

A more significant case of regionalizing has been the federal government's commitment, officially expressed by the Prime Minister shortly after the Quebec referendum of October 1995, to withdraw from several aspects of labour market policy, including training and employment-related measures. Human Resources Development Canada (HRDC), the leading federal government department for labour market activities, is shifting much of its traditional role in helping people develop skills for employment and find jobs to the provincial and territorial governments as well as Aboriginal associations, through bilateral agreements. This withdrawal includes apprenticeship programs, cooperative education, direct purchase of training, and workplace-based training. The federal government maintains a prominent labour market policy presence by virtue of the EI program and the Canada Labour Code (which deals with collective bargaining, health and safety, and other workplace issues in federally regulated industries and the federal public service).

Through 1996 and 1997, Ottawa negotiated bilateral labour market agreements with British Columbia, Alberta, Manitoba, Quebec, New Brunswick, Nova Scotia, Prince Edward Island, and Newfoundland and Labrador. The agreements are for three to five years and involve the transfer of over $5 billion funded through the EI account, and the transfer of 2,000 federal government employees, about 10 per cent of the HRDC's workforce, to these jurisdictions. National framework agreements have also been signed with First Nation, Métis, and Inuit authorities, and 11 regional bilateral agreements have been signed in the Northwest Territories for the design and delivery of programs and services by Aboriginal communities.

The expansion of provincial, territorial, and Aboriginal responsibilities in labour market policy is intended in part to reduce duplication in employment services with the federal government through such measures as integrated case management of people on EI, social assistance, and other provincial programs. Another aim is to increase cooperation among governments, employers, unions, and community organizations in developing responsive approaches to labour market needs at local levels. In terms of service to the clients, the agreements speak of offering convenient access to programs through the co-location of services; providing prompt, courteous, and accurate services; and emphasizing the individual responsibility of clients by involving them in decisions for the management of their own 'case plans'. There are no provisions in the agreements for the representation and participation of clients in the management committees or in the accountability and evaluation mechanisms. The agreements look to be more about administrative federalism and inter-sector partnerships than about control and empowerment on the part of clients. For the provinces, a related desired outcome is to reduce people's dependency on welfare as measured by the size of welfare caseloads and expenditures in their jurisdictions. These targets and this language reinforce old beliefs that reliance on a social service or benefit is a form of dependency, and commonly associate with the client the negative connotations of inactivity, personal inadequacy, and being a public burden.

REPAIRING THE SOCIAL UNION: 1997 AND BEYOND

The current phase of Canadian social policy development corresponds with the second Chrétien Liberal government and probably beyond. This phase is based on the greatly improved financial situation of the federal government and of most provinces as well. The sense in Ottawa at least is that the period of chronic deficits and deep program cuts is over. The federal Liberals are re-energized by having budgetary surpluses for governing and undertaking new policies and program initiatives. In typical Canadian political fashion, the debate on social programs so far in this post-deficit era focusses largely on intergovernmental relations under the rubric of the 'social union'. Social union is the latest term for the old problem of what the relationship should be between the two orders of government so that they can work effectively together in the areas of exclusive provincial jurisdiction—health, education, and welfare.

Federal surpluses are generating contending views of what such budgetary achievements represent. The concept of a fiscal dividend—the idea that new public money is available—has spawned multiple meanings that are at odds with one another.[46] One such perspective argues that the surplus is the result of excessive taxation both from the income tax system and from payroll taxes such as the EI premiums. A different perspective focusses on program spending cuts rather than tax increases as the cause of the dividend. From this perspective, the elimination of the federal deficit is due to years of retrenchment and offloading of social programs; consequently any fiscal dividend should be used to replenish past cutbacks in social programs and transfer payments.

The concept of a federal budget surplus is therefore a hotly contested idea. It is not generally self-evident that the surplus is new money available to the government for distributing as it sees fit. For many groups and other governments in the country, some if not all of the surplus belongs to them; it is old money, accounts repayable. For social policy, the post-deficit era involves a politics of reparation as well as a politics of allocating new resources. As the National Council of Welfare has noted, 'By the time the federal government started taking a second look at its role in social programs in 1996 and 1997, the new initiatives it supported paled beside the damage that had already been done.'[47]

A reparation agenda entails making good some losses suffered by a group as the result of retrenchment policies, policy mistakes, or historic injustices. It is about making amends and rectifying programs or transfers that are felt to be insufficient and fall short of some benchmark of adequacy or quality. Reparation is not usually about the full restoration of programs to their original form or expenditure levels, as that would undo the strategy of retrenchment and be an admission of wrongdoing by governments.[48] More commonly, policies of reparation seek to ease some of the private human and social costs associated with cutbacks, by offering replenished grants, tax relief, or renewed policy standards and goals. In addition to partially compensating victims of restraint and restructuring, reparatory initiatives keep many or most restraint measures in effect.

This strategy appears to be in line with public opinion in the late 1990s. Frank Graves's chapter on Canadian attitudes to government shows that there is some relaxation of fears about public finances and that there are evident concerns about the social costs of retrenchment policies. Moreover, there is renewed, though conditional, support for compassionate social policy and an active federal role, but one that is fiscally responsible and democratically transparent. The stealth style of social policy, in other words, is regarded unfavourably in the post-deficit era as exclusive and unaccountable. This orientation is likely connected with the greater awareness and critical stance of the media and think tanks toward partial indexing and the other tactics of stealth for balancing the federal budget and generating surpluses.[49]

The 1997 federal budget and *Main Estimates* for 1997-8 marked the turnaround. No new taxes and no further cuts to programs were announced in that budget. In his budget speech, the Finance Minister declared that 'having done what we had to do, we can see the worst is behind us, that brighter days lie ahead.' He added that the era of cuts is ending and 'we are now able to forge a new destiny for ourselves.'[50] Thus some selected tax reductions were introduced along with some program 'reinvestments' in higher education, research and innovation, health care, and child benefits. The 1997-8 expenditure plan proclaimed,

> These Main Estimates represent a watershed in controlling government expenditures and delivering modern, high quality public services. Just four years ago, it appeared to many that Canada's public finances were out of control. There was widespread talk of a fiscal crisis that would call into question Canada's ability to provide the services its citizens had come to expect. It was said that Canada had become too expensive, that we could no longer afford the society that our parents and grandparents had built.
> By 1998-99, the percentage of the gross domestic product (GDP) needed to support all federal government programs will be at its lowest level since 1949-50. While achieving this level will require determination to stay the course set out in the last four budgets, no new reductions are required.[51]

At the outset of the federal election campaign later that year, the Prime Minister announced an increase in the cash floor of the CHST. Though the CHST is a block fund, the increase was apparently for health care, and it was a reaction to growing concerns among Canadians and growing criticism of premiers and federal opposition parties about the quality of medical and hospital care. Hence, the transfer increased by $874 million for 1998-9 and $1.5 billion for 1999-2000 and 2000-1.

The 1998 and 1999 budgets were even clearer signs that in national terms, the post-deficit era had arrived. Both the relative size and the absolute level of the debt are coming down, as the result of economic growth and the allocation of half of any expected surplus to its reduction. Tax relief and reductions are another theme in this emergent era. Personal income taxes were reduced for many Canadians, some tax breaks were enhanced, and a new tax credit was introduced for individuals supporting elderly or infirm relatives. A more active and assertive federal government is readily apparent in the seven-pronged 'Canadian Opportunities Strategy'. The financial and policy heart of the strategy is the Canadian Millennium Scholarship Foundation, an independent body to manage a $2.5 billion initial endowment from the federal treasury to award scholarships to over 100,000 full- and part-time students. Awards start in 2000.

Behind these reparations and allocations to certain social programs, other policies continue to be subject to restraints and cutbacks, including old age pensions, labour market programs, and social housing. More than that, the federal government is striving to limit the scale of compensation on several issues. Examples include:

- the decision in 1998 to appeal a Canadian Human Rights Tribunal ruling on pay-equity requiring Ottawa to provide an estimated $3 billion to $4 billion in back pay and raises to thousands of public servants, most of whom are women;
- the agreement by the federal government and most provincial governments to limit payment to people who contracted Hepatitis-C through tainted blood between 1986 and 1990, but not before or after that period; and
- the reduction of EI premiums for 1998 and 1999 at a rate slower than that recommended actuarially or called for by many labour and business leaders.

By offering compensation to some groups affected but not others, and by restricting amounts payable, reparatory initiatives may alleviate adverse effects for some, but harden the discontent and negative consequences for others who are excluded.

POLICY SHIFTS AND PARADIGM LOST

Over the last two decades both the program terrain and the political theory or paradigm of social policy in Canada have been dramatically shaken and reshaped. The boundaries of the social policy field, and its content, have changed in significant ways. Certain policy instruments have declined in use, such as universality in income security, full indexation of the tax system and several benefits, and federal standards for welfare. Other instruments are now more prominent, among them conditionality of benefits and services to persons, tax expenditure measures, and partnerships with voluntary and community agencies.

The social policy field is marked by multiple and competing discourses, though talk of 'needs' and 'collective sharing of risks' has been declining, while talk of 'rights', 'duties', and 'opportunities' has been on the rise. We see this, too, in the reduced emphasis given to the metaphor of the 'social safety net', with its imagery of protection and a modicum of security, and the corresponding increased emphasis on the notion of the 'social trampoline', and active programs catapulting people back into the labour force. The language of federalism, it seems, is a constant in social policy-making in Canada. Over this whole period, clearly the dominant discourse, supported by political and economic elites, was that of deficit reduction or 'financial responsibility'. The residual status of social policy for most of these years is also apparent in 'echo terms' that reverberated off the dominant discourse. So, in response to talk of the fiscal deficit, human capital, and economic union, the concepts of the social deficit, social capital, and the social union were coined. In part, these concepts were coined by policy advocates and analysts to point out the partiality of the economic discourse, and in part to try to connect social policy to the dominant way of talking about public issues.

Despite claims that in our globalizing economy the nation-state is dead or dying, social policy in Canada remains very much a matter of domestic politics. Far more significant than any Americanization that may have taken place over the last 20 years, as a result of the Charter of Rights or the free trade agreements, has been the provincialization of social policy in this country. Internal shifts in the balance of spending and programming and identification with the public have been major trends in the recent history of the social union (welfare state) in Canada. Both federal and provincial social spending declined in real per capita terms through the 1990s, but the decline has been less severe in the provinces, who also obtained greater control over labour market and social housing program areas.

Over this period as well, the boundaries of Canadian social policy have become more transnational in scope and influence, so as to include the rights of the child or the status of Aboriginal peoples, women, or persons with disabilities. International governmental and non-governmental bodies increasingly network with domestic groups and monitor the implementation of United Nations conventions and covenants. Canadian governments have recently been criticized for not paying sufficient attention to the adverse consequences of cutting social expenditures for the population as a whole and for vulnerable and disadvantaged groups in particular.[52]

In many respects, in international terms, Canadians are doing well in human, economic, and social development. But of course the great social problems facing our country have not been solved. Some have in fact worsened over the last 20 years, and new problems have emerged as well. The problems mentioned in the quotation that opens this chapter are as pressing today as when the words were spoken, if not more so. In 1980 Canada had no food banks, but 20 years later there were more than 2,000. Homelessness and public begging on the streets of Canada's major cities are no longer fringe phenomena. At a structural level, economic growth and social well-being have become uncoupled and divergent in recent decades. Market-based incomes have become more unequal; the incidence of poverty among single-parent families, persons with disabilities, Aboriginal peoples, and even baby boomer families climbed in the 1990s. At the end of the 1990s, the claim of another Liberal Prime Minister, Sir Wilfrid Laurier, that the twentieth century would belong to Canada rings hollow to the many Canadians who are afraid of losing their jobs, falling through the safety net, and suffering the indignities of joblessness and poverty.

While I have discussed the 1980-2000 period in terms of four phases of development, the general trend has been cuts to programs, and challenges to their legitimacy as well as that of their clients. Social policy has not been an area of budgetary calm or political resilience. Some federal social programs are relatively intact and untouched by retrenchment and dismantling, but many programs have been altered in fundamental ways. If we compare the federal social programs in existence in 1980 with those of 2000, the overall pattern is one of change, generally toward retrenchment.[53] In seniors' benefits, the OAS became subject to a tax surcharge (1990) and then was de-universalized (1996). The other programs in this area, the Guaranteed Income Supplement and the Spouse's Allowance, have not seen a rise in the basic benefit since 1985. Federal contributions for social assistance, the safety net, were capped for Ontario, Alberta, and British Columbia (1990-6), and then the program was eliminated, with nearly all the federal conditions associated with that program. Federal social housing programming has been largely curtailed, expenditures frozen, and administration devolved to a number of provinces and the territories. Five rounds of cuts in this period battered UI/EI. The proportion of unemployed Canadians who draw benefits was halved. The once universal Family Allowance program is gone. The EPF agreement is gone, replaced by the smaller CHST. The CPP was modestly enhanced in the 1987 reforms, then modestly cut back in the 1998 changes. The Program for Older Worker Adjustment was terminated in 1997 with no replacement.

Against the backdrop of these changes and shifts are some prominent constants in social policy. Social expenditures remained the largest single program spending area of the federal budget over this entire period, as it had been in the 1960s and 1970s. The chief programs within the social sector continue to include seniors' benefits, transfers to the provinces and territories in respect to health, education, and welfare, and employment insurance. With respect to intergovernmental relations in social policy, what we presently call the social union, Ottawa's basic aims have not changed much over the last 25 years. These aims are to contain the open-ended nature of federal cost sharing, accept some of the demands for greater provincial flexibility and authority, and yet also maintain some federal standards and control. The goal and technique of targeting, that is, directing resources first to those most in need, was a steady refrain, as was thinking of the feasibility of social policy reform within the box of deficit reduction and fiscal restraint. In the words of a high-ranking veteran policy analyst, '[A] lot of the dynamics of social policy reform are real old: Quebec and the rest of Canada, interprovincial squabbling, feds versus provinces, class-based interests in terms of pension reform. I don't think that those categories have become any less relevant in talking about the politics of social policy reform.'[54] Other categories, such as 'employables' and 'non-employables', and 'the deserving' and 'the undeserving', retained an influence. The more the labour market and social programs changed the more the myths and stereotypes stayed the same. Old misconceptions about welfare and people on welfare persisted in the new economy and society.

Just as many social programs have undergone major changes, many of the assumptions and beliefs widely held about social policy-making by academics and advocates have been breached by events of the past 20 years. In 1980, conventional wisdom about social policy generally held, among other beliefs, that:

- universal programs are far more politically secure than selective programs and thus less likely to be cut;

- existing statutory spending programs develop strong inertial forces and are difficult to reduce;
- intergovernmental fiscal and policy agreements, given their complexity and the constituency of provincial and territorial governments, provide a form of stability against federal retrenchment efforts;
- new governments retain social programs even if they opposed them while in opposition, because the voting public and clientele groups expect continuity in and enhancement of benefits;
- economic growth will continue to expand opportunities, raise incomes, reduce inequalities and enlarge pension coverage for workers ;
- improvements in existing social programs and the introduction of new services are therefore also likely; and
- if one million or more workers in the Canadian labour force ever were unemployed the federal government would face a grave political crisis.

A blend of value assertions and political and policy predictions, these tenets are now antiquated. Social policy developments over the last two decades, as outlined in this chapter, have violated the expectations and aspirations associated with these beliefs. As a result, we are in need of new theorizing about the causes and consequences of change in the Canadian welfare state. We are in need of a wave of reflection and research by students and practitioners about the future role for social policy. We are in need of a new national policy agenda that reconnects economic growth with social growth. And we are in need of a far more democratic process for debating and designing tax and transfer programs. The time is long overdue to say farewell to social policy by stealth.

NOTES

1 William Shakespeare, *All's Well That Ends Well.*
2 Residualization is a process of reducing the social role of public policy and the state by orienting public provisions to a reactive approach of relieving problems, categorizing people as targeted client groups, and emphasizing personal responsibility through private institutions. See Michael J. Prince, 'At the Edge of Canada's Welfare State: Social Policy-

Making in British Columbia', in R.K. Carty, ed., *Politics, Policy, and Government in British Columbia* (Vancouver: University of British Columbia Press, 1996), 236-71.

3   See Grattan Gray, 'Social Policy by Stealth', *Policy Options* 11, 1 (March, 1990), 17-29; Ken Battle, 'The Politics of Stealth: Child Benefits Under the Tories', in Susan D. Phillips, ed., *How Ottawa Spends 1993-94: A More Democratic Canada...?* (Ottawa: Carleton University Press, 1993), 417-48.

4   There were also, of course, the brief ministries of Joe Clark in 1979-80, John Turner in 1984, and Kim Campbell in 1993. Each had some impact, though, on the structures and processes of social policy-making. Clark adopted the Policy and Expenditure Management System; Turner abolished the Ministry of State for Social Development and related committees; and Campbell oversaw the reconfiguration of federal departments and agencies, which resulted in the formation of the huge department Human Resources Development Canada.

5   Michael Howlett and M. Ramesh, *Studying Public Policy* (Toronto: Oxford University Press, 1995), 201.

6   Gray (a pseudonym for Ken Battle), 'Social Policy by Stealth'.

7   Battle, 'The Politics of Stealth', 447. Earlier applications of the concept of stealth to various aspects of public policy can be found in the Canadian literature. On the hidden costs of using regulations, see Douglas Hartle, *Public Policy and Decision Making and Regulation* (Montreal: Institute for Research on Public Policy, 1976), 91; on the hidden benefits of tax subsidies, see the National Council of Welfare, *The Hidden Welfare System* (Ottawa: Supply and Services Canada, 1976), 15; on ending universality gradually and increasing targeting of family benefits less obviously, see G. Bruce Doern, 'The Liberals and the Opposition: Ideas, Priorities and the Imperatives of Governing Canada in the 1980s', in G. Bruce Doern, ed., *How Ottawa Spends: The Liberals, the Opposition & Federal Priorities* (Toronto: Lorimer, 1983), 33; and on the slow and subtle whittling away at social programs, see Patrick Johnston, 'Images of the '80s: Food Banks, AIDS', *SPARC News* 6, 1 (Fall 1989), 2. In 'Constitutional Reform by Stealth' (Ottawa: Caledon Institute of Social Policy, May 1995), Battle noted that the phrase 'social policy by stealth' has become part of the discourse of Canadian public policy. Academics (including the present author), journalists, social advocates, and human service organizations have used the phrase, as has former Minister of Human Resources Development Lloyd Axworthy, and even Finance Minister Paul Martin.

8   For details see Michael J. Prince, *Designing Disability Policy in Canada: The Nature and Impact of Federalism on Policy Development*, Report for the Governance Aspects of the Social Union Project (Kingston: Institute of Intergovernmental Relations, Queen's University, 1999).

9 I wish to thank Leslie Pal for suggesting this line of analysis to me and for other valuable editorial comments.
10 See Battle, 'The Politics of Stealth'; Allan Moscovitch, '"Slowing the Steamroller": The Federal Conservatives, The Social Sector and Child Benefits Reform', in Katherine A. Graham, ed., *How Ottawa Spends 1990-91: Tracking the Second Agenda* (Ottawa: Carleton University Press, 1990), 171-217; Keith G. Banting, 'The Social Policy Review: Policy Making in a Semi-Sovereign Society', *Canadian Public Administration* 38, 2 (Summer, 1995), 283-90.
11 Johnston, 'Images of the '80s'. At the time of writing that article, Johnston was a senior policy advisor to the Ontario Premier, and was reflecting on his experiences in Ottawa as executive director of the Canadian Council on Social Development.
12 See Ramesh Mishra, *The Welfare State in Capitalist Society* (Toronto: University of Toronto Press, 1990), 71-3, and James J. Rice and Michael J. Prince, *Changing Politics of Canadian Social Policy* (Toronto: University of Toronto Press, 1999), chapters 3 and 5.
13 For a more detailed review of the social policy record of the 1980-4 Trudeau government, see Michael J. Prince, 'What Ever Happened To Compassion?: Liberal Social Policy 1980-84', in Allan M. Maslove, ed., *How Ottawa Spends 1984: The New Agenda* (Toronto: Methuen, 1984), 79-121.
14 Jim Coutts, 'Expansion, Retrenchment and Protecting the Future: Social Policy in the Trudeau Years', in Thomas S. Axworthy and Pierre Elliott Trudeau, eds, *Towards a Just Society: The Trudeau Years* (Markham: Viking, 1990), 200-1 and 178. See also Andrew Coyne, 'Social Spending, Taxes, and the Debt: Trudeau's Just Society', in Andrew Cohen and J.L. Granatstein, eds, *Trudeau's Shadows: The Life and Legacy of Pierre Elliott Trudeau* (Toronto: Random House, 1998), 223-42. Coyne describes Trudeau's social policy legacy as 'surprisingly modest', with mainly piecemeal adjustments to existing programs and few policy innovations. Like Coutts, however, Coyne concludes that Canada was a more just society in 1984, upon Trudeau's retirement, than in 1968, when Trudeau first became prime minister. Interestingly, Coyne omits consideration of the Constitution Act, 1982, with its Charter of Rights, and the Canada Health Act, 1984, as being part of the Trudeau social policy legacy.
15 Doern, 'The Liberals and the Opposition', 33.
16 Donald V. Smiley, *The Federal Condition in Canada* (Toronto: McGraw-Hill Ryerson, 1986), 181.
17 Michael J. Prince, 'The Tories and the NDP: Alternative Governments or Ad Hoc Advocates?' in G. Bruce Doern, ed., *How Ottawa Spends 1983: The Liberals, the Opposition & Federal Priorities*, 38.

18 W. Irwin Gillespie and Allan M. Maslove, 'The 1980-81 Estimates: Trends, Issues and Choices', in G. Bruce Doern, ed., *Spending Tax Dollars: Federal Expenditures, 1980-1981* (Ottawa: School of Public Administration, Carleton University, 1980), 41.
19 Michael J. Prince and James J. Rice, 'The Department of National Health and Welfare: The Attack on Social Policy', in G. Bruce Doern, ed., *How Ottawa Spends Your Tax Dollars: Federal Priorities 1981* (Toronto: Lorimer, 1981), 90.
20 G. Picot, G. Lemaitre, and P. Kuhn, 'Labour Markets and Layoffs During the Last Two Recessions', *Canadian Economic Observer* Cat. No. 11-010 (Ottawa: Statistics Canada, Mar. 1994), 4.1-4.12.
21 *Estimates 1984-84, Expenditure Plan Part I* (Ottawa: Minister of Supply and Services Canada, 1984), 20.
22 G. Bruce Doern, 'Liberal Priorities 1982: The Limits of Scheming Virtuously', in G. Bruce Doern, ed., *How Ottawa Spends Your Tax Dollars 1982: National Policy and Economic Development* (Toronto: Lorimer, 1982), 10.
23 Allan M. Maslove, 'Ottawa's New Agenda: The Issues and Constraints', in Allan M. Maslove, ed., *How Ottawa Spends 1984: The New Agenda*, 17.
24 See G. Bruce Doern, Allan M. Maslove, and Michael J. Prince, *Public Budgeting in Canada: Politics, Economics and Management* (Ottawa: Carleton University Press, 1988), ch. 1, and Donald J. Savoie, *Thatcher, Reagan, Mulroney: In Search of a New Bureaucracy* (Pittsburgh: University of Pittsburgh Press, 1994).
25 Michael H. Wilson, Minister of Finance, *A New Direction for Canada: An Agenda for Economic Renewal* (Ottawa: Department of Finance, 1984), 66-7.
26 Michael H. Wilson, Minister of Finance, *Budget Speech* (Ottawa: Supply and Services Canada, 1986), 12.
27 Frank McGilly, *An Introduction to Canada's Public Social Services* (Toronto: McClelland and Stewart, 1990), 326.
28 For details on these and other federal social policy measures of this period, see James J. Rice, 'Restitching the Safety Net: Altering the National Social Security System', in Michael J. Prince, ed., *How Ottawa Spends 1987-88: Restraining the State* (Toronto: Methuen, 1987), 211-36; Mishra, *The Welfare State in Capitalist Society*; and Ken Battle, 'Broader Base/Lower Rates: A Formula for Fair Tax Reform?' *Perception* 11, 2 (Nov./Dec. 1987), 15-18.
29 Gray, 'Social Policy by Stealth', 17.
30 Battle, 'The Politics of Stealth', 424-5.
31 These three themes are examined in greater detail in James J. Rice and Michael J. Prince, 'Life of Brian: A Social Policy Legacy', *Perception* 17, 2 (1993), 6-9, and 'Lowering the Safety Net and Weakening the Bonds of Nationhood: Social Policy in the Mulroney Years', in Susan

D. Phillips, ed., *How Ottawa Spends 1993-1994: A More Democratic Canada...?*, 381-416.
32 See Sean Fine, 'Yuppies Pose Day-Care Problem, Beatty Says', *The Globe and Mail* [Toronto] 24 Oct. 1990, A7.
33 See Susan D. Phillips, 'Rock-a-Bye, Brian: The National Strategy on Child Care', in Katherine A. Graham, ed., *How Ottawa Spends 1989-90: The Buck Stops Where?* (Ottawa: Carleton University Press, 1989), 165-208, and Katherine Teghtsoonian, 'Neo-Conservative Ideology and Opposition to Federal Regulation of Child Care Services in the United States and Canada', *Canadian Journal of Political Science* 26, 1 (Mar. 1993), 97-121.
34 *1995-96 Estimates Part I* (Ottawa: Supply and Services Canada, 1995), 28.
35 Paul Martin, Minister of Finance, *Budget Speech* (Ottawa: Public Works and Government Services Canada, 1995), 25, 27.
36 Jane Pulkingham and Gordon Ternowetsky, 'The Changing Landscape of Social Policy and the Canadian Welfare State', in Jane Pulkingham and Gordon Ternowetsky, eds, *Remaking Canadian Social Policy: Social Security in the Late 1990s* (Halifax: Fernwood, 1996), 15.
37 Ken Battle and Sherri Torjman, *How Finance Re-Formed Social Policy* (Ottawa: Caledon Institute of Social Policy, 1995), 10, 19.
38 David P. Ross, 'Who Will Speak for Canada's Children?' *Perception* 19, 2 (1995), 2-3.
39 National Council of Welfare, *Another Look at Welfare Reform* (Ottawa: Supply and Services Canada, 1997), 4, 1.
40 Chris Carter and Sue Clark, 'Unraveling the Social Safety Net', *Perception* 18 (1994), 3-4, 27-28.
41 Sandra Bach and Susan D. Phillips, 'Constructing a New Social Union: Child Care Beyond Infancy?' in Gene Swimmer, ed., *How Ottawa Spends 1997-98: Seeing Red: A Liberal Report Card* (Ottawa: Carleton University Press, 1997), 236, 241.
42 Ibid., 236.
43 Ibid., 255.
44 See Human Resources Development Canada, *An Analysis of Employment Insurance Benefit Coverage* (Ottawa: Applied Research Division, Oct. 1998); Pierre Laliberté, 'Setting New Priorities for Canada's Employment Insurance Program', *Perception* 22, 3 (Dec. 1998), 8-9; and Geoffrey E. Hale, 'Reforming Employment Insurance: Transcending the Politics of the Status Quo', *Canadian Public Policy* 24, 4 (Dec. 1998), 429-51.
45 Human Resources Development Canada, 'Federal Minimum Wage Alignment with Rates in Provinces and Territories', News Release, 96-35 (Ottawa, 18 Apr. 1996).
46 This is informed by Michael J. Prince, 'New Mandate, New Money, New Politics: Federal Budgeting in the Post-Deficit Era', in Leslie A.

Pal, ed., *How Ottawa Spends 1998-99: Balancing Act: The Post-Deficit Mandate* (Toronto: Oxford University Press, 1998), 31-55.
47 National Council of Welfare, *Another Look at Welfare Reform*, 1.
48 Exceptions may occur when one government reinstates a program or agency restrained or even eliminated by a different government, as was the case when the Chrétien Liberals restored the Court Challenges Program terminated by the Mulroney Conservatives. The cancellation in mid-1998 by the Liberals of their own proposed Seniors Benefit may be another variant of this strategy.
49 See Shawn McCarthy, 'Study Measures De-indexation's Pinch, 3.9 Million Canadians Have Been Pushed into Higher Tax Brackets, Caledon Institute Says', *The Globe and Mail* [Toronto], 3 June 1998, B2, and Diane Francis, '"Bracket creep": A Big Bonanza for Ottawa', *Maclean's* (20 July 1998), 44. The increased attention has likely been encouraged by Ken Battle's report, *No Taxation Without Indexation* (Ottawa: Caledon Institute of Social Policy, 1998). Another report calling for the restoration of full indexation to the personal income tax system is Finn Poschmann, *Inflated Taxes, Deflated Paycheques* (Toronto: C.D. Howe Institute Commentary 118, Dec. 1998).
50 Paul Martin, Minister of Finance, *Budget Speech* (Ottawa: Public Works and Government Services Canada, 18 Feb. 1997), 28.
51 President of the Treasury Board, *Getting Government Right: Governing for Canadians* (Ottawa: Public Works and Government Services Canada, 20 Feb.1997), 1.
52 In December 1998, for example, the United Nations Committee on Economic, Social and Cultural Rights issued a report on Canada's implementation of the Covenant. After noting some positive aspects of Canada's performance, the Committee went on to identify several subjects of concern, followed by a number of suggestions and recommendations (available at Web site: http://193.135.136.30/frames/unis/uniscdn.htm). Canada is expected to next submit a report to the Committee in 2003.
53 Important exceptions include the replacement of the Vocational Rehabilitation for Disabled Persons program in 1998 with the Employment Assistance for Persons with Disabilities program; the conversion of various regressive tax deductions and exemptions to credits; the entrenchment of the Charter of Rights and Freedoms in 1982; and the Canada Health Act, 1984.
54 Quoted in Leslie A. Pal, *Beyond Policy Analysis: Public Issue Management in Turbulent Times* (Toronto: ITP Nelson, 1997), 89.

6

Taking Stock: Canadian Federalism and Its Constitutional Framework

ROGER GIBBINS

The end of the century provides an opportunity, almost an obligation, to take stock of the Canadian federal state. By determining where we now stand it is possible to speculate on where we might be going, to identify potential trajectories of Canadian federalism for the early part of the next century. This enterprise, however, requires much more than a snapshot of the state of affairs in 1999, for any single snapshot is invariably blurred by a good deal of noise and rhetoric that may turn out to have little staying power. As I write, for example, the Ontario caucus of the federal Liberal party is articulating a centralist vision of federalism in which Ottawa would defend national programs, standards, and values from mean-spirited provincial governments, and would require the provinces to report to Ottawa in great detail about how they behave within their own constitutional domains. But a decade from now will any trace of this rhetorical attack be found in the constitutional framework, parliamentary institutions, or programmatic structure of the Canadian federal state? It is unlikely, and in any event is impossible to foretell.

It is essential, therefore, to conduct our stocktaking over a somewhat longer period of time. As Canadian historian Donald Creighton has explained, we have a better chance of anticipating the future if we pay careful attention to the past:

> The waves behind the vessel which is carrying humanity forward into the unknown ... can teach us where the winds of change are blowing and on what course the chief currents of our age are set. They can reveal to us the main direction of our voyage through time.[1]

The question remains, however, as to how far back we should look. The farther back we go, the more dramatic the change will be, but the less relevant the comparison will be for contemporary readers. For instance, an extended comparison of the late 1990s with the federal institutions and constitutional framework faced by Wilfrid Laurier's Liberal government in the late 1890s might leave many readers gasping, but not in pleasure. Conversely, a comparison of the status quo with the circumstances faced by Jean Chrétien's Liberal government in 1998 would be of little utility; perceptions of continuity would overwhelm perceptions of change. The point of comparison adopted here is 1967, Canada's centenary. By looking at patterns of continuity and change over the past 32 years I hope to establish a reasonable foundation upon which to base predictions for the *near* future. (I will resist predictions about the distant future; these should be left to those young enough to see if they're right, and to face the consequences.)

There is one final methodological caveat to address. Over a period of more than thirty years *everything* will change to some degree. Thus the discussion will focus on *relative* continuity and *relative* change; things for which change has occurred in modest proportion will be taken as evidence of continuity rather than change. And, of course, the analysis will be selective. Not all federal and constitutional elements can be considered in the limited space of a short chapter. Nonetheless, the reader should be aware that another writer might have included a different set of elements, and therefore have arrived at different conclusions. I would argue, however, that the differences would not be large, for the patterns of continuity and change explored below are neither subtle nor obscure.

THE NATURE OF FEDERALISM

Before tackling patterns of continuity and change in the Canadian federal state we should pause for a moment to consider the meaning of federalism. What is this concept that underlies so much of Canadian political life, that shapes our governing institutions and, at times, inflames our political rhetoric? What do we mean by federalism?

Unfortunately for the reader, but to the delight of political scientists, there is no simple or single answer. At one level federalism refers to a political system that divides the legislative powers of the state between two orders of government, provides a written account of that division, ensures that the division of powers cannot be unilaterally amended by any one order of government, and establishes an impartial dispute settlement mechanism to be applied when disagreements arise. Thus we have federal and provincial governments, a written constitution, formulas by which it can be amended, and a legal system culminating in the Supreme Court through which constitutional disputes can be resolved. Federalism, however, covers these bare bones with a great deal of flesh. It includes a vast maze of intergovernmental committees, agreements, fiscal transfers, and programs. It also includes a variety of mechanisms by which provincial and regional interests are represented within the parliamentary institutions of the national government, including the Senate and conventions of regional representation in Cabinet. And today it includes three territorial governments in the north and scores of Aboriginal governments across the country.

Even this description, however, is still too narrow in its focus on governments and their interactions. Federalism is also about the diversity that springs from Canada's regional and linguistic variation. It seeks to accommodate and celebrate that diversity, to avoid one-size-fits-all public policies and social programs. At the same time, federal systems try to foster unity in the face of this diversity, to nurture common values, goals, and aspirations. There are, then, two faces to federalism: a respect for diversity, wedded to an acknowledgment of the limits of diversity, a belief that the whole is not only the sum of its parts but more than the sum.

Linked to this are the multiple political identities characteristic of modern federal states. Citizens identify with their locality, province, region, and country. I am simultaneously a Calgarian, an Albertan, a western Canadian, and a Canadian, not to mention male, white, of British descent, and older than I like to think. All of these identities and more jostle for political space in federal states. Some enjoy the huge advantage of having governments to speak on their behalf,[2] while others do not. At times they compete, and at other times they complement and reinforce one another. Sometimes they lie dormant, and at other times flare up into political controversies and crises.

Federalism, therefore, is about governments, territory, values, and identity. There is even a case to be made for federalism as a moral framework for Canadian life.[3] Often, though, it is the governmental aspects that come most assertively to the fore, and we miss the complex stew of identities and values that underpin federal politics. In the pages to come we will fall into this trap to a degree. Nonetheless, it is important to remember that patterns of change and/or continuity among governments need not reflect and need not be reflected in the values, aspirations, and identities of citizens. Indeed, as we will see, patterns of change and continuity across the various dimensions of Canadian federalism are not moving in harmony. The articulation is loose at times, even disjointed. Canadians and their governments do not necessarily occupy the same political space.

The complexity of federalism, of course, complicates our task of taking stock. The task, however, is not beyond us. Let us turn first to patterns of continuity, against which we can then track elements of change.

PATTERNS OF CONTINUITY

The passage of decades may loom large in the lives of individuals, but it has limited impact on the basic demographic structure of a longstanding national community such as Canada's.[4] If we compare the 1966 census with that of 1996, we find only minor demographic shifts. Atlantic Canada's share of the national population dropped from 9.9 per cent to 8.2 per cent, Quebec's dropped from 28.9 per cent to 24.8 per cent, Ontario's share edged up from 34.8 per cent to 37.3 per cent, and the West's share increased from 26.3 per cent to 29.6 per cent, with all of this latter regional growth occurring in Alberta and British Columbia.[5] Over roughly the same time period (1961 to 1996), the proportion of Canadians identifying French as their mother tongue dropped from 28.1 per cent to 23.3 per cent. None of these changes are of sufficient magnitude to suggest that the demographic backdrop to Canadian federal politics in the late 1990s is dramatically different from that of the late 1960s.

There are, however, a few caveats to keep in mind. First, perceived change may be greater than actual change, and the former may have a political impact quite removed from any impact by the latter. Chronic western Canadian discontent, for instance, is fuelled by the *perception* that newcomers from other parts of Canada and abroad are flooding into the west, and that the region is booming relative to the rest of Canada. Western Canadians tend to see the world as tipped from east to West, with everything but political power rolling down the slope into the west. Second, political dynamics may focus on relative rather than absolute demographic changes. For example, Quebec nationalists may worry about the relative downward trend in Quebec's population, a worry not offset by absolute growth. In a similar fashion, the relative decline of the francophone population may cause concern for those who view the country within a binational or bilingual framework. Third, there has been an important change in the source of immigration into Canada. In both relative and absolute terms, immigration from Europe has declined while immigration from Asia Pacific and South Asia has increased. The racial composition of the Canadian population is thus becoming more diverse, although here too perceptions of change may exaggerate the reality of change. This increased diversity may alter federal dynamics by forging new transnational communities with relatively weak territorial identifications.

If we turn from demographics to politics we again find important aspects of continuity. Our basic political institutions remain intact, virtually unaffected by the passage of time. The House of Commons has essentially the same institutional norms and operating procedures as it had in 1967, indeed as it had in 1867. Provincial legislatures are, if anything, even more static. The conventions of responsible government and the attendant constraints of rigid party discipline remain in place despite modest procedural reforms, ones with little impact on public perceptions. The Senate remains resolutely unelected, unequal, and ineffective; perhaps all that has changed is that it today enjoys even less esteem than before, with a public torn between the options of abolition and reform. (The last defender of the status quo was reputedly sighted in 1991.) The electoral system is basically the same; MPs are still elected in single-member constituencies by a simple plurality of the popular vote, and, largely as a consequence, regionalism bedevils and fragments the national party system. The Supreme Court has the same institutional shape, and the ultimate power of appointment to the Court still rests with the prime minister, as does the power to appoint senators. If we consider federal elements more specifically, we find that the constitutional division of powers between the national and provincial governments is essentially unchanged from 1967. Apart from some modest strengthening in 1982 of provincial ownership and control of natural resources, the division of powers looks pretty much as it did in 1867, despite important changes in the nature of the Canadian society. Finally, and by no means least, there is still no formal constitutional recognition of Quebec as a distinct society despite 30 years of nationalist discontent and constitutional turmoil. In a *formal* sense, and particularly for the constitutional amending formula and division of powers, Quebec remains a province like the others.

The serious fiscal imbalance in the Canadian federal state remains in place. Simply put, provincial governments spend far more than they can raise through provincial tax revenues alone. As a consequence, Ottawa had emerged by the mid-1960s as a major funder of provincial programs relating to health care, social security, and post-secondary education. Thus the constitutional division of powers had been overlaid, and to some degree obscured and transformed, by massive financial transfers from Ottawa to provincial governments, transfers that have carried with them significant federal government encroachments into the legislative jurisdiction of provincial governments. The courts have ruled that although Ottawa cannot legislate directly in provincial areas of jurisdiction, it can spend in those areas, and can attach conditions to its financial largesse. In this way, the federal government can indirectly shape provincial programs and spending priorities. Admittedly, there has been a great deal of experimentation and change in the manner in which intergovernmental fiscal transfers are made. Conditional grants, through which Ottawa dictated programmatic standards to the provinces, and matching grants in which the level of federal transfers was driven by the size of provincial expenditures, have given way to unconditional grants and the greater transfer of tax points rather than cash. The Canada Health and Social Transfer (CHST), for instance, wraps federal grants for post-secondary education, health, and social services into a single block grant. However, the fiscal imbalance remains even if the remedies have changed. Moreover, the 1999 social union negotiations revealed considerable appetite in Ottawa for 'reconditionalizing' federal transfers, particularly with respect to health care expenditures. What had appeared to be a steady trend of increasing provincial autonomy is now very much in question for provinces other than Quebec. (More on this point shortly.)

This fiscal imbalance, incidentally, is replicated in spades in the relationships between provincial and municipal governments. Although public services such as education, social assistance, and health care are delivered through local governments and regional authorities, these governments and authorities generally have very limited powers of taxation. However, discussions of this particular fiscal imbalance have made little impact in a political culture fixated on the federal-provincial dimension of Canadian political life.

The 1967 centennial year was a time when neither public nor governmental concern with debts or deficits was apparent. Government expenditures were rapidly expanding both federally and provincially, and there appeared to be few financial constraints on the proclivity of Canadians to demand an activist government and for governments to respond with enthusiasm to that demand. In the early 1990s, concern over the magnitude of public debts and deficits finally took hold, and Canada entered a period of public spending cuts. The impact on federalism was immediate: Ottawa cut financial transfers to the provinces, the provinces downloaded cuts onto local governments and authorities, and both provincial and local governments argued that if senior governments were no longer paying the piper they should no longer call the tune. However, what first appeared to be a permanent change in the fiscal nature of Canadian federalism, and in the programmatic expectations of Canadians, has proved to be short-lived. Deficits have been eliminated, significant surpluses are being posted by both the federal government and most provincial governments, concern about the remaining debt has abated, and governments are now engaged in a lively debate on how best to spend new surpluses. Concerns over chronically high levels of taxation have failed to grip either political parties or governments. Thus we find more continuity than change; for better or worse, the fiscal environment of 1999 resembles more that of the late 1960s than it does that of the early 1990s. Governments again have 'jingle in their jeans' and a born-again belief that Canadians will support high taxes and public programs rather than place more money in their own pockets through tax cuts.

A final point of continuity, and at the same time an important source of change, is the nationalist movement in Quebec. For most of this century, provincial governments in Quebec have pursued a consistent constitutional agenda and federal vision: they have sought to defend the existing constitutional division of powers from encroachment by Ottawa, to expand Quebec's jurisdiction, and to achieve recognition of Quebec as a distinct national community. Differences within Quebec have centred on how best to achieve these consensual goals: through a reformed federation, through some form of partnership or sovereignty-association with the rest of Canada, or through the creation of an independent sovereign state. What stands out, however, has been the continuity of Quebec's demands—the consistent nature and direction of the pressure Quebec has exerted on the federal system. The intensity of that pressure has varied somewhat as the control of Quebec governments has alternated between federalist parties advocating a new deal within Canada and sovereigntist parties advocating a new deal with Canada, but the core message has transcended changes in the medium.

What has also stood out has been the inconsistent and at best subdued response from the rest of Canada. Although Canadians have been poised uncomfortably on the knife edge of Quebec separatism since the mid-1960s, the nature of this predicament is far from clear when we examine the formal evolution of federalism over the period explored in this chapter. The primary, virtually the only, constitutional response to the threat of separatism came with the Constitution Act of 1982, a response that in most respects rejected rather than accommodated the nationalist movement in Quebec. Thus the growing strength of the nationalist movement in Quebec, which might suggest change rather than continuity, has been matched by constitutional continuity outside Quebec.

It should be kept in mind, and not incidentally, that the identification of patterns of continuity should not be confused with a normative evaluation. It is very much an open question, for example, whether the conventions of party discipline should or should not be weakened, or whether Quebec's sociological distinctiveness should be recognized in the constitution. There are even those who would, allegedly, argue in support of the Senate status quo. The point, then, is to *acknowledge* the strong patterns of institutional and constitutional continuity that characterize the Canadian federal state. We live in a formal constitutional and institutional environment that in most respects has not been radically transformed. However, we should not assume that the citizens who live within this relatively static environment necessarily see the political world in the same way today as they did before. It may be the same zoo, but with different inhabitants.

If the founding fathers were to miraculously reappear for the millennium celebrations, they would recognize not only the broad outlines but many details of their 1867 institutional design. The prime ministers of the 1960s—John Diefenbaker, Lester Pearson, Pierre Trudeau—would be even more at home. Canadian governments may not be immune to the appeals of innovation and reform, but they have kept their enthusiasm well in check. To paraphrase William Lyon Mackenzie King, Canada's longest-lasting prime minister, 'Change if necessary but not necessarily change.'

PATTERNS OF CHANGE

It nevertheless will come as no surprise that a lot has also changed since 1967, more than can be mentioned and discussed in the limited space available. What I will discuss are some specific changes in the federal scheme of things, and some more general changes in the political environment within which federal dynamics play out. It is these latter changes that best signal changes to come as we prepare to move into the new century. Let me begin with changes to the formal constitutional structures, and then turn to the more dynamic, fluid aspects of federal politics.

Undoubtedly the most dramatic and important change came with the passage of the Constitution Act on 17 April 1982. The Act patriated the Canadian Constitution, which until that time was lodged within an act of the British Parliament, formally amendable only by that Parliament. As part of the process of patriation, the 1982 Act established Canadian amending formulas whereby parts of the Constitution could be amended by Parliament and seven of the ten provincial legislatures, provided that the latter represented at least 50 per cent of the national population, and other parts could only be amended by Parliament with the consent of all ten provincial legislatures. Changes to the division of powers, so long as such changes did not affect provincial control of natural resources, or derogate from the legislative powers, proprietary rights, or other rights or privileges of specific provinces, would be an example of the first type of amendment; changes to the amending formula itself would be an example of the second type, although, as things have turned out, even the amending formula has turned out to be open to unilateral modification. The 1982 Act also provided for the constitutional recognition of Aboriginal peoples (Indians, Inuit, and Métis) and treaty rights, and mentioned the foundational role of equalization payments. The acknowledgement of First Ministers' Conferences (FMCs) gave some constitutional cachet to intergovernmentalism.

When most Canadians think of the 1982 Constitution Act, however, the change that immediately comes to mind is the Charter of Rights and Freedoms. The Charter sets forth a broad array of rights (it says very little about responsibilities) in such areas as the administration of justice, freedom of conscience, speech, and religion, gender equality, official languages, and multiculturalism. Although it can be argued that many of the Charter's rights were by no means new, the Charter is nonetheless of great importance in the evolution of the Canadian federal state. It provides a coherent statement of the rights and values embedded in Canadian citizenship, and it guarantees them irrespective of the provincial or territorial community within which citizens might reside. This blanket application is of particular note within the context of a federal society, one that many argued was and *should be* characterized by significant value diversity across regional and linguistic communities.

The courts, as a direct consequence of the 1982 Constitution Act, have come to assume much greater influence in Canadian political life than before. Although the impetus for this particular change reaches back to the American civil rights movement of the 1960s and the growing judicial activism of Canadian courts in the 1970s, a sea change occurred when the Charter of Rights and Freedoms empowered the courts to strike down national or provincial legislation on grounds other than a violation of the federal division of powers. Canadian politics has become more judicialized and, inevitably, the Canadian courts have become more politicized, as judges wade into public policy debates and contest the law-making primacy of legislative assemblies.[6] The implication of this change for federalism is that judicial activism has the potential to impose a common public policy regime across the country, and across the constitutional division of powers. In the extreme, one not yet reached, the courts could render Canada a much less federal society by constraining public policy variation across provinces. Thus the Supreme Court as a national institution has far greater potential than Parliament to impose a degree of policy homogeneity from sea to sea to sea, for its jurisdiction is not limited to the federal sphere. Whether this potential is to be realized or not is one of the great federalism questions for the early decades of the next century.

The growing influence of the Court is also linked to the difficulty of making formal amendments to the Constitution. Canada, like other federal states, has adopted an amending formula that is appropriately difficult to use; a constitution that can be easily amended is little different from ordinary legislation. Certainly we saw in the failures of both the 1987 Meech Lake Accord and the 1992 Charlottetown Accord how difficult it is to formally amend the Constitution, although in the former case we came extraordinarily close. The only success stories have come from bilateral amendments applicable only to an individual province, such as the amendment to remove the religious foundation of the Newfoundland education system. However, the consequence of formal difficulty is that the courts play a larger role in fine-tuning and revising the meaning of the static constitutional text. The Constitution comes to mean what the courts say it means, and judges can change their minds far more easily than we can amend the formal constitutional text. Thus we find, for example, that the courts are erecting an elaborate constitutional architecture for Aboriginal rights, governments, and peoples. Virtually all the changes in these respects are court-driven; legislatures and electoral politics are at most interested bystanders.

If we continue to step back from institutional structures and constitutional provisions, we can also see a good deal of informal change in the nature and dynamics of Canadian federal politics. Provincial governments have grown, in terms of expenditures, program scope, and bureaucratic expertise, and are consequently on a more even footing with the federal government. The division of the Northwest Territories took place in 1999, and with it the creation of the new Nunavut Territory in the eastern Arctic with a public government under Inuit control. (The composition and character of government in the residual western Arctic, still known as the Northwest Territories, remain unclear.) Territorial governments in the North are now much more province-like in their autonomy, scale of program delivery, and incorporation into intergovernmental negotiations and discourse. Aboriginal governments across the country are taking on greater formal shape, jurisdictional control, and financial autonomy. Aboriginal peoples and governments have become much more active players across the spectrum of political life; we have travelled an immense distance from the 1969 White Paper on Indian Affairs, which recommended the formal abolition of Aboriginal rights, treaties, and constitutional status, to the 1995 Report of the Royal Commission on Aboriginal Peoples, which recommended a comprehensive entrenchment of Aboriginal rights and the constitutional recognition of self-governing Aboriginal communities.

Encompassing all of these changes has been the inexorable growth of intergovernmentalism as the defining characteristic of the Canadian federal state. Governments meet with one another constantly, and the interactions among governments have as much impact on the shape of public policy as do the interactions between governments and their electorates. The high-water mark of intergovernmentalism came with the 1999 social union framework, when, after more than a year of secret negotiations, the federal, nine provincial, and two territorial governments pledged to work in greater harmony.[7] Informing virtually every clause of the framework was the commitment to consult with one another before acting, and to continue this process of consultation while acting. Festive citizen parties in the street to celebrate this event were noticeably absent.

On balance, how should we weigh the patterns of continuity and change? Perhaps the simplest answer is that we have experienced a large measure of formal institutional and constitutional continuity, and an equally large measure of informal change in the way in which we and our governments live federalism. Whether this disjuncture between formal continuity and informal change can persist as the momentum of social change continues to grow is very much in doubt. At the very least, it is safe to conclude that the federal status quo at the end of the century is far from fixed or stable.

FUTURE CHALLENGES AND PROSPECTS

Fortune-telling is always a risky business, particularly when predictions are cast in printed text. Certainly I claim no special powers in this respect, and my record at predicting election outcomes is no better than what might come from reading the entrails of dead animals (or pollsters). The problems with crystal-ball gazing are illustrated in spades by the new social union framework. The outlines and consequences of the social union are murky, to say the least; the social union is simultaneously described as a device by which provincial governments can rein in Ottawa's propensity for unilateralism, a device by which Ottawa can impose greater accountability on provincial governments, a device for protecting national standards, and a framework for accommodating and facilitating regional policy diversity. It could take a generation for the dust to settle on this intergovernmental deal.

Somewhat greater clarity comes from a number of inescapable challenges gathering on the horizon. First, we will have to find some way to weave Aboriginal governments into the warp and woof of Canadian federal institutions and practice. That Aboriginal governments will grow in number, power, and autonomy in the years to come is not in question. What is far less clear is how those governments will be slotted into the intergovernmental mechanisms and programs that characterize the contemporary federal state. Take, for instance, the somewhat extreme but nevertheless illustrative example of FMCs, an intergovernmental mechanism that is replicated annually by hundreds of ministerial and deputy-ministerial meetings. The Royal Commission on Aboriginal Peoples estimated that we may soon have up to 70 First Nation governments, and this does not take into account potential developments with the large urban Aboriginal population or the Métis. How, then, will these governments plug into the FMC? Given that they cannot all have seats at the table or a formal role in decision-making, how will a more limited form of representation be designed? How will Aboriginal governments be accommodated in meetings of ministers, deputy ministers, or program officials? The rhetorical recognition of Aboriginal governments as a third order of government does not begin to address the incorporation of such governments into the ongoing and important processes of intergovernmental relations. Here it should be stressed that this particular challenge is more acute for Aboriginal peoples than it might be for the broader society. First Nation governments exercising newly won jurisdictional authority and political autonomy may have to relinquish some of that authority and autonomy to peak organizations along the lines of the Assembly of First Nations, organizations charged with the mandate to negotiate on their behalf within the matrix of intergovernmental relations. If such peak organizations do not emerge, or if they lack the political authority to impose deals on their constituent governments, it is difficult to see how Aboriginal governments can function effectively in an intergovernmental context. Thus while a legal framework for Aboriginal self-government is rapidly emerging, an effective federalism framework is not yet in sight.

A second challenge is that local governments will loom much larger in Canadian public life as we move into the next century. The mayors of Toronto, Montreal, and Vancouver represent political communities larger than six of the provinces, communities that dwarf the northern territories and First Nations, and the constituencies of the mayors of Calgary and Edmonton are almost as large. The population of the newly enlarged metropolitan Toronto government is larger than all but three of the provinces (including Ontario). Local governments, however, have no constitutionally-derived legislative authority and have access to a very limited tax base, even though they are increasingly the primary sites for the design and delivery of social services, and for the promotion of economic development. If we look at health policy reform, for example, we find that the most interesting and creative action is taking place at the local level. While the federal and provincial governments negotiate at tiresome length over how to divide up marginal increases in the global health care budget, it is local and regional health authorities that are making the policy decisions that touch the real lives of real people. Decisions about the length of hospital stays, the integration of acute care and home care services, the promotion of healthy living, and the more economical delivery of health services have little if anything to do with the Canada Health Act or intergovernmental compacts. In a similar fashion, the delivery of social services and the integration of such services with health care and the administration of justice have become increasingly localized as provincial governments decentralize to regional boards, local governments, and non-profit organizations. What happens in provincial governments has little immediate impact; what happens in Ottawa has even less.

There is a related, emerging school of thought, one associated with the ugly but insightful term *glocalism*, that argues that our cities will take on growing importance as a consequence of globalization. While individuals may enjoy playing on the global stage, they need a secure home base in which to have face-to-face interactions, find a good cup of coffee, raise families, and walk the dog. All of this can be provided by the local community. If that community has good airline connections and electronic links to the 'global village', the importance of the surrounding provincial and national communities may recede. In short, if we have both the local, and ready access to the global, the intermediate provincial and national communities, which have formed the building blocks of Canadian federalism, will recede in importance. They will not disappear, but their role in our political identities, passions, and policy debates will diminish. Where we live within Canada, and within provinces, will become more rather than less important in the wake of glocalism. The exception to this trend may be Quebec. For me, the 'local' in the glocalism dyad is more likely to be Calgary than Alberta, but for Quebec residents it may be Quebec itself, a distinct local community in the North American environment. Thus while glocalism may weaken provincial identities in the English-speaking provinces it *may* have the opposite effect in Quebec.

In the years to come, then, we can expect an intensified campaign for greater legislative scope, financial powers, and constitutional recognition for local governments. While this process may stop well short of the creation of city states, it seems unlikely that municipalities will remain simple creatures of their provincial governments. They will have become too important for the lives we lead and the public policies we construct. Citizens are likely to demand more local political control, and to resist the exercise of delegated power by appointed regional boards and cash-starved municipal governments.

If the glocalism hypothesis holds, and if the social union framework enhances the policy autonomy of provincial governments (an outcome that is by no means assured), then the consequence will be increased policy variance across and within provinces. Where someone lives within Canada will become more rather than less important in terms of public policies. We will become a more diverse, a more federal society. There will, of course, be a price to be paid. The notion of national standards will seem increasingly quaint, and the Canadian identity will no longer be defined by universal social programs. The upside is that we will unleash a great deal of policy creativity, innovation, and experimentation. Not all of it will be successful, but on balance we might well expect public policies that are more closely tuned to local communities. This can only happen if or more likely when we abandon the belief that a common citizenship entitles us to a common standard of social services.

Lest the reader fear that we may swing too far in the direction of regional and local diversity, it should be kept in mind that the courts will remain a vehicle through which many Canadians will pursue the universal application of rights and social programs. Thus the courts will continue to be a check on regional diversity. This check will be reinforced in turn by emerging political identities that are not tied to territorial communities. Feminists, environmentalists, religious communities, and new immigrant communities will forge political identities and alliances that are only loosely connected to the territorial features of Canadian federalism. There is no suggestion, then, that Canada is on the verge of balkanizing into discrete regional and local communities; many of the ties that bind the national community together will persist, and new ties are being created. Nevertheless, increased public policy diversity seems inevitable. The pervasive decentralization of program delivery and accountability—from Ottawa to the provinces, from the provinces to local governments and new regional authorities, from provincial agencies to non-profit organizations delivering contractually defined services—necessarily implies greater diversity in the programs ultimately reaching Canadian citizens. Canada will become less important as the container within which we construct our political identities and public policies.

A related point, and one touched on above, has to do with the progressive decline of territoriality in Canadian political life. Our political institutions were designed on the assumption, and have gone on to reinforce the assumption, that Canadians privilege territorial identifications above other forms of political identification. For instance, although my political perspectives are shaped to a degree by my age, occupation, sex, and ideological predispositions, it is assumed that my residence in Alberta will ultimately trump these other potential forms of political identification. This assumption, however, is now in question. Other forms of identity are pushing to the fore as Canadians begin to put more political weight on gender, ethnicity, ideology, and even religion. While we will continue to live within the territorial communities around which our constitutional and institutional structures have been built, those communities, particularly provincial communities, will have a weaker claim on our political loyalties and sensibilities. I can live within Alberta without necessarily being an Albertan in my political life.

This decline in territoriality is reinforced by the impact of new information technologies. E-mail and the Internet, along with cellphones and cheaper long distance tolls, have shattered the tyranny of territory. We build and live in new virtual communities that have no connection with the lines on maps, which still define our federal political communities and institutions. State structures are still built from territorial units, but our technological lives are not. Long distance telephone companies advertise that we live within a single North American neighbourhood. The same companies offer cellphone rates that make no distinction between calls next door and calls across the continent. When we call, moreover, we increasingly call a person and not a place; we no longer attach the person at the end of a cellphone conversation to a particular location. They could be anywhere, or nowhere. It would be surprising indeed if this sweeping technological and social change failed to make an imprint on the nature of Canadian federalism and its territorial foundations. Although our political institutions are crafted along territorial lines, our lives are not. Canadians are living outside the federalism box.

One of the most longstanding flashpoints of territoriality in Canadian politics has been the West, but even here pressure on the federal system and its parliamentary institutions will only abate in the years to come. The populist challenge to representative institutions[8] may wane as Reform transforms itself into a United Alternative committed to 'good government' or, more radically, 'better government'. More importantly, the North American Free Trade Agreement (NAFTA) has altered regional perceptions of the national government. Before, Ottawa wielded economic powers that were central to a region's economic well-being; these included the power to set tariffs, interest rates, trade policy, and freight rates. It was essential, therefore, that the region find more effective leverage on national politics. Hence the quest for institutional reform and the beautifully crafted slogan of the early Reform party: 'The West Wants In.' Today, however, Ottawa's economic powers have largely passed to the market or to international trade agreements within which Canada is a minor player. As a result, there is less in Ottawa to get in to; the national government is less relevant and so too is the need for institutional reform. This is not to suggest that NAFTA and globalization more broadly defined have strengthened the case for separatism, as they have in Quebec. 'Wanting in' has *not* become 'wanting out'. Rather, there is a sense of indifference to the national government and a slackening of territorial antagonism. Simply put, Ottawa has less capacity to hurt regional interests or to facilitate regional aspirations.

A further consequence of globalization may be that Canadian constitutional perspectives will come to be shaped by institutional innovation abroad. If Australia cuts its ties to the monarchy, will Canada consider the same when Prince Charles succeeds Queen Elizabeth II? If Britain reforms and modernizes the House of Lords, will Canadians continue to tolerate a Senate designed imperfectly for the nineteenth century, much less the twenty-first? Will we take pride in being the only remaining democratic federal state with a non-elected legislative chamber appointed at the whim of a single individual, the prime minister? If the new Scottish Parliament adopts procedures and architectural principles designed to minimize partisan divisions and maximize collaborative policy-making, will Canadians remain content with a political system in which partisan conflict permeates every nook and cranny? In short, will Canadians be embarrassed into pursuing constitutional and institutional change, or will we stand apart as loyal defenders of constitutional principles now abandoned by others? Will we be a bastion of constitutional conservatism in an emerging new world order?

Finally, there is the Quebec question. It is impossible to speculate about the future trajectory of Canadian federalism without coming to grips with Quebec's place within the Canadian federal state. Here, of course, any speculation is fraught with uncertainty and constrained by political sensitivities; suggestions that Quebec might indeed depart, and, even more, the suggestion that the rest of Canada might enjoy a prosperous future in some new form of partnership with an independent Quebec, are still frowned upon. Nonetheless, two points seem self-evident.

The first is that the nationalist movement in Quebec is not about to pack up its tent and silently drift away. The re-election of the Parti Québécois government in 1998, the PQ's dominant position among the francophone electorate, the limited enthusiasm displayed by young Quebecers for Canadian federalism, and the ongoing demographic erosion of Quebec's anglophone community all suggest that the prospects for a successful sovereignty referendum in the not-too-distant future are waxing, not waning. Admittedly, nothing is certain. However, when one reflects over the last thirty years and takes into account the reasonably robust state of the current nationalist movement and the PQ government, it is safe to conclude that Quebecers at the very least will not settle for a provincial status formally equivalent to that of other provinces. Quebec will continue to seek *national* recognition. About all that is uncertain is whether this recognition will be found inside or outside the Canadian federal state. On this point there is genuine ambivalence within Quebec, and hence the uneasy saw-off between the 'hard' and 'soft' nationalists.

The second point is that outside Quebec there is far less ambivalance. If we trace the evolution of constitutional thought and passion from the 1982 Constitution Act through the failed 1987 Meech Lake Accord, the failed 1992 Charlottetown Accord, and the 1997 Calgary Declaration, with its lukewarm endorsement of a modest recognition of Quebec's distinctiveness framed within the explicit context of provincial equality,[9] the rest of Canada is moving away from rather than toward the *constitutional* recognition of Quebec's distinctiveness. Perhaps inadvertently, Canadians outside Quebec have drawn their line in the sand. They agree that everything possible should be done to encourage Quebec to stay in Canada, but they stop short of the constitutional recognition of Quebec as a national community distinct from other provinces.

What does this mean for the future of Canadian federalism? In the short term, we appear to be deadlocked; there is no common ground between the constitutional visions of the two national communities. There is no solution that would satisfy the ambitions of nationalists in Quebec, including soft nationalists, and yet would still be acceptable outside Quebec. Thus constitutional reform is unlikely unless a sovereignty referendum passes in Quebec, but then the focus of constitutional reform will be on a reconstructed Canada-without-Quebec rather than on the Canada-Quebec relationship.[10]

Yet if we step back from a fixation on constitutional formalities we can see that a new federal order is emerging. Since the narrow win by federalists in the 1995 Quebec referendum, Prime Minister Jean Chrétien has fundamentally re-written Quebec's relationship with the rest of Canada, and he has done so in line with longstanding nationalist ideologies in Quebec. In 1996 Parliament unilaterally changed the amending formula to provide Quebec with a veto on future constitutional change. Although this was done by 'lending' Parliament's veto to Quebec, and incidentally to other provinces or groups of provinces, Quebec's demand for a constitutional veto has now been met in practice. Constitutional change in Canada can proceed only with the consent of the Quebec National Assembly. At almost the same time as this change to the amending formula, Parliament enacted legislation requiring all branches of the federal government to take Quebec's distinctiveness into account in programmatic or distributional decisions. Quebec's distinctiveness has also been recognized by provincial legislatures, albeit in muted terms, by the Calgary Declaration. Finally, and most importantly, the social union framework orchestrated by the Prime Minister clearly sets Quebec apart from the other provinces.[11] The other nine will interact as a group with the federal government, and their programs will be increasingly tied to federal accountability, interprovincial agreements, and perhaps more onerous financial conditions imposed by the federal government. Quebec alone will stand apart, its jurisdictional integrity uncompromised. It may still harmonize its programs with other governments, but it is under no obligation to do so. This autonomy, moreover, comes with no financial risks. As Stéphane Dion, the federal Minister of Intergovernmental Affairs, stated in the House of Commons, the government of Canada intends 'to ensure that Quebecers reap the full benefits of this agreement. To this end, it will offer its full cooperation to the Government of Quebec at every opportunity.'[12] Signing on to the social union would thus have been pointless, even counterproductive, for Quebec. The province's political clout in Ottawa and the remaining threat of separatism ensures Quebec 'most favoured nation' status in its bilateral, one might say binational, negotiations with the federal government.

The upshot of all of this is that the Prime Minister has achieved for Quebec what the majority of Quebec nationalists have sought for the past 30 years—a distinct position within the Canadian federal system in which Quebec is not a province like the others but rather has the de facto status of a separate national community, dealing one-on-one with the government of Canada. This has been achieved, moreover, with no loss of political power in Ottawa. The new 9-1-1 form of federalism, in which the nine provinces other than Quebec negotiate as a group with Ottawa, which then negotiates bilaterally with Quebec, is reinforced by partisan dynamics. Quebec is not necessarily hurt in the division of spoils by the leverage provided by the ongoing threat of separation, and it is this threat that helps maintain the Liberal party's lock on national office. So long as the threat exists, the Liberals can run as the one national party that can hold the country together, just as the PQ can run as the party best able to ward off encroachments from Ottawa. It can be argued that this new model of federalism can only be sustained by a prime minister from Quebec, and here the Liberals hold all the trumps.

But is this new federal structure stable in the long run? It may be within Quebec, for it delivers a form of de facto sovereignty-association without the risks of sovereignty. Quebec maintains its autonomy, is able to block constitutional change, and is able to use its political leverage in Ottawa to ensure that no financial costs are imposed. The rhetoric of sovereignty will not be abandoned, for this provides power in Ottawa and ensures that the Liberals remain in national power. If instability is to emerge its origins are more likely to come from outside Quebec, where Canadians may begin to question the incongruity of Quebec's de facto disengagement from Canada coupled with Quebec's continued dominance of the Canadian Parliament. In the short term, however, I suspect that the Prime Minister's new federal vision will endure. The Prime Minister may have delivered on the ultimate paradox: an independent Quebec within a strong Canada.

CONCLUSION

After more than a generation of constitutional crisis and debate, Canadian federalism appears to have settled into an uneasy if still somewhat fragile peace. Quebec's quest for formal constitutional recognition as a distinct society has come up short, but most of the de facto rudiments of sovereignty-association have been put into place without financial loss or diminished power in Ottawa. The West's quest for institutional reform has failed completely, but the region is prosperous and the relevance of the national government has been reduced by the inexorable dynamics of globalization. Although Aboriginal governments still lack full constitutional articulation, this does not appear to impose any significant political or legal constraint. Thus it appears that our inability to change the formal rules of political life has been effectively offset by a good measure of informal accommodation and change.

At the same time, we must keep in mind that the federal nature of the underlying society continues to be transforming at a rapid, indeed accelerating rate. Individuals have become enmeshed in a dazzling communications revolution that is radically altering the territorial dimensions of Canadian life. New political identities are pushing to the fore, identities that in many cases have no federalism anchor or point of reference. Canadians are stretching their political identities in ways that bear little relationship to formal federal structures. Urban and Aboriginal governments are seeking nothing less than a fundamental transformation of Canadian governance. All of this signals a growing disconnect between the political lives Canadians lead and the federal political institutions within which those lives are led. In the not too distant future that disconnect could ignite a new debate on the most basic features of the Canadian state and governance. Patterns of institutional continuity, therefore, must not blind us to ongoing and rapid change in the nature of Canadian society. The impact of this change on federalism can be delayed, but it cannot be denied over the long term.

NOTES

1 Donald Creighton, *The Passionate Observer: Selected Writings* (Toronto: McClelland and Stewart, 1980), 19.
2 The role that governments play in creating and nurturing social identities was first explored in the Canadian federalism context by Alan C. Cairns, 'The Governments and Societies of Canadian Federalism', *Canadian Journal of Political Science* 10 (1977), 695-726.
3 Samuel J. LaSelva, *The Moral Foundations of Canadian Federalism* (Montreal and Kingston: McGill-Queen's University Press, 1996).
4 Canada ranks among the oldest 25 countries in the current United Nations.
5 In relative terms there has been a greater demographic shift *within* the West—from Manitoba and Saskatchewan to Alberta and British Columbia—than there has been a shift into the region. In 1966, Manitoba and Saskatchewan combined had 9.6% of the national population, compared to 16.7% of the national population that lived in either Alberta or British Columbia. By 1996 these proportions had changed to 7.3% and 22.3% respectively.
6 See Rainer Knopff and F.L. Morton, *Charter Politics* (Scarborough: Nelson Canada, 1992).
7 For an insightful look at the social union rationale see Daniel Schwanen, 'More Than the Sum of Our Parts: Improving the Mechanisms of Canada's Social Union', *Commentary* 120, C.D. Howe Institute, Jan. 1999.
8 Rainer Knopff, 'Populism and the Politics of Rights: The Dual Attack on Representative Democracy', *Canadian Journal of Political Science* 31, 4 (Dec. 1998), 683-705.
9 The fifth of seven statements in the Calgary Declaration reads as follows: 'In Canada's federal system, where respect for diversity and equality underlines unity, the unique character of Quebec society, including its French-speaking majority, its culture and its tradition of civil law, is fundamental to the well-being of Canada. Consequently, the Legislature and Government of Quebec have a role to protect and develop the unique character of Quebec within Canada.'
10 For an initial discussion of the reconstruction of Canada-without-Quebec see Kenneth McRoberts, ed., *Beyond Quebec: Taking Stock of*

Canada (Montreal and Kingston: McGill-Queen's University Press, 1995). For a conceptual discussion of possible Canada-Quebec relationships see Roger Gibbins and Guy Laforest, eds, *Beyond the Impasse: Toward Reconciliation* (Montreal: Institute for Research on Public Policy, 1998).

11 The framework to improve the social union for Canadians was signed on 4 Feb. 1999, by the Prime Minister, all premiers other than Lucien Bouchard, and the two territorial leaders.

12 Statement by the Honourable Stéphane Dion, President of the Privy Council and Minister of Intergovernmental Affairs, House of Commons, Ottawa, 10 Feb. 1999.

7

'Coalitions of the Willing': The Search for Like-Minded Partners in Canadian Diplomacy

ANDREW F. COOPER

The search for partners persists as a central theme in Canadian diplomacy. As it has done throughout the post-1945 era, Canada plays the role of the quintessential joiner. The ingrained Canadian impulse has been to want not only to belong, but to play an active part in as many international organizations as possible.[1] Tactically, Canada has embraced coalition-building as its central mode of diplomatic operation. A constant principle of Canadian statecraft remains that Canada can do little by standing alone on the sidelines. The only way that Canada can influence the international agenda is through constructive involvement with other actors at the heart of the action. At one level, therefore, Canadian diplomacy has a considerable degree of continuity built into it. Yet, while it exhibits a solid core of recognizable features, Canadian diplomacy as conceptualized and practised at the end of the 20th century has undergone great changes. As in other areas of governance, shape shifting captures the essence of the uneven and multidirectional process found in Canadian diplomacy. What must be teased out, however, are both the changing sources and the distinctive accent of this activity. Embedded in an older architecture, Canadian diplomacy has been played out not only in a modified form but with a new scope and intensity. While much about the end results of this transition remains unclear, enough signals have come out to indicate that Canadian diplomacy is undergoing a process of transformation.

What stands out in this transformation is the fundamental duality of Canada's choice of diplomatic partners, a duality that has helped to balance Canada's core relationships. The dominant side of this search for partners has been expressed through association and joint activity with the United States and the other pivotal members within the Western alliance/industrial world. The institutional ties established through the North Atlantic Treaty Organization (NATO), the North American Air/Aerospace Defence Command (NORAD), and the Defence Production Sharing Agreement have traditionally positioned Canada as a loyal (if junior) partner. This set of strategically-oriented ties is embellished further by Canada's membership in a variety of mainstream economic forums, such as the General Agreement on Tariffs and Trade/World Trade Organization (GATT/WTO), the Organisation for Economic Co-operation and Development (OECD), the International Monetary Fund (IMF) and the World Bank, and the Group of Seven most industrialized countries (G7).

The motivation for this well-entrenched side of the search for partners is easily understood. By establishing a primary identification toward and running in tandem with this set of influential partners, Canada has gained a number of benefits. The image of Canada as a solid team player paid off in a number of ways throughout the post-1945 period. Canada's membership in the strategically-oriented Western alliance helped take care of Canada's own security needs. The wider set of arrangements, built up in the economic as well as the security domain, allowed Canada to sit at the high table of decision-makers. Canada's close association with the Western alliance or the 'Atlantic Community' also helped to alleviate the risks of estrangement from the US, Canada's central bilateral relationship and much larger neighbour in North America.

This interpretation of partnership, however, is one-sided; it needs to be expanded through a better appreciation of the other side of Canadian diplomacy. This alternative side highlights the tendency of Canada to cluster together with a very different group of countries, not the pivotal countries of the Western alliance/G7 but a loose network of so-called like-minded countries—the traditional candidates being Australia, New Zealand, and the Nordic countries—exhibiting a degree of common attitudes and common modes of diplomatic operation. From this less dominant perspective, Canada shares a sense of identity or belonging that is based not on close geographic proximity or the structure of power, but on an adherence to values and sentiments concerning the rules of the game within the international system. Traditionally, the hallmark feature of this like-minded group has been a bias toward institutionalism generally and multilateralism more specifically. Unquestionably, much of the impulse toward this alternative side for Canada derived from fear about entrapment by the US. All of the countries Canada tended to work with in this like-minded fashion were not those that were firmly attached to a single regional home, but rather those that straddled regions (Australia and New Zealand in Asia-Pacific, the Nordic countries in Europe). In addition to this attraction that was based on a shared situational dilemma, these countries were available because of their strong inclination toward good international citizenship. All of these countries were firmly attached to the ideals and operations of the United Nations and other international institutions.

The extent and impact of this alternative side of Canadian diplomacy should not be exaggerated. Structurally, the space available for these like-minded countries to make a difference was tightly constrained by the context of the Cold War and the system of bi-polarism. What influence these countries had in international affairs tended to be located at the margins of the global agendas. Situationally, the degree to which these like-minded countries opposed the great powers, especially the US, was limited. If willing to take on the US on selected issues, these countries remained supporters or even followers of the US. Even in disagreement, these countries could be considered the US's loyal opposition in the international system.[2]

Equally, though, the value of this like-minded diplomatic activity should not be underestimated. The explicit privileging of diplomacy is important here. Diplomacy and foreign policy are usually discussed as though they were synonymous, and there is some truth in this interpretation. The ends of diplomacy should be consistent with the ends of foreign policy. These ends, however, need to be separated from the means by which they are pursued. Diplomacy, from this more nuanced perspective, is about the set of instruments used in the conduct of international affairs; its techniques operate in the sphere of representation, information, communication, and negotiation. This refinement of emphasis highlights not only the institutional component (the work of the actual diplomats) but the machinery of diplomacy in the Canadian context.[3]

In terms of diplomatic practice, the like-minded countries could compensate in a collective fashion for their lack of structural capabilities and power resources by agility and a concentration of effort on specific issues. Their adoption of special functional roles such as bridge-building, mediation, and peacekeeping reinforced the notion that there is considerable value in the ability to play margins. Individually, an identification with this loose cluster of like-minded countries provided Canada with an extension of its sense of belonging. Although quite intangible in nature, this sense of belonging brings to the surface a larger and significant debate about the artificial or even the invented nature of this group identity. Certainly, an emphasis on belonging or shared identity in the relationship introduces serious questions about how much this alternative source of partnership has been based on the construct of an imaginary community not easily translated into diplomatic outcomes. At a more tangible level, conversely, this identification with the like-minded grouping may be interpreted as providing a key operational guide for more autonomous diplomatic activity. Determining who Canada 'is with' in the world, when examined through this different sort of lens, has significant behavioural implications. If Canada has another identity beyond that of being 'a safely predictable ally',[4] this more diffuse sense of belonging adds a greater element of nonconformity and spark to Canadian statecraft. As Arthur Andrew noted in his retrospective look at Canadian diplomacy after a long career in the Department of External Affairs, 'No Great power is going to encourage any country to play the role of gadfly, but the role is a necessary one and it can be played with an effect out of all proportion to the importance of the country doing it.... [This was a role Canada played] very effectively in co-operation with like-minded countries—the Scandinavians, Australia, New Zealand and others.'[5]

Nor, more significantly for this chapter, are there signs that this dualism is in the process of becoming a spent force in Canadian diplomacy. On the contrary, it may be argued that both of the two sides of this search for partners have become more closely defined. With the introduction of the Free Trade Agreement (FTA), followed by the North American Free Trade Agreement (NAFTA), the institutionalized nature of the first side of the search for partnership has been accentuated, in that this bilateral/regional approach has featured a more determined search for a tighter connection with the US. From this dominant perspective, estrangement in the Canada-US relationship is to be avoided at all costs. Denis Stairs goes so far as to say that there is only one imperative in Canadian foreign policy: 'the maintenance of a politically amicable, and hence economically effective, working relationship with the United States'.[6]

Paradoxically, as the dominant side of Canadian diplomacy has been tightened, there has been a corresponding opening up of the alternative design for diplomatic partners. That is to say, as the dominant assumption about the personality of Canada in international affairs has become more firmly solidified, many of the fundamental tenets about the subsidiary side of Canadian diplomacy have become more visible. With the shattering of the structural disciplines of the Cold War era, Canada has been provided with additional space for the creative use of statecraft across a fuller range of expanding global agendas. The greater salience accorded to multilateralism and institutions can be interpreted as contributing to the fuller expression of Canadian talents and outlooks. Along with and beside the more pronounced accommodationist strain in Canadian diplomacy associated with a tightened bilateralism/regionalism, this power shift brought with it a fresh tendency toward diversification and differentiation.

This evolutionary process is highlighted by the manner in which the issue of like-mindedness has been shape shifted, mutating significantly while hanging on to some of its older meaning. In the era of tight bi-polarity, like-mindedness was conceived and applied in a fixed or *table d'hôte* manner in terms of form, the range of actors involved, and intensity. In the looser post-Cold War period, by way of contrast, this side of Canadian diplomacy has taken on a more ad hoc character, with the concept of like-mindedness being transformed from a fixed to a diffuse or à la carte activity. In terms of definition and practice, the pattern of like-mindedness has been re-evaluated in the light of the changing context of international affairs. From a narrow and well-established cohort of countries, the scope of potential candidates for like-minded status has expanded. Even more strikingly, the concept of 'like-mindedness' is now more broadly defined. Although an array of like-minded countries remains at the core of selective coalitions of the willing, civil society generally and non-governmental organizations (NGOs) more specifically have become like-minded actors as well. Just as importantly, the intensity of this form of activity has increased greatly. From a cautious low-key style, like-mindedness has taken on a fast-moving quality. The role of gadfly long built into the concept of like-mindedness has become far more accentuated. With an engagement right across the spectrum of international affairs, the best-known of these coalitions of the willing has been directed toward nudging and tweaking the greats, especially the US, on selected issues in a determined and time-sensitive manner.

This pronounced (and unanticipated) component of the larger shape shift has arisen out of a combination of circumstances. In large part, the process became interconnected with the larger elements of transformation within global affairs. Many of these elements, it must be cautioned, did not come about just because of the end of the Soviet Union and bi-polarity. The number of both state and societal actors with a stake in international relations had expanded considerably through the 1960s and 1970s. During the same period, the agenda of international politics had opened up to a considerable extent—with the traditional dominance of the so-called 'high' security agenda relating to questions of war and peace being challenged by the ascendancy of the economic and social agendas. Without question, however, the pace and impact of these changes in the late 1980s and 1990s went well beyond those of the 1960s and 1970s. The scope of the international relations agenda became far more complex. Not only did the question concerning what the security agenda encompasses increasingly become the source of debate, but the economic and social agendas both widened and deepened. At the same time, the space for a wider group of actors to operate expanded considerably. The relaxation of the disciplines imposed by the Cold War not only provided greater opportunities for innovative action by secondary states, but also made more room available for a variety of sub-national/non-central actors as well as a host of non-state actors.[7]

The intensity of these features of international changes was reinforced by the spillover into diplomatic practice of new forms of technology and methods of communication. At the cutting edge of this shift was the highly publicized CNN effect, a media phenomenon that introduced a mixture of heightened focus and volatility into the public's perception of specific issues. Governments were pushed 'to do something' (or alternatively to pull away from doing something) because of the images presented by the media. In parallel fashion, NGOs could present their own alternative images and interpretations of issues and events.[8]

Finally, the role of personality must also be factored into this evolutionary process of shape shifting. The rise of like-mindedness in the late 1940s and early 1950s was closely associated with the Pearsonian era of Canadian diplomacy. In substance, this reference point for Canadian diplomacy corresponded to 'Mike' Pearson's own concerns about entrapment vis-à-vis the US. As he put it his *Memoirs*, 'In one form or another, for Canada, there was always security in numbers. We do not want to be left alone with our close friend and neighbour.'[9] The low-key style in which Pearson applied this principle went hand-in-hand with his preference for quiet diplomacy and behind-the-scenes problem-solving.

In his bid to launch a more active form of like-mindedness in the 1990s, Lloyd Axworthy as minister of foreign affairs has adopted an approach that is quite firmly embedded in the older architecture. Axworthy has frequently declared that Canadian diplomatic practice must be founded upon the notion of 'like-mindedness'. Addressing the question how best to adapt Canada's international contribution to a fast-changing global environment, Axworthy highlighted the centrality of this concept. As he suggested, 'In a globalized world ... co-operation with like-minded countries will be de rigueur.'[10]

Axworthy's interpretation of how this notion can and should be carried out, nonetheless, is very different from Pearson's. Indeed,

Axworthy's role as change agent includes a strange mix of the old and the new. Consistently with the older notion of diplomatic functionalism, Axworthy has placed great weight on issue-specific activity, or a logic of 'niche' selection vis-à-vis the process of coalition-building.[11] But Axworthy extended the boundaries of this focussed activity, and the speed with which it was applied. Functionalism, as practised in the Pearson era, legitimized the application of issue-specific strengths and skills. On the basis of this criterion, Canada should marshal its time and energy in a compartmentalized way. Instead of pointing Canada in a direction where it tried to 'do everything' and 'be everywhere', functionalism underscored the logic of Canada's defining its priorities, and calculating how its resources could be applied to maximum advantage.

Where Axworthy departed from the established tenets of the past was in his impatience with the static quality of the traditional form of like-mindedness. Explicitly, he wanted to liberate the like-mindedness concept from its identification with the fixed world view of the Pearson era to a more fluid focus on ad hoc issue-specific coalitions of the willing. This impatience was a longstanding condition, which may be traced back to Axworthy's younger days as a critical observer of Pearson's 'worth[y]' but 'grey and oh so solid' diplomacy. As neatly captured for instance in a series of newspaper articles Axworthy wrote for the *Winnipeg Free Press* in September 1965, this sense of impatience pointed toward diplomatic activity that was more noisy and public-oriented.[12]

THE TRADITIONAL PARADIGM OF LIKE-MINDEDNESS IN THE PEARSON ERA

When one looks more closely at Canadian diplomatic behaviour in the post-1945 period a number of features stand out that must be discussed in more detail. As rehearsed above, throughout the Pearson era (broadly defined as the period from the mid-1940s to the early 1960s) Canada adopted a dualistic pattern in terms of the countries it chose as diplomatic partners. John Holmes highlighted this mix in one of the many essays he wrote illuminating Canadian practices in international affairs: 'Canada has been encouraged to strengthen its independence by maintaining overlapping memberships in various clubs: NATO, the Commonwealth, and the shifting alignments of what the *Economist* called the "Sanitavian bloc" in the United Nations Assembly.'[13]

Holmes's phrasing alludes to the attitude that drives this search for a balanced diplomacy—what Andrew more bluntly calls 'a degree of cussedness in not accepting solutions or even "facts" as presented to us by the Powers, even by our friends'.[14] Yet, if motivated by a desire to offset the weight of the US and the other great powers, this behaviour was expressed in low-key words and deeds. In large part this mode of behaviour was conditioned by Canada's orientation toward problem-solving. Instead of being categorized as a system reformer, Canada is best described as a system maintainer. The key was to deliver results when and where they mattered, in times of crisis and deadlock.

With respect to where this type of balancing behaviour was located, pride of place was given to the UN system. Canada concentrated much of its efforts in international affairs upon working this system. Targeting and style went hand in hand, in that Canada's diplomatic approach was designed to be out of the public domain and uncontroversial. As George Ignatieff, Canada's UN ambassador in the mid-1960s, described the desired technique in one interview, 'No drama. No blood and guts. That's precisely what we try to avoid.'[15]

Reinforcing this UN orientation was the institutional-centrism of this diplomatic pattern. Certainly the experience of working together on a wide number of issues was encouraged by the structural design of the UN itself. Canada was placed in the catch-all 'Western Europe and Others Group' (WEOG), which included not only the United States and the Western European countries but Australia and New Zealand. Consequently, Canada had some considerable practical incentive for adhering to a sense of like-mindedness in addition to any perception of a shared outlook on ideas and values. To ensure that lobbying, the sponsoring of resolutions, and other diplomatic activity was effective, Canada needed to work together with selected members of this group on an ongoing basis.

As a result of the kudos received from outsiders, the design of like-mindedness has helped ingrain the cult of Canadian diplomacy (and the Canadian diplomat) in this so-called 'golden age' as a success story. Henry Kissinger, for example, extolled the high quality of Canada's diplomatic contribution: 'Canadian leaders had a narrow margin of maneuver that they utilized with extraordinary skills.'[16] This positive sentiment, in turn, contributed to the constant (and often nostalgic) refrain from participants and spectators about the need for a revitalization of like-mindedness. To quote Andrew again, the advice was that there will always 'be a need for a few "floaters"—well informed diplomatic operators who do not subscribe to any particular view of political or economic orthodoxy but who are willing to pay their dues and able to encourage the voices of reason.'[17]

Still, the robustness of this traditional aspect of Canadian like-minded diplomacy should not be oversold. Despite the occasional bursts of higher-profile activity (for instance, when Canada, New Zealand, and the Nordic countries made special pledges in the 1960s to make up the deficit in the UN peacekeeping fund), like-mindedness did not translate into deep engagement. The bulk of this activity appears to have been directed to the sharing of information, the exchange of views, the explaining of positions, and the floating of ideas. The main ingredient was the development of a habit of consultation. The character of the organizational structure was extremely loose, with a high tolerance for differences and rival ambitions. No secretariat existed. The obligations were minimal.

TRUDEAU TO MULRONEY

Although the traditional paradigm of like-mindedness is strongly identified with the Pearson era, it would be misleading to conclude that this notion faded away completely during the Trudeau and Mulroney years. Amid all the other controversies and tilts associated with the Trudeau ascendancy in the late 1960s and 1970s, the sense of like-mindedness not only survived but at least on particular issues actually flourished. A case in point was the Law of the Sea (LOS). Low on the priority list in the 1950s, this protracted round of multilateral negotiations came to the forefront of Canadian foreign policy in the 1970s. When building a coalition, Canada placed much store in working through a loose assembly of like-minded countries, the so-called Group of 12 (also known as the 'good Samaritans'), which comprised, in addition to Canada, Austria, Denmark, Finland, Iceland, Ireland, the Netherlands, Norway, Sweden, Switzerland, Australia, and New Zealand. At the same time, Canada patiently tried to tackle intricate technical (and increasingly scientific and legal) issues.[18]

As exhibited in the test case of North-South relations, however, Trudeau was no more interested than Pearson in extending like-minded diplomacy beyond traditional limits. By the late 1970s, a number of Canada's traditional like-minded allies (led by Norway and the Netherlands, with support from Sweden and Denmark) tried to push the boundaries of like-mindedness forward at the level both of structure and of action. Procedurally, this push was directed toward a more explicit recognition of this organizational form by the use of the label 'the Like-Minded Group of States'. Substantively, the focus was on a linkage between the activities of this like-minded group and, generally, the agenda of the New International Economic Order (NIEO) advocated by the Group of 77 developing countries, and, more specifically, such policies as a Common Fund, the purpose of which was a redistribution from the industrial North to the industrializing South.

Canada failed to support this attempt to stretch the boundaries of like-mindedness. Canada's sense of identity with this grouping of like-minded countries did not translate into a willingness to move the organizational format from a loose to a tight structure and to raise the level of policy co-ordination and interaction. The Canadian view of the like-minded grouping was that it should act as an informal assembly of countries rather than as a formalized coalition. Moreover, Canada's concerns about belonging to a tight partnership of like-minded countries were underscored by its cautious stance on the agenda to be pursued. The focus of Canada's diplomacy remained primarily the reduction of conflict and tension in the global arena through dialogue and confidence-building measures. Canada was reluctant, nevertheless, to be drawn into any action that entailed long-term obligations. When drawn in this direction, Canada pulled back to a less committed position on the North-South agenda. As one observer noted, 'In several cases, and especially in the important case of Canada, member-states in the Like-Minded Group totally ignored what had been advocated in the group's discussions when forming their policies on the Common Fund'.[19]

A similar blend of change and continuity persisted during the Mulroney period. Because of the FTA/NAFTA initiatives, the widespread opinion about the Mulroney government has been that it subordinated like-mindedness to the attraction of bilateralism. According to those who disagreed with his position, the Mulroney government had become fixated on the Canada-US relationship at the expense of all other options. This view is represented in the world of the practitioner/scholar by the stark assessment of Andrew that Canada had moved in the Mulroney years from 'the precariously balanced policies required of a Middle Power to become a safely predictable ally'.[20] From the world of journalism, frequent calls were made for Canada to return to the grouping 'we really belong to' by forming 'our own G-15 or G-20, a gang of the larger "middle powers" with the collective clout to make itself heard'.[21] From the world of partisan politics, critics tore into the Mulroney government for failing to seize the multiple opportunities available in alternative modes of diplomatic partnership because of its close and passive followership to the US. In the words of Lloyd Axworthy, from his position as opposition foreign policy spokesperson, this blinkered vision was seen especially in the Mulroney government's 'forgetting the need to seek out coalitions of like-minded nations now becoming more numerous'.[22]

There is no question at all that these critical assessments are correct in identifying the overall priorities of the Mulroney government. By design, like-mindedness was subordinated to the nurturing of an institutionalized special relationship with the US. Yet, even with this tilt, there remained some room at the margins for like-minded diplomatic activity on an ad hoc basis. One illustration that comes to mind revolved around the issue of UN reform and the 'new world order'. As part of its effort to help Boutros Boutros-Ghali, as UN Secretary General, develop the document *An Agenda for Peace*, Canada associated with the familiar like-minded countries. In January 1992, the CANZ (Canada, Australia, and New Zealand) and the Nordic countries submitted a joint brief to the UN Secretary General. This brief focussed on the need both for forward-looking assessments about potential crisis situations and for the Security Council to make greater efforts to involve other UN member states in its deliberations.[23] Another illustration comes out of the fisheries issue in the context of the agenda-setting stage of the 1992 Rio conference. From the outset of the UN Conference on Environment and Development (UNCED) negotiations, Canada concentrated on working with a small group of coastal countries, Iceland, New Zealand, Argentina, and Chile; Norway and Peru joined later on. This core group shared, to some extent at least, a similar diagnosis of the problem and a similar framework for solutions. After a number of preliminary meetings these countries co-sponsored the so-called Santiago resolution prior to the actual Rio meeting. Maintaining this mode of diplomatic partnership, John Crosbie, Fisheries and Oceans minister in the Mulroney government, convened a forum, explicitly labeled the 'Like-Minded States Meeting', that met 21-24 January 1993 in St John's, Newfoundland.

Here it needs to be added that some of the tilt away from like-mindedness by the Mulroney government came not by design but by default. The classic episode of this sort centred on the so-called Cairns group of agricultural trading countries. At the launching point of this coalition of smaller and middle-sized agricultural reformers, in August 1986, the Mulroney government embraced it as an effective mechanism to defuse and resolve the tensions of the export subsidy 'war' between the United States and the European Community/Union. As the Cairns initiative progressed, nonetheless, the Mulroney government's partnership commitments lagged. Initially, this reversal stemmed from the traditional Canadian reservations about belonging to a formal association of like-minded countries. Subsequently, these reservations turned to fear concerning the broadening of the agenda. With the ratcheting up of the demands by the other members of this grouping for not only external but also internal agricultural reforms (reforms that would cut into the Canadian supply management system of marketing boards, domestic quotas, and import regulations), Canada's continued membership in the coalition was called into question. These differences were finessed to the extent that at least one Canadian trade official could give a Mackenzie King-like answer to the question whether Canada belonged to the Cairns group or not: 'We're part of it, but we're not part of it.'[24] This diplomatic agility could not hide the feelings of some members of the Mulroney government that this episode demonstrated the need to more closely discern the extent to which like-mindedness actually existed in practice before any coalition-building exercise took place. The sting from this lesson could be felt in the words of Pat Carney, the former Conservative trade minister, on the Cairns experience: 'If you're dealing with coalitions you have to be careful you're not acting like a highwayman and dealing with a bunch of bandits you put together for certain issues.'[25]

From this brief review, it is apparent that the ingrained notion of like-mindedness could still act as a guide for Canadian diplomacy on specific issues long after the 'golden age' of the Pearson era. At the same time, though, the notion had not been advanced either conceptually or operationally in any new dramatic fashion. An embedded sense of convenience rather than a marked commitment underscored the approach. Rather than being a catalyst for a dramatic process of shape shifting, and a re-invention of Canada's diplomatic personality, this pattern of diplomacy had become thoroughly routinized. If like-mindedness still benefitted from a degree of comfort attached to its sense of familiarity, its foundations had become ripe for review.

THE RETURN OF THE LIBERALS AND THE EVOLUTION OF 'COALITIONS OF THE WILLING'

The overall performance of the Chrétien Liberal government since October 1993 has been marked by a number of policy reversals: a shift from opposition to NAFTA to accommodation with it; a shift toward deficit reduction rather than job creation; and a shift from a foreign policy oriented toward human rights to one centred on trade. Yet, alongside and amid these reversals has come a greater emphasis on like-minded coalitions. The re-emergence and transformation of like-mindedness, however, only occurred slowly. André Ouellet, during his tenure as foreign minister, provided little leadership in this direction. To a certain extent, this delay could be excused because of the immediate distractions that Ouellet faced. As the political minister for Quebec as well as minister of foreign affairs, Ouellet's attention was fixed firmly on the upcoming Quebec referendum. Harnessed to the tenets of the Liberal Red Book and its supplement, the Liberal Foreign Policy Handbook, Ouellet allowed for the possibility of like-minded diplomatic activity.[26] But his own preference was clearly for a cautious low-key mode of activity. As he suggested in an early appearance before the House of Commons Standing Committee on Foreign Affairs and International Trade, 'As a medium-sized country, it is obvious that we will not call the shots. We have to be humble enough to realize this. But in cooperation with others we could influence a lot of decisions.'[27]

The return of like-mindedness as a robust feature to Canadian diplomacy is often associated with Lloyd Axworthy, who took over the position of foreign minister from Ouellet in January 1996. Indeed, the renewal and reinvigoration of this notion has been identified as part of a coherent program that at least two commentators have termed the Axworthy doctrine.[28] In their depiction of this doctrine, Hampson and Oliver include the positioning of Canada at the core of a select grouping of like-minded (and high-minded) actors pursuing a form of 'moral multilateralism'.[29] There can be no doubt that Axworthy's personal views have strongly influenced the recent evolution in the concept of like-mindedness. As Liberal opposition spokesperson, Axworthy had contrasted the Mulroney government's 'forgetfulness' with his own adherence to an ambitious form of like-minded diplomatic activism. Even during his fairly short but extremely frustrating detour as minister of Human Resources Development, Axworthy found time to reiterate this theme. As he testified on one occasion, his belief in the need for a revitalized approach to diplomacy remained firm: 'There are similar countries who have similar interests. We should get together ... as a grouping, as a coalition, to try to move the agenda on some of these issues of structural employment ... and try to redefine the UN mandate in terms of these security issues as far as individuals are concerned.'[30]

To highlight Axworthy's position is not to ignore a number of contextual elements that facilitated the renewal of like-mindedness. In domestic structural terms, the concept of like-mindedness had become deeply embedded in the discourse and activity of the foreign policy bureaucracy going back to the Pearson era. As such, the search for alternative partners remained important. Politically, Axworthy's embrace of a more ambitious form of coalitions of the willing offered some compensation for the embrace by the Liberal government of a neo-liberal agenda, which was dominated by the Prime Minister's high-profile activity on Team Canada trade missions and Finance Minister Paul Martin's fight for deficit reduction. A diplomatic 'double vision' meshed well with the search for balance between economic and non-economic goals. Internationally, the erosion of the disciplines of the Cold War era meant not only a widened agenda but a greater constellation of potential like-minded actors who could tackle global problems issue by issue.

Nor, must it be added, should this privileging of 'like-mindedness' diplomacy minimize the other components of Axworthy's personal doctrine. Certainly, Hampson and Oliver have concentrated mainly on Axworthy's goals in the domain of human security: the focussing of security goals 'around human security and not state security', and 'the promulgation of new norms'. Although listed as means, some of the other components of Axworthy's doctrine are better analysed as having become ends in themselves. The obvious example of this blurring between how Canada should play its cards and for what purpose occurs on the question of 'soft' power (or the exercise of influence by the promotion of values and dissemination of information) as 'the new currency in international politics'.[31]

As we move from conceptualization to operation, it is valuable to examine three case studies as snapshots of this emergent type of like-mindedness or coalitions of the willing. The first of these cases is the Canadian-led initiative in the African Great Lakes region at the end of 1996. This case featured an attempt to put together a Multinational Force (MNF) to aid Rwandan refugees threatened by the escalating ethnic fighting/civil war centred in Zaire. Although highly controversial both in its motivation and its consequences, this initiative was portrayed by Axworthy as a good illustration of the ability of like-minded countries 'to get things done by building coalitions ... rather than by coercion'.[32] Axworthy's officials explicitly termed the 14-country Steering Committee put together after three weeks a 'coalition of the willing'.[33]

A second case features the coalition of the like-minded at the core of the campaign to ban anti-personnel land mines. As early as 1995, a core group of pro-ban nations was identified. Subsequently, these countries were 'brought together to plan further collaboration, and it was those nations that remained in the lead' through to the take-off point associated with a conference held in Ottawa from 3-5 October

1996, at which moment Axworthy challenged other countries to return to the Canadian capital in fourteen months (December 1997) to sign an international treaty.[34] This episode was widely regarded as an operational model, because of its transformational quality, in that this coalition was regarded as having 'the power to change the dynamics and direction of the international agenda'.[35]

The third case highlights the efforts of some 44 like-minded countries in pushing for progress on a charter for a strong and permanent International Criminal Court (ICC) in the run-up to and during the 1998 UN Rome conference on the issue. Dubbed by some as 'the Group of Lifeline Nations', this coalition sought an independent court with an independent prosecutor, as opposed to a body under Security Council control. This coalition held together from 1995 to 1998, a period in which the emphasis was on the development of a detailed draft treaty.[36]

At first glance, a sense of the traditional attributes of Canadian like-mindedness still lingers in all of these episodes. All three cases focussed on some form of shared activity directed toward the multilateral arena. Bilateral solutions, especially in respect to deals cut between the great powers, were uniformly treated with suspicion. The organizational mechanisms continued to be loose and flexible, with no formal structure such as a secretariat. At the heart of all of this sort of activity remained the traditional grouping of like-minded countries, featuring the Nordics, Australia, New Zealand, and some of the other smaller or medium-sized European countries. Canada kept in close contact with Australia, Norway, Sweden, Denmark, and the Netherlands as well as Spain and Belgium in developing the Zaire MNF. Australia, New Zealand, and the Nordic states were out in front with Canada on the ICC. On the land mines case, Canada, Belgium, the Netherlands, Austria, Norway, Denmark, Ireland, Australia, New Zealand, Germany, and Switzerland became part of the 'core group'.[37] Indeed, the comfort level was enhanced by a rough division of labour that developed between some of these core countries. Australia, for example, drafted the treaty text. Germany took on the compliance issues. Norway hosted the final treaty negotiations in September 1997.

When these episodes are looked at more closely, however, it can be seen that these ingrained components of like-mindedness had become overshadowed by the push for new forms of coalitions of the willing.

The fixed method of diplomatic activity was replaced by an ad hoc menu. As for their intensity, all of these campaigns featured a good deal of speed and energy. Instead of the reactive quality so firmly entrenched in traditional like-mindedness, the emergent coalitions of the willing of the 1990s have been activist and mission-oriented. Put another way, these episodes showcase a form of 'just in time' diplomatic practice. For example, one of the strongest images that comes out of the Zaire/Great Lakes intervention is the extensive use of telephone diplomacy by Prime Minister Chrétien—he repeatedly phoned leaders of the potential coalition countries to try to get the MFN initiative off the ground. Another image is the use of a form of 'virtual diplomacy'. An upgrading of the technological capacities of the Department of Foreign Affairs and International Trade (DFAIT) was seen as vital to enabling the 'mobility of our operations [to allow] rapid responses to emergencies and to situations which require temporary communications hookups ... during such crises as Zaire where Canada formed a virtual team with members in Africa, Ottawa, New York and Washington'.[38]

With respect to the trigger for action, all of these cases were influenced by the structural change found within the international system. Mobilization of coalitions of the willing was facilitated by the erosion of the discipline of the bi-polar system in the post-Cold War era. Autonomy of action was extended as the common enemy disappeared and the concept of security became extended to include non-military issues. In some cases, such as the Zaire/Great Lakes intervention, this autonomy allowed clear demonstrations of like-minded leadership behaviour. Frustrated by the lack of action on the part of the US and Britain, smaller and medium-sized countries tried to fill the gap. In other cases, such as those of the land mines and the International Criminal Court, this autonomy allowed more space for disagreement between the coalitions of the willing and the permanent members of the Security Council (and especially the US, France, Russia, and China).

At the same time, some of these episodes were triggered by specific events that raised the stakes and allowed mobilization to proceed. The clearest illustration of an external stimuli's acting as a catalyst for a coalition of the willing occurred in the Zaire/Great Lakes initiative. From the outset of this crisis, it was the need for the international community to do something (and do something quickly) about the refugee crisis in Central Africa that determined the tone of Prime Minister Chrétien's statements. In the press conference held on 12 November 1996 to announce the initiative, the Prime Minister declared, 'Canada may not be a superpower but we are a nation that speaks on the international scene with great moral authority.... Now is the time to use that moral authority to stop suffering, avert disaster.'[39] Domestic stimuli played a part as well, with highly visible segments of the Canadian public calling for quick action on all of these cases. In the case of land mines, for instance, public opinion was crucial in turning the activity of the coalition of the willing away from the stalled arms control negotiations in the UN Disarmament Commission toward alternative channels. Multilateral diplomacy 'of the many' was replaced by group activity 'with small numbers' to force the issue. As Maxwell Cameron has put it, 'Multilateralism is fine as long as states are prepared to move as fast as the slowest in the pack, but coalitions of the like-minded are preferable when the public wants results.'[40]

The range of actors involved in these coalitions of the willing has also been considerably expanded. One aspect of the change from a fixed to a more ad hoc expression is a reinforcement of the notion of cross-cutting coalitions, involving a greater array of countries not only from the developed but from the developing world. If the traditional core of like-minded countries remains necessary, they are no longer sufficient for the application of this mode of diplomacy. Although he framed the question more in the context of a coalition of the willing-big power differentiation, Axworthy picked up on this theme at the country level in his *International Journal* article on human security: 'The concept of a 'like-minded country' is assuming a whole new meaning. Though Canada will continue to work with established allies in many fields, it will increasingly work with new partners.... Issue-based coalitions will become as important to the management of Canadian foreign policy as the alliance structure once was.'[41]

This greater inclusiveness in the concept of the coalition of the willing provides both symbolic and tangible benefits. Working with a number of non-traditional countries helped increase the credibility and efficiency of these coalitions. At times, this activity also compensated for a decline in the support offered by the traditional like-minded, or for that matter any discomfort in that relationship (a discomfort brought to the fore by Axworthy's challenge in December 1997, to which countries such as Australia and Belgium responded negatively). One good example of this mixed pattern of coalition activity is South Africa's role on the International Criminal Court. South Africa brought not only a considerable degree of moral authority to the cause, but a wealth of practical experience (highlighted by the work of Judge Richard Goldstone on the trials of suspected war criminals in the former Yugoslavia). South Africa offered a viable means for extending the regional support for the ICC. Specifically, South Africa was instrumental in getting the Southern African Development Community (SADC) countries on side with respect to the ICC initiative. Another example was the support offered by a number of Latin American countries. The increased targeting of these countries as potential partners both inside[42] and outside[43] of government is a significant example of the expansion of the range of alternative diplomatic partnerships. Getting Mexico and many Central American countries on side was important for both the credentials and the operation of the land mines coalition. The support of Mexico, Argentina, and Costa Rica buttressed the ICC campaign.

In cases where it proved difficult to get non-traditional countries firmly on board, initiative diplomacy foundered. The prime case in point here is the Zaire/Great Lakes mission. Partially as a result of Prime Minister Chrétien's campaign of personal telephone diplomacy, which targeted President Nelson Mandela for special attention, South Africa had originally offered to provide support (possibly even including troops) for the operation.[44] Sensitive to charges that it was subordinating a comprehensive 'made in Africa' solution to an 'outside' (and inadequate) form of international intervention, however, South Africa soon pulled back from this initial burst of enthusiasm.

The other face of this change from a set to an ad hoc menu involves the increased scope of engagement taking place between governments and NGOs. At one end of the range of interactive behaviour,[45] NGOs have acted as catalysts for action, a pattern by which the activity of NGOs stimulates corresponding or complementary activities by governments. At the core of this dynamic is a triggering effect, in which out-in-front behaviour on the part of NGOs helps frame the agenda for action by government. It was the call for help from societal groups, loosely clustered around the Rwanda NGO Executive Committee, that did much to prepare the way for the Zaire/Great Lakes initiative. Organizations such as the Red Cross, Oxfam, Care Canada, and Médecins sans frontières all sent out early warnings that the refugee situation in Central Africa was deteriorating because of the changes on the ground in October and early November 1996. A number of NGOs, most notably Amnesty International, Human Rights Watch, and the Lawyers Committee for Human Rights, performed a similar triggering role on the ICC. For its part, the anti-land mines campaign provides a classic episode of this triggering effect. Beginning in the early 1990s, the International Committee of the Red Cross (ICRC) was mobilized into action against the 'scourge' of land mines by its field workers. Going beyond the organization's traditional low-key, technical mode of operation, the Red Cross took the lead in gathering a broad-based NGO coalition calling for a 'total ban on the production, export and use of anti-personnel mines'.[46] Eventually united under the auspices of the International Campaign to Ban Land Mines, this NGO coalition included the Vietnam Veterans of America, the German group Medico International, and the French group Handicap International, together with Human Rights Watch and Physicians for Human Rights.

At the other end of this interactive behaviour is some type of strategic alliance, through which know-how is shared and some mode of formal or informal division of labour established. Notwithstanding its problematic nature, the Zaire/Great Lakes initiative demonstrated the extent to which a form of partnership between government officials and NGOs could be forged. In the field, some military equipment (including transport planes) was made available to NGOs. And NGOs were included in MNF briefing sessions. Domestically, a Zaire NGO-Military Coordination committee was established with representatives from World Vision, Médecins sans frontières, the Canadian Red Cross, and Care Canada, together with officials from DFAIT, the Department of National Defence (DND), and the Canadian International Development Agency (CIDA).

More thoroughly, this sense of strategic alliance stands out on the land mines case. Axworthy and his DFAIT officials formed what amounted to a mutual admiration society with the NGOs. From one side, Axworthy talked of the campaign to ban land mines as a clear example of 'a new approach to international diplomacy ... a coalition of the willing, including governments and civil society as equal partners, united around a set of core principles'.[47] From the other side, Jody Williams, the 1997 Nobel Peace Prize winner, lauded the actions of Canada and other like-minded countries for challenging the status quo. At the October 1996 conference, she praised Axworthy for his 'courage to call the question'. After Axworthy completed his speech at the opening of the December 1997 conference, Williams led a standing ovation.

In operational terms, the activities of the governments and those of the NGOs in the land mines campaign complemented and supplemented each other. As readily acknowledged by the participants, these partners remained in close contact with each other through the negotiating process and the working out of the final form of a draft treaty. In the words of one official, 'There were daily phone calls with governments and the NGO partners. Anti-mine conferences, special events and concerts were planned and executed.'[48] At the same time, the NGO network helped bend public opinion toward the proposals offered by the coalition of the willing. Among other things, this network provided over the Internet 'The Good List' of Nations calling for a Comprehensive Ban on Antipersonnel Land Mines.

QUESTIONING CANADA'S PATTERN OF DIPLOMACY

Several questions must be asked about the implications of this shape shifting in Canadian diplomacy. The first turns on the issue of what this variable pattern of diplomacy means in terms of influence. As previously noted, the advocates of an extended form of like-minded diplomacy cast this activity in a positive light as the best way of breaking through inertia and top-down domination. The mutation toward an ad hoc approach is said to generate not only immediate benefits in terms of mobilization of support on specific issues but progress toward longer-term systemic reform. The key is to take risks through the activation and focussed targeting of a centrifugally oriented diplomacy.

Dissenting voices assess Canada's performance in a very different manner. Rather than raising Canada's position on the world stage, ad hoc coalitions of the willing are said to threaten Canada's status in international affairs. By identifying itself with a multi-faceted group of high-minded but not pivotal like-minded actors, it is argued, Canada has moved away from a more appropriate centripetal approach, to the margins of diplomacy. This sense that Canada's coalition behaviour is reducing its status comes out most forcefully in Conrad Black's stinging critique of this diplomatic pattern: 'Canadians tend to feel keenly that Canada is on the verge of becoming a country of the first rank but it is not widely perceived to be so. To be at the forefront of a large group of secondary powers such as the Scandinavians and the Dutch and even the Australians is something of an underachievement for a wealthy nation of some 30 million people.'[49]

Looking at the issue of influence from an instrumental perspective, the importance of this question can be exaggerated. Particular coalitions of the willing, such as that in the land mines case, may be viewed as providing opportunities for Canada and other non-big powers to make a difference on specific issues. Yet, even as this sort of issue has become higher-profile, its long-term impact remains contested. For some observers, the key issue is the legitimacy of the public diplomacy utilized by the coalitions of the willing. For others, it is an issue of whether diplomacy is becoming democratized through the participation of transnational NGOs, or, conversely, whether these actors have become co-opted by a concept and practice that is closely identified with the state and with patterns of inter-governmental relations. While resurgent, this alternative expression of Canadian diplomacy remains in any case only one side—and ultimately the far less crucial side—of Canada's personality in international affairs. The Axworthy doctrine and the cultivation of a more robust and multidimensional form of diplomatic style should not be seen as a break with the past, but as a corrective to the dominant side. Like-minded coalition partnerships remain, as in the past, a sign of a balancing component vis-à-vis Canada's core relationships with the US and its pivotal alliance and economic partners.

A second question about coalitions of the willing rests on the issue of resources. An argument can be made that ad hoc diplomatic initiatives provide not only a general defence against a retreat from internationalism but, more specifically, some leverage against a concentration of resources on the trade and economic dossiers in DFAIT.

Against the current of budget cuts, these initiatives have been able to draw on new pools of additional funding. In the run up to the Rome conference on the ICC, $46.8 million was given to the War Crimes section of the Justice Department to allow more effective searches for war criminals residing in Canada. The provisional MNF for the Zaire/Great Lakes initiative was allocated a budget of $11 million. At the time of the international signing conference of the Ottawa Convention in December 1997, a $100 million Canadian Land Mines Fund (CLF) was set up. A contribution of $300,000 was made from this CLF to the NGO Mines Action Canada.

Critics look at this ad hoc trend in Canadian diplomacy in a far more pessimistic fashion. Rather than viewing these initiatives as a means to secure adequate funding, they cast this form of mobilization and focussed activity as a drain, in budgetary terms. One of the most scathing aspects of the critique provided by Hampson and Oliver on the Axworthy doctrine is in respect to its financial implications. They charge that this activity has a distorting effect: '[T]hough [it is] rich in platitudes and expensive policy-planning exercises and mega-conferences', the net effect is 'nickel diplomacy'.[50] Kim Nossal, in one of his typical, evocative phrases, sums up the trend as 'internationalism on the cheap', or 'penny-pinching diplomacy'.[51]

These critics, identifying this form of ad hoc diplomacy as a component of a 'soft power' agenda, contrast the emphasis that has been placed on it with the lack of emphasis given to 'hard power' in the form of defence and intelligence assets. In principle, this connection makes sense. Few would disagree that the Rwanda/Great Lakes crisis can be used to indicate, not the expanded definition of the security agenda, but the ingrained significance of the military component of the security agenda. While Canadian strengths centred around diplomatic bargaining could be appreciated (and prove useful), these same strengths could be quickly sapped if and when placed in situations where military capabilities were vital. Yet, in practice, it is far more difficult to make the case that the absence of this initiative-oriented diplomacy would enable the defence budget to be strengthened. The problem of a lack of military capability is grounded in fundamental choices already made by the Canadian public. As Nossal himself contends, '"defence lite" [remains] pleasing to most Canadians (and their pocketbooks).'[52]

The resource question arises in a more serious way in relation to the issue whether these ad hoc initiatives have cut into other programs under the mandate of DFAIT. The main concern here is that these initiatives have drained funds away from established programs, namely development assistance. Nossal, for example, makes a broad connection between the rise of ad hoc initiatives and budgetary cutbacks: 'This notion [of selective internationalism] makes more understandable the apparent paradox of the minister of foreign affairs, Lloyd Axworthy, pursuing what appears to be an internationalist effort to ban anti-personnel land mines while at the same time allowing the development assistance budget to shrink toward the .3 per cent of GNP mark.'[53]

The accuracy of this line of criticism is reinforced by the appearance of a direct displacement effect on resource allocation away from development assistance programs to these ad hoc initiatives. Indeed, it has been argued by Cranford Pratt that spending on these forms of diplomatic engagement has come at the cost of spending on longer-term programs. He bluntly says that Axworthy has engineered a resource grab on CIDA by DFAIT: '[Axworthy] is ambitious that Canada should play a more prominent role on issues of common human security. His style is spontaneous, the focus of his interests shifts frequently, and he expects rapid and cooperative responses from the bureaucracy. However, many of the issues which concern him fall within CIDA's orbit. To finance initiatives which he desires, CIDA is therefore pressed to move funds away from activities that are integral to its existing programs.'[54]

A third and final question is whether or not there is a solid logic built into this alternative side of Canadian diplomacy. On the one side, there seems to be a good deal of justification for coalitions of the willing that are conducted by means of multiple but selective initiatives. The application of the principle of 'niche' selection has allowed Canada and its coalition partners to play to their specialized interests, task-related experience, and reputational qualifications. Collectively, this activity offers the possibility of building up constructive teams on a case-to-case basis. In Axworthy's own words, the purpose is to make a difference: 'I'm not advocating such partnerships as some sort of feel-good diplomacy. I'm advocating them because they work.'[55]

By way of contrast, commentators decidedly less enthusiastic about the practice of this mode of diplomacy focus not on its rationality but on its emotional and volatile flavour. From this critical standpoint, rather than providing a framework for structuring Canadian diplomacy on a rational basis, this approach imposes a sense of awkwardness and even ill-discipline. The built-in instinct is to look 'for a quick fix rather than developing a sustained, coherent, long-term strategy'.[56]

As was the case for the other questions, the answer to this question appears to be inconclusive. The campaigns on land mines and the ICC stirred passions. But the logic of the enterprise was widely appreciated. The Great Lakes/Zaire episode was far more problematic. At least in its public statements, DFAIT took the line that the initiative had proved a major instrumental success. Assistant Deputy Minister of Foreign Affairs Paul Heinbecker stated, for instance, 'We are quite satisfied we have achieved the largest part of our mission.'[57] Any image of success for the Rwanda/Great Lakes initiative, however, has remained highly contested. Some critics saw the lack of staying power of the initiative as symptomatic of the rise of a 'quick fix' mentality. Others highlighted the image of Canada as a coalition-leader and as an innocent abroad, 'bedeviled by international politics and, perhaps, naiveté on the part of Canadian diplomats and politicians'.[58]

Faced with internal criticisms like these it appears likely that this activist and ad hoc form of Canadian diplomacy will eventually subside. Notwithstanding Canada's ingrained adherence to the like-minded notion, a shift from its older, low-key habits to the targeting and selling of ambitious coalitions of the willing necessitates a major leap. The recent willingness and capacity to take lunges in this direction reflects the greater room for manoeuvre and margin of safety provided to Canada at the end of the 20th century. It also signifies that with Lloyd Axworthy there has been a Canadian foreign minister ready and eager to embrace the moment. Eventually, though, such a change in habits risks producing fatigue. More to the point, the fundamental structural limits placed on Canada's international activity will be imposed. Still, until these factors kick in, the altered yet familiar shape of Canadian diplomacy will likely continue to evolve in the near future. A case in point has been the suggestion that Canada should play a more supportive role for the so-called 'New Agenda coalition' in its bid to eliminate nuclear weapons. Although the details of this suggestion are unclear, any emergent proposal along these lines will offer a substantive test of the relative strength of the dominant and the alternative sides of Canadian diplomacy. Before Canadian diplomacy reverts to anything close to its familiar pattern, therefore, the emergence of new and robust like-minded partnerships will continue to produce international and domestic ripples.

NOTES

The support of the Social Sciences and Humanities Research Council of Canada is gratefully acknowledged. I would like to thank Leslie Pal, Jackie Carberry, and Stephen Clarkson for their comments and assistance.

1 Andrew F. Cooper, *Canadian Foreign Policy: Old Habits and New Directions* (Scarborough Ont.: Prentice Hall Allyn and Bacon, 1997), ch. 1.
2 Arthur Andrew, *The Rise and Fall of a Middle Power: Canadian Diplomacy from King to Mulroney* (Toronto: James Lorimer, 1993), 166.
3 For a good analysis of these nuances in contemporary diplomacy see Brian Hocking, 'Beyond "Newness" and "Decline": The Development of Catalytic Diplomacy', *Discussion Papers in Diplomacy* No. 10, Centre for the Study of Diplomacy, University of Leicester, October 1995.
4 Andrew, *The Rise and Fall of a Middle Power*, 166.
5 Ibid., 178-9.
6 Denis Stairs, 'Canada in the New International Environment'. Notes for presentation to the Inaugural Meeting of the Canadian Consortium on Asia Pacific Security (CANCAPS), York University, North York, 3-4 December 1993.
7 For one innovative account of these trends see J.N. Rosenau, *Turbulence in World Politics: A Theory of Change and Continuity* (Hemel Hemstead: Harvester, 1990).
8 On the effect of the media in cases involving humanitarian intervention see Warren P. Strobel, *Late Breaking Foreign Policy: The News Media's Influence on Peace Operations* (Washington DC: Endowment of the US Institute for Peace, 1997), and Nik Gowing, *Media Coverage: Help or Hindrance for Conflict Prevention?* (Washington DC: Carnegie Commission, 1997).
9 John A. Munro and Alex I. Inglis, eds, *Mike: The Memoirs of the Right Honourable Lester B. Pearson, Vol. 2: 1948-1957* (Toronto: University of Toronto Press, 1973), 32-3, 280.
10 Lloyd Axworthy, 'Canada and Human Security: The Need for Leadership', *International Journal* 52, 2 (Spring 1997), 193.
11 On niche selection see Andrew F. Cooper, ed., *Niche Diplomacy: Middle Powers After the Cold War* (Houndsmills/London: Macmillan, 1997).

12 Lloyd Axworthy, 'Canada's Role as a Middle Power', *Winnipeg Free Press*, 8-9 September 1965.
13 John Holmes, 'Is There a Future for Middlepowermanship?' in *The Better Part of Valour* (Toronto: McClelland and Stewart, 1970), 34.
14 Andrew, *The Rise and Fall of a Middle Power*, 173.
15 Quoted in Keith Spicer, 'Canada's Diplomat to the World', *The Globe Magazine*, 24 Sept. 1966, 7.
16 Henry Kissinger, *White House Years* (Boston: Little Brown, 1979), 383.
17 Andrew, *The Rise and Fall of a Middle Power*, 178-9.
18 Clyde Sanger, *Ordering the Oceans* (Toronto: University of Toronto Press, 1987), 25.
19 Asbjorn Lovbrack, 'International Reform and the Like-Minded Countries and the North-South Dialogue 1975-1985', in Cranford Pratt, ed., *Middle Power Internationalism: The North-South Dimension* (Kingston and Montreal: McGill-Queen's University Press, 1990), 44.
20 Andrew, *The Rise and Fall of a Middle Power,* 166.
21 Don McGillivray, 'Canada's Pretense Exceeds Its Stature', *The Ottawa Citizen*, 7 May 1986, A8.
22 'Canada and the Newly Developing Democracies', A Speech by the Honourable Lloyd Axworthy, PC, MP, to the International Relations Society, Trinity College, University of Toronto, Toronto, Ontario, 20 Nov. 1991, 14.
23 David Cox, 'Canada and the United Nations: Pursuing Common Security', *Canadian Foreign Policy* 11, 1 (Spring 1994), 63-78.
24 Quoted in Madelaine Drohan, 'Canada at Odds with Trade Group', *The Globe and Mail* [Toronto], 24 Oct. 1990, B3. See also Andrew F. Cooper, *In Between Countries: Australia, Canada and the Search for Order in Agricultural Trade* (Montreal and Kingston: McGill Queen's University Press, 1997), ch. 6.
25 Senator Pat Carney, statement to the Special Joint Committee of the Senate and of the House of Commons. Reviewing Canadian Foreign Policy, *Minutes of Proceedings and Evidence*, 21 June 1994, 46:37.
26 Liberal Party of Canada, *Creating Opportunity: The Liberal Plan for Canada* (Ottawa, 1993); Liberal Party of Canada, *Liberal Foreign Policy Handbook* (Ottawa, May 1993).
27 André Ouellet, testimony to the House of Commons Standing Committee on Foreign Affairs and International Trade, *Minutes of Proceedings and Evidence*, 16 Feb. 1994, 1: 34.
28 Fen Osler Hampson and Dean F. Oliver, 'Pulpit Diplomacy: A Critical Assessment of the Axworthy Doctrine', *International Journal* 52, 3 (Summer 1998), 379-406.
29 Ibid., 381.

30 Lloyd Axworthy, testimony to the House of Commons Standing Committee on Human Resources Development, *Minutes of Proceedings and Evidence*, 5 Apr. 1995, 73: 27.
31 Hampson and Oliver, 'Pulpit Diplomacy', 380.
32 Lloyd Axworthy, Minister of Foreign Affairs, 'Canadian Foreign Policy in a Changing World', Speech to the National Forum on Foreign Policy, Winnipeg, 13 Dec. 1996, *Canadian Speeches*, January/February 1997.
33 Paul Heinbecker, Assistant Deputy Minister at DFAIT, quoted in Hugh Winsor, 'Aid Mission On Move', *The Globe and Mail* [Toronto], 30 Nov. 1996, A1.
34 Steven Goose, *Minutes*, The Ottawa Process Forum, 5 Dec. 1997 (Ottawa, 1998).
35 Notes for an address by the Honourable Lloyd Axworthy, Minister of Foreign Affairs, to the Oslo NGO Forum Banning Anti-personnel Land Mines, Oslo, Norway, 10 Sept. 1997, 97/32.
36 Edward Mortimer, 'An End to Impunity', *The Financial Times* [London], 8 Apr. 1998, 12.
37 Norma Greenaway, 'Stopping a Scourge', *The Ottawa Citizen*, 29 Nov. 1997, B2.
38 'Cyber-Diplomacy', Speaking Notes for a speech by Mr. Gordon Smith, Deputy Minister, Foreign Affairs and International Trade, to the Technology in Government Forum, Ottawa Ontario, 18 Sept. 1996. This theme is also picked up in various speeches made by Minister of Foreign Affairs Lloyd Axworthy. See, for example, 'Canadian Foreign Policy in a Changing World', Speech to the National Forum on Foreign Policy, Winnipeg, 13 Dec. 1996, *Canadian Speeches*, January/February 1997, 19.
39 Transcript, Press Conference, Prime Minister Jean Chrétien, *CBC Newsworld*, 16:00, 12 Nov. 1996.
40 Maxwell A. Cameron, 'The Landmine Ban: Globalisation of Civil Society?' *Review: North-South Institute Newsletter* 2, 1 (1998), 8. On this issue see also Miles Kahler, 'Multilateralism with Small and Large Numbers', *International Organization* 46, 3 (Nov. 1992), 699.
41 Axworthy, 'Canada and Human Security', 193.
42 A key DFAIT official stated during the Review of Canada's international affairs that '[c]reative coalition building ... is increasingly important in foreign policy....That means a much broader horizon in terms of who we choose to work with on different issues. There should be different partners—many of these, I think, we'll find in Latin America and Asia Pacific—for different issues.' Keith Christie, testimony to the House of Commons Standing Committee on Foreign Affairs and International Trade, *Minutes of Proceedings and Evidence*, 21 June 1994, 46: 44.

43 See, for example, *Canada-Caribbean-Central America Policy Alternatives, Report Card on Canada's First Year in the OAS in the Light of Hemispheric Relations*, CAPA occasional paper, July 1990, 21.
44 Jeff Sallot, 'Canada Offers to Lead Aid Force', *The Globe and Mail* [Toronto], 12 Nov. 1996, A1, A14.
45 For a more detailed typology, see Andrew F. Cooper and Brian Hocking, 'Magic Bullets Meet the "Powerless State": Diplomacy and the Re-Calibration of State-Society Relations', paper presented at the Third Pan-European International Relations Conference and joint meeting with the International Studies Association, Vienna, 16-19 Sept. 1998.
46 Quoted in John R. English, 'The Landmine Initiative: A Canadian Initiative?' in Andrew F. Cooper and Geoffrey Hayes, eds, *Worthwhile Initiatives? Canadian Mission-Oriented Diplomacy* (Toronto: Irwin Publishing, forthcoming). See also ICRC, 'Land Mines Must Be Stopped' (Geneva, 1995).
47 Notes for an address by the Honourable Lloyd Axworthy, Minister of Foreign Affairs, to the United Nations Commission on Human Rights, Geneva, Switzerland, 30 Mar. 1998, 98/24.
48 Jill Sinclair, quoted in Greenaway, 'Stopping a Scourge', B2.
49 Conrad Black, 'Taking Canada Seriously', *International Journal* 53, 1, (Winter 1997-8), 1.
50 Hampson and Oliver, 'Pulpit Diplomacy', 388.
51 Kim Richard Nossal, 'Pennypinching Diplomacy: The Decline of "Good International Citizenship" in Canadian Foreign Policy'. Paper presented to the CNC-IISS Conference on Internationalism and Retrenchment in Canadian Foreign Policy, Toronto, 24-25 Apr. 1998, 5.
52 Louis Nastro and Kim Richard Nossal, 'The Commitment-Capability Gap: Implications for Canadian Foreign Policy in the Post-Cold War Era', *Canadian Defence Quarterly*, Autumn 1997, 21-2.
53 Nossal, 'Pennypinching Diplomacy', 5.
54 Cranford Pratt, 'DFAIT's Takeover Bid of CIDA: The Institutional Future of the Canadian International Development Agency', *Canadian Foreign Policy* 5, 2 (Winter 1998), 6.
55 Quoted in Allan Thompson, 'Axworthy Praises New World Teamwork', *The Toronto Star*, 3 Dec. 1997, A6.
56 Hampson and Oliver, 'Pulpit Diplomacy', 386.
57 Stephen Handelman, 'Canada to Halt African Mission', *The Toronto Star*, 14 Dec. 1996, A1, A23.
58 David Pugliese, 'PM's Bid for Glory Fades', *The Vancouver Sun*, 23 Nov. 1996, A9. See also Andrew F. Cooper, 'Between Will and Capabilities: Canada and the Rwanda/Great Lakes Initiative', in Cooper and Hayes, *Worthwhile Initiatives?*

8

Negotiating Canada: Changes in Aboriginal Policy over the Last Thirty Years

FRANCES ABELE
KATHERINE A. GRAHAM
ALLAN M. MASLOVE

For most Canadians, Aboriginal issues have flickered only episodically on the screen over the past thirty years. Perhaps the debates about Aboriginal rights that accompanied the patriation of the Constitution and the Meech Lake and Charlottetown accords, the national trauma of the Oka crisis, and some stereotypical images of Aboriginal people in cities come most quickly to mind as defining the relationship between Aboriginal peoples and Canada, both at the level of high politics, and 'on the ground'.

In reality, this relationship is fundamental to Canada as a society and as a nation-state. In public policy terms, the relationship between Aboriginal peoples and the government of Canada shapes the capacity of the federal government (and the provinces) to regulate land and resource use, to promote economic development, and to undertake many other basic functions. Canada's Aboriginal policy also has a direct and fundamental effect on social cohesion and the prosperity of Aboriginal people, collectively and as individuals. Ultimately, the health and fairness of the relationship between Aboriginal peoples and Canada affects all Canadians.

Changes over the last thirty years in this policy field have been remarkable. Aboriginal peoples have moved from a position of political irrelevance to a position of considerable importance in the policy process. Thirty years ago, the federal cabinet published a White Paper on Indian Policy that assumed the irrelevance of the founding treaties and argued for an end to any distinctions between Indians and other Canadian citizens; today, federal policy recognizes an inherent right to self-government for Indians, Inuit, and Métis. Thirty years ago, no treaties existed for over half the area of Canada; today, modern treaties (comprehensive claims agreements) have been negotiated for almost the entire country. The comprehensive claims agreements have constitutional protection, and they recognize the rights of Aboriginal peoples on their traditional lands and create a basis for new political arrangements that are having far-reaching effects. Aboriginal peoples' vision of Canada and proposals for the future of the federation have had a profound impact on public debate and upon the political map. The two new territories in the North (Nunavut and the new Northwest Territories) are the first political jurisdictions to be created as a result of Aboriginal peoples' political actions. And the federal department responsible for 'Indian affairs' has 'morphed' from an overseer and dominant intervenor in band governments to an advocate for Indians and Inuit in Ottawa. All of these changes have occurred almost entirely peacefully, and relatively gradually, but they represent a major shift in underlying philosophy, practice, and emphasis.

FOUR PARADIGMS

Canada's Aboriginal policy over the past thirty years has been guided by four paradigms, or perspectives. Each of these offers a particular 'definition of the problem', and each generates distinctive answers, prescriptions, and approaches. We use the terms 'paradigm' and 'perspective' rather loosely, as roughly synonymous terms meaning, in Jane Jenson's formulation, a shared set of interconnected premises which make sense of many social relations. [A paradigm] contains a view of human nature, a definition of basic and proper forms of social relations ... and specification of relations among institutions as well as a stipulation of the role of such institutions.[1]

The four paradigms in Aboriginal affairs may be sketched as follows.

The Problem Is Poverty
The *poverty paradigm* treats Aboriginal peoples primarily as members of a systematically disadvantaged and impoverished group. Having been in this circumstance for generations, Aboriginal peoples are stuck in an economic ghetto and require assistance to escape. The remedy that follows from this diagnosis includes a very wide range of measures intended to improve economic vitality (in the case of communities) and to promote education and improved employability (of individuals). The goal is the full participation of Aboriginal peoples as equals in Canadian society. This perspective does not assume that there will be economic equality *among* Aboriginal peoples; income stratification similar to that occurring in the greater society is expected.

The Problem Is a Culture of Complaint and Victimization
This might be called the *malcontents paradigm*. It holds that for various reasons, Aboriginal peoples have developed habits of criticism and complaint, and, accordingly, they shift responsibility for their life circumstances onto 'The Government' or 'White People'. Rarely explicit in official statements or in discussions among the policy elite, this perspective nevertheless occurs in public and private discussion. Something close to such a view may have influenced the 1986 Report of the study team examining federal programs and policies related to Aboriginal peoples, created as part of the newly elected Conservative government's Nielsen Task Force on Program Review. This document ignored general issues of the Aboriginal-Canadian relationship to focus on allegedly palatial housing on Indian reserves, and it recommended harsh prescriptions for containing federal costs related to Aboriginal peoples. Negative reaction to this viewpoint forced the Mulroney government to publicly repudiate the team's proposed policy direction.[2]

Media reports of poverty, failure, and protest and the relatively light treatment given Aboriginal economic and social success stories contribute to the misperceptions upon which this view is based. The 'Indian tragedy' theme in Canadian journalism also treats political conflict within Aboriginal communities as an unusual disorder, somehow worse or more newsworthy than political conflict elsewhere.[3] The thematic character of this reportage suggests it has some salience for at least a portion of the general Canadian population.

The Problem Is Unequal Individual Rights
For some, the problem is one of unequal citizenship or unequal rights. 'Discrimination' is seen to have produced and maintained inequality; resolution of the problem is a matter of ensuring that Aboriginal people, *as individuals*, enjoy full citizenship rights. One of the interesting features of this essentially liberal position is that it leads to two opposing prescriptions, depending upon the analyst's assessment of the empirical circumstances of Aboriginal peoples. One view identifies the Indian Act, the treaties, and all other 'special arrangements' for Aboriginal peoples as temporary measures, designed to deliver full equality to Aboriginal peoples and to disappear when that equality is in sight. The contrary view is that, far from temporary, the treaties establish the basis for equality between Aboriginal and non-Aboriginal citizens, because they recognize the distinctiveness of Aboriginal individuals and provide the support to Aboriginal societies that will allow them to participate fully in Canadian society, as distinct collectivities. As we will show, a central development in the last thirty years of federal Aboriginal policy has been the shift from the first to the second view—from a liberal view based upon individual rights to one that recognizes the importance of collectivities, and collective rights, to individuals' well-being.

The Problem Is the Relationship to Land
For some time, the view of almost all Aboriginal peoples, and a persistent minority view among non-Aboriginals, has identified the central problem as being one of land—of rights to its use and preservation, of attitudes to it, and of the inherent centrality of land to Aboriginal ideas of identity, nationhood, or peoplehood. The fact that this constitutes a minority view among the non-Aboriginal population, particu-

larly for the first part of the period under review, is significant. This minority view belies the centrality of land occupancy and title to much of the early and contemporary treaty-making between Aboriginal nations and the federal Crown. It also ignores the consistency with which Aboriginal peoples have asserted the centrality of land.

Ownership of or jurisdiction over land is at issue in the changing concept of Aboriginal self-government. The quest by Aboriginal peoples to have their right of self-government recognized and the policy dialogue that has resulted from this quest has been rooted in two of the paradigms that we have identified. The problem, from an Aboriginal perspective, has been grounded in the linked imperatives of recognition of the (collective) civil rights of Aboriginal peoples, and recognition of their land rights.[4]

HAS THERE BEEN PROGRESS?

The remarkable transformation in public policy concerning Aboriginal affairs during the last thirty years may be seen in the ways that the relative standing of the four paradigms has shifted. The shifts have had far-reaching importance both at the level of high politics—in constitutional discussions, in treaty negotiations, and in the aftermath of landmark judicial decisions—and in more localized 'on the ground' settings, as Aboriginal peoples have worked to improve their communities and to co-exist in peace and prosperity with non-Aboriginal Canadians.

There has been progress in defining the issues and advancing the relationship between Canada and Aboriginal peoples over the past thirty years. This progress is rooted in three developments:

- new Aboriginal policy dynamics within the federal government, as the roles and relationships among the Department of Indian Affairs and Northern Development (DIAND), various central agencies, and other line departments have evolved;
- increasing capacity by Aboriginal peoples themselves to undertake political advocacy in the arenas of constitutional and federal-provincial politics ('high politics') and to undertake developmental and remedial actions for people at the community level; and

- cross-fertilization between the domains of high politics and policy and the reality and aspirations of people 'on the ground'.

It is impossible to assess these developments without having an understanding of the general situation of Aboriginal peoples in Canada and the patterns of federal government expenditures on their behalf. We begin by providing this context. The chapter then examines the extent to which the four policy paradigms influenced federal government policy during the prime ministerships of Pierre Trudeau, Brian Mulroney, and Jean Chrétien. We conclude with a discussion of the factors that are likely to shape federal policy toward Aboriginal peoples in the new millennium.

Some basic definitions should be noted at the outset, as should some limitations of this chapter. It focuses principally on federal government policy as it relates to Canada's Aboriginal peoples and on the interplay between Aboriginal peoples in Canada and the federal government. The important influence of territorial, provincial, and, in the urban context, local government actions on Aboriginal peoples' lives should not be minimized.[5] These will, however, enter our analysis only tangentially.

The term 'Aboriginal peoples' also requires clarification. We are concerned with federal policy as it relates to four broad groups: status Indians (who are increasingly referred to as First Nations people), Indians who do not have status under the terms of the Indian Act, Métis, and Inuit.[6] Where appropriate, we have differentiated the public policy path followed for each group; in other cases we use the general term 'Aboriginal peoples'.

Finally, we must stress that a rough exploration such as this necessarily ignores some of the major accomplishments of individual Aboriginal communities and their governments. These are many and varied.[7]

THE CONTEXT: THE SOCIAL, CULTURAL, AND DEMOGRAPHIC LEITMOTIF

The period under review in this chapter is framed by two of the most comprehensive efforts to assess the well-being of Aboriginal peoples in Canada in order to inform public policy. Focussing exclusively on status Indians, the *Survey of the Contemporary Indians of Canada* (commonly known as the Hawthorn Report) was released in 1966.[8] Hawthorn wrote of the need for cultural revival, as a means of fostering new pride and a sense of identity in Indian communities, as a precursor to social rehabilitation and economic development.[9] Thirty years later the more broadly focussed *Report of the Royal Commission on Aboriginal Peoples* became public.[10] The Commission's assessment, which forms the basis for its subsequent recommendations, was that '[i]n the present circumstances of Aboriginal people in Canada, numerous impediments stand in the way of acquiring traditional wisdom and practising traditional ways.... Nevertheless, Aboriginal peoples are finding their way back.'[11]

Although some progress has occurred, some basic social and economic indicators demonstrate that there remains a considerable way to go.[12] On average, a Registered Indian male can expect to live ten years less than his non-Aboriginal counterpart; the gap between Aboriginal and non-Aboriginal women is only slightly less.[13] Aboriginal peoples are on average much poorer than other Canadians. In 1991, the average income of Indian men was half the Canadian average. Métis and Inuit men's incomes tended to be slightly higher, but were still less than 60 per cent of the Canadian average. For women, Aboriginal incomes were about two-thirds of those of their non-Aboriginal counterparts.[14]

High Aboriginal birth rates have produced a much younger population than the Canadian norm. In 1971, 45 per cent of Indians were under the age of 15, compared to 30 per cent of the Canadian population as a whole. In 1991 the corresponding figures were 37 per cent and 21 per cent respectively. In 1991, 43 per cent of Inuit were under fifteen. At the other end of the population pyramid, in 1971 only 4 per cent of Indians were 65 or older, compared to 8 per cent of non-Aboriginal Canadians. In 1991 the percentages were 3 and 12 respectively.[15] The age distribution must be considered alongside the tragically high suicide rates among Aboriginal peoples, particularly youths. The overall suicide rate of Indians is almost 3 times that of other Canadians. Among teenagers (15-19) the rate for Aboriginals is 93 per 100,000, compared to 13 for non-Aboriginals. For young people aged 20-24 the respective rates are 104 and 19 per 100,000.[16]

Aboriginal peoples are staying in school longer. In 1996-7, DIAND estimated that there were 27,487 Aboriginal students enrolled in post-secondary education, compared to 5,467 in 1981. In 1981, 41 per cent of Indians aged 15 and over had less than grade nine education; by 1991 this proportion fell to 21 per cent. (The corresponding percentages for non-Aboriginals were 20 per cent and 14 per cent.) In 1981, only 2 per cent of Indians had earned a university degree; by 1991 this had risen to 6 per cent. (The comparable non-Aboriginal percentages were 8 per cent and 11 per cent.)[17] This suggests potential improvement in Aboriginal peoples' employment prospects and incomes. The challenges remain significant, however, as a result of some of the other barriers in many Aboriginal peoples' lives and the fact that the Aboriginal labour force is growing at twice the Canadian rate.[18]

Without becoming swamped by these measurement issues, we briefly provide some contextual observations on federal spending here. Toward the end of the chapter we return to an overview of federal spending interpreted in light of our discussion.

Two aspects of federal spending are worth noting at this point. First, federal spending on Aboriginal affairs has been left relatively unscathed through the various episodes of expenditure restraint and cutbacks. For example, during the 1980s the annual rate of growth in this area was consistently in the range of 8 to 9 per cent, even though overall federal spending was frozen or cut during much of that decade.[19] Similarly, Aboriginal spending was left relatively unaffected through the expenditure-cutting years of the Chrétien government.

Second, the pattern of spending has markedly changed. In 1968-9, virtually all federal spending on Indian affairs and on the North was devoted to the delivery of services and the construction of facilities. Items that became prominent in budgets of later years, such as transfer programs that allowed for some local discretion, and the funding of self-government development, did not appear at all in 1968-9.

PARADIGMS, POLICY, AND POLITICS:
THE PAST THIRTY YEARS

Since 1969, three prime ministers and their governments have had a sustained opportunity to deal with the challenges of Canada's Aboriginal fact: the Liberal governments of Pierre Elliott Trudeau (1968-

84), the Conservative governments of Brian Mulroney (1984-93), and the Liberal governments of Jean Chrétien (1993 to the present).[20] The four dominant paradigms described earlier underlie federal Aboriginal policy in each of these three periods. The paradigms are not mutually incompatible, and in fact are often found in loosely related association, underlying policy choices and prescriptions.

With this framework and context in mind, we begin our review of Aboriginal policy over the past thirty years.

Aboriginal Policy in the Trudeau Era: Contestation and Collectivism
Aboriginal policy during the prime ministerships of Pierre Elliot Trudeau (1968-79 and 1980-4) was shaped to a considerable degree by the fundamental beliefs and aspirations of Trudeau himself and some key cabinet ministers. These included: a strong adherence to a liberal conception of equality, based on individual rights; reliance on the development of the Canadian nation-state as the vehicle for supporting the aspirations of individual Canadians; and a belief in social justice and a commitment to an active role for the state in the creation of a 'just society'.

There were two other important contextual factors shaping the specific content and tone of Aboriginal policy debates in this period. The first was the national and international preoccupation with energy supply and security. The oil crisis of 1973 launched a tempestuous decade of energy politics. The federal government's desire to open Canada's territorial North to petroleum and uranium exploration and development[21] and Quebec's response in developing massive hydroelectric facilities in James Bay brought the issue of unresolved Aboriginal land title to public debate. The federal government's stewardship of the resources and resource rents belonging to petroleum-rich Indian bands in Alberta also proved to be contentious.

Finally, particularly after 1981, this was the period in which the federal debt and deficit rose sharply. Institutional and fiscal reforms were designed to assist Cabinet in recognizing connections among expenditures and in slowing the flow of red ink. The former included the establishment of spending envelopes across broad policy areas. Aboriginal expenditures were included in the Social Development envelope. Spending controls included the '6 and 5' program of limited salary increases for public servants and the first across the board mid-year budget cuts. Despite these measures, however, government expenditure increases ranged from 7.6 per cent (the lowest rate of annual increase, from 1978 to 1979) to 28.8 per cent (the highest rate of annual increase, occurring from 1973 to 1974) during the Trudeau period.[22]

The key policy paradigms underlying the Trudeau government's actions in Aboriginal affairs were those concerning individual civil rights, and poverty.

The initial conception of Aboriginal rights was promulgated by the minister of the day, Jean Chrétien, in the infamous 1969 *White Paper on Indian Policy*.[23] It proposed the elimination of the Indian Act on the grounds that it was discriminatory, a proposal that reflected the individualistic basis of Trudeau liberalism. The apprehension that fundamental collective rights might be terminated led to protests by Indians across Canada. The National Indian Brotherhood (now the Assembly of First Nations [AFN]) emerged as a strong national political voice.[24] The need for resistance also strengthened Indian organizations working at the provincial level. The outcry was so strong that the government withdrew its proposals. Nonetheless, the spectre of the White Paper (and the liberal individualist ideology underlying it) shaped Aboriginal politics and policy for the duration of the Trudeau era and beyond.[25] Through their organizations, in consultative forums, in parliament, and elsewhere, Aboriginal peoples consistently sought recognition and security of collective Aboriginal rights.

A high point in their struggle was reached during patriation of the Canadian Constitution in 1979-82. To ensure that the Constitution Act itself and the new Charter of Rights and Freedoms would not ignore or erode collective Aboriginal and treaty rights, Aboriginal leaders made representations to the Supreme Court of Canada and the House of Lords in the United Kingdom. Heeding Aboriginal opposition, the Special Parliamentary Committee on the Constitution recommended in 1981: that Aboriginal rights and freedoms not be affected by the guarantees in the Charter of Rights and Freedoms; that Aboriginal rights be recognized in a specific constitutional provision; and that Aboriginal peoples be able to participate in a constitutional conference on their rights.[26] Realizing the intensity of Aboriginal views and the possibility that patriation might be scuttled, the government acquiesced. The Parliamentary Committee's recommendations were reflected in provisions of the Constitution Act that explicitly recognize and affirm existing Aboriginal and treaty rights (Section 35[1], which is unique in the international context), that speak to the Charter issue (Section 25), and that provided for at least two First Ministers' Conferences, in the five years following patriation, with representatives of the four Aboriginal groups to discuss 'matters that directly affect the Aboriginal peoples of Canada' (Section 37).

A strong theme during the Trudeau years—particularly the prosperous early years—was the elimination of poverty in Canada. The evident and disproportionate poverty of many Aboriginal communities became an important focus in this effort. Initiatives were undertaken to ameliorate Aboriginal poverty through education, economic development, and, ultimately, self-government.

Early in the period, the government engaged in an important dialogue with Indian and Inuit peoples on the issue of education. In 1971, the Fifth Report of the Standing Committee on Indian Affairs and Northern Development (the Watson Report) responded to concerns about high-school dropout rates and marginalization of Aboriginal peoples in the labour market. Aboriginal organizations had been quite active in making their concerns known and in seeking remediation. The committee's recommended response to the situation was to involve Aboriginal communities and parents more extensively and directly in education. In a seminal decision, the government accepted the principle of Indian control over Indian education. One important result was the phasing out of residential schools. The push for community control was taken one step further in 1973, when the National Indian Brotherhood argued forcefully for a legislative change in jurisdiction to give Indian parents and communities control over education.[27] The cumulative effect of these interventions was to shift government policy. The focus was now on helping Indian people help themselves to eradicate the consequences of low levels of educational attainment.

Similarly, federal economic initiatives for Aboriginal peoples emphasized community-based development. In part, this was consistent with other federal poverty eradication and social animation programs of the 1960s, such as the Neighbourhood Improvement Program and Opportunities for Youth. For a time, the community-based approach to federal initiatives for Aboriginal economic development was driven centrally, out of the Privy Council Office. In many sites across Canada, a relatively small group of federal public servants became public advocates for Aboriginal peoples, sometimes losing their jobs in the process.[28]

The final cornerstone of thinking about remedies for poverty came late in the Trudeau era. In 1983, the Report of the Special Committee of the House of Commons on Indian Self-Government (the Penner Report) was released. It advocated addressing the poverty and social conditions of Aboriginal peoples by giving them the power to control their own destiny through self-government. The committee arrived at this conclusion after extensive study of concerns related to education, child welfare, and health among Indian people. Although the report focussed on the problems of poverty, its recommended solution represented a new recognition of Aboriginal rights. Penner called for the constitutional entrenchment of the principle of self-government and for the enactment of federal legislation to establish self-government within its jurisdiction over 'Indians and lands reserved for Indians'. The Penner Report came at a crucial time for all Aboriginal peoples. The impending First Ministers' Conferences on Aboriginal issues, following patriation, would focus on the issue of Aboriginal self-government. Since the late 1970s, the Inuit of the central and eastern Arctic had been advancing their goal of a new public government corresponding to the territory covered by their Nunavut claim. The Métis of Western Canada were also developing their own models of governance. In both cases, the fundamentals of Penner's position were helpful.

The Trudeau era also saw ground-breaking developments in dealing with the problem of land and Aboriginal title. The most striking aspect of these developments is the apparent reluctance of the federal government to address the fundamental challenges of land and title directly. Instead, it was pulled into addressing land issues by court decisions and by pressures for northern resource development.

In many respects, the modern era of treaty-making begins in 1973, when the Supreme Court of Canada ruled in the Calder decision that Aboriginal land rights and title continued to exist in Canada,[29] without fully defining the rights. In response, Jean Chrétien, the Minister of Indian Affairs and Northern Development, issued the *Statement on Claims of Indian and Inuit People: A Federal Native Claims Policy* that same year. The 1973 policy has a number of important elements.

It recognized that there are parts of Canada where Aboriginal land interests had not been surrendered or extinguished by treaty, and that these interests must be settled. This would occur through establishment of a comprehensive claims process. Through a newly created Office of Native Claims in DIAND, the government would negotiate a quantity of land for Aboriginal use, based on traditional occupancy, and a monetary compensation package for traditional territory subject to other uses. Claims of this type were considered to be comprehensive, in that they could include land, hunting, fishing, and trapping rights, as well as other economic and social benefits. The policy also recognized 'specific claims', based on the alleged failure of the Crown to meet its lawful obligations in relation to Indian land and assets. These obligations are based in constitutional and common law, as well as in statutes and existing treaties.

There were three notable limitations to the 1973 Claims Policy. These limitations were fundamental and far-reaching, and they likely had the effect of making an already protracted process even longer. First, the bar was set very high for negotiations to begin. Claimants had to undertake exhaustive documentation of their claim and then queue up, since the government was only prepared to deal with a very limited number of claims. Second, the federal government insisted that the Aboriginal signatories to any agreement cede, release, and surrender all Aboriginal rights in perpetuity. This requirement was commonly referred to by Aboriginal peoples as a requirement for 'extinguishment' of rights and, by the Crown, as a requirement for 'surrender'. It may have made sense in property law but it did not work in politics: while certainty of land tenure and authority over the land was a development imperative, seeking extinguishment or surrender of Aboriginal rights to achieve this goal was highly inflammatory. To most Aboriginal peoples, Aboriginal rights, like human rights, are in principle inalienable. Third, the federal government compounded the problem by refusing to negotiate Aboriginal political rights, control over lands, and revenue-sharing from surface as well as subsurface resources. It maintained this approach through the early 1980s.[30]

These strictures of the federal policy regime concerning Aboriginal land and title were resisted by many claimant groups who, nonetheless, entered the claims process. For its part, the federal government seemed compelled more by the need to resolve outstanding land issues in order to enable natural resource development than by a desire for closure *per se*.[31] Because of the importance of northern resources on federal lands, key conflicts during this period occurred in the North. Two public inquiries focussed the debates. The Berger Inquiry into the proposed Mackenzie Valley pipeline and the Lysyk Inquiry into possible construction of a pipeline following the route of the Alaska Highway both reported in 1977. Both identified the need to resolve issues of Aboriginal title and to generate practical social and economic benefits for northern Aboriginal peoples as part of any plan to proceed. Arguably, however, the most remarkable aspect of these inquires was the opportunity provided to Aboriginal peoples in the North to explain their views concerning development and stewardship of the land. Also remarkable was the fact that many non-Aboriginal Canadians heard these views, and joined the opposition to the pipeline proposals.

The economic pressure on northern lands and the small opening created by the 1973 comprehensive claims policy led Aboriginal peoples across the North to commence negotiations. The Dene and Métis of the Northwest Territories, the Inuit of the central and eastern Arctic, represented by the Inuit Tapirisat of Canada (ITC), the Inuvialuit of the western Arctic, represented by the Committee for Original Peoples Entitlement (COPE), and the fourteen Indian bands in the Yukon, represented by the Council of Yukon Indians (CYI), all began land use and occupancy research and the preparation of negotiating positions. In the main, they sought political control over the decisions about development in their territories, and compensation for past damages.

The first comprehensive claims agreement (or modern treaty) was reached by the Cree and Inuit of northern Quebec in 1975, under extreme pressure from the impending James Bay hydroelectric project. No other agreement was reached until 1984, when the Inuvialuit of the Mackenzie Delta/Beaufort Sea signed.[32] In these and many other cases, however, the federal government's insistence on a surrender of rights and on separating land claims negotiations from discussions about self-government frustrated the progress of negotiations during this period.

Summing Up the Trudeau Era
The question of rights dominated Aboriginal-government relations during the Trudeau governments, beginning with the early conflict between the individualistic approach to civil rights articulated in the

1969 White Paper and the collectivist views held by Aboriginal peoples. Release of the White Paper triggered the rise of national and provincial/territorial organizations as advocates in the arena of high politics. Their role was reinforced through the process of constitutional patriation and conflicts over land and resource development.

The high politics of debates concerning Aboriginal rights and land were paralleled by a growing policy preoccupation with the poverty of Aboriginal peoples. This was driven by some of the central tenets of the 'Just Society', and the prescriptions offered were consistent with the community-development fashion of the time. A major breakthrough in thinking about the policy paradigm that was required for constructive and more fundamental change occurred near the end of the period, when the Penner Report suggested a new prescription, which linked the reduction of poverty to the right of self-government.

The prominence of constitutional issues on the government's agenda and the rise of national Aboriginal organizations as advocates of Aboriginal rights in the constitutional context contributed to more overt centralization in management of the Canada-Aboriginal relationship within the federal government. As federal-provincial relations were managed through the Privy Council Office and the Federal-Provincial Relations Office, so Aboriginal affairs were seen as the business of central agencies. The importance of the amelioration of poverty and community development to the government's agenda during Trudeau's first term in office reinforced this.

For its part, DIAND was a department in transition. The Trudeau period saw the beginning of a shift in the department's orientation from control of Indians and Inuit to a commitment to their development. This transition would not be easy, given the requirements of the Indian Act and the history of paternalism in Canada-Aboriginal relations. But the social activism of the 1960s did have a long-term impact on the department. Another factor loosening the reins of DIAND control over all things Aboriginal was the policy regime for resource development in place from the mid-1970s to the end of the Trudeau period. Despite its responsibility for the administration of Canada's territorial North, the department emerged as a relatively weak player in the Canada Oil and Gas Lands Administration, the agency established to implement the government's northern energy strategy. In addition, the government of the Northwest Territories and the Yukon territorial government began to seek a 'government-to-government' relationship with the federal centre. Both exerted influence in the post-patriation First Ministers' Conferences on Aboriginal issues, while seeking territorial political development and more province-like participation in northern resource development decisions and revenue.

Clearly, during the Trudeau governments, the intellectual basis that drove most policy initiatives was a determination to address the problem of unequal rights. In that, it reflected the perspective of the Prime Minister himself. One might read into the 1973 statement a step toward the recognition of the importance of land, but, in its call for surrender of rights as the price of settling outstanding issues, it was really a negation rather than an affirmation of the centrality of land to Aboriginal peoples' world view. Land was viewed as a commodity or an economic resource, not as a base for Aboriginal self-determination.

THE MULRONEY YEARS: HIDDEN ACHIEVEMENTS

Undoubtedly the most prominent features of Aboriginal policy through the Mulroney years (1984-93) are the political failure of the Meech Lake and Charlottetown accords and the horror of the Oka crisis. While these were defining events, it is also true that the period saw many quiet advances in Aboriginal policy. These included some fundamental changes in direction and some major concrete achievements.

The Rights Perspective
As had been the case during the Trudeau governments, during the Mulroney years public debates concerned Aboriginal rights. In fact, some issues were holdovers from the previous regime. The Mulroney government brought legislative closure to the long and bitter fight by Indian women who had married non-Indians to regain and retain status under the Indian Act for themselves and their children. In 1982, the Report of the Sub-committee on Indian Women and the Indian Act had provided a significant boost in parliamentary support for this reform. It was not until June 1985, however, that the passage of Bill C-31 brought about the removal of the offending provisions of the Indian Act and, also, a provision for increased control by Indian bands over their own membership. Bill C-31 had the immediate impact of restoring Indian status to an estimated 16,000 women and children. It

was accompanied by considerable controversy in some Indian reserve communities, which argued that scarce housing and other resources would be further stretched. Nonetheless, the C-31 amendments stand as an important accomplishment of the Mulroney government in the field of human rights.[33]

It fell to Brian Mulroney to chair the final First Ministers' Conference to define 'existing aboriginal and treaty rights' as required under the terms of patriation.[34] Discussions had increasingly focussed on representations by the national Aboriginal political organizations to have the inherent right of self-government recognized in the Constitution. The federal government accepted this position but, at the final First Ministers' meeting on the matter in May 1987, failed to broker the necessary provincial agreement.[35] This failure proved very costly, as it was to contribute to Aboriginal leaders' already deep concern over their exclusion from the negotiation of the June 1987 Meech Lake Accord, which was silent on the question of Aboriginal rights. We are left with the image of the Cree member of the Manitoba Legislature, Elijah Harper, scotching the Meech Lake Accord in 1990.

The Charlottetown Accord negotiations present an opposing case. Four national Aboriginal political organizations had a seat at the negotiating table—the AFN, the Native Council of Canada, the ITC, and the Métis National Council. Two other groups, the Native Women's Association of Canada (NWAC) and the chiefs of Prairie Treaty Nations, had loud voices in the debates, although they did not have formal standing. The final version of the Charlottetown Accord reflected a remarkable shift in the conception of Aboriginal peoples' place in Canada. It held out the prospect of a recognized Aboriginal order of government, fully engaged in the processes of Canadian federalism. National Aboriginal leaders seemed to have achieved remarkable success in the arena of high politics, only to sink into apparent irrelevance with Charlottetown's defeat.[36]

The Nielsen Detour
The high-level negotiations of political and constitutional rights probably dominated public perceptions of Aboriginal affairs, but programmatic change was also mooted. This initiative also met with failure. One of the first actions of the Mulroney government was to set up the Task Force on Program Review, commonly known as the Nielsen Task Force. Over the first two years of the government's mandate,

successive study teams, comprised of people from the private sector and public servants, conducted brief but intensive investigations into government activities. The goal was to reduce inefficiencies in government operations and spending. In 1985, the study team examining programs for Indian and other Aboriginal peoples reported. As indicated earlier, the tone of some sections of the report, such as that which dealt with housing conditions on some Indian reserves, edged toward the 'Aboriginal people as malcontents' paradigm. More importantly, the report recommended that the federal government shift responsibility for Aboriginal programs and services to the provinces and to Aboriginal communities. Federal funding should be contained and targeted, largely toward youth and education. The recommendations, plus an underlying fear that the logical extension of the report was a return to the policy direction of the 1969 White Paper, caused a major reaction among Aboriginal organizations and other interested social justice groups. A public servant in DIAND blew the whistle, leaking the so-called 'Buffalo Jump Memo', which indicated how the report could be implemented. The government was forced to officially repudiate the Nielsen recommendations. Nonetheless, suspicions remained that many subsequent actions of the Mulroney government reflected the policy agenda contained in the Nielsen report.[37]

Certainly, some of the Conservative initiatives related to Aboriginal economic development and education can be seen to be consistent with the Nielsen perspective. But they also implied that the federal government does have a role in both policy-making and programming to alleviate Aboriginal poverty.

Early in the first Conservative mandate, the Minister of the day, David Crombie, commissioned a report on Aboriginal economic development. The 1986 report's recommendations for a more coherent approach to Aboriginal economic development across the government and for easier access by Aboriginal entrepreneurs to capital were immediately accepted in principle by the Minister, and the chair of the task force was appointed to head up the department's efforts. In the early 1990s, the Mulroney government shifted the lead role in its Aboriginal economic development activities from DIAND to Industry Canada, when it created the Canadian Aboriginal Economic Development Strategy (CAEDS). CAEDS was noteworthy because it offered a comprehensive, long-term, and well-capitalized approach to economic development, in the five areas of traditional federal activity: migration to mainstream employment sites, especially urban areas; business development; sectoral development; human resources development; and community economic development.[38]

The Mulroney years were also characterized by an increasing level of Indian control over education and by greater federal spending on post-secondary education for status Indians and other Aboriginal peoples, as a matter of policy. The government was strongly criticized when it imposed limits on post-secondary funding in 1989 on the grounds of need for fiscal restraint, but the absolute number of Aboriginal students in universities and colleges did rise significantly during the period.

Confronting the Issue of Land

Perhaps the most important feature of the Mulroney years was the government's apparent willingness to confront issues of land. Doubtless, successive judicial decisions building on the Calder decision were an important catalyst. But the Mulroney government and successive Progressive Conservative ministers of Indian Affairs and Northern Development also showed a pattern of independent, pragmatic, and sometimes ground-breaking initiatives related to Aboriginal lands issues. This period was also characterized by a more explicit recognition that the issues of land and self-government were linked.

The first signal that the Conservatives were willing to contemplate changes to government policy concerning land and title was the establishment of the Coolican Task Force to review comprehensive claims policy. Reporting to David Crombie in 1985, the task force recommended recasting federal policy objectives by recognizing and affirming Aboriginal rights in claims agreements, rather than requiring the extinguishment of Aboriginal rights as a condition of settlement. The Coolican Task Force articulated a new perspective, in which the resolution of claims would be seen as a social contract, balancing the needs and rights of Aboriginal societies with those of governments, so as to ensure certainty of land ownership and appropriate development of land and resources. Finally, the Task Force recommended that the federal government compel the government of British Columbia to recognize the existence of Aboriginal title and to participate in the process of resolving long-standing claims that cover much of the province.[39]

Beginning in 1986, the Mulroney government issued a series of policy statements on both comprehensive and specific claims that suggest that the government understood Coolican's analysis and also needed to respond to ongoing criticism. The newly appointed Minister, Bill McKnight, announced a revised claims policy under which claimant groups would no longer be required to surrender all Aboriginal rights, title, and interests, but only those related to the use of and title to surrendered land and resources. The government's policy on extinguishment was further relaxed in a second policy statement just one year later. During his brief tenure as minister (1989-90), Pierre Cadieux convinced the premier of British Columbia that his government needed to recognize Aboriginal title and participate in a tri-partite British Columbia treaty process. In the case of specific claims, the government established a new negotiating regime, creating the arms-length Indian Specific Claims Commission in 1991 and dedicating $355 million to helping bands research their specific claims.

The momentum continued in the second mandate. In 1993, the government issued policy statements on comprehensive and specific claims that reaffirmed a commitment to settle claims expeditiously. In a remarkable shift from the position at the beginning of the period, the government indicated that it would negotiate comprehensive claims as 'main treaties that provide clear, certain and long lasting definitions of rights to land and resources'.[40] Thus, while there were significant conflicts over Aboriginal lands that were attributed to government foot-dragging during the Mulroney era (the grievances of the Lubicon Cree and the Oka crisis being two prominent examples), we do see evidence of increasing policy enlightenment in the recognition of the pressing need to deal with land issues, and to recognize the links between land rights and self-government.

This was a difficult step. Initially, the government sought to separate discussions on self-government from those on land. The government's approach to enhancing local control by Indian bands was articulated in a Community-based Self-government Policy, announced in 1986. This policy provided for the negotiation of multi-year transfer agreements between the government and bands to enable bands to deliver services on reserve. That same year, the government sanctioned a more far-reaching approach. Parliament passed the Sechelt Indian Band Self-government Act, which permits this British Columbia band to write its own constitution and govern its land base accordingly, with the support of a multi-year federal funding commitment. The Sechelt assumed delegated jurisdiction over non-band members residing in their territory, including the ability to tax for the provision of services to non-members. The Sechelt's initiative in seeking this legislation was loudly criticized by Indian leaders in other parts of the country as selling out to a municipal model of government. Nonetheless it does provide an important early example of enhanced governing authority, and anecdotal evidence suggests that a measure of success has been achieved in the promotion of overall community well-being.[41]

Important changes occurred in the territorial North, when the comprehensive claims negotiated by the CYI on behalf of fourteen Yukon First Nations and the ITC (later replaced by the Tungavik Federation of Nunavut as negotiator) on behalf of the Inuit of the central and eastern Arctic were resolved. In the Yukon, the 1993 agreement set a precedent by creating a constitutional obligation to negotiate self-government agreements with each of the fourteen Yukon First Nations. In an equally dramatic move, as one of the last acts of his prime ministership Mulroney signed the Nunavut Agreement in May 1993. That agreement settled the comprehensive claim and was followed only one month later by Parliament's passing of the Nunavut Land Claims Agreement Act and the Nunavut Act. The latter piece of legislation established the Nunavut government, with jurisdiction coterminous with the area covered by the Inuit claim. This public government assumed responsibility on 1 April 1999, ending a 23-year quest for self-government by the people of the region, approximately 85 per cent of whom are Inuit. The Sechelt, Yukon, and Nunavut initiatives all provide good examples of the interplay between high politics and policy, and the needs and aspirations of Aboriginal peoples in the communities in which they live. Progress was possible because the link between land tenure and ownership on the one hand, and self-government on the other, was recognized in policy and in practice.

Summing up the Mulroney Era
Major policy changes and some instances of dramatic (and positive) reversals mark the Mulroney years, yet the credit for progress in Aboriginal-Canada relations rarely 'sticks' to the period dominated by this most unpopular of prime ministers. Beyond the 'bad teflon' effect of Mulroney himself, we identify five other contributing factors:

- The accomplishments of the three main ministers of Indian Affairs and Northern Development during the Conservative years, David Crombie, Bill McKnight, and Tom Siddon, were obscured from public view.[42] Crombie served at the beginning of the period. He undertook a number of important initiatives, such as the Coolican review of comprehensive claims policy and the assessment of the government's approach to Aboriginal economic development. He also attempted to create a new, more equal relationship between himself, as minister, and Aboriginal leaders. To some degree, these new constructive steps were overshadowed by the Nielsen Task Force report and the ensuing fallout. Within the government, Crombie was recognized as an initiator, but he did not achieve policy closure, in the form of significant cabinet decisions, during his tenure. Of the three ministers, Bill McKnight accomplished the most. He is universally described as a 'straight shooter' who was not afraid to deliver tough news. Aboriginal leaders did not always like his message, but they thought that he delivered it with integrity. He enjoyed a similar stature among his cabinet colleagues, possibly a contributing factor in the policy progress of the time. In the public eye, Tom Siddon's tenure was overwhelmed by the Oka crisis and related events. This perception undervalues his achievements in overseeing the final advances in claims policy during the Conservatives' tenure and the important developments linking claims and governance in the Yukon and in Nunavut.
- The second factor contributing to the relative obscurity of the advances of the Mulroney years is the stratospheric level of political contestation and failure during the Meech Lake and Charlottetown processes. The stakes and consequences were certainly high for the federal government. These processes were equally consequential, however, for the national Aborigi-

nal political organizations—the AFN, the ITC, the Métis National Council, the Native Council of Canada, and the NWAC. As the saga of these two accords evolved, these organizations occupied an increasing amount of time on centre stage. Although they shared one common goal, recognition and protection of Aboriginal rights, including the right of self-government, they differed in important respects. Each had a different internal political dynamic, a different specific history with the government of Canada, and a different vision of a future relationship with Canada. There was also a sense, particularly among the Métis and within NWAC, that the negotiations would really take the form of a zero-sum game. Some groups' gains would be others' losses. All of this contributed to a rivalry among the Aboriginal political organizations that, ultimately, made the defeat of the Charlottetown Accord devastating for their leadership and for the health of the organizations themselves, when recriminations began. Observation of the interplay among Aboriginal groups during this time also prompted non-Aboriginal Canadians to revisit the question, 'What is the problem?' It is perhaps ironic that they sought a level of unanimity among Aboriginal peoples that other Canadians could not achieve during this period. Another unfortunate legacy of the supremely 'high politics' period of constitutional renegotiation was a significantly increased gap between the Aboriginal political leadership and the people they were representing. While political leaders negotiated with premiers and jockeyed for adequate news coverage of their goals, the recognition of 'on the ground' needs and problem-solving continued on a dynamic of its own in Aboriginal neighbourhoods, reserves, and communities. To an extent, national Aboriginal leaders' representations on issues related to land and a framework for the relationship between Aboriginal governments and the federation were disconnected from problems of poverty and disempowerment in communities. The Meech and Charlottetown processes thus provide an important illustration of the merits of connecting perspectives on land, rights, and poverty.

- Thus, a third factor that obscured the advances of the Mulroney years is that many of the good-news stories that were occurring were at the community level, out of public view. It was difficult to see these changes while national attention was captured by relations with Quebec and the constitutional question, tax reform and the battles over the Goods and Services Tax, the great debates over the Canada-United States Free Trade Agreement and the North American Free Trade Agreement, and deepening concern with the deficit. The positive local developments were led, in part, by a growing cadre of Aboriginal professionals who were actively committed to serving their communities as teachers, health care professionals, and so on. In addition to the specific program initiatives sustained by community activists, there were also a number of important examples of constructive local relations between Aboriginal communities and other governments or segments of the population. For example, in 1988 the City of Saskatoon and the Muskeg Lake First Nation signed a formal agreement governing their relationship concerning a new urban reserve within the city limits. This original agreement has been the foundation for a generally constructive and expanding relationship between the two parties ever since.[43] Similarly, the relationship between the St. Mary's First Nation and the City of Fredericton expanded during this time, as did the work of the City of Calgary Aboriginal Urban Affairs Committee. The constructive impact of these and other developments has received attention only recently, among Aboriginal peoples and the attentive public.[44] Widespread knowledge is still lacking.

- The fourth factor obscuring the view of the Aboriginal policy field during this time is the continuing metamorphosis of DIAND. Behind the limelight of high constitutional politics and ministerial initiatives, the department was going through a transformation that would lay the groundwork for a new role. The key words are downsizing and devolution. Consistent with the recommendations of the Nielsen Task Force and with the immediate political aspirations of Indian First Nations and territorial governments, the department shed much of its role in direct program delivery. More and more First Nations assumed responsibility for education, social services, and other programs in their communities. In the territorial North,

DIAND handed over numerous responsibilities and related staff to the territorial governments. Since the 1960s, DIAND's Northern Program Branch had been the overseer of the department's northern policy and its direct delivery role in the North. It had existed in perpetual tension with the territorial governments and other federal departments that had a northern interest. During the Mulroney years, it shrunk to a shadow of its former self.[45] This period is also characterized by the increasing sectoralization of Aboriginal policy within the federal government. The centre of action concerning Aboriginal economic development shifted to Industry Canada. The Department of Fisheries and Oceans became the uncontested steward of Aboriginal fishing policy within the federal government. Finally, as discussed earlier, DIAND was somewhat removed from the centre stage of constitutional politics. Increasingly, the Privy Council Office and the Department of Justice were serving as the central agency contact points for Aboriginal peoples. These institutional developments, within DIAND and within the federal government more generally, required that outside observers employ a new wide-angle lens to get a true picture of Aboriginal policy during the period. The fact that downsizing and devolution were the two dominant images of DIAND in this big picture obscured the fact that the department was contributing to some very important developments in the areas of claims and self-government agreements that would have a larger impact on the ground than the high politics that occupied the spotlight. This was also something of a formative period for the policy orientation of the department. It began to shed its long-standing role as paternal guardian of the federal Aboriginal interest. It began to get a new sense of itself as the advocate of Aboriginal interests within the federal government.

- Finally, the more positive developments of the Mulroney period were obscured by the images conjured up by one word—Oka.[46] The national agony surrounding the Oka crisis of 1990 is still easily remembered. For weeks, Aboriginal and non-Aboriginal Canadians and their governments were alternately galvanized and paralysed by the escalating protest by Mohawks and their supporters. In retrospect, however, the

Oka crisis contributed to some positive developments. First, it caused the centrality of land to the Aboriginal world view and to the paradigm of Aboriginal policy to come into full public view. Second, it prompted the establishment of the Royal Commission on Aboriginal Peoples, the most extensive review of Aboriginal policy since the Hawthorn Task Force of the mid-sixties.

In conclusion, the Mulroney era was accompanied by an awakening understanding among policy-makers and the general public of the centrality of Aboriginal perspectives on land and governance issues. Regrettably, it took scarring conflict to bring about a full examination of public policies and perspectives, through the Royal Commission.

THE CHRÉTIEN PERIOD: TALKING FAST, TAKING A DEEP BREATH, AND GATHERING STRENGTH...

When the Liberal government led by Jean Chrétien assumed office in 1993, the Royal Commission on Aboriginal Peoples was well underway. Born ostensibly out of the Oka crisis, the seven member commission[47] had been appointed by the Mulroney government on the specific advice of the retired Chief Justice of the Supreme Court, Brian Dickson. He had recommended a very comprehensive set of Terms of Reference for the Commission's work. The 16 items that the Commissioners were to examine dealt with issues of land, self-government, and political and social justice for Aboriginal peoples.[48] By 1993, the Commission had heard sometimes wrenching testimony around the country. It had also heard and seen evidence of achievement and hope. In parallel with its hearings, the Commission's research program was proceeding with the most comprehensive multi-disciplinary examination of the circumstances of Aboriginal peoples and their aspirations ever undertaken.

Talking Fast: The Irwin Years
Ron Irwin, the first Minister of Indian Affairs and Northern Development in the Chrétien government, would occupy the portfolio for the entire first term. Irwin chose to distance himself from the Royal Commission on Aboriginal Affairs, promoting an agenda of practical

action. His approach was viewed by some observers as a good antidote to the spectacular failures of the high politics of the Conservative era. In the words of one observer, 'Happily, Indian Affairs Minister Ron Irwin and the Chrétien government are untouched by the virus of constitutionalitis.'[49]

The cornerstone of Irwin's agenda was the assertion that the inherent right of self-government already existed under Section 35 of the Constitution. The time was ripe for this approach. The promise to recognize the inherent right was included in the Red Book campaign platform that had guided the Liberals to electoral success and had formed the basis for the government's priorities in office.[50] Mr. Irwin undertook three initiatives to bring this idea to life. First, in late 1994 he signed a so-called Framework Agreement with the Assembly of Manitoba Chiefs that was intended to guide the dismantling of the Manitoba Region of DIAND. The text of this agreement asserts, '[I]t is time to put in place a process that will lead both First Nations and Canada into a new relationship which is based on mutual respect and the recognition of First Nations' rights of government, management and control over their own lives, as recognized in the inherent right of the First Nations to self-government.'[51] The second development occurred in August 1995, when the Minister promulgated a policy statement on Aboriginal self-government. This statement formally launched a new process of negotiating Aboriginal self-government over a range of what elsewhere are municipal and provincial jurisdictions. This 'inherent right policy' asserts that Aboriginal governments can assume these responsibilities under Section 35 of the Constitution. Under this existing constitutional provision, the policy commits the federal government to negotiate 'practical' self-government arrangements. The policy provides for no further constitutional amendments on self-government, and recognition of a right to sovereign self-government, in the sense of international law. This policy provided the groundwork for the third element of the Minister's strategy—the negotiation of self-government agreements with individual First Nations and clusters of First Nations, commonly formed as Tribal Councils. By the end of his tenure, there were over fifty such negotiations underway.

The Irwin policy on self-government did not commit the government to deal with issues of land.[52] Generally, the fifty-odd negotiations often stalled. Reasons for this included a concern by First Nations that adequate fiscal resources would accompany transferred responsibility for particular governmental functions and, probably, a concern that negotiators at the small tables might cede points that would shortly be granted by evolving jurisprudence or by negotiations at other tables. Nevertheless, the number of negotiating tables and the amount of talk between the government and First Nations was presented by the Minister as an indication of progress.[53]

A major breakthrough of the period was the conclusion in 1996 of a tripartite Agreement-in-Principle among the federal government, the Nisga'a, and the British Columbia government to settle the Nisga'a land claim. This formed the basis for the final agreement in 1998 that includes recognition of Nisga'a government over the lands associated with this first British Columbia treaty. Two important characteristics of the agreement are the connection of land and governance, and the reliance on the legal concept of 'certainty' (whereby recognized Aboriginal rights are clearly enumerated). These two principles indicate how far federal Aboriginal policy has evolved since the 1960s. Recall the 1973 land claims policy, with its insistence on the separation of land and self-government issues and its requirement that extinguishment of all rights be a condition of land claims settlement.

There are other important aspects of the government's treatment of Aboriginal issues during this period. Métis, urban, and northern issues were more marginal during the first Chrétien government. In part, organizational upheaval in the national political organizations representing Métis and off-reserve Indians was a contributing factor.[54] In the case of urban people, the National Council of Native Friendship Centres, traditionally a service-oriented organization, felt compelled to undertake a stronger lobbying role as the Native Council of Canada became preoccupied with its transition into the Congress of Aboriginal Peoples. This was generally a difficult time for national Aboriginal political organizations. Relations between the Minister and the AFN were difficult at best, as the AFN tried to recommence more fundamental debates and to reassert itself in the wake of Charlottetown.

The government's northern agenda during its first term was largely confined to nudging along the implementation of the Nunavut Agreement and continued negotiations on self-government pursuant to the Yukon claims agreement. The complex circumstances in the western Northwest Territories seemed to defy progress or resolution, despite various local initiatives. A characteristic of all of the northern political initiatives was that they were proceeding at arms length from government (though they were all federally funded). For example, important work was undertaken by the Nunavut Implementation Commission, the Nunavut Planning Commission, and various co-management boards established under the land claims agreement. Recognition of the international character of many northern issues and the constructive role that Canadian northerners could play in the international realm was evident in the appointment of Inuit leader Mary Simon as Canada's first Arctic Ambassador.

Finally, we must consider the Department of Indian Affairs and Northern Development. During Irwin's tenure as minister, the department was marginalized, both in policy terms and in terms of managing implementation of the Minister's agenda. This was partly a result of the Minister's own 'shoot from the hip' style on policy matters. Among his tactics was to put items on the cabinet table without following the usual protocols regarding inter-departmental consultation or central agency clearance.

This review of the first Chrétien government's treatment of Aboriginal policy suggests a preoccupation with the issue of implementing Aboriginal self-government, generally at the level of the individual First Nation or Tribal Council, consistent with its general desire to avoid opening constitutional matters. The government was compelled to broaden its perspective at the end of its first term, when the report of the Royal Commission on Aboriginal Peoples was released.

As befits the iconoclastic role of royal commissions generally[55] and as a response to its own extensive terms of reference, the Royal Commission on Aboriginal Peoples focussed on the centrality of land as a foundation for a comprehensive approach to thinking about the future relationship between Aboriginal Peoples and Canada. In the Commission's view the relationship between Aboriginal nations and Canada should be based on treaties—those that exist, and modern treaties where required. Settlement of land issues and recognition of Aboriginal governments as legitimate stewards of the relationship between Canada and Aboriginal nations and other issues flow from this starting point. The Commission called for the regeneration of Aboriginal nations. The Commission defined a nation as a 'sizeable body of Aboriginal people that possesses a shared sense of national identity and constitutes the predominant population in a certain territory or collection of territories.'[56] The Commission estimated that there are between 60 and 80 Aboriginal nations in Canada and recommended that Aboriginal peoples work toward reconstituting these nations as the basis for self-determination within Canada. It elaborated a new relationship between Canada and Aboriginal peoples based on four principles: recognition, respect, sharing, and responsibility. Underlying these four principles is a view that Aboriginal peoples have distinctive rights and responsibilities as the original inhabitants and caretakers of the land.

Taking a Deep Breath and Gathering Strength
The government undertook to respond to the Commission's report in one year. The intervening election resulted in the appointment of a new minister, Jane Stewart, who brought a new considered and collaborative approach to the federal role. On 7 January 1998 Minister Stewart and the Federal Interlocutor for the Métis, Ralph Goodale, launched Canada's Aboriginal Action Plan, in response to the Royal Commission Report. They released the document *Gathering Strength*,[57] replicating the title of the third volume of the Royal Commission's Report.

The 1998 Action Plan is an important policy statement, because of its scope and because of its promises for the future. In many respects, the government has committed itself to the nation-to-nation, treaty-based approach advocated by the Royal Commission. The government's statement also recognizes the need to deal with the situation of Métis and off-reserve Aboriginal peoples. Finally, the plan indicates a new effort to deal with the social and economic problems faced by many Aboriginal people. Specific initiatives related to community-based healing and the development of a five-year Aboriginal Human Resources Development Strategy were announced on the day that the Action Plan was released.

There are, however, some important questions remaining about how the government will set in motion the process for fundamental renewal of the relationship between Canada and Aboriginal peoples. The Royal Commission had recommended a rather elaborate regime of recognition and renewal, beginning with a new Royal Proclamation to establish the fundamental nature of the Canada-Aboriginal relationship.[58] The Commission had also recommended companion federal and provincial legislative regimes and institutional arrangements to implement its proposed direction. The government's statement is, however, silent on these matters. Nor is the government committed to the recognition of the constitutional basis for Aboriginal self-government under Section 35 in the manner that the Commission had advocated. The government statement reads, 'certain provisions in self-government agreements with First Nations, Inuit, Métis and off-reserve Aboriginal peoples *could* be constitutionally protected as treaty rights under section 35 of the *Constitution Act, 1982*'(emphasis added).[59] This suggests that the government continues to rely on its 1995 inherent right policy, with its menu of municipal and provincial responsibilities for negotiation, as the foundation of its view of self-government. This contrasts with the Commission's view that 'the inherent right of self-government encompasses all matters relating to the good government and welfare of Aboriginal peoples and their territories.'[60] Finally, there was some immediate political fallout from the manner in which the government launched its new agenda, which may signal further difficulties ahead. The Statement of Reconciliation and Statement of Renewal that were read by Minister Stewart as the prelude to announcing the Action Plan were seen as an affront by two national Aboriginal political organizations, the Congress of Aboriginal Peoples and NWAC. They were critical of the failure of the Prime Minister to participate in the ceremony and argued that their issues were not adequately addressed by the new policy. The AFN did, however, show support for the government's efforts at the launch.

All of this aside, the year following the announcement of the new Action Plan was dominated by one achievement that reflected a new spirit of recognition—the conclusion of the Nisga'a Final Agreement. This agreement incorporates many features that speak to the fundamental political struggles of Aboriginal peoples to have their perspectives on land and governance both recognized and joined. It also holds promise for improving the objective circumstances of the Nisga'a people. The Nisga'a Agreement is a major milestone in the Aboriginal policy of the past thirty years.

HOW OTTAWA SPENDS ON ABORIGINAL PEOPLES

Changes in the pattern of federal government spending reflect three of the four perspectives we have discussed, and, more or less, suggest a progression over time. Until the early to mid-1970s, DIAND was largely a service delivery agency, responsible for direct delivery of programs to First Nations peoples. This was accomplished either through direct provision of education, social assistance, housing, and other services, or, somewhat later, through the distribution of funds to First Nation administrations. These payments were rigidly controlled; there was no opportunity at the local level for funds to be shifted from one function to another, and, indeed, in some cases, within the same functional area.

An immediate reason for this stringent regime was the minister's fiduciary responsibility; Ottawa's goal was to minimize risk that something would go seriously wrong in the provision of an important service to a community that would cause the minister or the government embarrassment and, if worst came to worst, force resignation. Thus, services were provided directly by Ottawa or via band administrations, but with a series of very tight controls. The consequence of this approach was that program design and administration was determined by officials in DIAND who were often out of touch with local conditions and needs. This approach exacerbated the sense of disenfranchisement and powerlessness that plagued the communities. In terms of the four perspectives, this regime in fact constituted a paternalistic version of the 'poverty' paradigm. The objective was to improve the conditions of First Nation communities by improving the services that were deficient. That is, it constituted an approach to alleviating poverty through assistance 'in kind'.

A later development (see Fig. 8.1) in federal spending was characterized by the transfer of funds to First Nation communities under agreements (such as Alternative Funding Arrangements [AFA] and Financial Transfer Agreements [FTA]) that allowed somewhat more (and sometimes a lot more) discretion on the part of the recipients. Community authorities had some discretion to transfer funds between functions, and in some cases to carry unspent funds into the next fiscal year. Since the early 1980s, when they made their appearance, AFA agreements have been secured with over 200 bands. FTA agreements, which date only from the mid-1990s, have also increased rapidly. The proportion of the DIAND budget accounted for by these programs has increased accordingly.

At one level this development was facilitated by a change in public attitudes such that there was support for First Nations peoples'

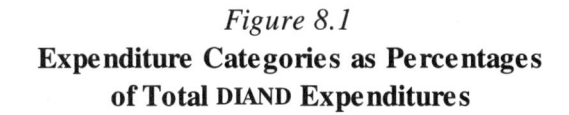

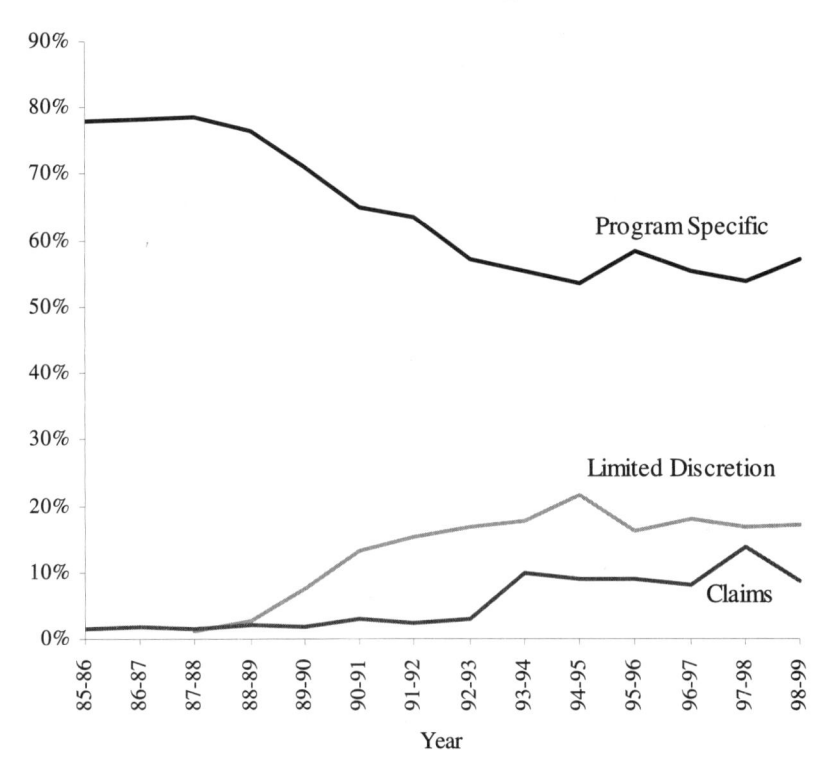

Figure 8.1
**Expenditure Categories as Percentages
of Total DIAND Expenditures**

assumption of greater responsibility for their own affairs. This made it easier for the Minister to relax regulatory control in the name of fiduciary responsibility. The trend toward grant regimes that permitted more local discretion is broadly consistent with the civil rights paradigm. That is, at least in terms of being responsible for local public services, First Nations peoples were to be treated more like non-Aboriginal communities. As this perspective became more accepted, the transfer regimes allowed progressively more local discretion.

The next stage that can be delineated is the movement toward self-government and land claims settlements, especially comprehensive settlements. This stage clearly corresponds to the land paradigm. Financial arrangements, which allow almost total First Nation autonomy, are negotiated as part of a comprehensive nation-to-nation settlement/ treaty. Ministerial responsibility is very muted if present at all; First Nations are regarded as self-governing peoples within Canada. Obviously, for individuals who view the 'Aboriginal issue' from any of the other three perspectives, this regime is unsatisfactory, because it accords to First Nations peoples privileges that other Canadians do not possess.

Much of this activity has been located in British Columbia, with the recently concluded Nisga'a agreement being the most prominent development. The Fiscal Financing Agreement negotiated under the umbrella of the Final Agreement provides for the transfer of funds to the Nisga'a to cover a range of services initially identified, and for the addition of other services at later dates. It also anticipates and provides incentives for enhanced fiscal independence over time through the development of own-source revenues.

SUMMING UP AND LOOKING FORWARD

We began by arguing that there has been progress in defining the relationship between Aboriginal peoples and Canada over the past thirty years. We suggest that the developments we have described show a somewhat remarkable progression in the federal government's conception of the appropriate paradigm for Aboriginal policy. We have moved from the concept of Aboriginal people as individualized citizens, impoverished because of a difficult and paternalistic past—the essence of the 1969 White Paper—to recognition of the collective identity of Aboriginal nations and peoples and of the need to resolve fundamental issues of land in order to achieve a more constructive future of self-control and improvement. This is the essence of the policy paradigm offered by the Royal Commission on Aboriginal Peoples and, as the new millennium nears, adopted to an important degree by the government in *Gathering Strength*.

What factors have contributed to this change? We identified one important factor at the outset and have dealt with it extensively in our review—the remarkable political mobilization of Aboriginal peoples over the past thirty years. We have observed the changing role played by the national and provincial/territorial Aboriginal political organizations in the arena of high politics over this period. Although our review has concentrated mainly on domestic high politics, the increasing role of Aboriginal advocacy in the international arena is also remarkable. Equally important has been the role of the Friendship Centre movement and community activists in working with Aboriginal peoples to improve their circumstances 'on the ground' both while high political battles were being waged and when the battlefields of high politics seemed empty.

Two other factors that have made a remarkable, but not surprising, contribution to policy learning and change are judicial activism and crisis events. Over this period, the courts, especially the Supreme Court of Canada, have rendered a number of landmark decisions concerning Aboriginal land and treaty rights that have induced change in government policy toward Indians and perhaps Inuit. The Métis, who have focussed on developing their own political structures and gaining public and political representation over the period are not on the verge of having judicial views on their legal rights illuminated. The changing situation of Métis in Canada will be a key issue as we move forward.

We dealt earlier with the catalytic effect of the Oka crisis. All crisis-influenced policy change was not, however, related to issues of land. Think of the effect on government policy of testimony on life in residential schools, the treatment of Aboriginal peoples by the justice system in Manitoba and Nova Scotia, and suicidal behaviour in Aboriginal communities. Limitations of space have not permitted us to deal with these issues extensively, but they should be remembered as influences on federal action, as well as on public perception of the paradigm of Aboriginal policy.

We suggest that the presence of these factors, plus, as we have shown, activist ministers in the Aboriginal portfolio, contributed to the evolution of a policy agenda that can be generally characterized as progressive. Changes in the role of DIAND and in the institutional regime for Aboriginal policy within the federal government have generally supported a move away from the paternalistic control of the past and encouraged fundamental policy debates. In the spirit of other ministries, for example the Department of Agriculture, that have become advocates on behalf of their constituencies, we now have a Department of Indian Affairs and Northern Development that sees itself as the voice for status Indians and Inuit people within the administrative state. In policy terms, the balance within DIAND between its role as overseer and its role as advocate has now shifted decisively in favour of the latter. Looking across the federal departments and agencies that now have designated responsibility for Aboriginal matters in their mandates (for example, Health Canada, National Resources Canada, Fisheries and Oceans Canada, and the Department of National Defence), we hypothesize that there are different views about the DIAND agenda and different levels of support. The situation for Métis and for non-status Indians, particularly in urban areas, is less clear, as DIAND is restricting its energies to Indians and Inuit and as advocacy and program support for Métis and non-status people is much more diffuse. Among other things it is entangled with provincial and sometimes municipal government priorities.

We must also remember the robustness of the Aboriginal spending envelope in the face of fiscal restraint during the 1980s and 1990s, and the significant shift from direct service provision to various forms of transfers.

Changing perceptions about land is a major development. Initially, the contrasting attitudes toward land could not have been more striking. A particular relationship to the land has traditionally been integral to Aboriginal belief systems, while non-Aboriginal society largely adopted the view of land as a market commodity with no special spiritual significance or relationship to nationhood. Over the past three decades there has been clear evidence of federal policy learning, as DIAND, and indeed the federal government generally, has come to appreciate more the Aboriginal perspective. But Aboriginal peoples have, at the same time, had their own debates about land as they confronted issues of meaningful self-determination and economic development. In the Aboriginal communities, the voices that argue that land is a resource to be exploited for economic progress have become stronger. These shifting and, in some respects, merging perspectives will be central to relations between Aboriginal peoples and the Canadian state in the future.

Amid all of this, it is undeniable that life for many Aboriginal people in Canada is perilous, even desperate. How might policy learning and high political debate make a difference on the ground? We conclude that the most constructive site for Aboriginal policy development over the next period will be in the middle ground of implementation. We are at the beginning of a new relationship, as articulated in *Gathering Strength* and as embodied in the creation of Nunavut, the Nisga'a Agreement, and the implementation of just treaty land agreements with Prairie Treaty Nations. Responsible, progressive policy-making will involve making these and similar commitments work, and building further on that process.

NOTES

For various and generous forms of assistance, we thank Marie Blythe, Julia Bracken, Amanda Coe, Peter Jull, George Kinloch, Leslie Pal, Phil Ryan, Lisa Seguin, and Samantha Tattersall, as well as the students in Public Administration 50.586 for much useful discussion: Rod Fowler, Malcolm Gibbs, Karen Patel, Jeff Potkins, Rod Windover, Demetrios Xenos and Tanya Zinterer.

1 Jane Jenson, 'Paradigms and Political Discourse: Protective Legislation in France and the United States Before 1914', *Canadian Journal of Political Science* 22, 2 (1989), 238. For a very thorough discussion of 'paradigm' and an interesting and somewhat complementary application of the idea to changes in the field of Aboriginal policy, see Michael Howlett, 'Policy Paradigms and Policy Change: Lessons from the Old and New Canadian Policies Towards Aboriginal Peoples', *Policy Studies Journal* 22, 4 (1994), 631-49.
2 Katherine A. Graham, 'Indian Policy and the Tories: Cleaning Up After the Buffalo Jump', in Michael J. Prince, ed., *How Ottawa Spends 1987-88: Restraining the State* (Toronto: Methuen, 1987), 237-67.
3 Recent examples include: Erin Anderson, 'Canada's Squalid Secret: Life on Native Reserves', *The Globe and Mail* [Toronto], 12 Oct. 1998, A1, and Peter Cheney, 'The Money Pit: An Indian Band's Story', *The Globe and Mail* [Toronto], 24 Oct. 1998. This series prompted a rebuke by the Grand Chief of the Assembly of First Nations. See Phil Fontaine, 'The Double Standard About First Nations Is Starting to Get Tedious', *The Globe and Mail* [Toronto], 3 Nov. 1998, A31.
4 Land and self-government have long been linked in jurisprudence. For example, the first decision in the landmark case Delagamuukw v. B.C. rejected the Aboriginal plaintiffs' efforts to use their traditional history as a basis for their claim to the title of lands in northern British Columbia. Chief Justice McEachern's dismissive treatment of oral history, and his depiction of Aboriginal peoples as having led 'short and brutish lives', as well as his judgment against the claim, were subsequently rejected in the landmark Supreme Court of Canada decision:

Delgamuukw v. B.C. (1997) S.C.R., Ottawa: 11 Dec. 1997. See also Dara Culhane, *The Pleasure of the Crown: Anthropology, Law and First Nations* (Burnaby: Talon Books, 1998).

5 See for example, Katherine A. Graham, 'Urban Aboriginal Governance in Canada: Paradigms and Prospects', in John Hylton, ed., *Aboriginal Self-Government in Canada: Current Trends and Issues*, 2nd edition (Saskatoon: Purich, 1999), forthcoming.

6 The Constitution Act (1982) identifies three categories of people whose 'existing Aboriginal rights' are recognized: Indians, Inuit, and Métis. Non-status Indians are not mentioned.

7 In all areas of human endeavour and in many communities, there has been a flowering of new Aboriginally-controlled institutions, dynamic portents of the future. To cite just a few examples, we note the activism and accomplishments of the Aboriginal Council of Winnipeg, whose Aboriginal Centre, located in the city's historic CPR station, will anchor redevelopment of Winnipeg's North Main Street, creating 'Neeginan' ('Our Place' in Cree); the successful Cree-owned regional airline, Air Creebec; the Mohawk Council of Akwesasne - Department of the Environment, and the Alkali Lake process, which assists small communities to regenerate.

8 H.B. Hawthorn, ed., *Survey of the Contemporary Indians of Canada* (Ottawa: Department of Indian Affairs and Northern Development, Indian Affairs Branch, 1966).

9 Centre for Policy and Program Assessment, School of Public Administration, Carleton University, *Public Policy and Aboriginal Peoples 1965-1992, Volume 2, Summaries of Reports by Federal Bodies and Aboriginal Organizations* (Ottawa: Royal Commission on Aboriginal Peoples, 1994), 10.

10 Royal Commission on Aboriginal Peoples, *Report of the Royal Commission on Aboriginal Peoples* (Ottawa: Minister of Supply and Services Canada, 1996).

11 Royal Commission on Aboriginal Peoples, *Volume 1: Looking Forward, Looking Back*, 664.

12 For context and for a discussion of trends as well as methodological issues, see Andrew J. Siggner, Eric Guimond, Gustave Goldmann, and Norbert Robitaille, 'Aboriginal Population Statistics: Are We Informed by the Aggregate Picture?' Presented at the Canadian Population Society Annual Meetings, 3 June 1998, University of Ottawa; E. Guimond, A Siggner, N. Robitaille, and G. Goldmann, *Aboriginal Populations in Canada: A New Demographic Perspective*, Census Analytical Studies Series (Ottawa: Statistics Canada, 1999).

13 Canadian Medical Association, 'Background paper on the health of Aboriginal peoples in Canada'. Submission to the Royal Commission on Aboriginal Peoples, 1993.

14 Profile of Canada's Aboriginal Population, 1991, Census of Canada; Selected Income Statistics–The Nation: 1991 Census of Canada, Statistics Canada.
15 Census of Canada data, 1971, 1981, and 1991, Statistics Canada.
16 Indian and Inuit of Canada Health Status Indicators 1974-83, Demographics and Statistics Division, Medical Services Branch, Health and Welfare Canada, 1986.
17 Census of Canada 1981 and Canada Year Book, 1997.
18 Census of Canada 1981 and Canada Year Book, 1997.
19 David C. Hawkes and Marina Devine, ' Meech Lake and Elijah Harper: Native-State Relations in the 1990s', in Frances Abele, ed., *How Ottawa Spends 1991-92: The Politics of Fragmentation* (Ottawa: Carleton University Press, 1991), 33-62.
20 The governments headed by Joe Clark, John Turner, and Kim Campbell should not be completely forgotten, but their impact on Aboriginal policy was minimal. Among the policies of these three governments, those of the Clark government with respect to natural resource development were probably the most important.
21 Massive incentives to oil and gas exploration on federally controlled Crown lands in the territorial north (the so-called 'Canada lands') were one aspect of the National Energy Program, which responded to the threats to offshore oil supplies in the 1970s.
22 Allan M. Maslove, 'The Public Pursuit of Private Interests', *How Ottawa Spends 1985: Sharing the Pie* (Toronto: Methuen, 1985), 12-13.
23 Minister of Indian Affairs and Northern Development, *Statement of the Government of Canada on Indian Policy* (Ottawa, 1969).
24 The genesis of the other major organizations—the Inuit Tapirisat of Canada, the Métis National Council, and the Native Council of Canada (now the Congress of Aboriginal Peoples)—is discussed below.
25 The seminal work on this period is Sally M. Weaver, *Making Canadian Indian Policy* (Toronto: University of Toronto Press, 1981). See also Katherine A. Graham, Carolyn Dittburner, and Frances D. Abele, *Soliloquy and Dialogue: Overview of Major Trends in Public Policy Relating to Aboriginal Peoples* (Ottawa: Minister of Public Works and Government Services Canada, 1995).
26 Government of Canada, *Final Report of the Special Parliamentary Committee on the Constitution*, 13 Feb. 1981.
27 National Indian Brotherhood, *Indian Control of Indian Education* (Ottawa, 1973).
28 See Joan Ryan, *Wall of Words: The Betrayal of the Urban Indian* (Toronto: PMA Books, 1978), and Sally Weaver, *Making Canadian Indian Policy*.
29 Supreme Court of Canada, Calder v. Attorney-General of British Columbia (1973) S.C.R.313, Ottawa: 1973.

30 Department of Indian Affairs and Northern Development, *In All Fairness: A Native Claims Policy* (Ottawa, 1981) and *Outstanding Business: A Native Claims Policy* (Ottawa, 1982).
31 See Edgar J. Dosman, *The National Interest* (Toronto: McClelland and Stewart, 1975).
32 Failure to achieve improvements in the living conditions of the James Bay Cree in the initial period of implementation of the James Bay and Northern Quebec Agreement caused some embarrassment for the government. See John Tait, *James Bay and Northern Quebec Agreement Implementation Review* (Ottawa: Department of Indian Affairs and Northern Development, 1982).
33 For a similar conclusion concerning another policy area during the Mulroney years, see Linda Freeman, *The Ambiguous Champion* (Toronto: University of Toronto Press, 1998).
34 The first conference occurred in 1983. It resulted in the addition of section 35(3) to the Constitution Act, 1982 to make it clear that treaty rights protected in 35(1) included 'rights that now exist by way of land claims agreements or may be so acquired'. This affirms the status of land claims as modern treaties.
35 A number of provincial premiers were unwilling to agree, arguing that they needed more specifics about what Aboriginal self-government actually meant before making such a commitment. See Frances Abele and Katherine A. Graham, 'Plus Que Ça Change...Northern and Native Policy', in Katherine A. Graham, ed., *How Ottawa Spends 1988-89: The Conservatives Heading into the Stretch* (Ottawa: Carleton University Press, 1988), 117.
36 J. Rick Ponting, 'Historical Overview and Background: 1970-96', in J. Rick Ponting, ed., *First Nations in Canada: Perspectives on Opportunity, Empowerment and Self-Determination* (Toronto: McGraw-Hill Ryerson, 1997), 46-7.
37 V. Seymour Wilson, 'What Legacy? The Nielsen Task Force Program Review', in Katherine A. Graham, ed., *How Ottawa Spends 1988-89: The Conservatives Heading into the Stretch* (Ottawa: Carleton University Press, 1988), 38.
38 Royal Commission on Aboriginal Peoples, *Volume Two: Restructuring the Relationship*, 791.
39 Task Force to Review Comprehensive Claims Policy (Murray Coolican, Chair), *Living Treaties, Lasting Agreements: Report of the Task Force to Review Comprehensive Claims Policy* (Ottawa: Department of Indian Affairs and Northern Development, 1985).
40 Government of Canada, *Federal Policy for the Settlement of Native Claims* (Ottawa, March 1993).
41 The Sechelt have concluded an agreement-in-principle under the British Columbia Treaty Process. This agreement does not alter the original Sechelt government agreement.

42 Pierre Cadieux served as minister from 1989 to 1990 and Pauline Browes served very briefly during the term of Kim Campbell in 1993.
43 T.M. Dust, 'The Impact of Aboriginal Land Claims and Self-government on Canadian Municipalities', *Canadian Public Administration* 40, 3 (1997), 481-94.
44 Some of these innovations were profiled by the Royal Commission on Aboriginal Peoples. Others were showcased at a national conference on Aboriginal Governance in an Urban Setting, held in Winnipeg in 1998.
45 Although not a DIAND responsibility, the devolution of responsibility for health care from Health Canada to the government of the Northwest Territories and the Yukon territorial government resulted in a significant reduction in the federal Aboriginal program envelope.
46 We should remember that the Oka crisis is one of a number of Aboriginal protests over land during the period covered by this review. Other notable protests include: the protest at Gustafson Lake BC, the Kettle Point protest in Ontario, and the protest over the Oldman Dam in Alberta, to name just three.
47 The original Commissioners included Co-Chairs René Dussault and Georges Erasmus, and Commissioners Allan Blakeney, Paul Chartrand, Viola Robinson, Mary Sillett, and Bertha Wilson. Less than two years after joining the Commission, Allan Blakeney resigned, to be replaced by Peter Meekison. Four of the Commissioners were Aboriginal: Viola Robinson (a Micmac who had been active with the non-status organization, the Native Council of Canada), Mary Sillet (an Inuk from Labrador), Georges Erasmus (a Dene leader who had also been National Chief of the Assembly of First Nations), and Paul Chartrand (a Métis law professor from Manitoba). Of the three non-Aboriginal members, two had judicial backgrounds. Bertha Wilson was a former Supreme Court Justice, and René Dussault was a judge on the Quebec Court of Appeal on his appointment. Both Blakeney and his successor Peter Meekison brought a western Canadian perspective to the job, as well as considerable experience in the national constitutional deliberations.
48 The full Terms of Reference are found in Royal Commission on Aboriginal Peoples, *Volume One: Looking Forward, Looking Back*, 699-702.
49 Jeffrey Simpson, 'The Grand Talk of Constitutional Reform for Aboriginals Is a Mirage', *The Globe and Mail* [Toronto], 15 Aug. 1995, A16.
50 The Red Book commitments on Aboriginal affairs were rooted in an elaborate consultative exercise, in which the Liberal party formed an Aboriginal Caucus of well-educated and active Aboriginal advisors.
51 Manitoba Northern Affairs, Native Affairs Secretariat, *Working in Partnership: Manitoba Policy on First Nation Government* (Winnipeg: Manitoba Northern Affairs, 1996), 5. It is interesting to note that the

Government of Manitoba was not party to the federal-Association of Manitoba Chiefs negotiations.
52 It should be noted that negotiations under the Tripartite British Columbia Treaty Process, begun under the Conservatives, did include land, because of the absence of treaties in British Columbia.
53 Speech, Ron Irwin, Institute of Public Administration of Canada annual conference, Regina 1995.
54 See, for example, Patty Fuller, 'New Name, Same Game?' *Alberta Report* [Edmonton], 21 Mar. 1994, 8.
55 For an excellent discussion of selected royal commissions in Canada, see Neil Bradford, *Commissioning Ideas* (Toronto: Oxford University Press, 1998).
56 Royal Commission on Aboriginal Peoples, *People to People, Nation to Nation* (Ottawa: Minister of Supply and Services Canada, 1996), 25.
57 Minister of Indian Affairs and Northern Development, *Gathering Strength: Canada's Aboriginal Action Plan* (Ottawa: Minister of Public Works and Government Services Canada, 1998).
58 This was to be a companion to the Royal Proclamation of 1763, which sets out the responsibility of the Crown for maintaining Aboriginal interests.
59 Minister of Indian Affairs and Northern Development, *Gathering Strength*, 17. Constitutional amendments represent a political minefield for the federal government, given provincial governments' role in approving amendments and the symbolic importance of amendments themselves.
60 Royal Commission on Aboriginal Peoples, *Volume 2: Restructuring the Relationship*, 225.

9

The Contested State: Canada in the Post-Cold War, Post-Keynesian, Post-Fordist, Post-national Era

STEPHEN CLARKSON
TIMOTHY LEWIS

However much the aspiration to professionalism may push social scientists toward a neutral style, metaphors persistently creep back in to enrich—but also to confuse—their writings. Take, for example, those who consider the sovereign state to have a size problem: it is at once too small to perform some functions, which are better left to supranational institutions, and too big to respond to the increasingly differentiated local and regional needs that are better met at sub-national levels of governance. Describing this as the 'Gulliver effect'[1] presents the state as immutable as was Gulliver when tied down by a thousand points of string in Lilliput. By implication, it is destined for irrelevance. Such an image is static, for it admits the possibility of change neither in the federal state's forms and functions, nor in its effects on its environment.[2] If a metaphor can help our understanding in this area, we prefer the Star Trek notion of shape shifting, which offers a more open-ended approach to conceptualizing recent mutations in the role of the sovereign state.[3]

The shape shifting metaphor conjures up the notion of constantly changing forms—an analogy appropriate for our understanding of the Canadian state, whose shape has shifted over the decades in remarkable ways. Thinking in terms of shape shifting encourages us to investigate the malleability of function as well as form. Indeed, forms often evolve in response to functional requirements, just as forms may themselves impose functional change. As shapes shift, so do roles. When a state's forms change, its traditional functions may be discarded and new ones acquired. For us, the idea of shape shifting suggests that there is something inherently adaptive about the state, which, unlike Gulliver, can move its limbs, lose limbs to other entities, and even grow new ones.

Such transformation responds to external forces as well as internal ones. Further, these changes can have effects on the world outside, particularly on other levels of governance. The shapes of continental or global levels of authority are themselves shifted by mutations in the Canadian federal state. The notion of shape shifting suggests that we should look out for changes in form and function, the external and internal forces that drive these changes, and their impact on other centres of power. In this endeavour we need to be prepared to find that many factors are both effects and causes of other phenomena, and may have contradictory characteristics, simultaneously centralizing and decentralizing, homogenizing and fragmenting the same political structure.

At the same time, we must recognize that any analysis of change presupposes some degree of continuity. Gulliver may be too static a metaphor, shape shifting perhaps too dynamic. The federal state is not wholly malleable. Its history, structural forces, institutional capacities, and constitutional framework comprise the core on which the forces of evolution have played. A glance back to Confederation reminds us that the federal state has already reconstituted itself in several palpably different incarnations, through a continual process of reconstructing its basic framework.

We begin our analysis of the Canadian state in the period when Lester Pearson and Pierre Trudeau (1963-84) attempted to complete and then sustain the social welfare state, which had been initiated during the last decade of the King/St. Laurent era. Although Canada has always been a fundamentally liberal country, sceptical of coercive and concentrated state action, except in times of war, we need to distinguish between two different ways of being liberal. John Ruggie has called the apparently stable system of the post-Second World War era one of 'embedded liberalism', in which market functions were woven into the social fabric, so that moderately liberalized trade and international capital movements under the pax Americana were subordinated to the interests of autonomous domestic macroeconomic management.[4] The wealth that this Keynesian welfare state redistributed emerged from the 'Fordist' consensus that granted organized labour a share in the returns produced by mass-production manufacturing and substantial growth in productivity.

The international financial order set up at Bretton Woods in 1944, along with the Keynesian and Fordist rationales for economic management that it presupposed, came under enormous strain following the disconnection of the American dollar from the gold standard in 1971 and the OPEC oil price and supply crisis of 1973. Following these shocks, when Canadian enterprise encountered difficulty competing in its own market because of declining tariff protection, it started expanding into the American market. The Trudeau governments' efforts in the late 1970s relied on relatively coercive interventions to deal with these shocks, but failed to mesh with an economy that was becoming increasingly continental in its orientation. The disjuncture reached politically catastrophic proportions with the short-lived National Energy Program of 1980.[5]

The election of the Conservative government in 1984 was more a rejection of Trudeau's successor, John Turner, than of the Liberal party's policy heritage, at least in regard to bilingualism and the Canada Health Act, which the Tory leader, Brian Mulroney, had taken great pains to endorse.[6] Once settled safely into the prime minister's office, however, he accepted the advice of his finance minister, Michael Wilson, and of the royal commissioner, Donald Macdonald, to initiate a neo-liberal transformation of the country that was ultimately endorsed by the Liberal party when it regained power under Jean Chrétien in 1993. In the fifteen years from 1984 to 1999, the Canadian state has been reduced in some functions and made much more subject to the market, but remains strong in other areas, so that it can discipline itself and society in the name of economic efficiency and individual liberty.

While it is indisputable that major political and cultural changes have occurred since the mid-1980s, we doubt the utility of describing them, in the words of much Canadian political economy discourse, as a shift from the paradigm of a 'nation-state' to one of a post-Keynesian, post-Fordist, post-sovereign, or even post-national state. Apart from 'post-modern', which contains a range of suggestive connotations concerning logic and reality in a world of interactive communications, multiple identities, and virtual realities, these 'post-' labels constitute an epistemological quagmire. They are empty of positive content, merely suggesting that a central phenomenon in human society has been pushed off the historical stage, but not indicating what has taken its place. While empirically 'lite', these 'post-' notions of the state are at the same time normatively heavy, infused as they are with nostalgia, apocalypse, and teleology.

Their nostalgic quality derives from the tendency to reify a late-lamented federal state by idealizing the regulatory capacity of what was in any case no more than a 'bastard' Keynesianism[7] and exaggerating the social harmony and stability in what was at best a 'permeable' Fordism[8], whose self-serving bargain between business and labour leaders excluded other social forces. The limitations of Fordism and Keynesianism were disguised in the post-war era by productivity gains and economic growth that allowed the dominant protagonists an ever-larger piece of an ever-larger economic pie. Present nostalgia is directed at the possibilities for social progress that this economic golden age created.

Besides looking backward with regret, the 'post-' labels look forward with despair. Their apocalyptic tone endows the present state with a terminal character: its proclaimed transmogrification into a neo-liberal monster implies that the Keynesian welfare state is history, its Fordist chapter closed. While it is true that politicians have systematically cut back welfare policies, the neo-liberal model has not achieved consensus as a desirable societal contract. Even if the public has come to accept as unavoidable the imperative of debt and deficit reduction, a balanced budget offers no general panacea. When forced by pressure from the financial markets, most governments have cut back programs reluctantly and in the hope that they can be restored once budgetary conditions improve. No sooner did the ultraconservative Klein government of Alberta find itself with a budget surplus than it increased its funding for education.

More troubling analytically, the 'post-' labels bear a teleological load that imputes to the state certain *a priori* functions that it ought to fill. One is given to understand that if the state does not perform them these services will not be provided at all, and the state itself will shortly lose its *raison d'être* and possibly self-destruct. This would have grave consequences in a country like Canada, whose weak historical and cultural underpinnings put the onus on the federal state to create a political community where no other form of community existed.[9]

We do not contest the proposition that the functions performed by the Canadian state have changed substantially over the course of three and a half decades. Rather, we wish to propose an alternative to the emptiness of these 'post-' conceptualizations. Instead of dwelling on the loss by the federal state of certain functions deemed to be its inherent properties, we will investigate how the location of some of these functions has shifted. We will examine economic issues (especially macroeconomic, industrial, and trade policy), and then turn to such political attributes of the federal state as its social and foreign policies in order to conclude with reflections on its democratic practice in the context of the Constitution's evolution. Before doing this, we need to reflect on the form within which Canada's state shapes are shifting.

RECONCEPTUALIZING THE CANADIAN STATE IN A MULTI-LEVEL FRAMEWORK

The evolution of the federal state from the social-democratic leanings of Lester Pearson and Pierre Trudeau to the neo-liberal proclivities of Brian Mulroney and Jean Chrétien can, we believe, be best understood by means of a nested, five-tier model. The emerging state reveals a disaggregated but integrated and interactive structure that operates from the municipal and provincial levels through the federal and on to the continental and global levels.[10]

While still showing dynamic potential, the *federal* state appears most reduced in its functions, having lost or transferred powers upward to the global and continental tiers, outward to the market, and downward to sub-national entities. Nevertheless, it has shown remarkable strength by taking bold steps both at home and abroad.

Above it, a market-driven *continental* regime has become institutionalized, first bilaterally between the United States and Canada, then trilaterally with Mexico. Although the federal state is the prime formal interlocutor in continental politics, the provinces play active roles beyond their borders with their sub-national counterparts, primarily in the US.

The *global* order comprises a set of supranational and inter-governmental institutions in whose agenda-setting and management the federal government actively participates as a sovereign state that consults the provinces according to their constitutional jurisdiction.

While these *provincial* governments have not developed a major international role, they have gained power from the federal level. At the same time they have lost capacity to the market and have off-loaded functions onto their cities.

At this, the *municipal* level of governance, cities have gained further responsibilities, but in some cases have lost the financial means necessary to meet them.

Not all of these levels of governance can properly be described as 'states'. In Canada only the federal and provincial levels have formal constitutional standing, municipalities remaining the colony-like creatures of their provinces. However, there has been sufficient institution-building at the other levels that governance functions with the quality of 'stateness' are performed at each tier in the model.[11] While the impact of change at each level is worthy of extensive investigation in its own right, our concern in this chapter is the federal state in Canada. Accordingly we will examine the other four tiers only as far as is necessary to understand Canada's federal level of authority.

The Federal State

The federal state started its shift toward neo-liberal governance some two years before the election of Brian Mulroney. The neo-liberal state is best identified with an off-loading of functions to lower levels of governance, an uploading of authority to the global and continental tiers, and a greater reliance on the imperatives of the marketplace.[12] Paradoxically, these apparent losses of power have occurred because the federal state has displayed considerable strength. It strove for many years to balance its budgets by taking steps that many entrenched interests, including the provinces, bitterly resisted, and it imposed structural reforms that favoured market outcomes constraining both state and civil society. In 1987, for example, the Bank of Canada announced its 'price stability' policy, which exerted substantial discipline on market actors and provincial governments.[13] In 1989 the government used its treaty power to create a new continental regime of accumulation, in which it has been an enthusiastically self-restraining participant. Successive federal governments cut and 'reinvented' social programs, reducing citizens' protection from the greater perils of the deregulated market. In each of these cases, discipline was exerted by Ottawa over the provinces, which were then forced to adjust. In short, to divest itself of authority the Canadian state had to take strong action.

The federal state also maintains an important role because it continues to nurture some vestiges of embedded liberalism. Part of the Chrétien Liberals' rationale for deficit elimination has been to ensure that the federal state can continue to play a role in social policy. In this regard it maintains the paradigm that prevailed under the Liberals of Pearson and Trudeau. While some may not approve of the life it is leading, reports of the federal state's demise appear greatly exaggerated.

The Global Order
The evolution of a global level of governance clearly diminishes the sovereign state's freedom to run its own affairs. Its loss of *internal* sovereignty may be partially offset by its capacity to exercise *external* sovereignty through participation in the deliberative process at the global level that establishes the norms, regulations, and disciplines it subsequently imposes on itself.[14] In 1990, during the Uruguay Round of trade talks, Canada was the country that proposed introducing the more authoritative institutional structure that transformed the famously ineffectual General Agreement on Tariffs and Trade (GATT) into the much more substantial World Trade Organization (WTO).[15] Ottawa believed that a mid-sized state was better off in a rules-based system with a dispute settlement mechanism strong enough to enforce those

rules. The same round of trade talks also yielded what had eluded the grasp of the Canadian government when negotiating the Canada-United States Free Trade Agreement (CUFTA). The WTO's comprehensive subsidy code promises to reduce the vulnerability of Canadian exports to the kind of American harassment that can arbitrarily allege unfair subsidies and impose stiff countervailing duties.

Canada experiences much of globalism's constraint as an extension of the US-dominated continentalism with which it has long had to deal. Two illustrations from the WTO make this clear.

1. Trade-related intellectual property rights (TRIPs) were adopted after years of sustained lobbying from the American information, entertainment, and pharmaceuticals sectors. First incorporated in the Uruguay Round's Dunkel draft, then embedded at US insistence in the North American Free Trade Agreement (NAFTA), they ultimately became part of the WTO's General Agreement on Trade in Services. With TRIPs now enshrined in the trade order, Washington, supported by the EU, pressured Ottawa to adopt the new norms. Its compliance gave the foreign-owned pharmaceutical subsidiaries generous protection for their branded drugs and eliminated the legal base for the Canadian public health system's much cheaper generic drug suppliers.[16] Canada's autonomous drug policy was thus undermined by its own concurrence with a US-initiated reconstitution of both the continental and global regulatory regimes.

2. Although CUFTA had grandfathered such Canadian cultural policies as the interdiction of split-run editions of American magazines appearing in Canada with Canadian advertising, Time Warner induced Washington to lodge a case at the WTO against Ottawa's barring the distribution of a Canadian edition of *Sports Illustrated*. The WTO dispute panel and appellate body rulings reached back into Canadian political history to declare cultural policies that were democratically legislated years—even decades—ago to be invalid according to Geneva's 1995 trade rules.[17] In this case Washington's aggressive invocation of global rules that it had itself largely designed helped it approach the goal of unfettered access to its northern

neighbour's magazine advertising market. Such internationalization of US power extends the deep integration with the American system that the Canadian state has long experienced as a member of a previous *de facto* continental regime.

The Continental Regime
The projection abroad of governmental, societal, or entrepreneurial actors also characterizes the development of governance at the continental level. If an integrated North American market is being forged by corporations that operate continentally thanks to NAFTA's new investment and trade rules,[18] and if a halting evolution of continental norms can be detected in the work of dozens of working groups beavering away on specialized issues such as the transportation of dangerous chemicals,[19] one might think that the Canadian state was on the road to irrelevance. But NAFTA was carefully designed to prevent any supranational form of continental governance from developing. Far from NAFTA's encouraging greater political integration, its two English-speaking member states are carefully monitoring their borders to obstruct immigration from Mexico and to restrict general labour mobility. In the name of their national autonomy, the three governments have already taken steps to hobble NAFTA's putatively autonomous Commission for Environmental Cooperation (CEC). In the interests of securing this autonomy they are also resisting the creation of a North American monetary union that might clone Europe's EMU.[20]

The growth of a continental form of governance has effects on the Canadian state similar to those of globalism. The most controversial are the limits on the range of permissible government action imposed by NAFTA and CUFTA on many policy areas formerly considered to be at the sovereign discretion of the federal or provincial states. This inhibition is equivalent to the integration that characterizes the European Union's market-centred and state-limiting processes[21]—integration that occurs because member states are prohibited from actions that impede trade and capital flows across national boundaries—but its actual constraint on Canadian governments has been hard to measure. A contemporaneous shift in the managerial philosophy of both elected and bureaucratic policy-makers away from a big-is-better activism in favour of a small-is-best disengagement makes it difficult to determine whether a reduction in interventionist practices by federal and provincial governments is due to officials' fear of falling afoul of the new continental rules or to their own proclivity for neo-liberalism. Non-decision-making is notoriously resistant to scholarly observation: analysts can rarely tell to what extent NAFTA has prevented state actions that might have been taken in its absence. Furthermore, Canadian governments may be renouncing industrial policies that support national enterprises because of their compulsion to eliminate budget deficits, not because of NAFTA's national treatment principle.

Provincial Governments
As a rule, federal off-loading has increased both the *de facto* and *de jure* jurisdiction of the provinces, which have welcomed the extra power when the financial implications were neutral but have had mixed reactions when federal off-loading has meant less money. When off-loading has been accompanied by general cuts in transfer payments, all provinces have protested. When cuts in transfer payments have disproportionately favoured the equalization-receiving, have-not provinces, their otherwise better-off cousins have objected vociferously.

Since the Canadian government negotiates trade treaties but can implement them only in areas of its own constitutional jurisdiction, provincial involvement has been needed in the pursuit of more liberalized trade. For this reason, Ottawa has encouraged increased provincial participation since the Tokyo Round of the GATT negotiations first brought non-tariff barriers to the bargaining table.[22] Paradoxically, increased provincial involvement in trade policy-making has resulted in decreased regional industrial policy capacity, because principles such as national treatment or the right of establishment diminish a sub-national government's ability to foster its own enterprises' competitiveness through traditional programs targeted at indigenous firms. While provincial influence over trade policy has increased, it remains the case that Canada's global and continental trade initiatives have been driven by the federal government.[23] The growing authority of global and continental governance over areas of provincial jurisdiction suggests that increased provincial trade policy capacity results more from federal initiatives and uploading than from federal off-loading or independent 'province-building'.

The provinces' increasing fiscal weight since the 1970s has given them greater authority in what used to be the federal preserve of macroeconomic management, but the use of this authority has been strongly influenced by the federal state. For example, the federal government's 1990 transfer cuts precipitated choleric criticism in the provincial capitals, which then proceeded to bring down just the kind of tough, deficit-cutting budgets Ottawa had sought to provoke.[24] Monetary policy is a matter of federal jurisdiction and has also been used to influence provincial fiscal policy, particularly via the Bank of Canada's price stability policy. All those attempting to swim against this monetary-policy tide eventually fell into line, particularly Ontario.[25] In sum, while provinces have acquired increased capacity and authority relative to the federal state, they have done so in a neo-liberal context that has been largely shaped by the federal state.

The Municipal Level
One consequence of federal cuts in inter-governmental transfers has been provincial off-loading to the municipalities. Provinces have jealously guarded their jurisdiction over local government, so Ottawa's relations with municipalities are far weaker than Washington's with US cities, where local governments are also a constitutional jurisdiction of states.[26] The effects of provincial restraint policies on municipalities have been dramatic, again especially in Ontario, where Toronto has suffered a virtual putsch at the hands of Queen's Park.

Their constitutionally subordinate status does not mean that Canadian cities are cut off from the international political economy. Indeed, a principal mechanism through which the global and continental orders work is a network of international cities that act as growth nodes and connectors to other cities and their regional hinterlands.[27] This global-local interface, captured by the notions of 'glocalization' and 'glurbanization', has been affected by the federal government insofar as it has promoted or resisted globalization. In promoting globalization, for example through the WTO, Ottawa has enhanced the position of its international cities through which trade is organized, particularly Toronto, Vancouver, and Montreal. By refusing the application of four chartered banks to merge into two superbanks, the federal state has implicitly declared its determination, in the face of globalization, to retain a regulatory authority that may help ensure Toronto's survival as a second-tier global financial centre.

FROM PAUL MARTIN TO PAUL MARTIN: FROM WELFARE TO WORKFARE

Keeping this nested, five-tiered interconnection of governing structures in mind, we will proceed to investigate the changes from the Pearson/Trudeau era to the Mulroney/Chrétien era, starting with the domain of economic policy.

The activist state was clearly what Lester Pearson's coterie of ministers and advisers—the economic nationalist, Walter Gordon, the Fabian democrat, Tom Kent, and the social welfare advocate, Paul Martin—thought they had been elected to construct in the mid-1960s. Pierre Trudeau's writings display a related belief in equity-oriented social engineering as the proper role for the modern state. His promise of a 'just society' was clearly premised on the belief that, although government had no business in the bedroom, state action was necessary if social justice was to prevail over the inequities caused by laissez-faire capitalism.[28] By contrast, what makes the current epoch *post-modern* is its scepticism about the notion that states can be rationally and purposefully run to achieve any specific ends. If government is more likely to be the problem than the solution, then it has no business in either the bedrooms or the boardrooms of the nation.

The degree to which the Keynesian vision has been superseded by the neo-liberal model is indicated by such changes as these:

- the long run prevails over the short run as the policy focus;
- controlling inflation trumps reducing unemployment as an immediate priority;
- direct government intervention is viewed as inappropriate, because an economy is believed to reach its optimal equilibrium through the play of market forces;
- the supply side as opposed to the demand side of the economic equation is emphasized; and
- deficit finance is considered an unacceptable policy tool.

None of these characteristics in itself defines the character of economic policy, and to some extent traces of both policy approaches can always be found. Nevertheless, the neo-liberal vision tends to delegitimate the state's use of direct, short-term, demand-based, deficit-supported measures. Emphasizing structural, long-term, supply-side, fiscally balanced policy, the neo-liberal governor has neither a capacity for nor an interest in day-to-day economic intervention.

In Canada changes in macroeconomic policy, industrial policy, and trade policy have been closely connected. Under neo-liberalism these three fields share a diminished concern with the demand side of the economy in favour of engineering permanent, structural solutions. As attention has turned toward the international competitiveness of the Canadian economy, expanding trade has displaced deepening domestic demand as a prime goal of public policy.[29] The shift from one paradigm to the other can be understood as a movement away from a Fordist regime of accumulation (the set of arrangements through which capitalist accumulation functions during a particular historical stage) and from a concomitant Keynesian mode of regulation (the institutional framework within which this accumulation was realized). Just as demand manipulation through fiscal and monetary policy became politically incorrect, high wage levels on the Fordist model lost their cachet as a means for supporting domestic demand. The Swedish high-wage, high-tech success story, so attractive to Canadians with a post-Keynesian mind-set,[30] was dismissed by neo-liberals, who believed high wages impaired the country's international competitiveness. The focus on trade has depreciated the importance of both industrial policy and discretionary, interventionist macroeconomic policies. It has also shifted the levels in the multi-tier model at which governance functions occur. Control over industrial policy, for example, now resides at least as much in NAFTA's interdictions and the WTO's dispute settlement body as in provincial capitals.

Macroeconomic Policy
For three decades after the Second World War Ottawa believed that, by adjusting both monetary and fiscal levers, government could moderate the ups and downs of the business cycle.[31] By the late 1960s, Keynesianism had become associated with the notion, embodied in the Phillips Curve, that inflation and unemployment were direct tradeoffs: if one variable was high, the other would be low.[32] The emergence of 'stagflation' in the 1970s—the coexistence of high inflation and high unemployment—necessarily called into question this

relationship and so Keynesianism's credibility. It also prompted three important policy changes in the mid-1970s that heralded the beginning of the end of the Keynesian era.[33] The imposition of the Anti-Inflation Program (AIP) by Finance Minister Donald Macdonald, the introduction of 'monetary gradualism' by the Bank of Canada, and the restriction of growth in federal spending to no more than trend growth in GNP signalled the post-Keynesian effort to rescue the Keynesian mode of regulation.[34]

These changes did not imply that Keynesian practice was completely rejected in Canada. The persistent deficits that began in 1975 were presented at the time as primarily countercyclical responses to an economic underperformance that was not yet understood to result from a secular decline in growth and productivity rates. While countercyclical demand management had been fettered, budget documents through to 1984 still defended deficit financing as an appropriate policy to offset cyclical economic underperformance.[35] Keeping federal spending within the GNP growth trend was explicitly argued to be consistent with deficit spending in a down year: when growth was beneath the previous trend, spending at the trend level that year would be stimulative.[36] There were no constraints placed on the tax cuts, known as 'tax expenditures', which became the primary mechanism used in the 1970s to stimulate the economy. In the context of stable spending on social welfare, these concessions to business and to middle- and upper-income taxpayers significantly lowered federal revenues and became the direct source of what hindsight would demonstrate were structural deficits.[37] Although the means for what was conceptualized as countercyclical deficit finance had shifted somewhat during the 1970s, the norms remained as alive and well as they had been before 1975.

While marking important alterations of the policy prescribed by the prevailing consensus, the AIP and monetary gradualism were designed to deal with inflation without harming the short-term employment levels that were both a Keynesian and post-Keynesian concern. By controlling wages and prices directly, the federal government sought to reduce inflation without creating higher unemployment.[38] Monetary gradualism was articulated as a longer-term complement to the AIP in the sense that, with respect to its effect on employment, a steady reduction in money supply growth was preferable to a harsh monetary contraction.[39] Along with deficit financing, these policies made sense only in terms of a Keynesian concern for the short-term employment effects of a rapid reduction in demand. In a difficult economic situation they supported the notion that social justice required that state action protect against economic dislocation.

These changes did not imply a reduction of the federal state's role in the economy. On the contrary, the AIP extended the federal state's power to a sphere with which it had little previous experience. Significantly, the courts legitimized this increased federal jurisdiction in the face of provincial protests.[40] The Trudeau government's intractability in its dealings with the provinces, its distrust of continental integration as manifested by the 'third option' with respect to trade, its creation of the Foreign Investment Review Agency (FIRA), and its commitment to the National Energy Program showed that Ottawa refused to abdicate its role. Indeed, the 1983 'recovery budget' presented by Finance Minister Marc Lalonde was probably the most Keynesian budget of the post-war era. It proudly boasted of its high deficit as a means to boost employment and facilitate recovery from the 1981-2 recession.[41]

Although consistently defended by Prime Minister Trudeau and his government, the federal role was nevertheless challenged by the province-building that had begun in 1960 with Quebec's Quiet Revolution and had spread in the 1970s to the western provinces. Provincial governments were becoming more important economic actors, both in absolute terms and relative to the federal government.[42] The friction with business and the provinces caused by Trudeau's coercive intervention in micro-level decisions created a generalized obloquy in the private sector, some provincial capitals, and the media over any policy that impacted upon corporate or provincial autonomy. The resulting delegitimation of interventionist policy by the early 1980s created political opportunities for Brian Mulroney's neo-liberalism, which advocated a state that would provide a context for private sector growth without making decisions for it. Having campaigned in part on restraint in government, the Tories deplored the deficit financing of the previous decade.[43] The official disavowal of the Keynesian consensus in Canada was signalled shortly after the

Progressive Conservatives took office when the new minister of finance, Michael Wilson, presented a document that defined the economic doctrine for the new government's mandate.[44] *A New Direction for Canada* no longer conceptualized deficit finance as an appropriate response to economic underperformance during the business cycle; now it was seen as dangerously inflationary. Deficit reduction was identified as an important part of the comprehensive reforms that the Mulroney government believed would restore competitiveness to the Canadian economy.

In the event, the Tories did not come close to attaining their deficit reduction goal, even though, or rather because, they implemented other politically costly changes. The Bank of Canada's price stability policy[45] combined with CUFTA brutally to exacerbate the impact of the 1990-1 world recession.[46] This economic slowdown actually engendered increased government spending (particularly in the form of unemployment insurance payments and debt servicing charges) and resulted in major tax revenue reductions—and consequently a rising deficit. Procrastination in introducing the Goods and Services Tax (GST) made fiscal balance still more elusive.

Structural reform was presented by the Mulroney government as necessitated by the federal state's loss of power: international economic forces had eroded Ottawa's capacity to intervene effectively in either Keynesian or post-Keynesian terms. Canada should not be insulated from global change, but should embrace it. The GST exemplified this attitudinal shift: it liberated domestic producers from a manufacturers' tax that harmed their competitive position. A consumption tax, though regressive, was a lesser, and much preferred, evil. Price stability policy disciplined wages both by reducing inflation and by creating enough unemployment to weaken the bargaining position of labour.

Neo-liberal restructuring also had definite implications for the balance of power between the federal government and the regimes below and above. Price stability, the GST, and free trade required a federal state strong enough to face down the objections from various provinces that suffered serious regional effects from these tough-love policies.

The alienation of jurisdiction by the federal government to the global and continental trade and investment regimes impeded Ottawa's efforts to balance its budget. By hobbling economic performance and raising debt-servicing charges, these structural policies contravened the government's fiscal goals even though the rising deficit in the early 1990s exacerbated the perceived urgency of deficit reduction. Moving authority to global and continental regimes worsened Ottawa's fiscal condition. This became a crucial reason for the movement of state functions downward to lower levels in the multi-tier state. Caught in this dilemma, Ottawa made substantial cuts 'by stealth' to its own social programs[47] and off-loaded some of its fiscal problems by cutting transfers, particularly to the 'have' provinces. In this way both deficits and responsibility for social policy were shifted down to the sub-national tier, which in turn tried to pass its problems on to the municipalities. Off-loading responsibilities to the provinces (environment), deregulating services (transportation), downsizing (cuts to the federal civil service's employment base), and privatization (sale of crown corporations such as Air Canada) reduced the functions and the structures of the federal state.

Despite these measures, which appeared drastic at the time, the fiscal position of the federal government was worse when the Mulroney government left office than when it took power. Nevertheless, the Progressive Conservatives did create the political conditions that would allow Jean Chrétien's finance minister, Paul Martin Jr, to eradicate the deficit. The recession of the early 1990s, and the very slow recovery that followed, accelerated and deepened a trend toward delinking the perceived interests of the Canadian mass public from the Keynesian welfare state and the deficits that had come to support it. High unemployment, declining real incomes, and the shift of employment from unionized to non-standard work undermined the sense of mutual aid that had once generated public support for a more generous state. Instead, the combination of great personal economic stress among the general public and its sense that the welfare state benefited only privileged bureaucrats and special interests elicited a turn inward for self-protection. In addition, there was a growing apprehension among the public that the welfare state would not long survive to help people, even when they ultimately qualified for support.[48] This changed consciousness allowed deficit reduction to be credibly presented as a matter of the 'general' interest. Wide public support for the endeavour allowed cutting to be done openly rather than by stealth, and gave the Liberals the public support for deficit reduction that had eluded Brian Mulroney.

The Liberals had several other advantages. The structural transformation of the economy and the massive dislocation of the manufacturing sector engendered by free trade was largely completed by the time the Progressive Conservatives were routed from office. The GST was in place by 1991 and became an indispensable source of increasing revenue. The government could at least plan around a predictable level of underperformance (particularly high unemployment) rather than have to cope with a deep recession and rebuild the revenue structure. NAFTA merely consolidated continentalism; it did not constitute a change in kind. When interest rates started to fall after 1995, the Liberal government reaped big rewards in the form of lower debt-servicing charges.

The Liberals purged Keynesian notions from their public rhetoric to a greater extent than had their Tory predecessors. Deficit reduction was to be permanent, not simply confined to the upside of the business cycle.[49] Even if the government believed that demand contraction following from fiscal retrenchment would have a negative impact on growth or employment, it was not so foolish as to admit this. The political space for the government's fiscal agenda widened to the extent that the public no longer thought deficit elimination would undermine the economy.

The combination of the inherited Mulroney measures, public acquiescence, and the final purge of Keynesian ideas surrounding deficit finance meant that the fiscal question could become the dominant theme of public debate during the Liberal tenure through to 1998. Policy of every stripe was filtered through its relationship to the government's budget-balancing priority. While Paul Martin's insistence on making prudent assumptions and keeping a contingency reserve certainly facilitated deficit reduction, the real explanation for his success in balancing the budget and then running surpluses was the Liberals' remarkably disciplined commitment to the goal, even in the face of concerted provincial opposition to transfer payment cuts. Their tenacity proved possible because it was electorally viable and brilliantly marketed. No unfinished neo-liberal structural reform remained to push the government off its track.

From one perspective, the logic of neo-liberal deficit elimination required substantial and permanent reduction in key federal responsibilities. For example, no longer would the state take responsibility for the national transportation system. Federal transfer payments that had matched provincial payments for social assistance dollar for dollar under the Canada Assistance Plan (CAP) were combined with the Established Program Financing block transfers for health and education in 1996 to produce the Canada Health and Social Transfer (CHST), which cut federal transfers by over $6 billion. The CHST's fixed sum vitiated the automatic countercyclical content of the CAP. With its diminished funding came reduced federal control over the content of social policy.

Another interpretation of the Liberal record is that the government reluctantly cut programs to preserve its social policy power in the longer run. Only if the books were balanced, some Liberals maintained, could social programs be saved and ultimately strengthened. Once budgetary surpluses were achieved, it would be possible both to reduce tax burdens and to 'reinvest' in social policy. On this view, fiscal retrenchment was a means to higher social goals, and could be conceptualized as participating in embedded liberal visions of the secure society that the government purported to be fostering. This argument is consistent with Paul Martin's advocacy of a reinvigorated international 'architecture' with strengthened Bretton Woods institutions.[50] His efforts at the International Monetary Fund hearkened back to Canada's role in the creation of the post-war order, and, if successful, would also help embed macroeconomic regulation in higher levels of governance. The endeavour could be understood as moving authority up to the global level so that the federal state could be salvaged, along with its domestic policy objectives.

This reasoning may assuage the guilt of some left Liberals, but the Chrétien regime's liberalism proved itself in practice to be distinctly more 'neo' than 'embedded'. Social programs now do more to facilitate market functions than to protect citizens from them. Having lost their justification as automatic stabilizers of demand, they have acquired a supply-side rationale as 'bridges' to employment. The federal fiscal structure has become much less sensitive to variations in economic conditions than was the case even in the early 1990s.

Keynesian demand management is now dismissed in the rhetoric of budget documents. Concerns about short-term employment have disappeared from policy-makers' discourse. Yet, while the Liberal fiscal agenda was of primarily neo-liberal stock, the need to justify retrenchment as a mechanism to save social programs was certainly part of what animated the government's actions. Some of the cutting was manifestly reluctant rather than enthusiastic, and with budgetary balance some reinvestement started to emerge. Federal fiscal policy did reveal strands of an embedded liberal DNA.

Industrial Policy
Industrial or sectoral policy also distinguishes the Pearson/Trudeau state from its Mulroney/Chrétien incarnation. Under the earlier regime, government was deemed responsible for intervening to save troubled industries and protect national economic players. The 1970s crisis of Canada's macroeconomic management was directly linked to its fractured regime of accumulation. In the Fordist post-war compromise between labour and capital, high wages for workers in assembly line industries made possible the mass consumption that generated enough demand to keep these manufacturing processes growing. As productivity increased, wages rose—thanks to government-sanctioned collective bargaining. This regime of accumulation shattered in part because it failed to develop linkages between the extraction of natural resources and their processing into finished products. Instead, resources were exported to the American market in massive quantities and manufacturing for the national economy was largely controlled by branch plants of US transnational corporations, which typically imported high-cost components for local assembly. In the process, Canada received minimal rents for its resources and contributed to higher returns in the US. At the same time the branch-plant economy led to a rising financial drain of management charges, royalties, and dividend payments to the US head-office economy. With tax revenues from this truncated economic system kept permanently low, the welfare aspect of the federal state never reached European levels in protecting citizens from the vicissitudes of industrialism. Dependence on American capital acted as one constraint; a relatively low level of worker mobilization was another. National unity and

nation-building rather than class struggle provided the dominant axis along which social consciousness was organized.[51]

As GATT-negotiated declines in Canada's tariffs proceeded to reduce protection for territorially based manufacturing through the 1970s, and as the federal government's efforts at maintaining an interventionist economic role failed by the early 1980s, the logic justifying a century-old import substitution industrialization strategy collapsed. The Canada Development Corporation, Petro-Canada, FIRA, and the National Energy Program had expressed the faith that the government could and should control developments within its own economic territory, particularly for the benefit of the industrial heartland in Ontario. But with new Canadian direct investment abroad having exceeded the entry of new foreign direct investment since 1975, Canada's continentally-oriented regime of accumulation could no longer sanction a national mode of regulation that had become intolerable to those, such as the western provinces, who had never been its beneficiaries.[52]

Under Mulroney, intervention in the national market under the guise of an industrial strategy became unacceptable. Instead, the government took pride in negotiating international rules that were to replace and even prohibit the old ways of affecting the nature of the economic game. The federal government steadily withdrew from microeconomic policy-making. This retreat originated in the Mulroney government's belief that previous efforts to formulate a national industrial strategy under the Trudeau Liberals had failed. Retreat accelerated during the Chrétien Liberals' attack on their inherited deficit. The resulting program cuts have radically restricted use of federal funds to enhance either innovation or productivity.

The welfare state was cut back partly to reduce budget deficits, but also to provide the greater labour 'flexibility' that business in Canada was demanding. CUFTA made it easier to move plants to the US or Mexico, and put pressure on trade unions to make wage concessions. Supporting this competitive imperative, the Canadian state whittled down the social wage, reducing unemployment insurance benefits, cutting assistance to people on welfare, and generally doing less to protect citizens from the economic circumstances it was engendering. As corporations responded to free trade, the foreign-owned branch plants evolved into hollowed-out subsidiaries,[53] and Canadian-owned national champions, which once served the domestic market, restructured to serve the continental market.

Discourse among most of the political elite by the late 1990s contended that what used to be microeconomic, firm-, or sector-centred industrial policy should now focus on 'investing' in education for skills development and in infrastructure for attracting footloose investment to locate in Canada. In this optic, government should no longer be a hierarchically superior organization connected through a vertical relationship with the market. Instead it should become a heterarchically articulated agency nourishing a horizontal, information-sharing, and morale-boosting relationship with the private sector. Such re-thinking of government's proper role emphasizes the move away from Fordist mass production assembly plants toward more specialized, more dynamic clusterings of very flexible, knowledge-based firms with a less permanent, less structured workforce.

Under this approach, subnational regions become more natural loci than the federal tier for the needed public sector encouragement of private sector partnerships and alliances. Hence, provincial governments may constitute the preferable administrative tier for establishing innovative systems that galvanize private-sector initiatives with a techno-economic, lean production mission.[54] Ottawa's partial evacuation of the industrial policy field has obligingly created space for provincial activity in the field, but the 1999 federal budget's post-deficit investment in creating, diffusing, and commercializing knowledge is symbolically very important. Not the neo-liberal tax-cutting for which elites clamoured in the name of productivity, it appears to be of a coordinating, Ottawa-affirming character. Ironically, just days after the government enriched its Technology Partnerships Canada program as part of this investment, the WTO issued an interim decision invalidating the program, and, at the same time, rubbing in the point that the federal state was no longer master in its own house.[55]

Trade Policy

The primary mechanism through which the neo-liberal federal state has engaged in industrial policy is the subjection of the Canadian economy to the disciplines of international competition. While not a fully proactive, 'anticipatory' industrial strategy, the use of trade policy in lieu of an industrial policy is more than a merely reactive approach.[56]

It is a non-invasive way of precipitating ongoing industrial restructuring, devolving authority to both higher and lower levels of governance, and further empowering non-national capital.

By the early 1980s, when nationalists in the Trudeau government had lost their battle to enhance the interventionist thrust of federal industrial policy, the government's focus was already moving to commercial policy.[57] In effect, free trade was an industrial policy designed to force firms to become competitive, under the threat of extinction. The emerging neo-liberal paradigm knitted macroeconomic, industrial, and trade policy together into a coherent pattern: in a relatively small and increasingly open market, domestic demand was not to be the economy's driver.

Trade policy was distinguished from the two other pillars of the neo-liberal platform by its dependence on negotiating with other governments norms that directly affected the scope of what had previously been the state's strictly internal policy domain. The federal government's implementation of the bilateral CUFTA in 1989, followed shortly by the trilateral NAFTA in 1994 and the multilateral WTO in 1995, signalled the effort to institutionalize a continental and global mode of regulation appropriate for an increasingly globalized and continentalized regime of accumulation. From the viewpoint of the Canadian state system, these trade agreements have created an 'external constitution' that establishes new limits on the permissible actions of Canadian governments and creates new rights, primarily for corporations, and most notably foreign transnational companies, vis-à-vis the three internal tiers of the Canadian state.

At the same time these bilateral, trilateral, and multilateral agreements extend the sphere of operation of the Canadian state, whose civil servants—and, on occasion, NGOs—participate in transnational policy-making. The GATT was so weak as a forum for arbitrating trade conflicts that it was dubbed sarcastically the 'general agreement to talk and talk'. Successive rounds of trade talks did succeed in reducing global tariff levels significantly. GATT's replacement in 1995 by the more muscular WTO—which has an autonomous, supra-national capacity and an integrated structure with legal personality designed to impose the discipline of collectively negotiated rules on even the most powerful sovereign state—suggests a substantial change at the global level of governance in the institutionalization of the trade policy function.[58]

Along with the other trading nations, Canada participated with considerable effect in the creation of this new system and has continued to play an active role in the negotiations, which have extended the WTO's norms to telecommunications, informational technology, and beyond. The construction of trade rules has now become an endless cycle of confrontation, negotiation, adjudication, and bargaining, followed by renewed disputation and negotiation. As an energetic participant in this cycle, Canada has tried to affect the ongoing trade agenda (which now includes rules for environmental, labour, and human rights along with conditions for the admission of Russia and China), while bargaining separately to achieve bilateral trade deals with Israel and Chile. All the while it is continuously interacting within its primary continental regime, NAFTA, through its ongoing, daily involvement in Washington, where every roaming lobbyist and the least expected congressional hiccup can spell trouble for the world's largest dyadic trade relationship.

The implications for the state's structure and function in this ever-broadening scope of trade policy come into starker relief once the distinction between 'foreign' and 'domestic' policy breaks down. Such nominally domestic policy areas as the regulation of anti-trust and financial services now overlap with external trade and investment norms. The inclusion of cultural, environmental, food, and health policies within the scope of trade disputes signals a new phase of deeper interpenetration between the global and the national.

Given the strengthening of the connection between the flow of commerce and the flux of capital, rules governing trade practices cannot be isolated from norms specifying the treatment of foreign capital. Codes on investment were initiated at the continental level with CUFTA, which reduced the capacity of Investment Canada (formerly FIRA) to regulate foreign takeovers of Canadian companies. With the federal state's ability to screen foreign investment minimized, NAFTA moved toward giving foreign investors rights over the Canadian state in its Chapter 11. This innovation has given foreign firms powerful new rights to challenge almost any regulatory action that might 'expropriate' their future earnings. The federal government's withdrawal of its legislated elimination of the gasoline additive MMT in the face of a legal challenge by Ethyl Corporation of Virginia, the producer of the octane enhancer, showed how dramatically power had been lost to the foreign marketplace.

This increase in the powers of foreign corporations over the Canadian state points to the need to follow how players in the private sector interact horizontally with the state. In the domain of international trade politics, the transnational corporation (TNC) is playing a growing and contradictory role, alternately undermining and reinforcing the sovereign state in its participation in global governance. For instance, the same export-oriented corporation that calls for the privatization of crown corporations and the deregulation of the economy in Canada may also be soliciting municipalities to create fully serviced industrial parks in which to locate its plants, importuning provincial governments to increase the supply of technically skilled graduates, lobbying the federal government to negotiate a phrase change in an international agreement that will favour its interests, and working directly with Canadian officials in Washington or Geneva as they strategize over a trade dispute within NAFTA or at the WTO. TNCs, whether foreign- or Canadian-owned, will be pressing officials in Ottawa to respond to their needs, needs that may be articulated by special interest groups lobbying for big business (Business Council on National Issues), a business sector (Canadian Manufacturers Association), importer or exporter associations, a particular industry such as steel, or an industrial sector such as auto parts.[59] What was once an arcane bureaucratic dossier looked after by trade officials haggling over customs codes is now a congested public policy field crowded further by organizations of many kinds that are representing constituencies in civil society suddenly made aware that their interests are affected by the new phenomenon of deep integration.[60]

Environmental issues dramatize most clearly how national policy-making has become simultaneously internationalized and localized. That provincial environmental regulations can be dragged onto the international agenda was shown when Ontario attempted to require that all beer be sold in recyclable bottles. This move sparked accusations of protectionism from outraged American breweries (which sold their product in cans) and resulted in an adverse ruling by a GATT panel, the implementation of which was mediated by the federal government.[61] Greenpeace is the flagship for the new post-modern, anti-statist NGO that is able to mobilize transnational coalitions against particular domestic targets, ranging from British Columbia's practice of clear-cut logging to Newfoundland's seal harvesting.[62] By intervening in global and continental forums these NGOs are stimulating the crystallization of a supranational consciousness that is linking trade questions to environmental issues. Ecological questions have already become annexed to trade issues at the continental level in NAFTA's Commission for Environmental Cooperation, whose mandate is to reconcile the goal of controlling protectionism with that of sustainable development.

The transnational qualities of environmental politics clearly transcend the scope of the old nation-state, but attachment to sovereignty dies hard. Federal-provincial conflicts still determine whatever collective inter-governmental action is taken—as the disappointing follow-through from the Rio and Kyoto environmental summits confirmed. Most provinces have declined to sign the North American Agreement on Environmental Cooperation, NAFTA's environmental side agreement. It is an indication of the federal government's greater commitment to trade than to the environment that it uses its treaty power aggressively in the former case and tentatively in the latter, even though it has comparable constitutional authority in each area. Provinces also favour trade over the environment, but they have limited constitutional leverage over Ottawa in these areas. In both the spheres of environment[63] and trade and commerce,[64] the Supreme Court has expanded federal regulatory jurisdiction.[65] Using the same logic the Supreme Court has increased federalism's centripetal tendencies by ruling that the nature of telecommunications requires jurisdiction be lodged at the pan-Canadian level.[66]

Complicating the federal state's new trade-policy function is the reinforcement of already strong regional governments. The broad, constitutionally entrenched jurisdiction of Canadian provinces over natural resources, transportation, education, and social policy makes the federal state able to do little more than speak on their behalf in international forums on these issues. Nevertheless, CUFTA and NAFTA committed the federal government to take 'all necessary measures' to ensure provincial compliance, a stronger requirement than the 'reasonable measures' standard prevailing under GATT. In the process of courting foreign investment in the hope of attracting projects that will generate tax revenues and jobs, provinces and cities offer subsidies and concessions that can give rise to claims of unfair trading when they successfully lure an investor away from another jurisdiction. Such bidding wars show that, while sovereign states may be actively engaged in trade liberalization, their sub-national jurisdictions can flout such resulting norms as the WTO subsidy code with considerable impunity.

There is also a question as to how far the provincial state can go in representing its interests abroad. Even though these governments may have a considerable potential for international relations in a globalizing world, practical budgetary constraints and formal problems of recognition limit provinces in this ambition. Taking a feather from the cap of Germany's *Laender*, they could demand from the courts guarantees that they be able to reverse federal government actions alienating any of their powers in the course of international negotiations at which they are not directly represented.[67] They could even insist on direct representation in the new continental and global regimes. But there is surprisingly little discord in this dossier. Indeed, provincial voices readily sing as part of a federal chorus when 'Team Canada' sallies forth on federal-provincial trade missions in Asia, Latin America, or Europe.

If their bureaucratic capacity is inadequate to project their regions' interests abroad, provinces may need to rely on the federal state to represent them in intergovernmental forums even in areas of provincial jurisdiction. Cutbacks of the provinces' quasi-embassies abroad confirm that provinces are experiencing real limits to their capacity for direct participation in global affairs. Continental governance has generated little in the way of the 'region states' that some observers expected.[68] Contrary to expectations following the signing of NAFTA, long-standing transnational linkages of Canadian provincial governments with contiguous states of the US are not expanding to include equally close relations with states of the Mexican federation.[69] Indeed, even Ontario's relations with the Great Lakes states have withered.

If our analysis has accurately depicted the economic shape of neo-liberalism in Canada, we can conclude that it has:

- changed the way that the state's role in the economy is applied;
- rearranged the distribution of power among the five levels on which state functions are fulfilled; and

- seriously affected the impact of social programs on the distribution of income and well-being.

Since these changes have been effected by both major national parties in Canada, they can be taken to constitute a paradigm shift among the country's ruling elites, who, in conjunction with their ideological counterparts in most other developed and developing countries, have facilitated the spread of a globalized market and opened their borders to its impact at home. Our next task is to determine whether neo-liberalism has by the same token transformed the Canadian state's political face.

THE CONTRADICTORY POLITICAL FEATURES OF THE NEO-LIBERAL STATE

Social Policy

The advocacy state of the Pearson and Trudeau period offered public support to help the marginalized find their political voice through programs such as the Company of Young Canadians, Official Languages legislation, Opportunities for Youth, and the Local Initiatives Program. A prime beneficiary of such an empowerment approach to participatory politics has been the women's movement.

In the late 1960s a path-breaking royal commission established an ambitious agenda for government action to reduce the flagrant inequalities experienced by women in the political economy. The 1970s witnessed some considerable progress on this dossier. Most notable was the success of politicized women during the early 1980s debate on the Charter of Rights and Freedoms in having affirmative action constitutionally protected and gender equality exempted (along with Pierre Trudeau's coveted minority language education rights) from the controversial 'notwithstanding' clause, which allowed legislatures to override most Charter provisions. By 1984 women's voices were strong enough to command a nationally televised debate on their issues during that year's federal election campaign. Women's groups opposed Brian Mulroney's government, even though, as is now acknowledged by active feminists, more progress was made on women's issues during his tenure than before it. This hostility was due to their interpretation of the impact of his government's structural economic policies upon the interests of women, especially in its second term.[70] Substantial subsequent budget cuts under the Chrétien Liberals led to a reining in of the various agencies set up in the heyday of the women's movement. The official response to women's movement outrage has been efforts to delegitimate such criticism by labelling it as whining by a 'rude, belligerent, ignorant' special-interest group no longer seen as worthy of public financial support.[71]

Neo-liberal budget cuts have had an analogous chilling effect on the social security system. Established in the Pearson/Trudeau years, it delivered payments through social insurance and demogrants to individuals according to universalistic standards rationalized as rights of equal citizenship. The Mulroney/Chrétien years have seen payments income-tested, targeted, and increasingly made conditional on the recipient's engaging in work or training.[72] These changes in the direction of policies toward individuals affect the nature of civil society by subverting the integration of the working class in the national community and undermining a pan-Canadian sense of identity based on social justice. In its place a *sauve qui peut* attitude has permeated a society increasingly polarized according to income levels, undermining the capacity of the federal state to integrate Canadians by identifying social justice with Canadian citizenship.

With the emergence of an economic policy that focusses increasingly on investment in human capital, the distinction between economic and social policy is becoming more and more blurred.[73] As Ottawa has cut back its social policy transfers to the provinces, so too have national standards been weakened. The old CAP, for example, required that welfare be available to everybody in need, that there be an appeals process, that the provinces provide certain basic information to the federal government, and that no provincial residency requirements be imposed on recipients. The sole surviving condition in the CHST is the prohibition on residency requirements. Canada Health Act principles are still operative, but erosion in the comprehensiveness of coverage has occurred as funding has declined. This provincialization of social policy, the costs of which can in turn be off-loaded to municipalities, has a disintegrating impact on Canadian society. Since equalization has been built into many programs, the divergence of interests between the equalization-receiving and equalization-giving provinces and populations has risen, although the decision in the 1999 federal budget to return CHST entitlements to a per capita basis will mitigate this tendency. The divergence of interests has also increased as equalization payments to the worse-off provinces are spent more on imports and less on the production of the better-off provinces.[74]

An embarrassing result of these changes was a damning report issued by the United Nations Committee on Economic, Social and Cultural Rights, which condemned Canada for allowing serious social problems to fester, including the deterioration of human rights, the conditions on native reserves, and homelessness. While referring specifically to the years from 1989 to 1994, the committee raised grave questions about further worsening following the drastic cuts in Paul Martin's 1995 budget. The role of the Canadian NGOs that used this global forum to exert pressure on their domestic politicians clearly illustrates the connection between the five levels of the state. These non-state participants included the Charter Committee on Poverty Issues, the National Anti-Poverty Organization, the National Association of Women and the Law, the Grand Council of the Crees, the Ad Hoc Committee on Trade and Investment, the Inter-Church Council on Immigrants and Refugees, and Toronto's Parkdale Community Services.[75] This example shows how, when social policy authority was off-loaded, civil society flexed its muscle by turning to the global level of the multi-tier state as part of its strategy to pressure the federal level to reverse its reduction of welfare standards.

Constitutional Politics
The impact of constitutional politics on the tension between centrifugal and centripetal forces is ambivalent. The 1982 Charter of Rights and Freedoms both sustains social-democratic norms and supports the emerging values of the neo-liberal order. On the one hand it has fostered a sense of entitlement for all Canadians (at least in Canada outside Quebec) as holders of individual rights. On the other hand, the Charter continues to be rights-enhancing and status-enhancing for minority groups and collectivities organized around gender, ethnicity, language, and sexual orientation. These developments enhance the role of the courts relative to all legislatures, whether federal or provincial. They also bolster federal power vis-à-vis the provinces,

because Charter rights are identified with the federal government, which fought for them—against the provinces' resistance—in the early 1980s, and because they are rights held through membership in the Canadian political community, not through being part of a province.[76]

To the extent that individual rights are protected by virtue of individualism, the Charter disaggregated the Canadian political community. To the extent that collective rights are protected by virtue of membership in a particular group, the Charter's centralizing pan-Canadian vision was not attached to notions of collective provision or mutual aid. Under the Charter, individuals were Canadianized but isolated from each other; groups were Canadianized, but not by participating in a common interest. A distinct identity as Canadians came at the expense of a sense of social obligation to Canadians. The notion of responsible parliamentary government as the locus of the general interest and of the protection of rights diminished in favour of the courts as the new guarantor of these constitutional, rights-based values. The parliamentary state, in which politicians from the two main national parties were empowered by periodic elections, had been altered by the growing political role of judges and the accompanying 'Charter consciousness'.

The Constitution Act of 1982 was negotiated by a prime minister with a deep commitment to a specific vision of a pan-Canadian state.[77] However, as is all too well known, the Constitution was patriated without the premier of Quebec's signature. This failing allowed Brian Mulroney to campaign in Quebec on a platform of restoring the province to the Canadian constitutional family 'with honour and enthusiasm'. As Mulroney's federalism was more decentralized than Trudeau's, he was able to negotiate with the provincial premiers at Meech Lake an accord that accepted Quebec's demands and extended their decentralizing provisions to the other provinces as well.

The extent to which participatory, pan-Canadian Charter values with respect to constitutional change had taken hold in Canada outside Quebec was not well understood at that time. The closed processes of executive federalism by which the Meech Lake Accord was negotiated, its decentralizing tenor, and the 'distinct society' clause raised public ire outside Quebec, particularly when Trudeau in retirement launched his virulent attack on the deal.[78] Newfoundland and Manitoba did not ratify the Accord within the three-year time frame, causing it to be stillborn. This failure to negotiate the Canadian state's constitutional decentralization precipitated the fracturing of the federal party system. A small group led by Lucien Bouchard, calling itself the Bloc Québécois (BQ) and dedicated to achieving sovereignty for Quebec, split from the Tory caucus. In the west, Preston Manning founded the Reform party as a neo-conservative, populist movement animated in no small part by hostility to Quebec. The Quebec-Prairie axis of the Mulroney coalition collapsed over the failure to reconcile agendas that were superficially compatible in terms of a common wish for decentralization, but that were fundamentally animated by different national understandings of Canada.[79]

A further outcome of the Meech Lake debacle was a new level of nationalist rage in Quebec, which prompted Mulroney's second effort at constitutional reform. As much as the Meech process was closed, the Charlottetown process was open, but by then the positions of Quebec and of Canada outside Quebec (particularly the west) were too polarized for reconciliation, and the new Charlottetown Accord failed to gain approval by referendum in 1992 either in Quebec or in the rest of Canada. In constitutional terms, the centralizing norms of Trudeau's Charter had prevailed over the decentralized federal agenda Mulroney sought in part as a complement to his continental economic vision. The political result was a regionally-based party system. In the 1993 federal election, the Progressive Conservatives were reduced from two successive large majorities to a mere two seats in the House of Commons.[80] The BQ became the official opposition, even though it held no seats outside Quebec. Reform was the third party, with just one seat east of Manitoba. Along with the Progressive Conservatives, the NDP lost official party status, and while the Chrétien Liberals won seats in every province of the country, their sweep of 98 of Ontario's 99 ridings constituted their base of support. Mulroney's coalition had exploded in the wake of the failed Meech and Charlottetown accords, the FTA, the GST, and a devastating recession. In the process, the party system, which once played a unifying role in the national polity, now mirrors and reinforces both inter-federal and inter-class conflict. The near victory of the Yes forces in Quebec's 1995 referendum on sovereignty only emphasized the territorial and national divisions in Canadian politics.

The attack on interest groups and recipients of social assistance as 'special' and 'privileged' has emerged from a related, rightward-leaning populism that seeks to retrieve more direct forms of democracy—

the restoration of control to a mass public through referendums, recalls, and initiatives—from what is seen as co-optation by representative democracy.[81] This anti-elitism is given political expression by the Reform party in national politics and by the Conservative provincial governments of Ralph Klein in Alberta and Mike Harris in Ontario. It is visible in accountability legislation that fetters the discretion of elected representatives in many provinces by requiring balanced budgets, and in public reaction against the political content of judicial decisions such as those relating to crime and pornography.

At a time when the whole world is being wired to an interactive communications system that empowers the individual with information in unprecedented quantities and at dazzling speeds, the upper reaches of the multi-level state offer the most limited and indirect forms of popular control. Radical, even xenophobic populism in the politics of countries as different as France and Australia is already expressing this disenchantment with the democratic deficit as the global and continental levels of the multi-level state appear unable to resolve the problems left behind by its sovereign Fordist, Keynesian, and modernist predecessor.

Foreign Policy

A curious paradox of the democratic deficit in the face of globalization can be found in the most elitist of all public policy fields. Levels of citizen participation in Canada's foreign policy formation are higher than ever before, thanks to the federal government's encouragement of grass roots contributions to discussions of Ottawa's diplomatic initiatives. The astonishing examples of NGO mobilization at several world summits, such as the Asia Pacific Economic Cooperation (APEC) leaders' meeting in 1997, and against the Multilateral Agreement on Investment (MAI) at the OECD in 1998, demonstrate falling levels of tolerance for elite behaviour at the global level if it is not based on extensive consultation.

In this conjuncture of enhanced participation, the federal government has also retrieved some authority in foreign policy. The collapse of the Soviet Union relieved Canada of having to toe Washington's anti-communist line and play a secondary military role fully integrated in the NATO alliance system. The end of the East-West nuclear stand-off has shifted the locus of foreign policy authority from a continental or multilateral level back to the federal state.

The ideational corollary of the end of the Cold War is a noticeable shift in official discourse from traditional realpolitik notions of defence to more holistic language about 'human security'.[82] Although US coercive power has become even more irresistible, the disappearance of the Soviet threat has enabled the Canadian government to take a lead on such issues as the international treaty to abolish land mines, the institution of an international criminal court, and even the consideration of NATO's nuclear disarmament—all in defiance of its neighbour, the global superpower on whose economy and culture it has never been more dependent.

During the Cold War, 'multilateralism' described Canada's strategy of active participation in inter-governmental bodies to offset its asymmetrical bilateral dependency on the US. In the post-Cold War period, when intergovernmental institutions have become more global than Atlantic in scope, Canada's ranking in the international hierarchy has become vulnerable. Although it has retained its place as the seventh largest economy, following Russia's economic disintegration, the country's relative importance has diminished, because of the rise of various Third World economies. The threatened loss of membership in the 'great power club' may have served to stimulate rather than diminish the Canadian state's efforts to participate in a global governance for which its diplomatic culture as a mid-sized, federal, binational power gives it a historical predilection. A new version of multilateralism—building coalitions with other sovereign states and exploiting with them the machinery established by the available international institutions—has become an increasingly important thrust of the Canadian government's diplomatic practice, which is increasingly focussed on low-cost, high-visibility, symbolic politics and decreasingly willing to spend public dollars on serious and expensive aid to destitute Third World zones.[83]

Participation in a continental regime necessarily limits the sovereignty of the members, for whom it at the same time provides forums for expanded diplomatic action. The Organization of American States (OAS) is a bi-continental organization in which Canada plays happy soldier in order to demonstrate its commitment to the Western hemisphere. As a multilateral network with a renewed dynamic, the OAS offers Canada an additional mechanism for distinguishing its identity from that of its dominant neighbour through coalition-building with the Latin states. A dramatic example of such self-assertion through association in this traditionally US-dominated organization was Ottawa's successful initiation of a resolution that condemned the US Congress's Helms-Burton bill. Canada is also participating in the pre-negotiations for the Free Trade of the Americas Agreement (FTAA), targeted by the Miami Declaration of 1994 as an extension of CUFTA and NAFTA. If successfully negotiated, the FTAA will both further limit Canadian sovereignty and increase the federal state's role in hemispheric affairs. Beyond North America–South America intercontinentalism, Canada engages enthusiastically in APEC, the budding consultation forum among states sharing frontage on the Pacific Ocean. APEC shows how Canada's old multilateralism, which focussed on NATO's military operations, has taken on a more globally directed, trade-centred form that offers the federal state greater room for manoeuvre than it had under NATO's constraining nuclear umbrella.

CONCLUSION

This review confirms that substantial changes have taken place in the functions and structures of the Canadian state, from the activist, relatively generous practices of the Pearson and Trudeau governments to the regressive stances of neo-liberal politics. Federal shapes have shifted in response to a changing environment and have helped to shape that environment. The federal state is different from its modernist predecessor both because of its neo-liberal traits and because it has become so tightly interconnected with governance above and below that it is now just one tier in an evolving and nested multi-level state structure. While there has been change, its nature is not always obvious and its consequences are not always consistent. Continuities with earlier eras also exist. Finally, there is some evidence of a return to a more active federal state, and the insufficiency of the neo-liberal model itself creates the basis for further evolution.

The boundaries between state, market, and civil society have become more porous. It does not follow that the state is declining just because, for example, airlines administer immigration procedures at their check-in counters, or because advertisers take on the job of policing their own practices. These developments could simply be an indicator of sensible delegation. Similarly, the transnational activity of social movements, epistemic communities, and NGOs may complicate inter-governmental relations but may not *ipso facto* threaten the *raison d'être* of sovereign states.[84] While strong states might lose some of their monopoly control over foreign affairs, weaker, more decentralized states like Canada may gain by exploiting 'their' NGOs' transnational endeavours to project the national interest.

The conceptual question, 'How can we describe the sovereign state?' does not deal with the normative question about how to sustain the quality of the social and political life achieved under the modernist, Fordist, Keynesian welfare state of the first post-Second World War decades. To be sure, the phenomenon of globalization may be a process through which capitalism is liberating itself from political control and engendering ever-increasing disparities between rich and poor both within and among countries.[85] Although a decline in the level of social services for the citizenry, a weakening of the power of trade unions to defend workers, and a diminished capacity to redistribute wealth on egalitarian principles seem to be indicators of social regression inherent in neo-liberalism, these do not appear to be logically necessary characteristics of the emerging multi-level state. Even though the shapes of governance are shifting, the world of federal states may not be as 'global' as both proponents and critics of globalization assume.[86]

If some variant of the proposed Tobin tax on international capital flows were instituted, redistribution in favour of poorer countries might become possible through some form of global governance. A citizens' version of the MAI is being proposed by the Council of Canadians, an NGO that has developed an international coalition to demand that rights given TNCs be balanced by obligations that foreign investors create jobs with high labour standards, maintain the level of environmental regulations, and protect national cultural distinctiveness.[87] The European Union has shown that social welfare and worker rights can be defended in principle—though very imperfectly in practice—at the continental level. Asian capitalism offers an alternative, less individualistic political model for achieving economic competitiveness and social solidarity.[88] In short, capitalisms vary, as do popular responses to it. The post-modern, multi-level state is far from synonymous with a reprise of pre-modern, Dickensian practices.

The danger inherent in any claim that a sea change has occurred in Canada's state forms is that the features of continuity that persist from the putatively discarded paradigm may be ignored. Consider, for example, those achievements that Trudeauphiles claim to be his lasting legacy and that continue to shape the Canadian polity:[89] the Charter of Rights and Freedoms; the patriation of the Constitution; multiculturalism and bilingualism; and the long struggle to establish native land claims. Other continuities exist that may result in a different, but reinvigorated, role for the Canadian state. Inter-regional equalization has been remarkably resistant to retrenchment and has actually been extended through fiscal federalism in such measures as the 'cap on CAP' (embedded until the 1999 budget in the CHST), Employment Insurance, and other programs that discriminate in favour of the less prosperous provinces at the expense of the richer. Canada's new Social Union Framework Agreement may result in a new species of co-operative federalism in which the federal government reclaims some of its earlier functions by enriching its transfer payments and working in tandem with the provinces, although Quebec is again not a signatory. While the rhetoric of consensus concerning these talks disguises inevitable political and jurisdictional disagreement, the National Child Benefit, which was their first product, indicates that some movement has taken place. The 1999 federal budget placed the social union project in the context of an ongoing consultative process even though Paul Martin—as Lucien Bouchard vociferously claimed—arguably violated the Agreement's requirement of consultation one year prior to Ottawa's making significant changes to existing social transfers by moving to per capita entitlements under the CHST.[90]

A close reading of how Prime Minister Chrétien interpreted his promises during the 1995 Quebec referendum to renew the federation also suggests that, even under the unprecedented twin pressures from separatism and fiscal retrenchment, the federal government had a vision that would modify but maintain Ottawa's relevance. Two results of these promises in late 1995 were a House of Commons resolution to recognize Quebec as a distinct society, and a law requiring substantial provincial consent before Ottawa would concur in most constitutional amendments. But the prime minister had also promised greater decentralization,[91] and in the 1996 Speech from the Throne the federal government announced it would no longer use its spending power to create new shared-cost programs in areas of exclusive provincial jurisdiction without the consent of a majority of the provinces. Those not consenting would be compensated if they operated an equivalent or comparable initiative. This promise was further defined by the Social Union Agreement, which went further than the Meech Lake Accord in its restrictions on the spending power. Ottawa also promised in 1996 to withdraw from labour market training, forestry, mining, and recreation. Partnerships with provinces in other areas were recommended. But it was clear that the federal government still envisioned an important, if altered, role for itself. The spending power promise, while important, was only a moderate constraint on federal action.[92] While always pledging to work with its provincial partners, the federal government still claimed it had a major role to play with respect to both the economic and the social union. It would work for unhampered mobility between provinces and unfettered access to social benefits across the country. It would seek to enhance labour mobility. It would try to liberalize internal trade. And with interested provinces it would work to create a Canadian securities commission, a single food inspection agency, and a national revenue collection agency. The process emerging from the 1996 Throne Speech is ongoing, and while some of the decentralizing pledges have been kept, the commitments with a centralizing thrust continue to animate much federal behaviour. If tensions on the national unity front do not reignite, further federal assertion can be anticipated as the fiscal problem recedes.

The effort of some factions to 'unite the right' in federal political parties also reveals as much continuity with an earlier era as change from it. This endeavour, led primarily by the Reform party and some Progressive Conservatives, seeks to repair the fracturing of the party system and create a second national party that could challenge the Liberals on the Canadian political landscape. The form such an arrangement might take was hotly disputed[93] and the divisions between the 'right' parties were extremely deep.[94] Success was far from assured, even as agreement to move the unification agenda forward was reached at a convention in February 1999. But the desire for unification suggested an atavism regarding the Canadian political system, particularly for the Mulroney coalition of Quebec and the West. Indeed, the willingness of the right in Canada outside Quebec to court not only nationalists but also separatists in Quebec for partisan political gain indicated that perhaps too much of the past was being retrieved.[95]

A final danger dogs those who would declare the former paradigm dead and buried. With substantial resistance to neo-liberalism gaining expression both at home (with the distress in hospital and educational services brought on by the cutting back of the state) and abroad (with the crisis of the globalized financial market system in 1997-8), no new point of equilibrium has been reached. The neo-liberal model leaves the state without an obvious role to play as a buffer against the short-run economic vicissitudes that characterize capitalist economies. Having abdicated this function, the federal state exists with a void at its centre.

The neo-liberal model has clearly been the winning approach since the Mulroney government took office in 1984, but the silence at its heart renders it incomplete. It is unable to be both true to itself and responsive to the social needs to which governments may feel compelled to respond. Because politicians have deprived themselves of the tools and the rationales for discretionary intervention, citizens demanding a more activist state must speak from outside the neo-liberal ideological loop. Over time the neo-liberal vision is subject to contestation against which it has only weak arguments. Indeed, considerable authority and legitimacy having been located elsewhere, the federal government may try to reassert itself in ways it had earlier abandoned and reclaim some of the authority and legitimacy it had previously alienated. Given the inability of the neo-liberal model to respond to some of these concerns, the pendulum may even be poised to swing back toward a state less reluctant to exercise its power to regulate the market and to provide civil society with the services it desires. New health money and other provisions in the 1999 budget were consistent with the emergence of a more involved federal state. Automatic stabilizers and measures to maintain aggregate demand remain in the policy arsenal. Calls for government action to create physical and human infrastructure are continually heard. Suggestions for government action to re-establish order in the world's financial markets imply enhanced roles for states co-operatively to achieve exchange rate, as well as nuclear, stability. As a result, the potential for contestation and further change remains within the federal political space.

The post-war consensus was characterized by its relative stability. At the turn of the millennium a prime characteristic of the Canadian state is its level of flux. If it suffers from chronic instability, this is largely because the citizenry who have borne the brunt of neo-liberalism's 'reforms' are clamouring for their reversal. But it is also because the corporate sector, in its endless efforts to merge and acquire to protect itself from global market vicissitudes, is also running scared. If the Canadian state manages to find a new shape between embedded and neo-liberalism, it will only be after passing through its present phase of being constantly contested.

NOTES

1 Gilles Paquet, 'Institutional Evolution in the Information Age', in Thomas J. Courchene, ed., *Technology, Information and Public Policy* (Kingston: Queen's University, The John Deutsch Institute for the Study of Economic Policy, 1994).
2 For a thorough critique of the notion of the 'Gulliver effect', see François Rocher and Christian Rouillard, 'North American Integration Ten Years Later: Economic Efficiency vs Federal Principles in Canada', unpublished manuscript (1998).
3 When we speak generally, we will use the term 'sovereign state' to describe internationally recognized national states. It is very difficult to apply the concept of nation-state to Canada, where Québécois and Aboriginals identify themselves as nations or peoples. When we refer specifically to Canada's national state, as opposed to its federal system, we will employ the term 'federal state' or 'Canadian state'.
4 John Gerard Ruggie, 'International Regimes, Transactions, and Change: Embedded Liberalism in the Postwar Economic Order', in Stephen D. Krasner, ed., *International Regimes* (Ithaca: Cornell University Press, 1983), 195-231; 'Embedded Liberalism Revisited: Institutions and Progress in International Economic Relations', in Emanuel Adler and Beverly Crawford, eds, *Progress in Postwar International Relations* (New York: Columbia University Press, 1991), 201-34; and 'Trade, Protectionism and the Future of Welfare Capitalism', *Journal of International Affairs* 48, 1 (Summer, 1994), 1-11.
5 Stephen Clarkson, *Canada and the Reagan Challenge: Crisis and Adjustment, 1981-85*, 2nd edn (Toronto: James Lorimer, 1985).
6 Stephen Clarkson, 'The Dauphin and the Doomed: John Turner and the Liberal Party's Debacle', in Howard Penniman, ed., *Canada at the Polls, 1984: A Study of the Federal General Elections* (Durham NC: Duke University Press, 1988), 97-119.
7 David Wolfe, 'The State and Economic Policy in Canada, 1945-75', in Leo Panitch, ed., *The Canadian State: Political Economy and Political Power* (Toronto: University of Toronto Press, 1977), 251-88.

8 Jane Jenson, '"Different but not exceptional": Canada's Permeable Fordism', *Canadian Review of Sociology and Anthropology* 26, 1 (Feb. 1989), 69-94.
9 Donald Smiley, 'A Note on Canadian-American Free Trade and Canadian Policy Autonomy', in Marc Gold and David Leyton-Brown, eds, *Trade-Offs on Free Trade: The Canada-U.S. Free Trade Agreement* (Toronto: Carswell, 1988), 442-5.
10 In this paper, 'regional' will apply to sub-national jurisdictions, and 'continental' to groupings of several sovereign states that encompass most of a continental land mass.
11 We use 'state' to refer to the enduring if evolving ensemble of political, judicial, administrative, and coercive institutions. 'Government' will refer to the executive, legislature, and bureaucracy that enjoys the current electoral mandate.
12 John Shields and Stephen McBride, *Dismantling a Nation*, 2nd edn (Halifax: Fernwood Press, 1997).
13 Observers often describe this policy as one of 'zero-inflation'. In fact, it is directed to 'price stability', which may or may not constitute zero-inflation. For example, if prices rise in one year but not the next, inflation in the second year would be zero, but prices would not have been stable. The Bank is only beginning to turn its collective mind to the question of precisely what should count as price stability (Interviews by Timothy Lewis with Bank of Canada officials, 2 June 1998). See also Proceedings of a conference held by the Bank of Canada, May 1997, *Price Stability, Inflation Targets, and Monetary Policy* (Ottawa: Bank of Canada, Feb. 1998).
14 Wolfgang Streeck has suggested a similar hypothesis for the member states of the European Union, arguing that they have compensated for what they have lost in internal sovereignty by what they have retained in their inter-governmental bargaining in the EU's various institutions—though decision-making deadlocks and democratic deficits at the continental level of governance are high prices to pay for this exchange. Wolfgang Streeck, 'Public Power Beyond the Nation-State: The Case of the European Community', in Robert Boyer and Daniel Drache, eds, *States Against Markets: The Limits of Globalization* (London: Routledge, 1996), 299-315.
15 Michael Hart, *Fifty Years of Canadian Tradecraft: Canada at the GATT, 1947-1997* (Ottawa: Centre for Trade Policy and Law: 1998), 191.
16 Christopher Kent, 'The Uruguay Round GATT TRIPs Agreement & Chapter 17 of the NAFTA: A New Era in International Patent Protection', *Canadian Intellectual Property Review* (1994), 711-33.
17 Ted Magder, 'Franchising the Candy Store: Split-Run Magazines and a New International Regime for Trade in Culture', *Canadian-American Public Policy* 34 (Apr. 1998), 1-66.

18 Stephen Blank, Stephen Krajewski, and Henry S. Yu, 'US Firms in North America: Redefining Structure and Strategy', in *North American Outlook* 5, 2 (Feb. 1995).
19 Commission for Environmental Cooperation, *NAFTA's Institutions: The Environmental Potential and Performance of the NAFTA Free Trade Commission and Related Bodies* (Montreal: CEC, 1997).
20 Stephen Clarkson, 'The Joy of Flux: What the European Monetary Union Can Learn from North America's Experience with National Currency Autonomy', in Colin Crouch, ed., *After the Euro: Shaping Institutions for Governance in the Wake of European Monetary Union* (Oxford: Oxford University Press, 1999).
21 Fritz W. Scharpf, *Negative and Positive Integration in the Political Economy of European Welfare States* (Florence: European University Institute, 1995).
22 On the role of provinces in trade issues, see Douglas M. Brown, 'The Federal-Provincial Consultation Process', in Peter M. Leslie and Ronald L. Watts, eds, *Canada: The State of the Federation 1987-88* (Kingston: Institute of Intergovernmental Relations, Queen's University, 1988), 77-93; 'Canadian Federalism and Trade Policy: The Uruguay Round Agenda', in Ronald L. Watts and Douglas M. Brown, eds, *Canada: The State of the Federation 1989* (Kingston: Institute of Intergovernmental Relations, Queen's University, 1989), 211-35; and 'The Evolving Role of the Provinces in Canadian Trade Policy', in Douglas M. Brown and Murray G. Smith, eds, *Canadian Federalism: Meeting Global Economic Challenges?* (Kingston: Institute of Intergovernmental Relations, Queen's University, 1991), 81-128.
23 Ian Robinson argues that CUFTA and NAFTA are centralizing in their effects. See 'NAFTA, the Side-Deals, and Canadian Federalism: Constitutional Reform by Other Means?' in Ronald L. Watts and Douglas M. Brown, eds, *Canada: The State of the Federation 1993* (Kingston: Institute of Intergovernmental Relations, Queen's University, 1993), 193-227, and 'Trade Policy, Globalization, and the Future of Canadian Federalism', in François Rocher and Miriam Smith, eds, *New Trends in Canadian Federalism* (Peterborough Ont.: Broadview Press, 1995), 234-69.
24 Robert M. Campbell, 'Federalism and Economic Policy', in Rocher and Smith, *New Trends in Canadian Federalism*, 200.
25 The major exceptions are British Columbia and Nova Scotia. British Columbia was not hit very hard by the recession in the early 1990s, but its economy has struggled in the late 1990s, and it now has a substantial deficit. Nova Scotia's position, like that of the other Atlantic provinces, is much improved because of ballooning equalization payments, which originate in the strength of Ontario's economy over the last year, but a fiscal shortfall is still projected.

26 Richard Simeon, 'Canada and the United States: Lessons from the North American Experience', in Karen Knop, Sylvia Ostry, Richard Simeon, and Katherine Swinton, eds, *Rethinking Federalism: Citizens, Markets, and Governments in a Changing World* (Vancouver: UBC Press, 1995), 251.
27 Thomas J. Courchene, 'Glocalization: The Regional/International Interface', *Canadian Journal of Regional Science* 18, 1 (Spring, 1995), 1-20.
28 Stephen Clarkson and Christina McCall, *Trudeau and Our Times. Volume 2: The Heroic Delusion* (Toronto: McClelland and Stewart, 1994), 339-40.
29 Daniel Drache, 'Globalization: Is There Anything to Fear?' Unpublished manuscript (Toronto: Robarts Centre, York University, 1998).
30 Wallace Clement and Rianne Mahon, eds, *Swedish Social Democracy: A Model in Transition* (Toronto: Canadian Scholars' Press, 1994).
31 The argument in this section is based upon Timothy Lewis, *The Political Economy of Debt and Deficit Politics in Canada* (Ph.D. Dissertation, University of Toronto, 1999).
32 The Phillips Curve was not actually a strict application of the Keynesian model, but rather an empirical observation that countries with higher inflation rates had lower unemployment rates and vice-versa. Given the priority in Keynesian thinking of employment concerns over moderate levels of inflation, it did function to legitimate Keynesian efforts to 'buy' lower employment at the price of higher inflation.
33 See Robert M. Campbell, *Grand Illusions: The Politics of the Keynesian Experience in Canada, 1945-75* (Peterborough Ont.: Broadview Press, 1987), 6, and David A. Wolfe, 'The Rise and Demise of the Keynesian Era in Canada, 1930-1982', in *Readings in Canadian Social History* 5 (Toronto: McClelland and Stewart Ltd., 1984), 71-2.
34 For more on the character of Canada's postwar Keynesianism, the forces that unravelled it, and the policies that replaced it, see Robert Campbell's chapter in this volume.
35 The major exception was the 1979 budget, for which the short-lived Clark government could not gain the confidence of Parliament. See John Crosbie, *Budget Speech* (Ottawa: Department of Finance, 11 Dec. 1979).
36 Donald S. Macdonald, *Budget Speech* (Ottawa: Department of Finance, 25 May 1976), 21.
37 H. Mimoto and P. Cross, 'The Growth of the Federal Debt', *Canadian Economic Observer* (June 1991), 3.1-3.17.
38 For an explanation of the economic thinking underlying the Anti-Inflation Program, see Department of Finance, *Canada's Recent Inflation Experience* (Ottawa: Department of Finance, Nov. 1978).
39 See Gerald K. Bouey, 'Remarks by Gerald K. Bouey, Governor of the Bank of Canada', *Bank of Canada Review* (Ottawa: Bank of Canada,

Oct. 1975), 28, and 'Statement by Gerald K. Bouey, Governor of the Bank of Canada', *Bank of Canada Review* (Ottawa: Bank of Canada, Nov. 1975), 4.

40 Anti-Inflation Reference, [1976] 2 S.C.R. 373.

41 Marc Lalonde, Minister of Finance, *Budget Speech* (Ottawa: Department of Finance, 19 Apr. 1983). For another document that also vindicated deficit finance as an appropriate mechanism to improve upon cyclical economic underperformance see Marc Lalonde, *The Federal Deficit in Perspective* (Ottawa: Department of Finance, April 1983).

42 The federal government nonetheless sought to direct the provinces toward policies that were consistent with its economic philosophy. In 1973 Finance Minister John Turner used his budget speech to try to persuade provinces that they too had responsibilities for countercyclical demand management. John N. Turner, *Budget Speech* (Ottawa: Department of Finance, 19 Feb. 1973), 20.

43 Peter Aucoin, 'Organizational Change in the Management of Canadian Government: From Rational Management to Brokerage Politics', *Canadian Journal of Political Science* 19, 1 (March, 1986), 3-27, and Donald J. Savoie, *The Politics of Public Spending in Canada* (Toronto: University of Toronto Press, 1990), 163.

44 Michael Wilson, *A New Direction for Canada: An Agenda for Economic Renewal* (Canada: Department of Finance, 8 Nov. 1984).

45 The Governor of the Bank of Canada argued in 1987 that the Bank should direct itself to the goal of price stability. See John W. Crow, 'The Bank of Canada and Its Objectives', *Bank of Canada Review* (Apr. 1987), 21-2.

46 Duncan Cameron, 'Introduction', in Duncan Cameron and Mel Watkins, eds, *Canada Under Free Trade* (Toronto: James Lorimer and Company, 1993), xiv-xv.

47 Ken Battle and Sherri Torjman, *Federal Social Programs: Setting the Record Straight* (Ottawa: Caledon Institute for Social Policy, Spring 1993).

48 Edward Greenspon and Anthony Wilson-Smith, *Double Vision: The Inside Story of the Liberals in Power* (Toronto: Doubleday Canada Ltd, 1996), 349-50.

49 Paul Martin, Minister of Finance, *Budget Speech* (Ottawa: Department of Finance, 6 Mar. 1996), 8.

50 For some exposition on Canada's vision for the future of international economic institutions, see Department of Finance, *The Economic and Fiscal Update: Strong Economy and Secure Society* (Ottawa: Department of Finance, 14 Oct. 1998), 9.

51 Jenson, 'Canada's Permeable Fordism', and Thomas Legler, *A Comparison of Canadian and Mexican Postwar Development (1945-1994): More than at First Meets the Eye* (México: Centro de Investigationes Sobre América del Norte, 1995), 14-15.

52 Stephen Clarkson, 'Disjunctions: Free Trade and the Paradox of Canadian Development', in Daniel Drache and Meric S. Gertler, eds, *The New Era of Global Competition: State Policy and Market Power* (Montreal: McGill-Queen's University Press, 1991), 103-26.
53 Harry Arthurs, 'The Hollowing Out of Corporate Canada', unpublished paper, 1998.
54 David Wolfe, 'The Emergence of the Region State', in Thomas J. Courchene, ed., *The Nation State in a Global/Information Era: Policy Challenges* (Kingston: John Deutsch Institute for the Study of Economic Policy, 1997), 205-40.
55 Heather Scoffield, 'Ottawa's High-tech Strategy is Illegal, World Panel Rules', *The Globe and Mail* [Toronto], 20 Feb. 1999, A1.
56 On the distinction between 'reactive' and 'anticipatory' industrial policies, see Michael M. Atkinson and William D. Coleman, *The State, Business, and Industrial Change in Canada* (Toronto: University of Toronto Press, 1989), 23-7.
57 Stephen Clarkson, *Canada and the Reagan Challenge: Crisis and Adjustment, 1981-85* (Toronto: Lorimer, 1985), 57-81.
58 Gilbert R. Winham, 'International Trade Policy in a Globalizing Economy', *International Journal* 51, 4 (Autumn, 1996), 638-50.
59 Alan M. Rugman, 'Why Business Supports Free Trade', in John Crispo, ed., *Free Trade: The Real Story* (Toronto: Gage, 1988), 95-104.
60 Michael Hart, *Fifty Years of Canadian Statecraft: Canada at the GATT, 1947-1997* (Ottawa: Centre for Trade Policy and Law, 1998).
61 John Kirton, Alan Rugman, and Julie Soloway, *Environmental Regulations and Corporate Strategy: A NAFTA Perspective* (Oxford: Oxford University Press, 1999).
62 Stephen Dale, *McLuhan's Children: The Greenpeace Message and the Media* (Toronto: Between the Lines, 1996).
63 R. v. Crown Zellerbach Ltd., [1988] 1 S.C.R., 401; Friends of the Oldman River Society v. Canada (Minister of Transport), [1992] 1. S.C.R., 3.
64 General Motors of Canada Ltd. v. National City Leasing, [1989] 1 S.C.R., 641.
65 On this point, see Robert G. Richards, 'The Canadian Constitution and International Economic Relations', in Brown and Smith, eds, *Canadian Federalism*, 57-63.
66 *Alberta Government Telephones v. Canada* (Canadian Radio-television and Telecommunications Commission), [1989] 2 S.C.R., 225; Téléphone Guèvremont Inc. v. Québec (Régis des télécommunications), [1994] 1 S.C.R., 878.
67 Thomas Hueglin, 'Globalization Without Citizens: A Critique of Reinicke's *Global Public Policy*', unpublished paper, 1999, 8.
68 Thomas J. Courchene, with Colin R. Telmer, *From Heartland to North American Region State: The Social, Fiscal and Federal Evolution of Ontario: An Interpretive Essay* (Toronto: Monograph Series on Public

Policy, Centre for Public Management, Faculty of Management, University of Toronto, 1998).
69 Don Munton and John Kirton, 'Beyond and Beneath the Nation-State: Province-State Interactions and NAFTA', paper for the International Studies Association, San Diego, Apr. 1996.
70 Sylvia Bashevkin, 'Losing Common Ground: Feminists, Conservatives and Public Policy in Canada during the Mulroney Years', *Canadian Journal of Political Science* 29, 2 (June 1996), 211-42.
71 John C. Crosbie, *No Holds Barred: My Life in Politics* (Toronto: McClelland and Stewart, 1998), 276.
72 Keith Banting, 'The Internationalization of the Social Contract', in Thomas J. Courchene, ed., *The Nation State in a Global/Information Era: Policy Challenges* (Kingston: John Deutsch Institute for the Study of Economic Policy, 1997), 255-86.
73 Courchene, 'Glocalization', 7.
74 These points regarding equalization are emphasized in Courchene and Telmer, *From Heartland to North American Region State*.
75 Margaret Philp, 'UN Committee Lambastes Canada on Human Rights', *The Globe and Mail* [Toronto], 5 Dec. 1998, A7.
76 Alan Cairns, 'The Charter and the Constitution Act, 1982', in *Charter Versus Federalism: The Dilemmas of Constitutional Reform* (Montreal and Kingston: McGill-Queen's University Press, 1992).
77 Kenneth McRoberts, *Misconceiving Canada: The Struggle for National Unity* (Toronto: Oxford University Press, 1997).
78 For the content of Trudeau's objections, see Donald Johnston, ed., *Pierre Trudeau Speaks Out on Meech Lake* (Canada: General Paperbacks, 1990).
79 See R.K. Carty, 'On the Road Again: The Stalled Omnibus Revisited', in R.K. Carty, ed., *Canadian Political Party Systems: A Reader* (Peterborough Ont.: Broadview Press, 1992), 639.
80 This was also a result of perceptions of graft during the two Mulroney administrations, the pain caused by the structural economic reforms that these governments implemented, widespread dislike of the Prime Minister on a personal level, and the terrible campaign run by Mulroney's successor, Kim Campbell. Jean Chrétien proved able and willing to profit from the mistakes of her campaign.
81 For an account of these issues, see David Laycock, 'Reforming Canadian Democracy?: Institutions and Ideology in the Reform Party Project', *Canadian Journal of Political Science* 27, 2 (June 1994), 213-47.
82 Mark Neufeld, 'The Political Economy of Security Discourse: Reflections on Canada's "Security with a Human Face"', in Ken Booth, ed., *Security, Community and Emancipation: Critical Security Studies and Global Politics* (Boulder: Lynne Rienner, 1999).

83 See Andrew Cooper's chapter in this volume.
84 Thomas Risse-Kappen, *Bringing Transnational Relations Back In: Non-state Actors, Domestic Structures, and International Institutions* (New York: Cambridge University Press, 1995).
85 Stephen Gill, 'Globalisation, Market Civilisation, and Disciplinary Neoliberalism', *Millennium: Journal of International Studies* (Tokyo: United Nations University, 1994), 399-423.
86 On the argument that the world is not as global as is often thought, and that even if it is, downward policy harmonization does not follow, see William Watson, *Globalization and the Meaning of Canadian Life* (Toronto: University of Toronto Press, 1998), and Paul Hirst, 'The Global Economy: Myths and Realities', *International Affairs* 73, 3 (1997), 409-25.
87 Heather Scoffield, 'Groups Pitch Alternative to MAI', *The Globe and Mail* [Toronto], 8 July 1998, B4.
88 Richard Stubbs, 'ASEAN's Distinctive Capitalism: Implications for International Trade Rules', in William D. Coleman and Geoffrey R.O. Underhill, eds, *Regionalism and Global Economic Integration: Europe, Asia and America* (London: Routledge, 1997).
89 Andrew Cohen and J.L. Granatstein, eds, *Trudeau's Shadow* (Toronto: Random House, 1998).
90 See 'A Framework to Improve the Social Union for Canadians: An Agreement between the Government of Canada and the Governments of the Provinces and Territories', 4 Feb. 1999.
91 Chrétien committed his government to decentralization, recognition of Quebec as a distinct society, and a veto on constitutional change for Quebec for any amendment affecting its jurisdiction in his Verdun speech of 24 Oct. 1995 and in his address to the nation the next night.
92 Notice and consultation provisions notwithstanding, the Social Union Agreement, like the Throne Speech promise, did not fetter the raw power of the federal government to use its spending power in areas of shared jurisdiction or for programs such as the 'Millennium Scholarship Fund', that transferred money directly to Canadians. Indeed, the Social Union Agreement gave formal administrative recognition to the legitimacy of the use of the federal spending power.
93 Brian Laghi, 'United Alternative Looks at Split into Five Blocks', *The Globe and Mail* [Toronto], 8 Jan. 1999, A1; Sheldon Alberts, 'New United Alternative Proposal Includes Strong Regional Launching Pad', *The National Post*, 8 Jan. 1999, A5; Henry N.R. Jackman, 'Suppose the Tories and Reform Chose the Same Candidates', *The Globe and Mail* [Toronto], 8 Jan. 1999, A19.
94 Ted Byfield, 'Not Exactly the Great White Hope: Western Reformers Are Dismayed at Tory "Terms" for United Alternative', *The National Post*, 8 Jan. 1999, A13.

95 Joel Ruimy, 'Reformers, Separatists Drawn to Rally to Unite the Right', *The Toronto Star*, 8 Jan. 1999, A6; Andrew Coyne, 'Separatist Footsie, à la Reform', *The National Post*, 11 Jan. 1999, A19.

APPENDIX A

CANADIAN POLITICAL FACTS AND TRENDS

Canadian Political Facts and Trends presents a snapshot of key political developments between June 1998 and March 1999, particularly those events that are related to chapters in this year's edition. It was compiled and written by Sandra Bach, relying primarily on news reports published in *The Globe and Mail*.

1998

5 June: British Columbia survivors of Indian residential school abuse win a major court victory that could result in more litigation by victims across Canada. Despite a bid by both the federal government and the United Church to deny in court any responsibility for the Alberni Indian Residential School, the BC Supreme Court rules that the school was a 'joint venture', so both should pay for the abuses that occurred.

15 July: It is reported that relocating the Innu of Davis Inlet to nearby Sango Bay could cost $16 million more than the $80 million earmarked by Ottawa. The federal government announced in 1994 that it would relocate the 550 residents of Davis Inlet to Sango Bay. Davis Inlet leaders had long attributed their chronic social problems to the isolation of the island settlement where they were relocated in the 1960s from their traditional hunting grounds in the Sango Bay area.

A landmark treaty is reached in British Columbia giving the northern Nisga'a people title and self-government for over 2,000 square kilometres of their ancestral lands in northwestern BC, and $500 million in cash and government programs. This treaty is the first signed in BC since 1859, and the settlement of the first of more than 50 outstanding native land claims covering the entire province.

20 August: Recent dissent in the ranks of the Reform party is described as a blessing in disguise. Some party faithful claim that the best result of the tensions may be a realization among Reformers that the party can't win an election on its own.

4 September: A group of federal Tory and Reform party activists announce the creation of a committee to pursue dialogue between the two conservative rivals.

9 September: Internal police documents reveal that Indonesian authorities had gone so far as to ask the RCMP what would happen if bodyguards accompanying former President Suharto were to shoot anti-Suharto demonstrators during the 25 November Asia Pacific Economic Cooperation (APEC) summit meeting in Vancouver. RCMP told the Indonesians that Suharto's bodyguards would be permitted to carry weapons, but that shooting demonstrators would not be tolerated.

10 September: Insisting that they are not rejecting the Progressive Conservative party or the Reform party, a group of Progressive Conservatives and Reformers announce that they have formed a committee to plan a United Alternative convention in Ottawa the third week of February 1999.

17 September: In a speech on economic matters made during the 12-13 September weekend, Prime Minister Chrétien emphasizes debt repayment, stating that it would be above the $3 billion suggested in the last budget. He re-affirms the government's plan to proceed with modest tax cuts and health care spending, but warns that surpluses would not be as big as previously projected. Government officials claim that the arithmetical basis of the 50-50 plan was not tenable.

9 October: A lawyer for the APEC protesters calls for the shutting down of the tribunal probing police handling of his clients. He charges that Solicitor General Andy Scott's overheard conversation during an airline flight revealed that the outcome of the RCMP Commission's investigation had been prejudged by the Minister.

14 October: The APEC inquiry runs into serious trouble when one of the lawyers for the complainants quits the hearing, and another states that he would leave if the government refused to pick up the students' legal fees.

30 October: Prime Minister Chrétien's leadership comes under scrutiny as Liberals debate whether the Prime Minister is one of Quebec Premier Lucien Bouchard's 'winning conditions' for holding another referendum. His comments on not formally re-opening the Constitution during a routine interview with *La Presse* jeopardizes the federal government's plans to maintain a low profile in the Quebec election.

3 November: Quebec Premier Lucien Bouchard announces that if his government is re-elected, it will inject $2.1 billion into the province's health care system.

5 November: Students argue that their tactics at the 25 November 1997 APEC summit in Vancouver were illegal but nonviolent. Among other things, they swarmed a police line to force mass arrests, pulled down part of the security fence, and tried to form human roadblocks on motorcade routes. Police argue they had to use pepper spray because the site was difficult to defend.

6 November: Indonesian Foreign Affairs Minister Ali Alatas argues that Indonesia did not seek or expect special security treatment for former President Suharto at the APEC summit.

10 November: It is reported that the government would be seeking ways to avoid paying down millions of dollars on the national debt, preferring to focus upon health care and tax cuts. The Liberals show signs of difficulty in keeping their election promise to divide future surpluses equally between new spending initiatives, and a combination of tax cuts and debt repayment.

11 November: Prime Minister Chrétien acknowledges for the first time that his government has drifted off course in its promise to split future surpluses 50-50 between new spending, and tax cuts and debt repayment.

13 November: The federal government plans to tighten residency requirements for immigrants seeking Canadian citizenship. According to immigration lawyers, the proposed new law would ensure that, before applying for citizenship, all immigrants must remain within Canada for a cumulative total three years during a five-year period.

Final weekend results of the Nisga'a referendum show that over 70 per cent of those who voted supported the treaty with the federal and provincial governments.

16 November: Michel Trudeau, the youngest son of former Prime Minister Pierre Trudeau, drowns after an avalanche sweeps him into the Kokanee Lake, BC while he is skiing.

The federal government balks on its promise to set up an independent land-claims tribunal because of fears that the new process could lead to increasing damage awards for native bands. After one and a half years of negotiations, the tribunal's future is stalled over money.

In a unanimous decision, the Federal Court of Appeal overturns the Federal Court of Canada ruling by Mr. Justice Francis Muldoon in March. Judge Muldoon had overruled the Canadian Human Rights Commission's decision that it could hear seven pay-equity complaints filed by unions representing Bell Canada employees.

23 November: Solicitor General Andy Scott resigns over allegations that he compromised the APEC inquiry during an in-flight conversation.

27 November: The APEC hearings are postponed indefinitely. Mr. Justice Nadon agrees to halt the hearings while the Federal Court of Canada rules on the argument that the inquiry's chairman, Gerald Morin, is biased. An

RCMP officer swore in an affidavit that he overheard Mr. Morin tell a companion that he had some concerns about police conduct at the summit.

30 November: Quebec Premier Lucien Bouchard wins a comfortable majority in the provincial election, but the Parti Québécois falls short of the popular support it would require to stage a winning referendum.

The federal government is set to announce a $1 billion reduction in Employment Insurance (EI) premiums after reaching a deal with the federal EI commission. Finance Minister Paul Martin had agreed to lower EI premiums by 15 cents per $100 of employees' insurable earnings, beginning 1 January 1999.

3 December: The Organization for Economic Co-operation and Development warns that Canada's standard of living could fall far behind those of other industrial nations.

9 December: In a unanimous decision, the country's premiers state that Ottawa's restoration of $6 billion in federal cash contributions for health care should take precedence in the social union discussions.

12 December: While in Quebec City, Preston Manning faces political pressure to work with the Bloc Québécois and to refrain from running 'United Alternative' candidates in Quebec.

18 December: Two of the last remaining panelists on the APEC inquiry resign, claiming that a number of allegations have harmed the integrity of the RCMP Public Complaints Commission hearing. The federal government rejects calls for a full judicial inquiry into the APEC affair.

1999

7 January: Delegates to a convention aimed at uniting Canadian conservatives decide to avoid issues like the Triple-E Senate and official bilingualism to ensure that the movement is not divided before it begins.

9 January: The United Alternative's latest proposal for regional blocs gains the attention of Quebec separatists. A top Bloc Québécois adviser claims that the concept of a confederal party made up of five regional blocs is the clearest sign yet that separatists are being courted in the conservative attempt to oust the federal Liberals from power.

13 January: The federal government makes a new offer to place limits on its spending power in the creation of new national social programs. The offer is extended privately by Justice Minister Anne McLellan in an attempt to break the stalemate in politically sensitive negotiations aimed at creating a new partnership on Canada's social union.

21 January: Maude Barlow of the Council of Canadians argues that Canada's social union talks may cause permanent damage to social programs, and that there is a risk that national social program standards will be dismantled.

26 January: In a letter to provincial premiers, Prime Minister Chrétien commits the government to a significant increase in health funding in the next budget.

The federal and BC governments unveil their agreement with the Sechelt Indian band, the province's second modern-day land claims treaty. The 900-member Sechelt First Nation receives a financial settlement of $42 million and ownership of 933 hectares of land.

27 January: Quebec Deputy Premier Bernard Landry makes it clear that his province's traditional position on the discussion of a health care agreement with Ottawa has not changed.

A new study conducted by the Canadian Labour Congress (CLC) claims that a record low number of jobless Canadians collected EI in 1997, including only a quarter of the unemployed in Ontario. In a news conference, CLC president Bob White says that the percentage of unemployed covered by EI in 1997 was less than half of what it was in 1989, falling to 36 per cent from 74 per cent.

28 January: Quebec Premier Bouchard rejects Ottawa's proposal for an accord on health care, stating that Prime Minister Chrétien has no choice but to give Quebec its fair share of new federal health care money. Provincial negotiators voice unhappiness with new federal social union proposals that would allow provinces greater flexibility in designing new national social programs but would not compensate them if they opted out.

30 January: Federal and provincial negotiators engage in intense negotiations over the social union agreement. The provinces present Ottawa with a new bargaining position. Provincial officials give some ground on the federal demand to reduce inter-provincial barriers between social programs, such as student loan schemes that don't support residents studying in another province. However, the provincial paper ignores Ottawa's attempts to get around the controversial opting-out provision, a core Quebec objective in the talks.

2 February: Finance Minister Paul Martin states that his upcoming budget will include some tax relief, but that the government will not sacrifice key programs to do so. Martin also emphasizes that health spending will be in the spotlight.

In a new Angus Reid poll, Canadians rank health care as the top priority for leaders' attention, with 43 per cent of respondents putting the issue first on a list of concerns. Canadians continue to support debt reduction over new spending or tax cuts when asked in a Globe/Angus Reid poll what the Liberal government's main budget priority should be.

4 February: The social union agreement, which is agreed to by all provinces and territories other than Quebec, includes provisions allowing the federal government to initiate social programs with the approval of a majority of provinces and provision of three months notice prior to implementation.

9 February: Quebec Premier Lucien Bouchard says that the rest of Canada will face political consequences in a Quebec referendum for signing the social union accord without Quebec's consent. Bouchard argues that Quebec and Canada are moving further apart and that Ottawa is prepared to impose its vision of a centralized state on Quebec.

Prime Minister Chrétien dismisses the newest string of allegations that he had a hand in the security arrangements for the APEC summit.

10 February: Premier Brian Tobin promises to pay more attention to health care and education after Newfoundland voters do not give him the landslide election victory he had hoped for, but reduce his majority government. The Liberals win 32 seats, a drop of five from 1996, the Progressive Conservatives 14 seats, and the New Democrats two.

15 February: Residents of the eastern Arctic choose the first government of Nunavut.

The federal government agrees to pay for the lawyers of the protesters who were directly involved in RCMP pepper-spraying and the confrontations at the 1997 APEC summit in Vancouver.

16 February: Finance Minister Paul Martin delivers a much-demanded boost for Canada's health care system in his sixth budget, while also providing Canadians with some broad-based tax cuts. Martin focuses on three core areas: health spending, tax cuts, and money for research and development.

24 February: Ottawa imposes restrictions on its offer to cover the legal fees of students who clashed with police at the 1997 APEC summit in Vancouver. Solicitor General Lawrence MacAulay outlines criteria for students to get government help in a letter to Ted Hughes, head of the public inquiry into the affair.

25 February: The Quebec government launches a $250,000 advertising campaign to denounce Paul Martin's budget as "anti-Quebec".

26 February: The Supreme Court of Canada rules that a sexual act becomes a criminal act if a person objects to it. In overturning the sexual-assault acquittal of an Alberta man, the court states that the first time a 17-year-old woman said 'no' to Steve Brian Ewanchuk, his advances should have ceased.

2 March: A group of more than 1,000 native Canadians who attended residential schools as children launch multi-million dollar lawsuits against the federal government and churches.

6 March: Paul Okalik is elected as the first premier of Nunavut.

9 March: The House of Commons passes a controversial bill that critics claim gives band councils too much power to expropriate land and decide how matrimonial property on reserves gets divided in a divorce. The bill allows band councils to distribute leases and licenses, and to set up property management codes.

Statistics Canada reports that, after five years of job cuts, employment in the public sector started to stabilize in 1998, falling only 0.6 per cent from 1997.

BC Premier Glen Clark announces that he will not resign over allegations that he had been involved in the granting of conditional approval from the government for a charity casino owned by his neighbour, a man who was subsequently charged with running an illegal gaming house.

11 March: Justice Minister Anne McLellan introduces proposed legislation to change the way Canada handles youth crime, giving adult sentences to the most serious, violent offenders, and requiring probation for every incarcerated youth. It would also steer minor, non-violent cases away from jail, and, in some cases, away from the courts.

16 March: Members of Parliament pass Canada's controversial magazine legislation. Bill C-55 purports to protect the $600 million-a-year domestic magazine advertising market by barring advertisers from buying ads in Canadian editions of US magazines.

Ottawa plans to pre-empt a court fight on gay rights by extending spousal benefits to the gay and lesbian partners of federal employees.

22 March: The Nisga'a land claim treaty is stalled, because of Ottawa's reluctance to push ahead with the agreement in Parliament when its passage in the BC legislature is uncertain.

24 March: NATO forces prepare to begin air attacks against Yugoslavia after President Milosevic refuses the NATO peace proposal for Kosovo.

25 March: NATO begins aerial attacks on Yugoslavia, striking targets in Belgrade and throughout Serbia. Six Canadian CF-18s take off from their Canadian bases to participate in direct bombing attacks, marking the first time since 1945 that Canada has taken part in armed conflict without the sanction of the United Nations.

APPENDIX B

FISCAL FACTS AND TRENDS

This appendix presents an overview of the federal government's fiscal position, and includes certain major economic policy indicators for 1989-98, as well as some international comparisons.

Facts and trends are presented for federal revenue sources, federal expenditures by ministry and by type of payment, the government's share of the economy, interest and inflation rates, Canadian balance of payments in total and with the United States in particular, and other national economic growth indicators. In addition, international comparisons on real growth, unemployment, inflation, and productivity are reported for Canada, the United States, Japan, Germany, and the United Kingdom.

The figures and time series are updated each year, providing readers with an ongoing current record of major budgetary and economic variables.

Table B.1
Federal Revenue by Source
1988-89 to 1997-98

As a Percentage of Total

Fiscal Year	Personal Tax [a]	Corporate Tax	Indirect Taxes [b]	Other Revenue [c]	Total Revenue	Annual Change
1988-89	55.1	11.3	24.8	8.9	100.0	6.6
1989-90	55.1	11.5	24.8	8.7	100.0	9.3
1990-91	58.9	9.8	21.9	9.4	100.0	5.0
1991-92	62.8	7.7	20.6	8.9	100.0	2.2
1992-93	63.0	6.0	21.7	9.4	100.0	-1.4
1993-94	60.1	8.1	23.0	8.8	100.0	-3.7
1994-95	61.0	9.4	22.0	7.6	100.0	6.0
1995-96	60.4	12.2	20.4	7.0	100.0	5.4
1996-97	59.0	12.1	20.7	8.3	100.0	7.5
1997-98	58.5	14.7	20.1	6.7	100.0	8.8

Revenue by Source is on a net basis.

a Employment Insurance contributions are included in the total.
b Consists of total excise taxes and duties.
c Consists of non-tax and other tax revenues.

Source: Department of Finance, *Fiscal Reference Tables*, November 1998, Table 3.

FISCAL FACTS AND TRENDS 353

Figure B.1
**Sources of Federal Revenue as a
Percentage of Total, 1997-98**

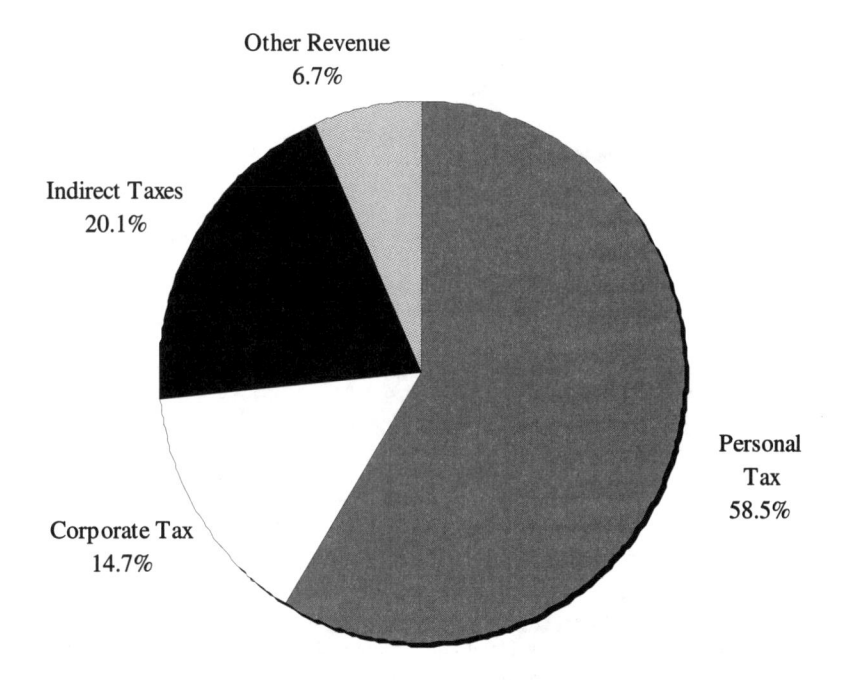

Other Revenue
6.7%

Indirect Taxes
20.1%

Personal Tax
58.5%

Corporate Tax
14.7%

Source: Department of Finance, *Fiscal Reference Tables*, November 1998, Table 3.

Figure B.2
Federal Expenditures by Ministry
1999-2000 Estimates

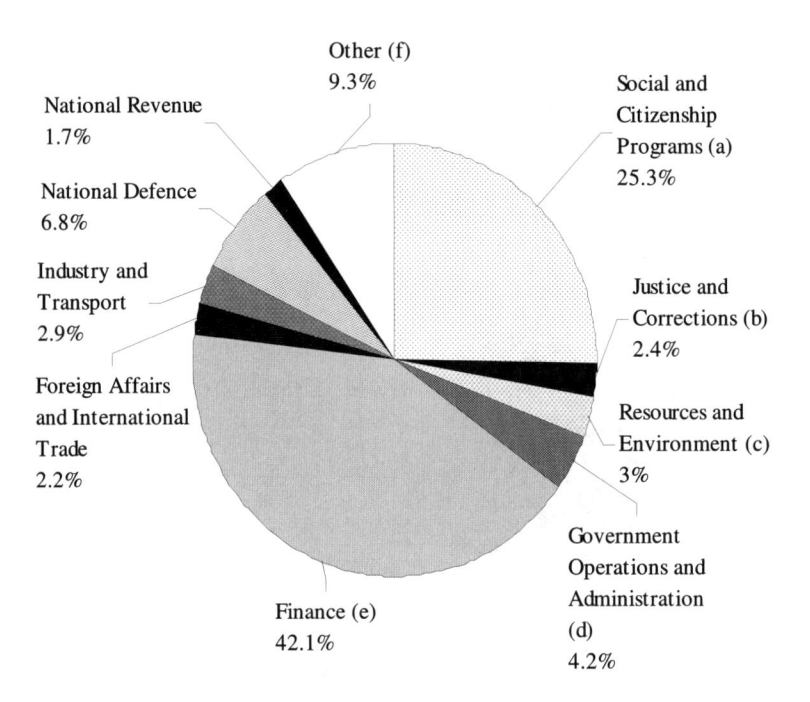

- Other (f) 9.3%
- National Revenue 1.7%
- National Defence 6.8%
- Industry and Transport 2.9%
- Foreign Affairs and International Trade 2.2%
- Finance (e) 42.1%
- Government Operations and Administration (d) 4.2%
- Resources and Environment (c) 3%
- Justice and Corrections (b) 2.4%
- Social and Citizenship Programs (a) 25.3%

(a) Social and Citizenship programs include departmental spending from Canadian Heritage, Citizenship and Immigration, Human Resources Development, Veterans Affairs, Health, and Indian Affairs and Northern Development.
(b) Justice and Corrections includes spending from the Department of Justice and the Solicitor General.
(c) Resources and Environment includes departmental spending from Agriculture and Agri-Food, Environment, Fisheries and Oceans, and Natural Resources.
(d) Government Operations and Administration spending includes that from Public Works and Government Services, the Governor General, Parliament, the Privy Council, and Treasury Board.
(e) Finance expenditures include, but are not limited to, spending on public interest charges and social transfers to the provinces.
(f) Other includes the consolidated specified purposes account (Employment Insurance).

Source: Department of Finance, *Main Estimates, Budgetary Main Estimates by Standard Object of Expenditure*, Part II, 1999-2000, 1-20 to 1-27.

FISCAL FACTS AND TRENDS 355

Figure B.3
Federal Expenditures by Type of Payment
1994-95 to 2000-01

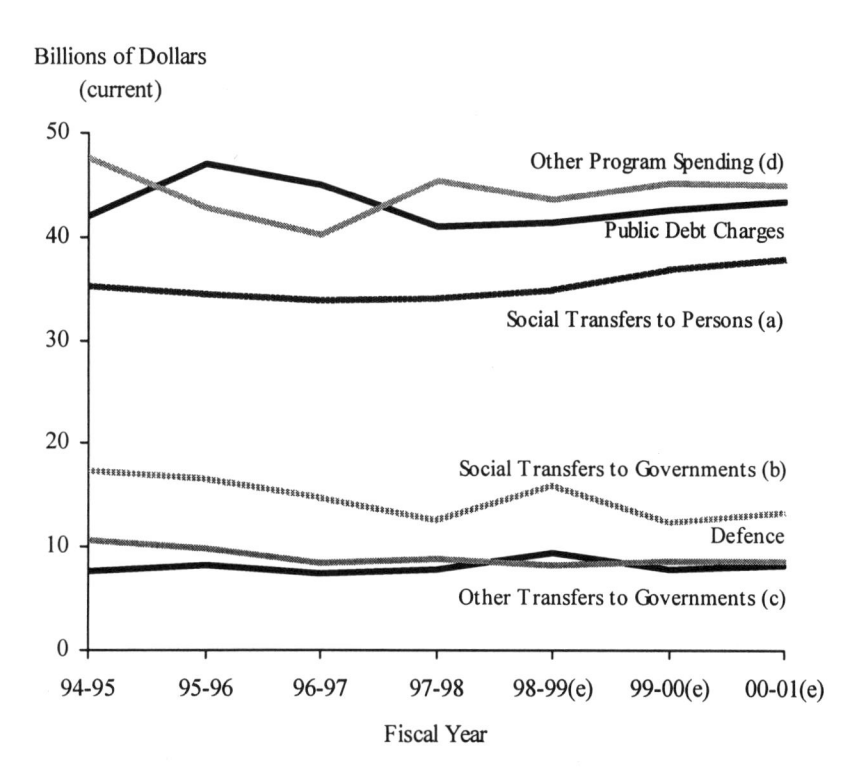

Billions of Dollars (current)

[Line chart showing federal expenditures from 94-95 to 00-01(e) with lines for: Other Program Spending (d), Public Debt Charges, Social Transfers to Persons (a), Social Transfers to Governments (b), Defence, and Other Transfers to Governments (c)]

Fiscal Year

(a) Includes elderly benefits and Employment Insurance benefits.
(b) Consists of the Canada Health and Social Transfer (CHST). Prior to the CHST, two separate social transfers existed: Established Programs Financing for health and post-secondary education expenditures, and the Canada Assistance Plan for welfare and welfare services. The CHST figures include cash transfers to the provinces, and do not include the value of the tax point transfer.
(c) Includes fiscal equalization and transfers to Territories, Alternative Payments for Standing Programs, and "other" fiscal transfers.
(d) Includes all other federal non-defence operating and capital expenditures.
(e) Figures for these years are budgetary estimates.

Source: *Budget Plan 1999*, 16 February 1999; *Public Accounts of Canada*, Vol. I, External Expenditures by Type, various years.

Figure B.4
Federal Revenue, Program Spending, and Deficit/Surplus as Percentages of Gross Domestic Product 1990-91 to 1999-2000

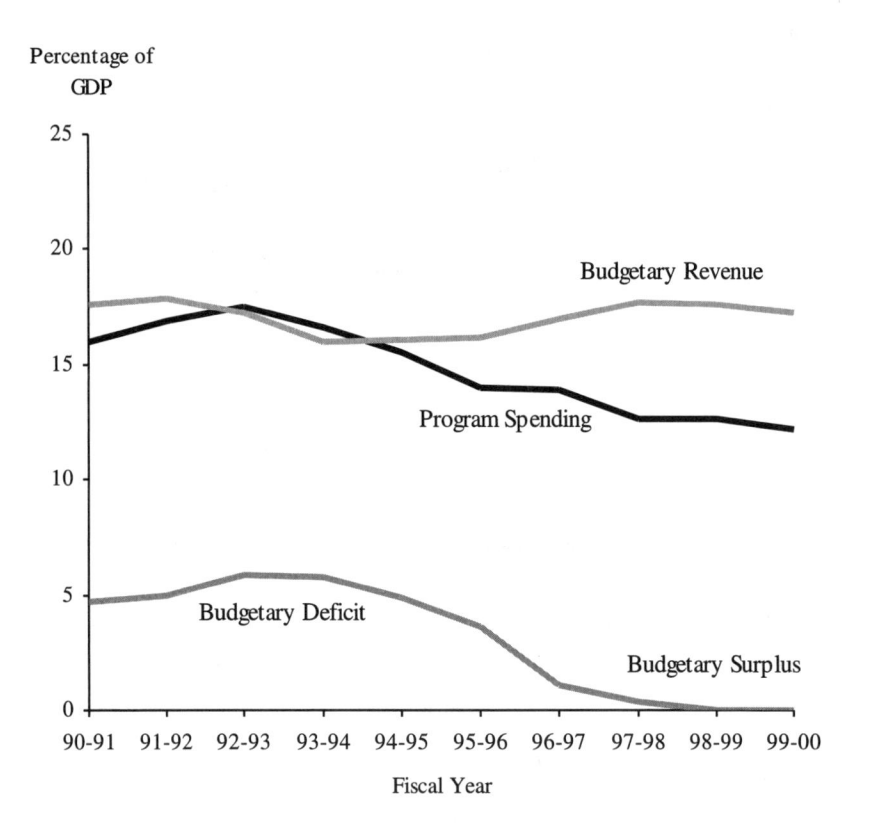

Notes:
Budgetary revenue and program spending are based upon fiscal years, while GDP is based on the calendar year. Revenues, program spending, and the deficit are on a net basis. Program spending does not include public interest charges. GDP is nominal GDP.
Beginning in 1997-98, the budgetary deficit trend line changes to indicate a budgetary surplus as a percentage of the GDP.

Source: Department of Finance, *Fiscal Reference Tables*, November 1998, Table 2; *Budget Plan 1999*, 16 February 1999, Table 3.3, 55.

Table B.2
Federal Deficit/Surplus
1990-91 to 2000-01

Billions of Dollars (current)

Fiscal Year	Budgetary Revenue	Total Expenditures	Budgetary Deficit/ Surplus	Annual % Change	As % of GDP
1990-91	119.4	151.4	-32.0	10.7	4.8
1991-92	122.0	156.4	-34.4	7.5	5.1
1992-93	120.4	161.4	-41.0	19.2	5.9
1993-94	116.0	158.0	-42.0	2.4	5.9
1994-95	123.3	160.8	-37.5	-10.7	5.0
1995-96	130.3	158.9	-28.6	-23.7	3.7
1996-97	140.9	149.8	-8.9	-68.9	1.1
1997-98	153.2	149.7	3.5	-61.0	0.4
1998-99[a]	156.5	153.5	0.0	-100.0	0.0
1999-00[a]	156.7	153.7	0.0	0.0	0.0
2000-01[a]	159.5	156.5	0.0	0.0	0.0

a Figures for these years are estimates.

Note:
While revenue, expenditures, and deficit categories refer to fiscal years, nominal GDP is based upon a calendar year. Total expenditures include program spending and public debt charges.

Source: Department of Finance, *Fiscal Reference Tables,* November 1998, Tables 1 and 2; Department of Finance, *The Budget Plan 1999,* 16 February 1999, Table 3.3.

Figure B.5

Federal Revenue, Expenditures, and the Deficit/Surplus 1991-92 to 2000-01

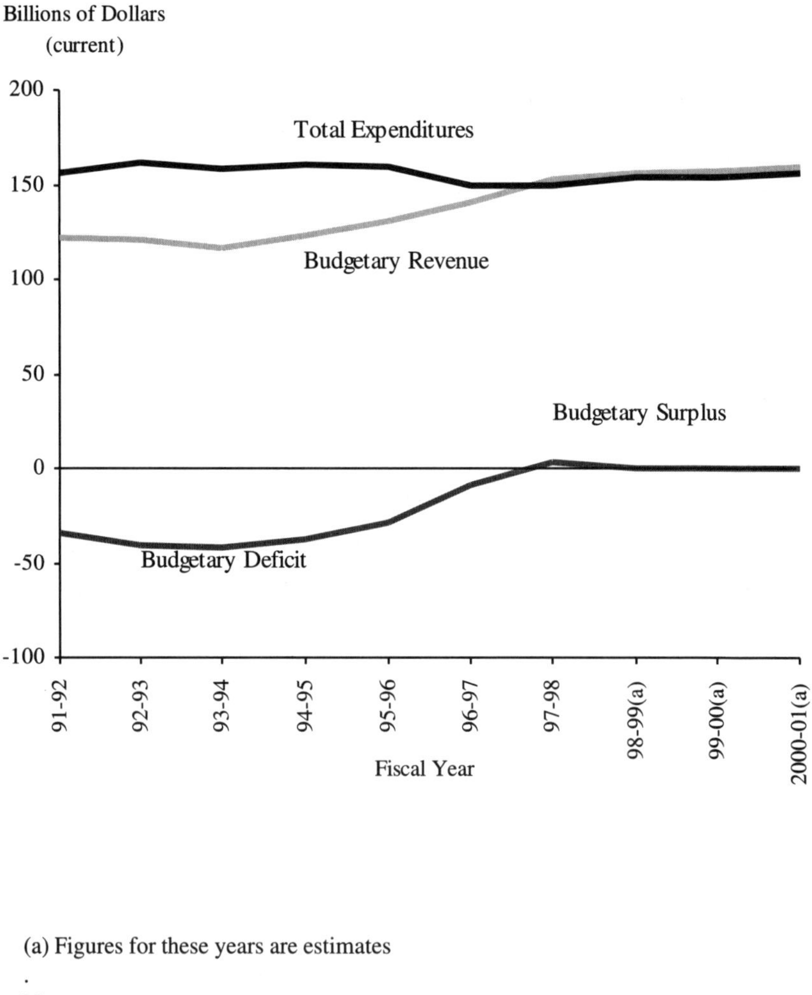
Billions of Dollars
(current)
200
150
100
50
0
-50
-100
Total Expenditures
Budgetary Revenue
Budgetary Surplus
Budgetary Deficit
91-92
92-93
93-94
94-95
95-96
96-97
97-98
98-99(a)
99-00(a)
2000-01(a)
Fiscal Year

(a) Figures for these years are estimates

Note:
Expenditures include program spending and public interest charges on the debt.

Source: Department of Finance, *Fiscal Reference Tables*, November 1998, Tables 1 and 2; Department of Finance, *The Budget Plan 1999*, 16 February 1999, Table 3.1; *Public Accounts of Canada*, Statement of Revenues and Expenditures, various years.

FISCAL FACTS AND TRENDS 359

Figure B.6
**Growth in Real GDP
1989 to 1998**

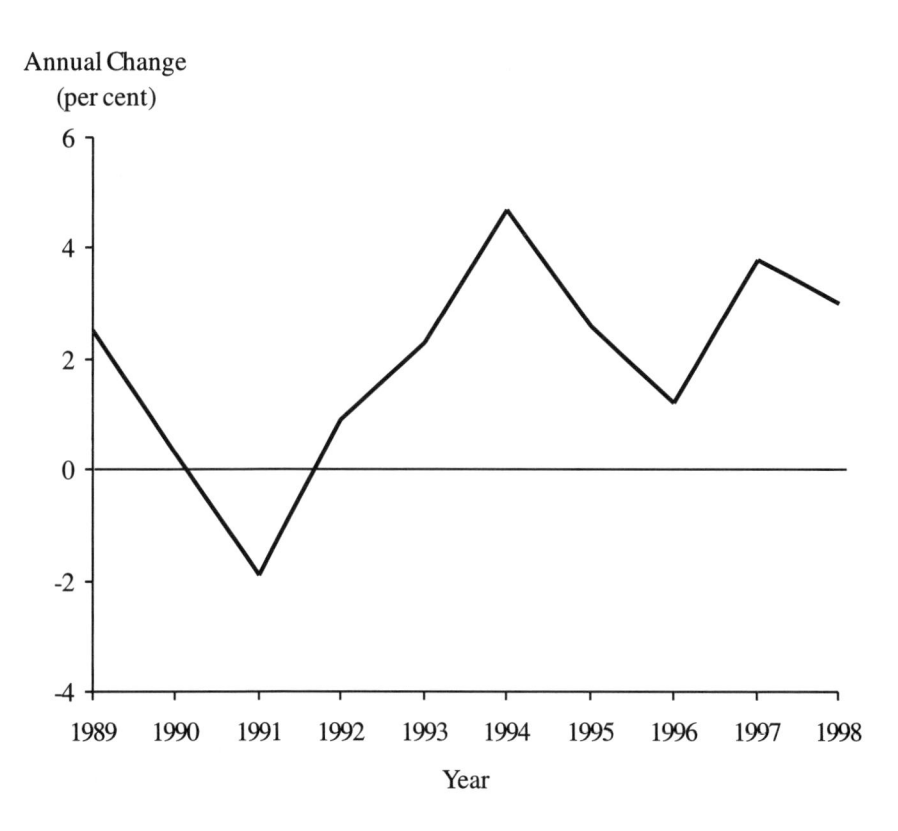

Annual Change
(per cent)

Source: Statistics Canada, *The Daily*, Cat #13-001, various years, and based upon updated figures as at March 10, 1999.

Figure B.7
Rates of Unemployment and Employment Growth
1989 to 1998

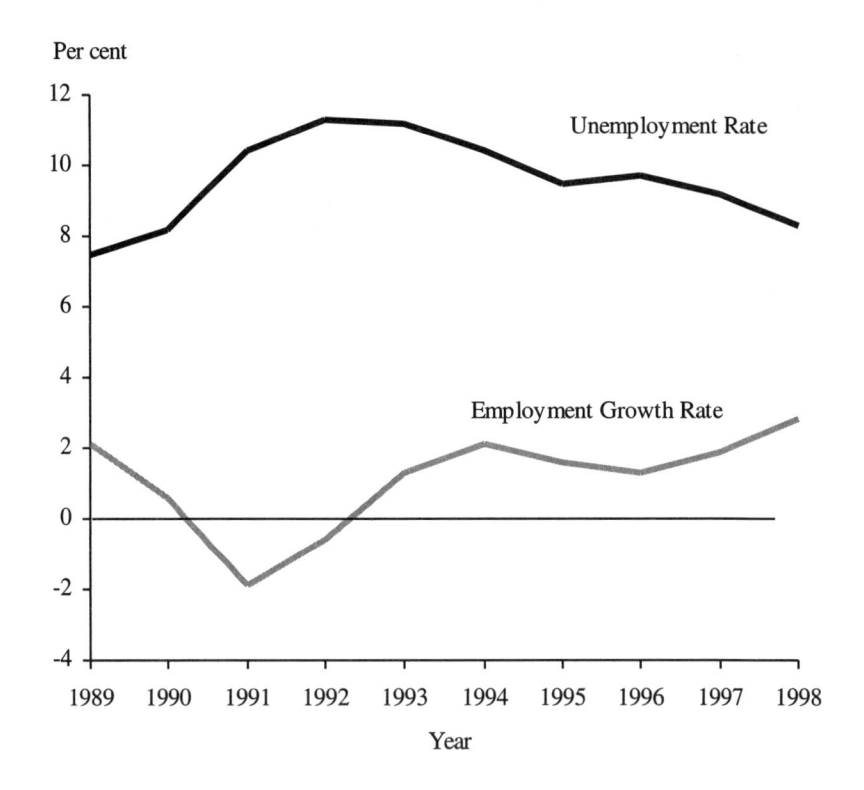

Note:
Employment growth rates and the unemployment rate apply to both sexes, 15 years and older, and are seasonally adjusted.

Source: Statistics Canada, *Historical Labour Force Statistics* (71-201), various years.

FISCAL FACTS AND TRENDS 361

Figure B.8
**Interest and Inflation Rates
1989 to 1998**

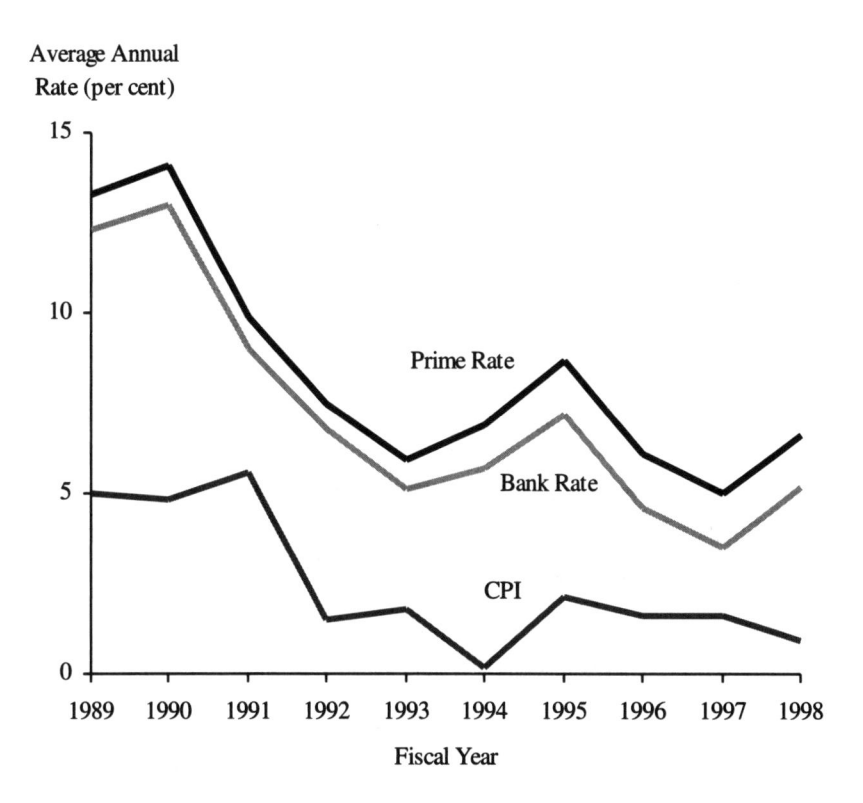

Average Annual Rate (per cent)

Note:
The Consumer Price Index (CPI) is not seasonally adjusted. The Prime Rate refers to the prime business interest rate charged by the chartered banks, and the Bank Rate refers to the rate charged by the Bank of Canada on any loans to commercial banks.

Source: *Bank of Canada Review*, Table F1, various years; Statistics Canada, *The Consumer Price Index*, Cat. #62-001, various years.

362 HOW OTTAWA SPENDS

Figure B.9
**Productivity and Costs
1988 to 1997**

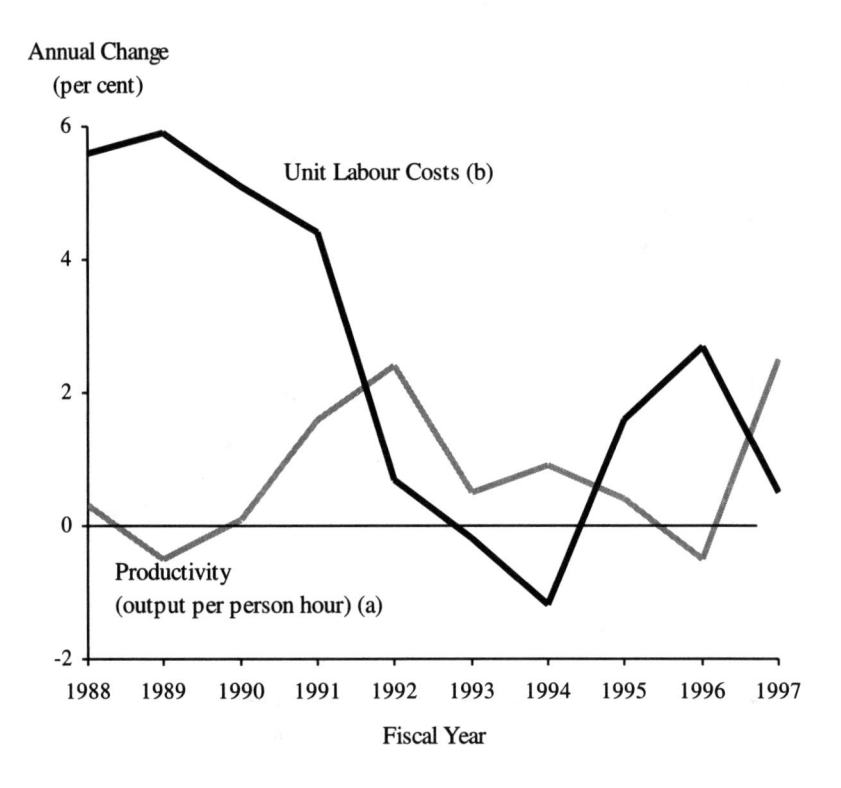

(a) Output per person hour is the real GDP per person hour worked in the business sector, and is a measure of productivity. This trend shows the annual percentage change of this indicator. Real GDP is based on constant (1986) prices.
(b) Unit labour cost in the business sector is based on the real GDP, in constant 1986 prices. This trend shows the annual percentage change in this indicator.

Source: Statistics Canada, Cat. #15-204, various years.

FISCAL FACTS AND TRENDS 363

Figure B.10
**Balance of Payments
1988 to 1997**

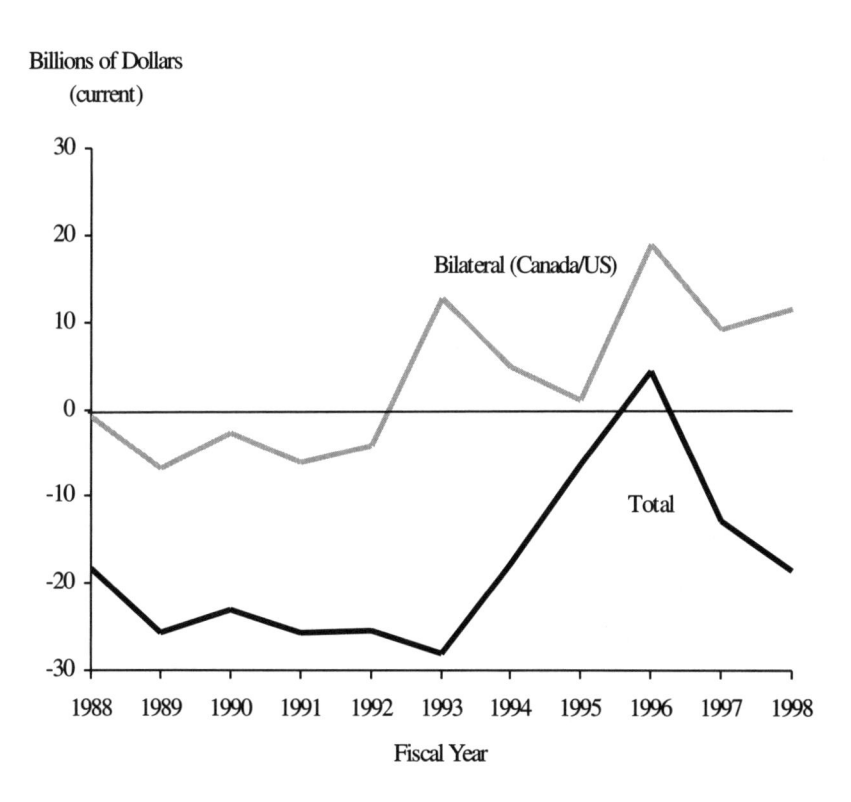

Source: Statistics Canada, Cat. #67-001, various years.

364 HOW OTTAWA SPENDS

Figure B.11
**Growth in Real GDP
Canada and Selected Countries
1988 to 1997**

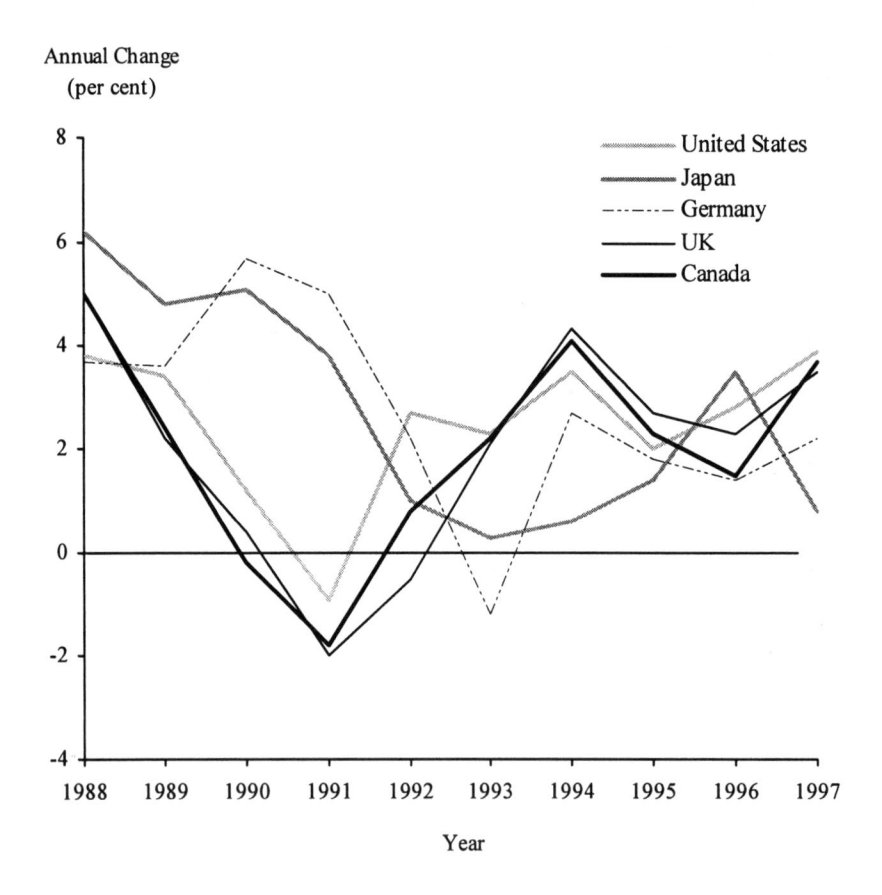

Source: Organization for Economic Cooperation and Development (OECD), *Economic Outlook*, December 1998, Annex Table 1, A4.

Figure B.12
**Unemployment Rates
Canada and Selected Countries
1988 to 1997**

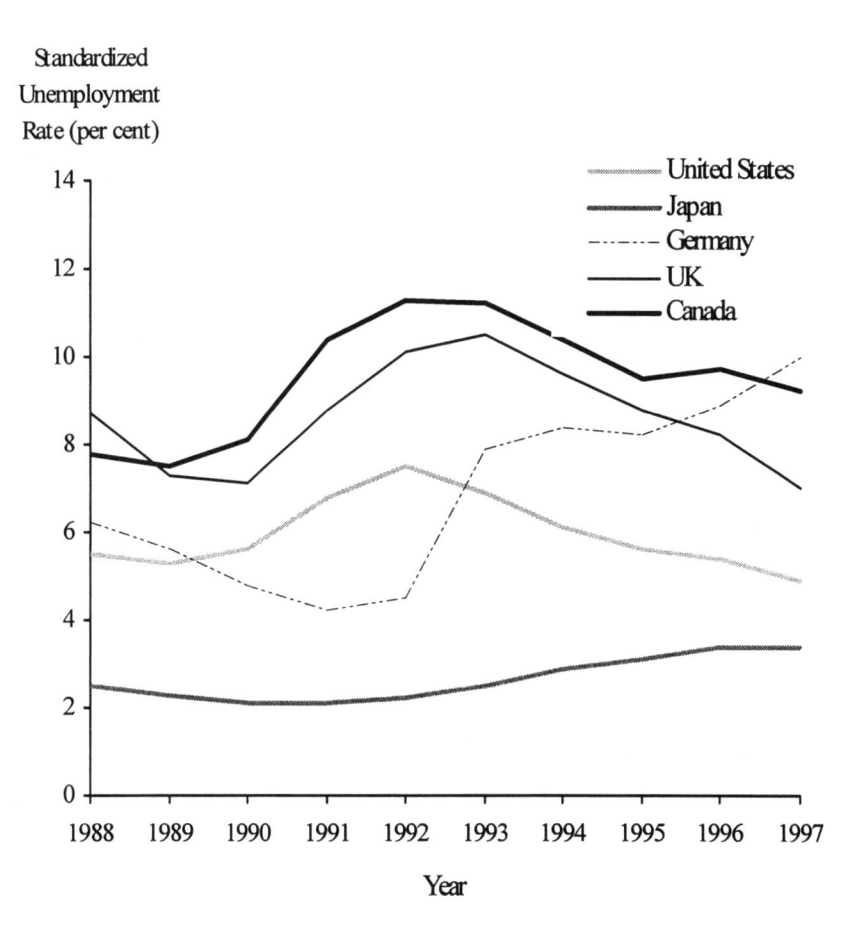

Source: *OECD Economic Outlook*, December 1998, Annex Table 22.

Figure B.13
**Annual Inflation Rates
Canada and Selected Countries
1988 to 1997**

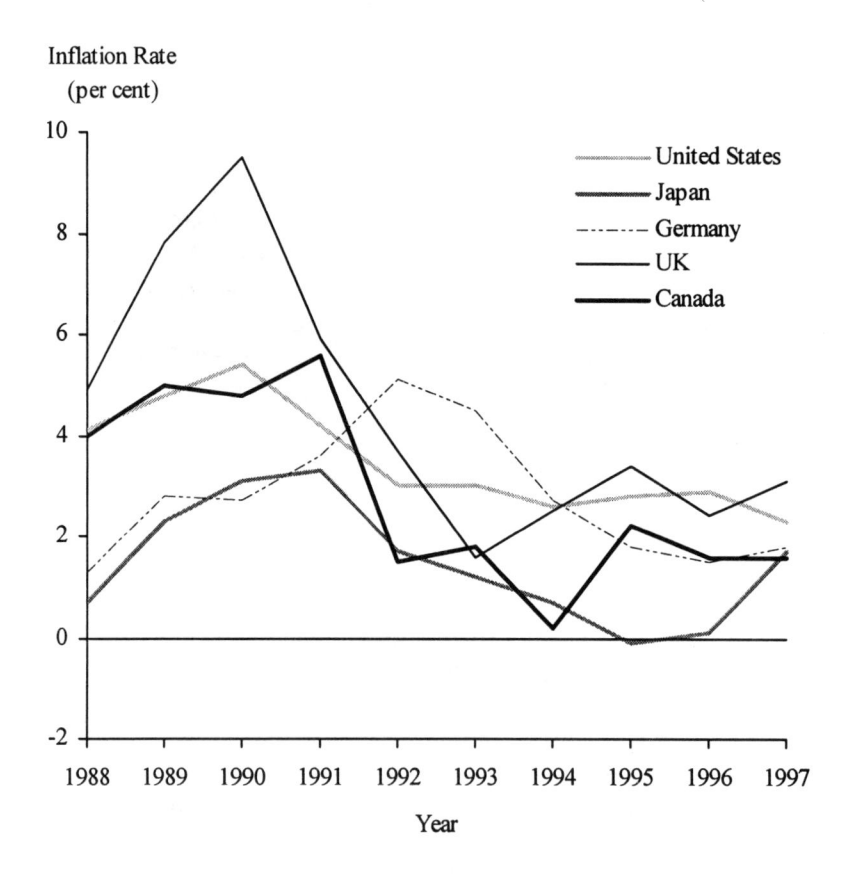

Source: *OECD Economic Outlook*, December 1998, Annex Table 16.

FISCAL FACTS AND TRENDS 367

Figure B.14
Unit Labour Costs
Canada and Selected Countries
1988 to 1997

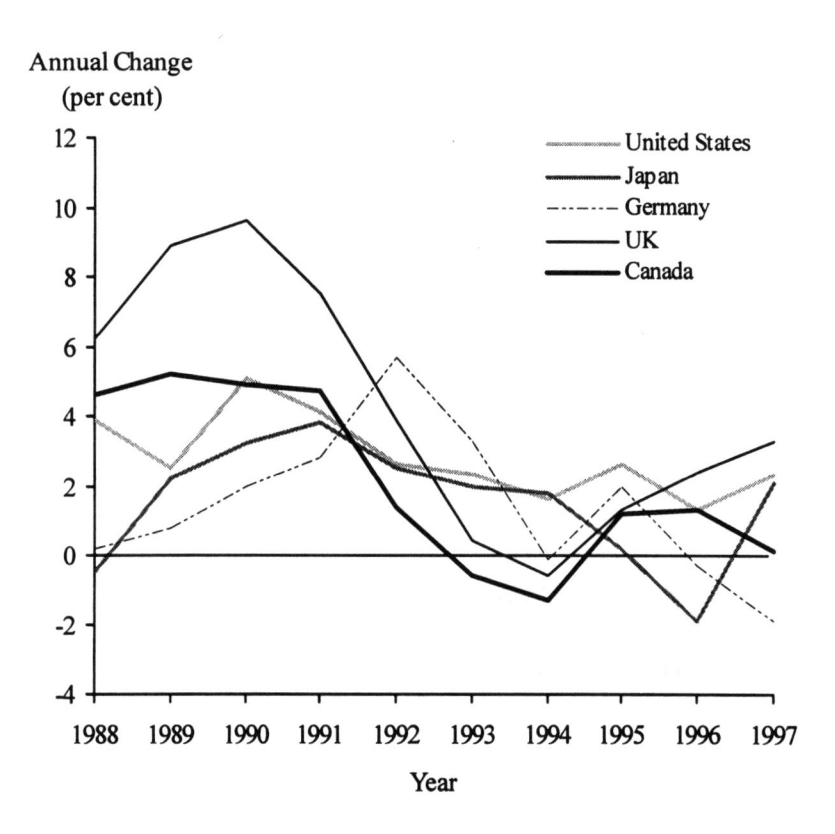

Annual Change
(per cent)

Source: *OECD Economic Outlook*, December 1998, Annex Table 13.

Table B.3
International Comparisons
1988 to 1997

Percentage Change from Previous Year

Growth in Real GDP

	1988	1989	1990	1991	1992	1993	1994	1995	1996	1997
Canada	4.9	2.5	0.3	-1.9	0.9	2.5	3.9	2.2	1.2	3.7
US	3.8	3.4	1.2	-0.9	2.7	2.3	3.5	2.3	3.4	3.9
Japan	6.2	4.8	5.1	3.8	1.0	0.3	0.6	1.5	3.9	0.8
Germany	3.7	3.6	5.7	5.0	2.2	-1.2	2.7	1.2	1.3	2.2
UK	5.2	2.1	0.6	-1.5	-0.1	2.3	4.4	2.8	2.6	3.5

Unemployment Rates

	1988	1989	1990	1991	1992	1993	1994	1995	1996	1997
Canada	7.8	7.5	8.1	10.4	11.3	11.2	10.4	9.5	9.7	9.2
US	5.5	5.3	5.6	6.8	7.5	6.9	6.1	5.6	5.4	4.9
Japan	2.5	2.3	2.1	2.1	2.2	2.5	2.9	3.1	3.4	3.4
Germany	6.2	5.6	4.8	4.2	4.5	7.9	8.4	8.2	8.9	10.0
UK	8.7	7.3	7.1	8.8	10.1	10.5	9.6	8.8	8.2	7.0

Increase in Unit Labour Costs

	1988	1989	1990	1991	1992	1993	1994	1995	1996	1997
Canada	4.6	5.2	4.9	4.7	1.4	-0.6	-1.3	1.2	1.3	0.1
US	3.9	2.5	5.1	4.1	2.6	2.3	1.6	2.6	1.3	2.3
Japan	-0.5	2.2	3.2	3.8	2.5	2.0	1.8	0.2	-1.9	2.1
Germany	0.2	0.8	2.0	2.8	5.7	3.3	-0.1	2.0	-0.3	-1.9
UK	6.2	8.9	9.6	7.5	3.9	0.4	-0.6	1.3	2.4	3.3

Source: *OECD Economic Outlook*, December 1998, Annex Tables 1, 13, 22.

ABSTRACTS/RÉSUMÉS

Frances Abele, Katherine A. Graham, and Allan M. Maslove
Negotiating Canada: Changes in Aboriginal Policy over the Last Thirty Years
Since 1969, three prime ministers and their governments have had a sustained opportunity to deal with the challenges of Canada's Aboriginal fact: the Liberal governments of Pierre Elliott Trudeau, the Conservative governments of Brian Mulroney, and the Liberal governments of Jean Chrétien. Our review suggests a somewhat remarkable progression in the federal government's conception of Aboriginal policy. The federal government has moved from its earlier view of Aboriginal people, which saw them as individualized citizens, impoverished because of a difficult and paternalistic past. Its 1998 response to the Royal Commission on Aboriginal Peoples recognizes the collective identity of Aboriginal nations and peoples and the need to resolve fundamental issues of land for a more constructive future of self control and improvement. We identify three factors that have contributed to this change: the remarkable political mobilization of Aboriginal people over the past thirty years; judicial activism, and crisis events. We also trace the changing role of the Department of Indian Affairs and Northern Development, federal spending, and the institutional regime for Aboriginal policy-making in the federal government over the period. Developments within the federal government have also had an impact on policy learning.

Depuis 1968, trois premiers ministres et leurs gouvernements ont eu l'occasion prolongée de relever les défis du fait autochtone au Canada: les gouvernements libéraux de Pierre Elliott Trudeau, les gouvernements conservateurs de Brian Mulroney et les gouvernements libéraux de Jean Chrétien. Notre examen suggère une progression assez remarquable dans la conception qu'a le gouvernement fédéral d'une politique autochtone. Celui-ci s'est en effet éloigné de sa première vision des autochtones, d'après laquelle il s'agissait de citoyens individualisés, appauvris à cause d'un passé difficile et paternaliste. La réponse du gouvernement fédéral en 1998 à la Commission royale sur les peuples autochtones reconnaît l'identité collective des nations et peuples autochtones et le besoin qu'il y a de résoudre les questions territoriales fondamentales en vue d'un avenir plus constructif comportant autonomie et progrès. Nous identifions trois facteurs qui ont contribué à ce changement: la mobilisation politique remarquable du peuple autochtone au cours des trente dernières années; l'activisme judiciaire et des événements de crise. Nous discutons également pour cette période les changements intervenus, dans le rôle du ministère des Affaires indiennes et du Nord, les dépenses fédérales, et le régime institutionnel pour les décisions en matière de politique autochtone au sein du gouvernement fédéral. Les événements au sein du gouvernement fédéral ont eu un impact sur l'apprentissage politique également.

Robert M. Campbell
The Fourth Fiscal Era: Can There Be a 'Post-Neo-conservative' Fiscal Policy?
The chapter presents the 1999 budget as a metaphor for the emerging fourth fiscal policy era, which follows the Keynesian, post-Keynesian, and neo-conservative eras. While other eras had defining features, the new era, lacking a distinctive characterization to this point, reflects past policy experiences. The 1999 budget foreshadows its shape shifting character, as familiar and unfamiliar, transitory and contradictory. This era will be informed by scepticism about policy capacity and an appreciation of international policy constraints. Disillusionment about the modest results of the neo-conservative era will ensure a perpetual tension between the market and the public purpose. As in the 1999 budget, the agenda will be framed by fiscal balance and debt and tax reduction and comprise active and pragmatic initiatives. The goal of the fourth fiscal policy era will be an approach to economic and public policy that is flexible, and capable of making fast adjustments to international and competitive changes while responding positively to economic opportunities.

Ce chapitre présente le budget de 1999 comme métaphore pour la quatrième ère fiscale qui émerge, à la suite des ères keynésienne, post-keynésienne et néo-conservatrice. Si d'autres ères avaient des traits définis, cette nouvelle ère manque d'une caractérisation distinctive jusqu'ici et ne fait que refléter les expériences du passé en matière de politiques. Le budget de 1999 vient en présager le caractère changeant, le côté familier et inconnu, transitoire et contradictoire. Cette ère sera informée d'un scepticisme sur la capacité politique et une appréciation des contraintes en matière de politiques internationales. Une désillusion devant les résultats modestes de l'ère néo-conservatrice créera une tension perpétuelle entre le marché et les objectifs publics. Comme dans le budget de 1999, le programme sera cadré par l'équilibre fiscal ainsi que la réduction de la dette et des impôts et il sera composé d'initiatives actives et pragmatiques. Le but de la quatrième ère de politique fiscale sera d'élaborer une approche en matière de politique économique et sociale qui soit flexible, et capable de s'adapter rapidement aux changements tant à l'échelle internationale qu'en matière de concurrence tout en répondant de façon positive aux possibilités économiques.

Stephen Clarkson and Timothy Lewis
The Contested State: Canada in the Post-Cold War, Post-Keynesian, Post-Fordist, Post-national Era
Politics in Canada can no longer be characterized simply in terms of the division of powers between the provinces and the federal government. We maintain that the forms and functions of Canada's evolving system of government are best understood in terms of a 'multi-level state' whose loci of authority have been shifting vertically, upwards or downwards, to other levels, as well as horizontally, outwards and inward, to and from civil society or the market.

The federal order of government has been the originator of many of these changes and has acquired new functions in the process. After identifying the nuances since the early 1960s of these shifts in macroeconomic, industrial, and trade policy along with changes in democratic practice and in social and foreign policy, we conclude that the Canadian state retains substantial power, even though many of its services have shrunk. But since neo-liberalism under globalization has failed to deliver higher employment levels and greater well-being, the shifting shapes of the multi-level state remain highly contested.

On ne peut plus caractériser la politique au Canada en fonction du simple partage des pouvoirs entre les provinces et le gouvernement fédéral. Nous maintenons que les formes et les fonctions du système de gouvernement au Canada, en pleine évolution, sont le mieux comprises en fonction d'un "État à plusieurs niveaux" dont les lieux d'autorité se déplacent verticalement, vers le haut ou vers le bas, pour atteindre d'autres niveaux, ainsi qu'horizontalement, vers l'extérieur ou vers l'intérieur, en direction ou en provenance de la société civile ou du marché.

L'ordre fédéral du gouvernement a été l'initiateur d'un bon nombre de ces changements et a ainsi acquis de nouvelles fonctions. Après avoir identifié les nuances, depuis le début des années 1960, de ces changements en politique macro-économique, industrielle et commerciale ainsi que les changements dans la politique démocratique et en politique sociale et étrangère, nous concluons que l'État canadien conserve un pouvoir considérable, même si plusieurs des services fournis par celui-ci ont été réduits. Mais puisque le néo-libéralisme à l'ère de la mondialisation n'a pas pu créer des niveaux d'emploi plus élevés ni un plus grand bien-être, les formes changeantes de l'État à plusieurs niveaux restent très contestées.

Andrew F. Cooper
'Coalitions of the Willing': The Search for Like-Minded Partners in Canadian Diplomacy
This chapter explores the evolving character of Canadian diplomacy through the lens of partnership. Special attention is paid to the search for like-minded partners as a distinctive but mutating expression in Canadian diplomacy. In terms of motivation, the dominant rationale of this approach remains that of balancing Canada's core relationships with the United States in particular and the western alliance/industrial world more generally. In terms of targeting, much of the focus has remained on a loose network of traditional like-minded countries, especially Australia, New Zealand, and the Nordics. Yet, if solidly grounded in older habits and an ingrained architecture, Canadian like-minded diplomacy has been played out in the late 1990s with a new scope and intensity. These changes are teased out through a comparison of the fixed and low-key style of like-minded diplomacy, as practiced through the Pearsonian era; with the adoption of a more robust and issue-specific mode of 'coalitions of the willing' associated with Lloyd Axworthy. As captured by way of snapshot

references to the recent initiatives on land mines, the International Criminal Court, and the Zaire/Great Lakes humanitarian operation, this process of shape shifting has meant both an opening up of like-mindedness to a greater array of countries and the inclusion of non-governmental organizations. While expanding the range of alternative partnerships, nevertheless, this privileging of like-minded partnerships in Canadian diplomacy has become highly contested. The chapter concludes, therefore, with an overall assessment of the approach.

Ce chapitre explore le caractère changeant de la diplomatie canadienne en ce qui concerne les partenariats. Nous accordons une attention particulière à la recherche de partenaires d'optique commune comme expression distinctive mais changeante de la diplomatie canadienne. Quant à sa motivation, le raisonnement sous-tendant cette approche reste celle d'équilibrer les relations essentielles qu'entretient le Canada avec les États-Unis en particulier et l'alliance de l'Ouest et le monde industriel plus généralement. Quant au ciblage, celui-ci porte encore sur un réseau relâché de pays traditionnellement d'optique commune, surtout l'Australie, la Nouvelle-Zélande et les pays nordiques. Pourtant, si cette diplomatie s'appuie sur de vieilles habitudes et une architecture enracinée, la diplomatie axée sur les optiques communes a été poursuivie à la fin des années 1990 avec une étendue et une intensité nouvelles. Nous démontrons ces changements en comparant le style figé et discret de la diplomatie axée sur les optiques communes, telle que pratiquée à l'époque de Pearson, avec l'adoption d'un mode plus robuste et axé plutôt sur les questions de l'heure, sur des "coalitions selon la volonté", style pratiqué par Lloyd Axworthy. Nous démontrons par des instantanés illustrant les initiatives récentes relatives aux mines terrestres, au Tribunal criminel international et à l'opération humanitaire du Zaire/ Grands lacs que ce processus d'évolution formelle a mené à une ouverture de l'approche axée sur les optiques communes pur inclure une gamme plus large de pays, ainsi que des organisations non gouvernementales. Si la gamme de partenariats éventuels s'en est trouvée élargie, il n'en reste pas moins que le fait de privilégier les partenariats avec les pays d'optique commune à fini par être très contesté. Ce chapitre conclut donc par une évaluation générale de cette approche.

Roger Gibbins
Taking Stock: Canadian Federalism and Its Constitutional Framework
The last thirty years have witnessed dramatic change in the nature of Canadian society, coupled with limited formal change in federal institutions. Although the 1982 Charter of Rights and Freedoms has made a huge impression on political life, the most serious political controversies of the past few decades have failed to leave an institutional mark. Quebec's quest for constitutional recognition as a distinct society has come up short, and although western Canadian discontent has transformed the party system, it has left no mark whatsoever on parliamentary institutions. At the same time, there has been a good deal of informal change, particularly with respect to Quebec's relationship with the broader Canadian community. What remains to be seen is whether the institutional status quo will persist in the face of unrelenting social change. The discontinuity between the lives individual Canadians lead at the dawn of the 21st century and political institutions imperfectly designed for the 19th century steadily increases.

Depuis trente ans on assiste à des changements dramatiques dans la nature de la société canadienne accompagnée de changements formels limités dans les institutions fédérales. Même si la Charte de droits et libertés de 1982 a fait une grande impression sur la vie politique, les controverses politiques les plus importantes des dernières décennies n'ont pas laissé de marque institutionnel. La recherche, de la part du Québec, d'une reconnaissance constitutionnelle comme société distincte n'a pas réussi, et si le malaise de l'Ouest a transformé le système des partis, il n'a laissé aucune marque sur les institutions parlementaires. En même temps, il y a eu bien des changements informels, en particulier en ce qui concerne la relation qu'entretient le Québec avec la communauté canadienne. Il reste à voir si le statu quo institutionnel persistera face aux changements sociaux implacables. La discontinuité entre, d'une part, la vie menée par les Canadiens individuels à l'aube du XXIe siècle, et, d'autre part, des institutions politiques imparfaitement conçues pour le XIXe, ne cesse d'augmenter.

Frank Graves
Rethinking Government **As If People Mattered: From 'Reaganomics' to 'Humanomics'**
The chapter discusses the changing relationship between Canadians and their government, with a focus on the period since the current government took office in 1993. Graves relies on data and analysis drawn from *Rethinking Government*, a major longitudinal research study, and demonstrates that, in post-deficit Canada, the public has chosen active human investment instead of the more 'neo-conservative' agenda based on trickle-down economics, minimal government, and broad tax relief. He outlines the shifts in public attitudes that have accompanied the transition from the welfare state to Reaganomics, and now the emerging search for a new 'humanomic' state. While the public wants a more active federal government to address its concerns, they also want to play a more decisive role in the decision-making process of government. Given that a 'normative rupture' exists between the values of elites and the broader public, a major challenge for government in the 21st century will be to find a more open and transparent way to include Canadians in the governing process.

Ce chapitre discute l'évolution de la relation entre les Canadiens et leur gouvernement, en se concentrant sur la période depuis l'arrivée au pouvoir du gouvernement actuel en 1993. Le chapitre s'appuie sur des données et des analyses tirées de Repenser le gouvernement*, une importante étude longitudinale, pour démontrer que, dans le Canada post-déficitaire, le public a opté pour un investissement actif dans les êtres humains plutôt que pour le programme "néo-conservateur" basé sur l'économique des effets de retombée, une présence minimale du gouvernement et des allégements fiscaux généralisés. L'auteur résume l'évolution des attitudes du public qui a accompagné la transition de l'État-providence à la politique reaganomique, et la recherche naissante, à l'heure actuelle, d'un nouvel État "humainomique". Si le public désire voir un gouvernement fédéral plus actifs, attaquer à ses préoccupations, il veut également jouer un rôle plus important dans les prises de décisions gouvernementales. Étant donné la "rupture normative" entre les* *valeurs des états et celles du grand public, un défi majeur que devront relever les gouvernements au XXI{^{e}} siècle sera de trouver une façon plus ouverte et transparente d'inclure les Canadiens dans le processus relié à l'acte de gouverner.*

Leslie A. Pal
Shape Shifting: Canadian Governance Toward the 21st Century
A review of the last twenty years of *How Ottawa Spends* shows how the shape of the Canadian policy landscape has shifted in important ways. Key themes include the gradual emergence of a consensus on tackling the deficit; the emerging support for decentralization and partnership among governments; changes in modes of governance (downsizing, and more orientation toward the market); globalization as the primary context for Canadian policy-making; the concern with the impact of these policy changes on community, cohesion, and democratic practice; and, finally, the increasing concentration on the social and economic union.

The current government operates in a substantially changed context, and its successes on issues such as the budget and the federation have obscured the ambivalence that lies at the core of its policies. The year began with the first balanced budget in a generation, and in February 1999 Paul Martin's budget predicted surpluses for three more years. The key challenge for the Liberals in this last year—one that generally they have been successful in meeting—was to take account of the change and continuity in Canadian policy and institutions over the last two decades, and forge acceptable responses. This challenge will, if anything, increase in the future.

Un examen des vingt dernières années de How Ottawa Spends *fait ressortir les changements importants survenus dans la politique canadienne. Parmi les thèmes clés: l'apparition graduelle d'un consensus sur la nécessité de s'attaquer au déficit; l'appui croissant donné à la décentralisation et à un partenariat entre les gouvernements; l'évolution des modes de gouvernance (réduction des effectifs, et une orientation accrue en fonction du marché); la mondialisation comme contexte primaire des décisions politiques au Canada; les préoccupations au sujet de l'impact de ces changements en matière de politiques sur la communauté, la cohésion et les pratiques démocratiques; et finalement, la concentration croissante sur l'union sociale et économique.*

Le gouvernement actuel fonctionne dans un contexte assez nouveau, et les succès qu'il a remportés sur des questions telles que le budget et la fédération ont obscurci l'ambivalence qui se trouve au coeur de sa politique. L'année a commencé par le premier budget équilibré depuis une génération, et en février 1999 le budget Martin a prédit des surplus pour les trois années à venir. Le défi clé que les libéraux avaient à relever au cours de l'année dernière - et qu'en général ils ont réussi à relever - était de tenir compte de l'évolution et de la continuité dans la politique et les institutions canadiennes au cours des deux dernières décennies, et d'élaborer des réponses acceptables. Ce défi risque d'être encore plus grand à l'avenir.

Gilles Paquet
Tectonic Changes in Canadian Governance
The pattern of governance has shifted gradually in Canada over the last few decades. This transformation is ascribable to major transnational and technological changes, to the epiphany of a culture of diversity that has undermined the traditional foundations of social cohesion, and the interaction between these sets of forces which has acquired a dynamics of its own. The paper argues that this corresponds to a tectonic change in the Canadian governance regime and presents (1) evidence of a *reframing* of the philosophy of governance (from egalitarianism to subsidiarity), (2) evidence of a *restructuring* of the governance process (a new division of labour among the three sectors—private, public, and civic—a new emphasis on sub-national forums, and a significant increase in the range of relevant stakeholders), and (3) evidence of a *retooling* of public management and of the ways in which the public sector is administered. The paper also documents some of the ongoing resistance to this transformation.

Le pattern de gouvernance s'est modifié graduellement au Canada au cours des dernières décennies. Cette transformation est attribuable à certains changements transnationaux et technologiques, à l'émergence d'une culture de la diversité qui a miné les fondements traditionnels de la cohésion sociale, et à l'interaction entre ces deux ensembles de forces qui ont enclenché une dynamique particulière. Cet article suggère que cela s'est traduit par des changements tectoniques dans le pattern de gouvernance au Canada et présente certains éléments de preuve: (1) le recadrage de la philosophie de gouvernance (de l'égalitarisme vers la subsidiarité), (2) la restructuration du processus de gouvernance (une nouvelle division du travail entre les trois secteurs—privé, public, et civique—une nouvelle importance des forums infra-nationaux, et un élargissement de l'éventail des intervenants pertinents) et (3) le changement dans l'outillage du management et de l'administration publics. Le texte met aussi au dossier la preuve qu'il y a résistance active à cette transformation.

Michael J. Prince
From Health and Welfare to Stealth and Farewell: Federal Social Policy, 1980-2000

Social policy has not been an area of budgetary calm or political resilience over the past 20 years in Canada. At the national level, Conservative and Liberal governments both have actively engaged in restraining, reforming, and retrenching social programs. Canadian social policy has been on the defensive for this entire period. Federal social policy in the 1980s was deeply conservative, first, in its struggle to maintain social programs in the face of a major economic recession and rising deficits, and second, in its attempt to restrain the growth of social expenditures. For much of the 1990s, change to federal social policy has been abrupt and transformational.

In addition to exploring changes in the practice of social policy, this chapter considers how the theory behind Canadian social policy has also been challenged. Through the 1990s, it became additionally obvious that federal social spending programs were far more bendable and vulnerable than conventional social policy theory held or hoped. The time is long overdue to say farewell to social policy by stealth as a style of governing. The author concludes that we are in need of a new national agenda that reconnects economic growth with social growth.

La politique sociale n'a pas été un domaine de calme budgétaire ni de robustesse politique au cours des vingt dernières années au Canada. Au niveau du pays, les gouvernements soit conservateurs soit libéraux se sont occupés à restreindre, à réformer et à réduire les programmes sociaux. La politique sociale canadienne a été sur la défensive pendant toute cette période. La politique sociale fédérale des années 1980 était profondément conservatrice: premièrement dans sa lutte pour maintenir les programmes sociaux face à une récession économique majeure et des déficits croissants, et deuxièmement dans sa tentative de restreindre la croissance des dépenses sociales. Pendant une bonne partie des années 1990, les changements survenus dans la politique sociale fédérale ont été brusques et transformationnels.

En plus d'explorer les changements dans la pratique de la politique sociale, ce chapitre considère la façon dont la théorie sous-tendant la politique sociale canadienne a été aussi mise en question. Au cours des années 1990, il est devenu évident que les programmes de dépenses sociales du gouvernement fédéral pouvaient être beaucoup plus facilement pliés ou altérés que ne l'avait estimé ou espéré la théorie conventionnelle de la politique sociale. Le temps est venu, depuis longtemps, de dire adieu à la politique sociale furtive comme style de gouvernement. En conclusion, le chapitre maintient qu'il nous faut un nouveau programme national qui rétablisse le lien entre croissance économique et croissance sociale.

CONTRIBUTORS

Frances Abele is the Director of the School of Public Administration at Carleton University.

Robert Campbell is a Professor of Political Studies at Trent University.

Stephen Clarkson is a Professor of Political Economy at the University of Toronto.

Andrew Cooper is a Professor of Political Science at the University of Waterloo.

Roger Gibbins is the President of the Canada West Foundation and a Professor of Political Science at the University of Calgary.

Katherine Graham is an Associate Dean of Public Affairs and Management at Carleton University.

Frank Graves is the President and founder of Ekos Research Associates.

Timothy Lewis is a doctoral candidate in Political Science at the University of Toronto.

Allan Maslove is the Dean of Public Affairs and Management at Carleton University.

Leslie Pal is a Professor of Public Administration at Carleton University.

Gilles Paquet is a Professor of Economics and Public Management at the University of Ottawa.

Michael Prince is the Lansdowne Professor of Social Policy and an Associate Dean in the Faculty of Human and Social Development at the University of Victoria.

THE SCHOOL OF PUBLIC ADMINISTRATION
at Carleton University is a national centre for the study of public policy and public management.

The School's Centre for Policy and Program Assessment provides research services and courses to interest groups, businesses, unions, and governments in the evaluation of public policies, programs, and activities.

The *How Ottawa Spends* Series

How Ottawa Spends 1998-99: Balancing Act: The Post-Deficit Mandate
edited by Leslie A. Pal

How Ottawa Spends 1997-98: Seeing Red: A Liberal Report Card
edited by Gene Swimmer

How Ottawa Spends 1996-97: Life Under the Knife
edited by Gene Swimmer

How Ottawa Spends 1995-96: Mid-Life Crises
edited by Susan D. Phillips

How Ottawa Spends 1994-95: Making Change
edited by Susan D. Phillips

How Ottawa Spends 1993-94: A More Democratic Canada...?
edited by Susan D. Phillips

How Ottawa Spends 1992-93: The Politics of Competitiveness
edited by Frances Abele

How Ottawa Spends 1991-92: The Politics of Fragmentation
edited by Frances Abele

How Ottawa Spends 1990-91: Tracking the Second Agenda
edited by Katherine A. Graham

How Ottawa Spends 1989-90: The Buck Stops Where?
edited by Katherine A. Graham

How Ottawa Spends 1988-89: The Conservatives Heading into the Stretch
edited by Katherine A. Graham

How Ottawa Spends 1987-88: Restraining the State
edited by Michael J. Prince

How Ottawa Spends 1986-87: Tracking the Tories
edited by Michael J. Prince

How Ottawa Spends 1985: Sharing the Pie
edited by Allan M. Maslove

How Ottawa Spends 1984: The New Agenda
edited by Allan M. Maslove

How Ottawa Spends 1983: The Liberals, The Opposition & Federal Priorities
edited by G. Bruce Doern

How Ottawa Spends Your Tax Dollars: National Policy and Economic Development 1982
edited by G. Bruce Doern

How Ottawa Spends Your Tax Dollars: Federal Priorities 1981
edited by G. Bruce Doern

Spending Tax Dollars: Federal Expenditures, 1980-81
edited by G. Bruce Doern